Social Influence Network Theory

M000115551

Social influence network theory presents a mathematical formalization of the social process of attitude change as it unfolds in a social network of interpersonal influences. This book brings the theory to bear on lines of research in the domain of small group dynamics concerned with changes of group members' positions on an issue, including the formation of a consensus and of settled disagreement, via endogenous interpersonal influences, in which group members are responding to the displayed positions of the members of the group. Social influence network theory advances a dynamic social cognition mechanism, in which individuals are weighing and combining their own and others' positions on an issue in revising their own positions. The influence network construct of the theory is the social structure of the endogenous interpersonal influences that are involved in this mechanism. With this theory, the authors seek to lay the foundation for a better formal integration of classical and current lines of work on small groups in psychological and sociological social psychology.

Noah E. Friedkin is Professor of Sociology at the University of California, Santa Barbara. He is the author of *A Structural Theory of Social Influence* (Cambridge, 1998), which received the award for Best Book in Mathematical Sociology from the Mathematical Sociology Section of the American Sociological Association, as well as articles in various scholarly journals, including the *American Sociological Review*. *American Journal of Sociology, Social Psychology Quarterly, Advances in Group Processes*, and *Journal of Mathematical Sociology*. Professor Friedkin's areas of research specialization are social psychology, mathematical sociology, and formal organizations.

Eugene C. Johnsen is Professor Emeritus of Mathematics, former Vice Chair of Mathematics, and former Director of Summer Sessions at the University of California, Santa Barbara. His mathematical publications have appeared in journals such as the *Canadian Journal of Mathematics, Linear and Multilinear Algebra, Mathematische Zeitschrift*, and the *Journal of Combinatorial Theory*, and his social science publications have appeared in such journals as *Social Networks*, the *Journal of Mathematical Sociology, Sociological Methods and Research*, and *Advances in Group Processes*. Professor Johnsen's research has been in the areas of linear algebra, combinatorics, social networks, and mathematical sociology.

Structural Analysis in the Social Sciences

Mark Granovetter, editor

The series *Structural Analysis In The Social Sciences* presents studies that analyze social behavior and institutions by reference to relations among such concrete social entities as persons, organizations and nations. Relational analysis contrasts on the one hand with reductionist methodological individualism and on the other, with macro-level determinism, whether based on technology, material conditions, economic conflict, adaptive evolution or functional imperatives. In this more intellectually flexible structural middle ground, analysts situate actors and their relations in a variety of contexts. Since the series began in 1987, its authors have variously focused on small groups, history, culture, politics, kinship, aesthetics, economics and complex organizations, creatively theorizing how these shape and in turn are shaped by social relations. Their style and methods have ranged widely, from intense, long-term ethnographic observation to highly abstract mathematical models. Their disciplinary affiliations have included history, anthropology, sociology, political science, business, economics, mathematics and computer science. Some have made explicit use of "social network analysis," including many of the cutting-edge and standard works of that approach, while others have eschewed formal analysis and used "networks" as a fruitful orienting metaphor. All have in common a sophisticated and subtle approach that forcefully illuminates our complex social world.

Recent books in the series

Philippe Bourgois, *In Search of Respect: Selling Crack in El Barrio*
  (Second Edition)
Nan Lin, *Social Capital: A Theory of Social Structure and Action*
Robert Franzosi, *From Words to Numbers*
Sean O'Riain, *The Politics of High-Tech Growth*
James Lincoln and Michael Gerlach, *Japan's Network Economy*
Patrick Doreian, Vladimir Batagelj, and Anujka Ferligoj, *Generalized*
  Blockmodeling
Eiko Ikegami, *Bonds of Civility: Aesthetic Networks and Political Origins of*
  Japanese Culture
Wouter de Nooy, Andrej Mrvar, and Vladimir Batagelj, *Exploratory Social*
  Network Analysis with Pajek
Peter Carrington, John Scott, and Stanley Wasserman, *Models and Methods in*
  Social Network Analysis
Robert C. Feenstra and Gary G. Hamilton, *Emergent Economies, Divergent*
  Paths
Martin Kilduff and David Krackhardt, *Interpersonal Networks in*
  Organizations
Ari Adut, *On Scandal: Moral Disturbances in Society, Politics, and Art*
Zeev Maoz, *The Networks of Nations: The Evolution and Structure of*
  International Networks, 1815–2002

Social Influence Network Theory

A Sociological Examination of Small Group Dynamics

NOAH E. FRIEDKIN
University of California, Santa Barbara

EUGENE C. JOHNSEN
University of California, Santa Barbara

CAMBRIDGE
UNIVERSITY PRESS

CAMBRIDGE
UNIVERSITY PRESS

32 Avenue of the Americas, New York NY 10013-2473, USA

Cambridge University Press is part of the University of Cambridge.

It furthers the University's mission by disseminating knowledge in the pursuit of education, learning and research at the highest international levels of excellence.

www.cambridge.org
Information on this title: www.cambridge.org/9781107617674

First published 2011
Reprinted 2012 (twice)
First paperback edition 2013

A catalogue record for this publication is available from the British Library

Library of Congress Cataloguing in Publication data

Friedkin, Noah E., 1947–
Social influence network theory : a sociological examination of small group dynamics / Noah E. Friedkin, Eugene C. Johnsen.
  p. cm. – (Structural analysis in the social sciences ; 33)
Includes bibliographical references and index.
ISBN 978-1-107-00246-3 (hardback)
1. Small groups – Research. 2. Social influence. 3. Social psychology.
I. Johnsen, Eugene C., 1932– II. Title.
HM736.F75 2011
302.3´4–dc22   2010041889

ISBN 978-1-107-00246-3 Hardback
ISBN 978-1-107-61767-4 Paperback

Contents

List of Tables and Figures

Tables

ix

List of Tables and Figures

Figures

Acknowledgments

This book could not have been completed without the support of our wives, Rene Friedkin and Marjorie Johnsen, who put up with our intense, even obsessive, engagement with this endeavor over a period of many years. We are deeply grateful for their understanding and devotion.

We dedicate the book to Dorwin "Doc" Cartwright, with whom we spent many enjoyable hours discussing issues, ideas, and findings related to social networks. When Doc retired to Santa Barbara, he joined a faculty seminar on social networks in the Sociology Department at the University of California. We met regularly on Mondays from 3 to 5 p.m. for more than 15 years. Watching Doc's mind at work was instructive and stimulating as he juggled formalization and empiricism in productive and interesting ways. Doc's 1965 book, *Structural Models: An Introduction to the Theory of Directed Graphs*, co-authored with Frank Harary and Robert Norman (New York: Wiley), served as a standard reference for many of us in the field of social network analysis. Our commitment to the advancement of a network approach to group social structure and process, embedded in the field of social psychology, was secured by Doc's interest in and support of this project. Doc passed away in Santa Barbara on 18 July 2008.

The data analyzed in this book were gathered with support from the National Science Foundation under Grants SES85–10450 and SES85–11117 (N. E. Friedkin and K. S. Cook). In the collection of these data, we gratefully acknowledge the contributions of Karen Cook, Shawn Donnelly, Channing Hillway, and Joseph Whitmeyer.

Preface

Social influence network theory presents a formalization of the social process of attitude changes that unfold in a network of interpersonal influence (Friedkin 1986, 1991, 1998, 1999, 2001; Friedkin and Cook 1990; Friedkin and Johnsen 1990, 1997, 1999, 2002, 2003). In this book, we bring the theory to bear on lines of research in the domain of small group dynamics that are concerned with changes of group members' positions on an issue, including the formation of a consensus and of settled disagreement, via endogenous interpersonal influences, in which group members are responding to the displayed positions of the members of the group. Newcomb (1951) has suggested, and we agree, that the occurrence of endogenous interpersonal influence is among the basic postulates of social psychological theory:

> Any observable behavior [e.g., a displayed position on an issue] is not only a response (on the part of a subject) which is to be treated as a dependent variable; it is also a stimulus to be perceived by others with whom the subject interacts, and thus to be treated as an independent variable. (Newcomb 1951: 34)

Social influence network theory advances a dynamic social cognition mechanism, in which individuals are weighing and combining their own and others' positions on an issue in the revision of their own positions. The influence network construct of the theory is the social structure of the endogenous interpersonal influences that are involved in this mechanism.

With this theory, we seek to lay the foundation for a better formal integration of classical and current lines of work on small groups in psychological and sociological social psychology. We explore a terrain that lies between two traditions – the analysis of social cognitions, and the analysis of social structures. Our book is addressed to our colleagues in the social sciences, and to the increasing number of scholars in the physical sciences, who are engaged with the mathematical formalization of endogenous interpersonal influences that unfold in social networks. The theoretical scope of our approach is not limited to small groups. Small groups are simply the setting in which we are currently studying the mechanism upon which the theory is based. We investigate the merits of our postulated mechanism in small groups, assembled under experimental conditions, because such groups allow (a) measures of group members' initial positions on an issue, (b) control over the moment at which discussion on the issue is opened, (c) measures of the influence network in which group members are responding to the positions of other group members, and (d) measures of the revised positions that arise from such responses. However, the work in this book is also motivated by an agenda of theoretical integration in the field of research on small groups.

With the cognitive revolution in social psychology, which began in the late 1950s as a reaction to behaviorism, a misleading theoretical disjunction has emerged between the investigation of social cognition mechanisms and the investigation of small group social structures. The former is focused on the problem of how individuals process social information. The latter is focused on the implications of the structures of social relations. We want to reduce this disjunction. We intend to do so by revisiting lines of work on group dynamics with formal and empirical analyses that are based on a postulated social cognition mechanism unfolding in an influence network. Our analyses attend to (a) the classic work on group dynamics by Sherif, Asch, Newcomb, Cartwright, French, Festinger, and other investigators, whose empirical and theoretical work dramatically advanced the field of social psychology; (b) the more recent work of psychologists who have investigated majority–minority influences, social decision schemes, and choice shifts in small groups; and (c) the current work of sociologists on social structures of interpersonal sentiments and interpersonal influences in small groups. The bearing of a simple social cognition mechanism on these disconnected lines of inquiry suggests that their formal integration need not be a chimera, that is, a grotesque combination of mismatched parts. Hence, although our most fundamental focus is on whether the mechanism presents empirically supported predictions in small group settings, we also aim to foster the mathematical foundations of an approach to interpersonal influence that is widely applicable to various lines of research in social psychology. We hope that our colleagues in both psychological and sociological social psychology will appreciate this agenda, even though they may disagree with certain features of the approach that we have developed.

The bulk of the work on small group dynamics is in psychology. We bring a sociological perspective to bear on parts of this literature via the construct of an influence network. The social networks of interpersonal contacts that fascinated Cartwright, Festinger, French, Moreno, and

Newcomb now rarely appear as an important theoretical construct in the work of cognitively oriented social psychologists. This neglect is understandable given the promising frontiers opened by the cognitive revolution and the failure of the group dynamics tradition to incorporate social cognition into studies of the implications of social networks. Cartwright and Harary's (1956) formal theory of structural balance was a seminal effort to link social cognitions and social networks, and French's (1956) formal theory of social power was a seminal effort to link social networks and group members' positions on issues. Neither of these advances led to the incorporation of social networks as an important theoretical construct in the cognitive revolution. The connection of social networks to the core concern of social cognition – how people process social information – was not developed.

The theoretical status of social networks is secure within sociology. However, in the three core journals of sociology (*American Sociological Review*, *American Journal of Sociology*, and *Social Forces*), where social networks frequently appear as an important theoretical construct, a surprisingly small fraction of publications deal with empirical data on entire social networks, specifically the intact $n \times n$ matrix of social relations that exists among the members of a group of size n. Among studies that do deal with entire networks, a small fraction of them employ a clear specification of a social process that unfolds in the network; sociological work has been mainly focused on the structural features of social networks, such as the structural centrality of individual members and the differentiation of the network into subgroups. Our analysis of influence networks is based on the specification of a dynamic social cognition mechanism that describes how persons' attitudes on an issue are affected by their own and others' attitudes on the issue. The network construct that we deal with emerges from the specification of this cognitive mechanism.

Our work is situated at the interface of two disciplines with different emphases, and we present an approach in which neither emphasis alone is viewed as theoretically sufficient to explain individuals' positions on issues when individuals are embedded in groups. This work is addressed to scholars with an interest in the employment of mathematical formalizations of social phenomena. A serious reader, without the requisite mathematical background, may also find our empirical results of interest; in each chapter, we try to separate our formal and empirical analyses. Although we draw only on linear algebra and a discrete-time social process, our analysis sometimes becomes detailed as we elaborate the steps that move us from the postulated individual-level mechanism to its implications for group dynamics and outcomes. Our work presents an intimate dance between formal analysis and empirical findings in which we privilege both partners. This dance occurs in various different substantive venues that require separate introductions to substantive problems, depending on the particular line of work we are analyzing. We organize the book as follows.

Beyond the Part I introductory Chapters 1–4, we focus each of the remaining Chapters 5–12 on prominent topics of substantive inquiry. Chapters 5–12 in Parts II and III may be read independently and in any order. We have placed some of our mathematical analyses in appendices and refer to them where appropriate.

Chapters 5–9 in Part II deal with five classic lines of work: (a) the formation of consensus in group discussions of issues; (b) the special properties of the smallest group, the dyad; (c) the social comparison hypothesis that interpersonal influences are importantly affected by group members' initial positions on issues; (d) the majority influence hypothesis that individual and group outcomes are importantly affected by the group's initial faction structure; and (e) the group polarization hypothesis that small group discussions reinforce the average initial inclination of the group's members on an issue. These five lines of work, mainly developed by psychologists, intersect in important ways, with their focus on the account of an emergent consensus, in their emphasis on the initial positions of group members, and in their treatment of group discussion as a condition that has a main effect on individual outcomes. We show how our formalization bears on each of these lines of work.

Chapter 5 presents an analysis of the emergence of consensus via attitude changes that unfold in influence networks and related empirical findings on dyads, triads, and tetrads. A consensus may or may not be formed in a group. When it is formed, the consensus may be located at one of the two initial boundary positions of the initial range of positions in a group, or at an initial position between these boundary positions, or at a compromise position that is not one of the initial positions. All of these outcomes arise in our experiments, and we show how our formalization accommodates them. Disagreeing individual positions and collective consensual positions rarely fall outside the range of a group's initial positions; the exceptions are concentrated in dyads.

Chapter 6 focuses on dyadic influence systems. The smallest group presents certain unusual formal properties and our empirical evidence on dyads suggests that they have, in some respects, potentially more complex influence systems than those in larger groups. An influence process that involves superaccommodative group members necessarily exhibits particular unusual formal properties in a dyad, which only arise in very special cases in larger networks. In addition, our empirical evidence indicates that dyads are more likely than larger groups to generate settled positions on issues that are more extreme than any of the initial positions of group members. We present a viewpoint that relates the unusual formal properties of superaccommodative dyads and these observed breaches of initial ranges of positions.

Chapter 7 is addressed to Festinger's social comparison theory and to the broader literature dealing with the effects of group members' initial positions on an issue on their influence networks. Our findings indicate that, except in special cases, the distribution of initial positions on an issue is not informative of the influence network that is formed in a group and, in turn, is not generally informative of the final position(s) of group members on an issue. In the absence of a *direct measure* of the influence network of a group, models that seek to predict group members' final positions from a measure of group members' initial positions do not appear to substantially advance our understanding of group dynamics. We find that two prominent models that have attempted this – the consensus model of Davis (1996) and the meta-contrast-ratio model of McGarty, Turner, Hogg, and Wetherell (1992) – fail to advance the prediction of small group discussion outcomes beyond the baseline prediction that group outcomes converge to the mean of initial positions.

Chapter 8 is related to the focus of Chapter 7 and concentrates on the implications of initial attitudinal factions (e.g., majorities and minorities) in groups. We develop a formal perspective on the literature concerned with such factions. We show that initial factions do not fix the positions of their members, but do constrain their attitude changes. Factions are rarely broken and their members are usually "fellow travelers" during the course of the influence process.

Chapter 9 presents an analysis of choice shifts and group polarization. The literature on group polarization has taken group discussion as a condition that may shift the average initial position of group members in a particular direction. The network of interpersonal influences in which discussion on an issue unfolds is not directly dealt with as a basis of choice shifts and group polarization, although Cartwright (1971) pointed to the influence network as an important construct in his review of the developing literature on these phenomena. We show that choice shifts and group polarization are not main effects of group discussion but phenomena that may be generated by an influence process (one process) unfolding in an influence network. Some networks will generate choice shifts and group polarization; others will not.

Based on these analyses and empirical findings, it is difficult to escape the conclusion that the extant literatures in the group dynamics tradition have been limited by their lack of attention to the influence network construct and that the neglect of influence networks has impeded an integrative perspective. We advance a perspective wherein particular conditions and experimental paradigms may be formalized as special cases of social structures in which one fundamental social cognition process unfolds that can have different implications for different structures.

Part III concludes the book with Chapters 10–12, in which social influence network theory is linked with three prominent formal theories.

Chapter 10 brings our approach to bear on the social decision scheme theory hypothesis that group outcomes may be understood in terms of heuristic formal rules that directly transform group members' initial positions on an issue into a consensus position. Chapter 11 dovetails our theory with expectation states theory and affect control theory. Chapter 12 extends Blau's (1977) analysis of the implications of macro-level sociodemographic heterogeneity by introducing small group dynamics as a source of social integration in large-scale differentiated communities.

Chapter 10 concentrates on social decision scheme theory, arguably the most prominent approach among psychologists to group decisions, and this theory's application to jury outcomes. The extant literature on social decision scheme theory indicates that groups behave as if different decision schemes are invoked to reach a collective decision, depending on the type of issue with which the groups are dealing. We show that a social influence network perspective provides a unifying formal framework. A single social process is consistent with different decision schemes and suffices to account for the issue-contingent results that have been noted in the literature.

Chapter 11 shows how influence networks may form and change based on group members' attitudes about each other, and presents an integrative viewpoint on two prominent lines of research in sociological social psychology – expectation states theory and affect control theory. Expectation states theory emphasizes the effects of sociodemographic or personal characteristics of group members on their interpersonal influences. These effects are mediated by consensual perceptions of the relative competence of group members. Affect control theory emphasizes the effects of individuals' sentiments in interpersonal interactions. These sentiments are assumed to be consensual for persons in identical situations. Both theories invoke assumptions of prior consensus, and neither presents a framework that grapples with the implications of influence networks. We dovetail these two theories by relaxing the assumption of prior consensus that is involved in both theories and generalize expectation states theory under the assumption that broader interpersonal sentiments (attitudes about particular others) govern the formation of influence networks in small groups. We show how a group's influence network and matrix of interpersonal sentiments may coevolve over time, each affecting the other.

In Chapter 12, our final chapter, we develop a perspective on the implications of small group dynamics for macro-level sociological theory. We elaborate Blau's (1977) analysis of large-scale social structures, in which he hypothesizes that homophilous contacts contribute to macro-level social integration. Blau's insight is that an in-group relation on one sociodemographic dimension is frequently also an out-group relation on other sociodemographic dimensions. His theory is structural in that he does not delve into what occurs in interpersonal contacts. For Blau, contact presents integrative opportunities. We dovetail Blau's macro-level structural analysis with the meso-level of subgroups and with the micro-level interactionist tradition in social psychology that attends to small group dynamics. We show how gender-homophilous contacts in disjoint small groups may contribute to a macro-level reduction of the variance on issue positions in the population, due to the effects of the influence networks in the small groups of which the population is composed.

The book is a collaborative effort of a sociologist and a mathematician, but the substantive and mathematical work is not divided along these lines. Our collaboration has been successful and satisfying in part because we each contribute to both the substantive and the mathematical aspects of our research. To be sure, there is some natural asymmetry in this interaction – Friedkin more often bringing Johnsen to ground on substantive issues, and Johnsen more often bringing Friedkin to ground on mathematical issues. The experience of these corrections has underscored for us the value of this collaboration. Friedkin's (1986) initial foray into the development of the theory was followed by Friedkin and Johnsen's (1990) more general formalization. Since 1990, we have spent many enjoyable hours pursuing further generalizations, implications, and applications of one deceptively simple formal model. The result has been a series of publications on various topics (Friedkin 1991, 1998, 1999, 2001; Friedkin and Johnsen 1997, 1999, 2002, 2003). This work has been motivated by the realization that scholars in different disciplines have converged, sometimes independently, on an approach with strikingly similar formal features. We fold revised and extended versions of some of these publications into the present book, and present numerous new developments on the general formal properties and implications of the model, and on the model's application to small group dynamics.

The present book may be viewed as a companion to Friedkin's (1998) application of the model to the Durkheimian problem of social integration in large, complexly differentiated social structures. In that work, the constructs of the model were operationalized with structural measures, based on features of the communication network among group members. Here we apply the model to the micro settings of small groups engaged in a discussion of an issue, and the operationalization of the theory stays close to the *cognitive foundation of the formalization*. The influence process is the same in both applications – the study of large differentiated populations and the study of small groups; we have *one process* that unfolds in networks of different sizes and structural complexity. The bearing of our model on topics related to small group dynamics, we believe, is straightforward and informative.

Part I

Introduction

1

Group Dynamics: Structural Social Psychology

In this chapter, we present an overview of the group dynamics tradition that is our substantive focus, and we present our case for the advancement of this tradition via analysis of the attitude change process that unfolds in interpersonal influence networks. The idea that motivates this book is that some of the important lines of work on attitude change in small groups developed by psychologists (e.g., their work on social comparison, minority–majority factions, group polarization and choice shifts, and group decision schemes on attitudes) may be advanced if a social network perspective is brought to bear on them. In addition, we show how certain lines of current work in sociological social psychology may be advanced with our approach. Sociologists are more likely to pursue these advances than psychologists, given the current emphasis in psychology on social cognition. However, as we emphasize, the influence network and process specified by our theory are a social cognition structure and process. Thus, we seek to move the two orientations into closer theoretical proximity and to build a theoretical interface that speaks to both psychological and sociological social psychologists. By attending to the classic foundations of modern social psychology, to the theoretical perspectives, hypotheses, and findings that constituted the group dynamics tradition, we hope to advance current work on small group social structures and social processes. We revisit the classical past, pursuing an agenda of formal unification, in order to reshape perspectives and trigger new research.

1.1 The Field of Group Dynamics

The field of group dynamics is currently in an odd state. It consists of two disconnected subgroups of researchers, corresponding to the two disciplines – sociology and psychology – that have contributed to it.

3

It contains lines of inquiry that were developed by psychologists, and then abandoned by them during the cognitive revolution in psychology, and lines of work that never managed to interest sociologists, although they deal with key features of social groups. Recently, social identity and self-categorization theorists in psychology have sought to revisit and advance many of the lines of work on group dynamics. Their approach is based on the social cognition paradigm that has come to dominate psychological social psychology, and this paradigm is very different from the theoretical foundations on which the field of group dynamics was built. At the same time, sociologists who have advanced work on social networks, a construct that was theoretically central in the classical work on group dynamics, have not systematically applied these advances to the further development of these lines of work. Although attitudes are a core construct in social psychology, the development of a formal theory of attitude change in influence networks has not been vigorously pursued in sociology. We briefly review this strange state of affairs. We argue that a sociological approach, which attends to the influence networks that are formed within groups, may provide a useful platform for better theoretical integration of sociological and psychological work on group dynamics and advancement of particular lines of work in this field.

1.1.1 A Brief History of the Field

In the formative period of the field of group dynamics, psychologists were concerned with the origins and effects of interpersonal networks (Cartwright and Zander 1968; Festinger, Schachter, and Back 1950; Newcomb 1961). During the 1950s, psychologists pursued a research program on social communication and influence that focused on the bases of power and influence in groups (including determinants of pressures toward uniformity in groups, pressures to communicate with and influence others in a group, and persons' susceptibility to interpersonal influences), the structural conditions of groups (including group size, composition, cohesion, patterns of interpersonal communication and influence, and internal differentiation), and the effects of these group conditions on individual and collective outcomes. In 1958, the Society for the Psychological Study of Social Issues (a division of the American Psychological Association) gave its Kurt Lewin Memorial Award to the *group* of investigators associated with the Research Center for Group Dynamics at the University of Michigan, who developed this program of research (Cartwright 1958).

The field of group dynamics continued to grow during the 1960s (Cartwright and Zander 1968; Shaw 1961). Shaw (1961), reviewing the rapid growth of group dynamics during the preceding decade, wrote, "The future looks bright!" Steiner (1964) concurred with this assessment;

however, he noted that the field was fragmented into theoretically isolated areas. Although empirical work was abundant, the absence of integrative theoretical advances also was noted by Gerard and Miller (1967). Several key investigators began to shift their attention away from small group processes toward intra-individual processes, in particular, to the development of the theory of cognitive dissonance (Festinger 1957, 1964) and attribution theory (Kelley 1967).

By the 1970s, interest in the field of group dynamics had begun to wane, and this decline has continued to the present. Helmreich, Bakeman, and Scherwitz (1973) presented a highly critical viewpoint on the state of theory in the field, although not all subsequent reviewers have agreed with their assessment (Davis, Laughlin, and Komorita 1976; Zander 1979). Steiner (1974) commented that the study of group dynamics had declined, but he suggested that a resurgence of the field might be in the offing; subsequently, he concluded that his optimism had not been confirmed (Steiner 1986). McGrath and Kravitz (1982) reiterated the concerns that had surfaced during the 1970s:

> While the increased use of formal models will certainly tip the field more toward a concern with theoretical matters, the field is still a long way from having a proper balance among theory, method, and data. The dominance of atheoretical (even antitheoretical) viewpoints in the group area, virtually since the days of Lewin, still persists. We hoped to find signs of abatement of such views but did not. . . . Without the guiding hand of theory, it seems likely that the field will continue to move from one fashionable topic to the next, with fashions determined more by availability of paradigms than by conceptual import of the issues. (McGrath and Kravitz 1982: 219)

By the 1990s, Levine and Moreland (1990: 620–21) had concluded that the most active lines of research on small groups were no longer to be found in social psychology but in organizational psychology. However, even in organizational psychology, there has been a decline of work in the human relations and group dynamics traditions exemplified by Likert (1967) and Katz and Kahn (1978). During the 1990s, there was more work on intergroup relations, based on social cognition approaches, than on intragroup relations, in which the structural features of groups are acknowledged and dealt with (Mackie and Skelly 1994). In their review of these developments, Levine and Moreland state:

> The fact that more social psychologists are now studying small groups is encouraging, and intergroup relations is clearly an interesting and important area of research. Moreover, social cognition approaches to studying groups and their members have

produced some exciting discoveries and brought small group research closer to the current center of social psychology. At the same time, however, it is disturbing to watch research on intragroup relations move out of social psychology into other disciplines, such as organizational psychology (*cf.* Levine & Moreland, 1990). And much of the new research on intergroup relations has a very individualistic flavor. Few attempts are made to study actual social behavior, and many of the groups that are studied are minimal in nature. If such research replaces traditional work on small groups, which is more difficult to perform, then valuable insights into groups may be lost. (Levine and Moreland 1998: 416)

The field of group dynamics within psychology declined during the years of the cognitive revolution and, although the concepts of group membership and group effects have been retained, psychologists now rarely deal with the social network structure of groups, the social processes that unfold in these networks, or the contributions of these network structures and processes to individual and collective outcomes. A notable exception is the work of Latané (1981; 1996). The interests of psychologists have increasingly become concentrated on the study of individual perception and cognitive process.

1.1.2 Recent Activity in Self-Categorization Theory

Recently, British and Australian social psychologists working within the social cognition paradigm have revisited many of the classical lines of work that were developed in the field of group dynamics (Abrams and Hogg 1990b; Hogg and Abrams 1988; Turner 1991; Turner, Hogg, Oakes, Reicher, and Wetherell 1987; Turner and Oakes 1989):

The small-group dynamics tradition lost popularity, largely to attribution, social cognition, and intergroup relations research, during the 1960s and early 1970s.... However, since the late 1980s there has been a revival of a new and different form of group processes research within social psychology, that articulates with developments in social cognition and the study of intergroup relations and social identity. (Hogg and Tindale 2001: 57)

Self-categorization theory focuses on how persons categorize themselves and others (including the definition of social identities) and how this categorization process serves as a basis for group behavior. According to self-categorization theory, the depersonalization of individuals that is, for example, entailed in the categorization of persons into *in-groups* and *out-groups*, is a fundamental process underlying group phenomena. Once individuals are depersonalized, group phenomena can be understood on the basis of *prototypes*:

> For self-categorization theory, a prototype is a cognitive representation of the defining features of a social category. It is a relatively nebulous or fuzzy set of properties that the individual group member believes defines the category. Prototypes... are embodied as a reified image of a "most prototypical" group member – an ideal or representative category member. Prototypes encompass the whole range of interrelated properties that define the group and differentiate it from relevant outgroups, or from people who are not in the group. The prototype is the cognitive representation of the group norm or the group stereotype. (Hogg 1992: 94)

> Categorization, therefore, accentuates perceived similarities between self or fellow group members and the prototype. This is what is meant by depersonalization: self and others are perceived not as unique persons but as embodiments of the prototype. Since prototypes are, by definition, shared among group members, one consequence of the depersonalization process is relative intragroup uniformity of perceptions, attitudes and behavior. In this way the self-categorization process accounts for conformity to group norms. (Hogg 1992: 94)

Hence, in this theory, social influence boils down to group members' convergence on the prototypical position of the group. Members of outgroups have no influence on the members of an in-group.

The categorization process and the construction of prototypes are driven by individuals' efforts to reduce uncertainty and construct coherent or meaningful cognitive structures that "pattern the social world into discrete, well-defined and meaningful social units" (Hogg 1992: 103). Persons define themselves as belonging to a particular social category, ascertain the norms of that social category, and bring their attitudes and behaviors into conformity with those norms. This process is more or less powerful depending on the salience of persons' category membership; for instance, categorization theorists explain that an intergroup context fosters *in-group out-group* distinctions and makes social category assignments and prototypes salient. In self-categorization theory, prototypes are not formed from the process of interpersonal influence but from a *shared perception* of the distribution of group positions on an attitudinal or behavioral dimension:

> Consider a salient social comparative dimension (attitude scale, behavior dimension, etc.) which represents ingroup, including

self, and outgroup or non-group members. The relevant ingroup
norm is that position on the dimension which simultaneously
maximizes intergroup differences and minimizes intragroup differences. The ingroup member occupying this position, the most
prototypical group member, is the person who is simultaneously
most different to the outgroup and least different to the ingroup.
(Hogg 1992: 97)

If there were not a shared perception of the distribution of persons'
attitudinal or behavioral positions, then there might not be a shared
definition of the group's prototype.

Self-categorization theorists have systematically explored the application of their theory to a variety of group dynamics phenomena, including
conformity, polarization, leadership, social influence, deindividuation,
and cohesion. They view their approach as a radical departure from
classic explanations of group dynamics phenomena that emphasize interpersonal relations involving attraction, communication, and influence.

The structure of interpersonal interaction in a group was a prominent, if
not the core, theoretical construct in most of the classic work. In contrast
to self-categorization theory, we pursue an integration of group dynamics
phenomena on the basis of a refined theory of social influence networks.
We share the sense of self-categorization theorists that a better integration
of the field is possible and worth pursuing, but we believe that the early
structural foundations of the field should not be discarded.

1.1.3 Enlarging the Scope of Structural Social Psychology

The cognitive revolution in psychology has contributed to the decline
of group dynamics as a field of study, and few psychologists are now
engaged in refining the classical tenet that the *social structure* of groups
(in particular, the network of interpersonal influences that is formed
among the members of a group) is an important theoretical construct in
explanations of individuals' thoughts, feelings, and behaviors. However,
the pursuit of a more refined specification of structural effects, which
involves an elaborated theoretical understanding of how interpersonal
processes unfold in more or less complexly configured social structures,
is a goal that has remained relevant in many fields of sociological inquiry.
This goal has helped to support the enduring interest of sociologists in
social network structure and process.

Sociologists' work on social networks increased during the same period
in which psychologists' work on social networks diminished. The formation of social networks and the effects of these networks on persons'
attitudes and behaviors have been long-standing concerns of sociologists

(Coleman, Katz, and Menzel 1966; Davis 1970; Homans 1950; Lundberg and Lawsing 1937). Currently, the social network construct appears in numerous sociological publications. Remarkably few of these publications actually deal with the structure of interpersonal relations in which persons are embedded, i.e., an $n \times n$ matrix realization of a social network. Among the few publications that do grapple directly with the implications of network structure, a small fraction entertain models of an interpersonal influence process that affects network members' attitudes and interpersonal agreements. Most of the network models that do touch on these constructs (attitudes and agreements) are simulation models for which no direct empirical support is provided.

We believe that the field of group dynamics will be advanced by a sociological perspective that focuses on how attitudes are formed in influence networks. In the remainder of this chapter, we present our case for this approach. Our method is dialectical. We describe three points of theoretical tension or opposition in social psychology, how these tensions are manifested in social influence network theory, and how social influence theory helps to reconcile and synthesize them. To make our points, we draw on the scalar equation of our *standard model*, upon which most of the analysis in this book is based. Here we present only the bare bones of the model. The reader will have questions about where this mechanism comes from, its theoretical heritage, the assumptions that it involves, and its operationalization. We present a formal exegesis of the model in Chapter 2 and an operationalization of its constructs in Chapter 3. In Appendix A we collect the key equations, construct definitions, and measurement models developed in Chapters 2 and 3.

Our standard model describes a mechanism by which persons weigh and integrate their own attitudes and the attitudes of others on an issue:

$$y_i^{(t+1)} = a_{ii} \sum_{j=1}^{n} w_{ij} y_j^{(t)} + (1 - a_{ii}) y_i^{(1)}, \qquad (1.1)$$

for each $i = 1, 2, \ldots, n$ and $t = 1, 2, \ldots$. The n group members' time t positions on an issue are $y_1^{(t)}, y_2^{(t)}, \ldots, y_n^{(t)}$, and these positions include their initial set of positions $y_1^{(1)}, y_2^{(1)}, \ldots, y_n^{(1)}$. Group members' individual susceptibilities to interpersonal influence are $a_{11}, a_{22}, \ldots, a_{nn}$, where $0 \leq a_{ii} \leq 1$ for all i. The relative interpersonal influence of each group member j on i is $w_{i1}, w_{i2}, \ldots, w_{in}$, where $0 \leq w_{ij} \leq 1$ for all i and j, $\sum_{j=1}^{n} w_{ij} = 1$, and $w_{ii} = 1 - a_{ii}$ for all i. Note that $\sum_{j=1}^{n} a_{ii} w_{ij} + (1 - a_{ii}) = 1$, so that i's attitude at time $t + 1$ is formed as a *weighted average* of the attitudes of others and self at time t, and i's initial position.

Individual differences are allowed in persons' susceptibilities to interpersonal influence and in their profiles of accorded interpersonal influences. If a person i's susceptibility is $a_{ii} = 0$, then i's position on the issue does not change. If $a_{ii} = 1$, then i attaches no weight to his or her initial position, and i's initial position may be modified by the interpersonal influences of one or more other members of the group. The relative weights of others' positions, and the positions that they take on the issue at time t, determine the modification. If $0 < a_{ii} < 1$, then i's initial position on the issue has some weight in any modification of i's position that occurs.

Here, we draw on our standard model to make our points with sufficient formal precision so that the reader may see how a formal synthesis of each of the tensions that we address is afforded by our approach. In this chapter, we seek to motivate theoretical interest in an individual-level social-cognition mechanism that includes endogenous interpersonal influences. The influence network construct that is involved in this mechanism is the social structure of such endogenous interpersonal influences. The potential theoretical advances that may be achieved with an influence network construct are the generic payoffs of a class of models of which our standard model is a specific instance.

1.2 Particularities versus Ideal Types

The first tension is between particular and general features of groups in explanatory models (Nagel 1961: 547–8) and stems from the idea that we must either plunge into a detailed ethnographic analysis of particular groups (i.e., adopt an idiographic approach) or else rise to a higher level of abstraction with a formal model that might be applied to many groups (i.e., adopt a nomothetic approach). We show how the formal apparatus of social network theory allows information about the particularities of a group to be taken into account in explanations of individual and group outcomes and how the theory also may be employed to make more general predictions about the effects of group social structures.

Sociology has long struggled with the question of the relative merits of investigating the particular or general features of groups in an effort to explain and predict individual and group outcomes. Weber recognized that

> As in the case of every generalizing science the abstract character of the concepts of sociology is responsible for the fact that, compared with actual historical reality, they are relatively lacking in fullness of concrete detail. (Weber 1947: 109)

Weber argued that the construction of *ideal types* of social structures and processes, abstracted from historical reality and causal complexity, was an essential theoretical tool of sociology. Unfortunately, although an ideal-type or formal model may be desired and pursued, it may not be attained or attainable. Because sociological models involve considerable abstraction, we are continually faced with the difficult problem of assessing whether a high degree of abstraction is acceptable as a meaningful representation of reality or whether it involves a simplification that is unacceptably misleading.

Social influence network theory deals with this tension between the particular and general by allowing for both. In order to understand the social dynamics of particular groups, we must grapple with the actual, realized network structures of these groups. Social influence network theory allows the representation of particularities in the structure of the social situation in which the attitude change process occurs. These particularities are represented in the individual differences among group members' susceptibilities to influence, interpersonal influences, and initial attitudes on particular issues, i.e., the three constructs of the theory. A detailed ethnography of a group is needed by our theory to describe members' initial attitudinal positions, susceptibilities, and interpersonal influences. Such a detailed ethnography is especially crucial when idiosyncratic features of the group's social structure (for example, a single relationship of interpersonal influence between the members of two subgroups) are consequential for an explanation of the observed individual and collective outcomes of the group. In our theory, all effects on persons' attitudes are transmitted through one of three variables – persons' susceptibilities to interpersonal influences, interpersonal influences, and initial positions. Hence, antecedent conditions, including idiosyncratic features of a group, are moved into the background. Moreover, our theory involves a dramatic simplification and abstraction of the process of interpersonal influence and, in this respect, it asserts the existence of a *general* process.

Social influence network theory also allows the analysis of *abstracted* structural conditions in groups (e.g., forms of influence hierarchy and patterns of differentiation) or ideal types of social structures (e.g., center–periphery influence networks and conformity situations). Such analysis is accomplished with *special cases* in which group members' susceptibilities, influences, and initial positions are constrained analytically or by an experimental design. In the analysis of special cases, the theoretical focus is on a *type* of social structure and its implications, whereas in a detailed ethnography of a particular group the focus is on the observed social structure (in whatever form it takes) and on the implications of that structure for past and future outcomes.

We will show how the formal apparatus of social network theory allows both ethnographic and ideal-type analyses. The analysis of particularities will be illustrated with data on small discussion groups for which we obtained measures of the influence networks and initial attitudes of the members. The analysis of ideal-type structures will be illustrated throughout the book and especially in our work on special cases of the theory. An example is the special case of a minority of one, i.e., a group with three or more members in which all the members save one have a fixed unanimous initial position on an issue. This is the situation dealt with in the experiments conducted by Asch, and represents an ideal-type deviance vs. conformity circumstance. Another example is the special case of a consensually stratified influence network, i.e., a group with two or more members in which the profiles of influences on each group member are the same for each member; this is the structural condition that is assumed to obtain in the task-oriented groups dealt with by expectation states theory. Another example is the case of an ideal-type accommodative group, i.e., a group with two or more members each of whom adopts the mean initial position of the group; this special case is a prominent baseline model in psychological social psychology.

These special cases, and others, will be formally described and analyzed. Some of these cases describe classic experimental paradigms upon which research has been based. Others are constrained situations that might be (but have not yet been) operationalized in the laboratory, for which there are deducible predictions. Still others are difficult (perhaps impossible) to operationalize in the laboratory, but may (or do) occur outside it. With suitable measures of persons' susceptibilities, influences, and initial positions on an issue, we can work in a theoretically coherent way in both laboratory and field settings.

1.3 Social Structure versus Social Process

The second tension is between social structure and process. Here we situate our network theory of social influence in the ongoing tension between theoretical approaches that focus strictly on social process and those that focus strictly on social structure. The former approach includes processes that operate within and between individuals (such as mechanisms dealing with information integration and social conflict), and the latter approach includes structures of stable social relations (such as the authority hierarchy in formal organizations and enduring influence networks in groups). In psychologists' research on mechanisms of attitude change (Eagly and Chaiken 1993), social structures rarely appear as important explanatory constructs, and in sociologists' research on the effects of social structures on persons' attitudes, the process of attitude change is rarely attended to in any detail. For the psychologist, the attitude change mechanism that is specified by social influence network theory may be more interesting than the social influence network in which the process unfolds. For the sociologist, the structural effects of the social influence network may be more interesting than the process that produces these effects. However, the effects of the social process and of the network structure cannot be fully understood without taking both into account, and this is what we shall do.

Our analysis of groups is based on a model of a micro-level *social process* that unfolds in a macro-level *social structure*. The social process is described by (1.1). We say that the social process is at the micro-level because it describes how individuals cognitively combine and integrate the attitudes of other group members with their own attitudes. The social structure is the influence network described by the matrix

$$
\mathbf{W} = \begin{bmatrix}
w_{11} & w_{12} & \cdots & w_{1n} \\
w_{12} & w_{22} & \cdots & w_{2n} \\
\vdots & \vdots & \ddots & \vdots \\
w_{n1} & w_{n2} & \cdots & w_{nn}
\end{bmatrix},
\tag{1.2}
$$

with $a_{ii} = 1 - w_{ii}$ for $i = 1, 2, \ldots, n$. We say that the social structure is at the macro-level, even if it is the structure of a small group, because it describes the entire group network of interpersonal influences, potentially of large size, in which each group member is embedded. The implications of the influence network depend on the social process that is unfolding in it. The implications of the social process depend on the network in which it is unfolding. Hence, we treat social structure and social process as dually important.

1.3.1 Social Process with Minimal Social Structure

The attitude change mechanism that is specified by social influence network theory states that the attitude held by person i at time $t + 1$ is a weighted average of i's and others' influential attitudes at time t and i's attitude at time $t = 1$. It is a model of what is going on in the head of person i, and it describes a particular *cognitive algebra* by which person i reconciles or integrates discrepant attitudes. Taken in isolation, i.e., for one person, the scalar equation of the model (1.1) describes a cognitive process for the focal person who is responding to the attitudes of significant others – a minimal social structure. This process could be investigated without attending to the larger influence network in which it is embedded, i.e., the complete network described by $\mathbf{W}$.

For example, the immediate $t = 2$ response of person i to the initial $t = 1$ positions of group members on an issue is

$$y_i^{(2)} = a_{ii} \sum_{j=1}^{n} w_{ij} y_j^{(1)} + (1 - a_{ii}) y_i^{(1)}, \tag{1.3}$$

so that the *change* in i's attitude from $t = 1$ to $t = 2$ is

$$y_i^{(2)} - y_i^{(1)} = a_{ii} \left(\sum_{j=1}^{n} w_{ij} y_j^{(1)} - y_i^{(1)} \right). \tag{1.4}$$

The model predicts that i's initial change of attitude is a proportion (a_{ii}) of the distance between i's initial position and his or her weighted average of the group's initial positions. The proportion is i's *susceptibility* to influence, and the *weighted average* is i's social construction that may not be shared by others in the group. Thus, an investigation might strictly focus on a subject's one-time (immediate) response to the displayed initial attitudes of all members of the group.

But there is a limitation to focusing only on the direct response of an individual – the implications of the social process unfolding over time in the group of n individuals are ignored. If everyone in a group is subject to the same process and may be revising their attitudes, then a given person may find that the influential attitudes to which he or she is responding also may be changing; and these changes may trigger further changes in the focal person's attitudes. Hence, the sequence of attitude changes in the group as a whole becomes crucial to understanding how the group members have come to settle on particular attitudes. Put another way, for a more general understanding of the origins of group members' attitudes on an issue, we must deal with the *complete social structure* of group members' direct responses to one another and to the flows of interpersonal influence among them over time.

1.3.2 Social Structure without Social Process

By the same token, without attending to social process, it is also difficult to predict the attitudes of the members of a group strictly on the basis of the social structure of the group. Consider the representation of the interpersonal influence network of a group as a directed graph with persons $(1, 2, \ldots, n)$ and lines ($\rightarrow$) indicating their direct interpersonal influences on each other. Information on members' initial positions and on the configuration of positive interpersonal influences, i.e., the pattern of $w_{ij} > 0$ values for i and j in $\mathbf{W}$, gives us no reliable basis for predicting the equilibrium attitudes of the group's members. The configuration of positive interpersonal influences does not indicate the degree of each group member's susceptibility to interpersonal influence, nor does it indicate the presence of heterogeneity in the relative strength of the interpersonal influences. It does not indicate how many times persons will revise their opinions, nor anything about the sequence of interpersonal influences. Most importantly, it does not indicate how persons combine the various influences upon them. In short, the configuration of positive interpersonal influences does not indicate anything about the process of attitude change that might unfold in the structure.

Without social process assumptions, the implications of a configuration of positive interpersonal influences are ambiguous. This may be a hard pill to swallow for those sociologists who believe that a science of social networks can be developed that attends only to the structural configuration of relations among social units. However, a focus on structure alone will not significantly advance our explanation of group dynamics unless it is coupled with formal theories of the social processes that occur in networks. We doubt that there are any structural effects on individual outcomes that are not contingent upon social processes, because different social process assumptions may lead to different structural effects. If we cannot fully comprehend the implications of a social structure without attending to the social processes that are operating in it, then sociological theories concerned with social network structures need to be elaborated to include models of social processes.

Although some attention to social process is apparent in lines of work in structural social psychology (e.g., on social contagion, social exchange, and social movements), the sociological analysis of network structures has neglected the specification of the processes that occur within these structures. One need only peruse Wasserman and Faust's (1994) well-known reference work on network analysis to confirm this neglect. If every hypothesis of a structural effect is contingent on implicit social process assumptions, then a fully refined science of social networks will be one in which the intimate relationship between social structure and social process in the determination of individual and collective outcomes is explicitly and formally specified.

1.3.3 Social Structure in Social Process

We depart from the structural emphasis of social network analysis and place our emphasis on social process. We *start* with a formal model of endogenous interpersonal influences on attitudes and *derive* both our definition of a "group" and our hypotheses about structural effects on attitudes *from the process*, as it plays out in a network of interpersonal influences.

The relationship between this approach and other approaches to attitude change (Eagly and Chaiken 1993) may be conceptualized in terms of the social process equation of our standard model (1.1),

$$y_i^{(t+1)} = a_{ii} \sum_{j=1}^{n} w_{ij} y_j^{(t)} + (1 - a_{ii}) y_i^{(1)},$$

which describes the immediate (unmediated) responses of persons to the attitudes of influential others including themselves. Social psychological theories of attitude change and persuasion concentrate on such immediate responses, on the processes by which they occur, or on the conditions that affect these responses (Eagly and Chaiken 1993; Petty, Wegener, and Fabrigar 1997). Social influence network theory extends current theories of attitude formation by taking into account sequences of endogenous interpersonal influence and, in doing so, *immediately implicates social structure*. That is, if we start with the cognition mechanism (1.1) and collect the n weights $w_{i1}, w_{i2}, \ldots, w_{in}$ for the direct unmediated influences of the time t attitudes on person i's time $t + 1$ attitude for *each* of the n members of a group, we get the matrix realization of a valued network $\mathbf{W} = [w_{ij}]$. Our theoretical approach does not begin with a network of interpersonal communications or social exchanges and then address their bearing on interpersonal influences; instead we begin with the social process mechanism, in which weights on self and others' attitudes appear as theoretical constructs. Positive weights may or may not be restricted to relations of direct communication or social exchange, although the latter may be employed as structural indicators of such positive weights. Moreover, the theory points to the importance of the relative magnitudes of these weights.

Thus, although social influence network theory is predicated on a social cognition function that describes what is happening within the head of a person, the theory does not support a reductionism in which collective outcomes (such as consensus or disagreement) are explained in terms of a simple aggregation of individuals' independent responses to their situations. The theory rests on a model of how individuals cognitively integrate conflicting attitudes, but the outcomes of this process depend upon (and cannot be understood apart from) the social structure that is implicated in the process. Social structure is in the process. If the structure is fixed, as in our standard model, the influence network may be viewed as a structural context in which the process of interpersonal influence unfolds; along these lines, the network may be a preexisting structure in which the social influence process is activated. However, the assumption of stability may be relaxed (Friedkin and Johnsen 1990) and, when it is, the social structural transformations become part of the group dynamics on an issue. We do exactly this in our integration of expectations states theory, affect control theory, and social influence network theory.

In terms of this influence process, a *social group* is defined as the set of individuals $(i = 1, 2, \ldots, n)$ for whom the process is operating over time $(t = 1, 2, \ldots)$,

$$y_1^{(t+1)} = a_{11} \sum_j^n w_{1j} y_j^{(t)} + (1 - a_{11}) y_1^{(1)}$$

$$y_2^{(t+1)} = a_{22} \sum_j^n w_{2j} y_j^{(t)} + (1 - a_{22}) y_2^{(1)} \qquad (1.5)$$

$$\vdots$$

$$y_n^{(t+1)} = a_{nn} \sum_j^n w_{nj} y_j^{(t)} + (1 - a_{nn}) y_n^{(1)},$$

such that the set of n group members includes all persons who directly or indirectly (i.e., via intermediaries) influence each other's attitudes. Thus, a group is defined on the basis of the endogenous interpersonal influences that occur on an issue. An *éminence grise* (e.g., Rasputin) must be included in the analysis of an influence system. This definition is consistent with a number of prior definitions of groups (Hogg 1992: 4). In our theory a group is a "collection of individuals who are *interacting* with one another" (Bonner 1959: 4; Freeman 1992; Homans 1950: 1; Stogdill 1959: 18); it also is "a collection of individuals who are *interdependent*" (Cartwright and Zander 1968: 46; Lewin 1951: 146); and it also is "a collection of individuals who influence each other" (Shaw 1976: 11). We do not require that group members "perceive themselves as belonging to a group" (e.g., they need not be solidary, cohesive, or group-oriented), or that they have "joined together to achieve a goal" (e.g., they need not be task-oriented), or that they are "trying to satisfy some need through their joint association" (e.g., they need not be homogeneously motivated), or that their "interactions are structured by a set of roles or norms" (e.g., they need not be formally organized). For instance, the extensively ramified network of a large population might not satisfy any of these properties, yet might satisfy our definition of a group if the positive weights of the population's members were restricted to the population.

Although we do not stipulate that identifications, goals, needs, or norms are implicated in the process of attitude change, we do require a common engagement with an object or set of objects (e.g., an issue, person, or event) toward which persons' attitudes are being formed. Our definition of a social group implies that different groups may exist for *different* issues that arise in a population of persons, that different groups may exist on the *same* issue, and that the same group may be engaged with different issues.

1.4 Individuals versus Groups

The third tension is between groups and individuals as analytical units. Social influence network theory simultaneously implicates the group and the individual and provides a consistent analysis of both individual- and group-level phenomena. Influence networks are the ubiquitous context in which persons' expressed positions on issues are modified. Understanding the role of such networks in the attitude change process is crucial to an understanding of how group members resolve their disagreements and settle upon attitudes toward the various objects in their social environment. Even if we thoroughly understand the *direct attitudinal response* of individuals to various conditions (including the influential attitudes of others), a structural sociological perspective on attitude formation and change suggests that there is more to be learned.

First, the conditions that affect persons' attitudes are not randomly distributed, and sociologists emphasize that there is a social structure of conditions that importantly contributes to an explanation of why persons who are located in different parts of the structure may hold different attitudes toward the same objects. Second, if the important conditions that affect persons' attitudes include the attitudes of other persons, then individuals may be situated in a changing landscape of attitudes. If some person j who is influential for person i changes his or her attitude on an issue, then i is confronted with a new situation. Hence, as each group member responds to the attitudes of others, some of the attitude changes that occur may importantly alter the conditions under which an attitude formation process in the group unfolds. A sociological perspective draws attention to the social structure of such endogenous interpersonal responses and emphasizes its explanation of the movement of persons' attitudes over time and their final destinations, including their convergence to consensus. Social influence network theory is a formalization of the interpersonal influence process that occurs in a social structure of endogenous interpersonal responses to the changing attitudes of others.

1.4.1 Studying Individuals or Groups

When social psychologists refer to the problem of integrating groups and individuals, they do so in one of two distinct ways. Either a distinction is made between the study of groups and the study of individuals (group-level versus individual-level units of analysis) or a distinction is made between types of variables (group-level versus individual-level variables) that may affect individual outcomes. Allport argued that "there is no psychology of groups which is not essentially and entirely a psychology of individuals" (1924: 4).[1] Homans argued that "groups are not what we study but where we study it" (1961: 7). Along the same lines, we believe that it is worthwhile to base an understanding of social psychological phenomena in groups on formal models of social process that describe how *individuals* respond to the more or less dynamic (changing) conditions in which they are situated. Groups, large and small, are where we study the process of interpersonal influence on individuals' attitudes, and we aim to derive conclusions about the effects of group structure and other group-related phenomena from this influence process.

F. Allport remarked that

> The study of groups is, in fact, the province of the special science of sociology. While the social psychologist studies the individual in the group, the sociologist deals with the group as a whole. He discusses its formation, solidarity, continuity, and change. (1924: 10)

The idea that psychologists should be concerned with individuals and sociologists should be concerned with groups was probably never defensible, and it is certainly outmoded now in the minds of most sociologists. Social psychologists sometimes refer to the problem of integrating groups and individuals in terms of a distinction between group-level and individual-level *variables* that may affect individual outcomes. With respect to these two types of variables, psychologists' interest has become increasingly focused on the cognitive conditions and intraindividual processes that explain individuals' thoughts, feelings, and behaviors. Sociologists have been more interested in the effects of sociodemographic conditions on individuals in their environments.

The integration of group and individual-level explanatory variables is typically accomplished with contextual-effects models of individuals' thoughts, feelings, or behaviors. For instance, a linear model of the form $y = X\beta + u$ may be referred to as a contextual-effects model when the individual-level units of analysis are situated in various groups and the set of explanatory variables, X, that are hypothesized to influence the individual outcome, y, include both individual-level and group-level variables. A group-level variable may be an aggregated measure of individual-level variables (e.g., the average income or age, or the percentage of males or college graduates in a group) or a measure that is independent of individual-level variables (e.g., characteristics of a group's task). There are more elaborate forms of this genre of contextual analysis (e.g., Bryk

---

1 Note that Allport is arguing that an understanding of *social psychological* phenomena in groups must rest on the study of individuals. He is not suggesting that all types of group dynamics can be understood strictly in terms of individuals' thoughts, feelings, and behaviors.

and Raudenbush 1992), but the basic approach is much the same as in the standard contextual-effects model. Groups and individuals are integrated in this form of contextual analysis when the variable features of both are dealt with simultaneously in the same model.

In the experimental studies of psychologists on small groups, a *group discussion* of an issue is frequently treated as a contextual condition that has an effect on the individuals who are situated in the group. We will see this approach manifested in several of the lines of work addressed in this book, where the social structure of the group (the network of interpersonal influences among a group's members) is not attended to. Social influence network theory not only allows an analysis of standard contextual effects (direct effects of group-level conditions on the attitudes of persons), but also refines such an analysis by taking into account the network of interpersonal influences of a group. Group members may differ in the weight that they accord to particular persons and the attitudinal positions they advocate. The pattern of such interpersonal influences mediates the effect of a *group discussion* on individual responses. Moreover, these interpersonal influences are implicated in a social process that produces the responses not as a main effect of *group discussion* but as an outcome that depends on the implications of the process unfolding in the influence network that may be configured in different ways. Social influence network theory refines the contextual construct of a group discussion.

In addition, social influence network theory extends the classical contextual effects model by allowing the particular circumstances (local environments) of some persons to affect the attitudes of other persons who may be situated in very different circumstances (local environments). If endogenous interpersonal influences are affecting attitudes, then persons' attitudes are being affected by the attitudes of others that, in turn, are being affected by their individual and contextual circumstances. Hence, persons' attitudes may be indirectly affected by the contextual circumstances of other persons. Such effects are predicted when group members' initial positions on an issue are linked to a set of individual and contextual conditions that are not shared by all members, i.e., $y^{(1)} = X\beta$. In the next chapter, we will show that the interpersonal influence process in a group may result in a set of total (all direct and indirect) interpersonal influences, which we denote by an $n \times n$ matrix $V = [v_{ij}]$, where v_{ij} is the total influence of j on i that results from the influence process unfolding in the group. We will show that the transformation of group members' initial positions on an issue into their final positions may be formally described as a transformation that is mediated by V; i.e., $y^{(\infty)} = Vy^{(1)}$. With the linkage $y^{(1)} = X\beta$, the effects of X also are mediated by V; i.e., $y^{(\infty)} = VX\beta$. Hence, a person may come to hold an attitude that is more consonant with the social circumstances of some other person or reference group than with his or her own immediate personal circumstances. The total effects of endogenous interpersonal influences V may importantly *reorganize* the associations between persons' sociodemographic conditions and their attitudes.

For each individual, the influence process implicates a subset of persons who are directly influencing him or her and, more broadly, a larger subset of persons who may have an indirect influence via intermediaries. Potentially, the influence network of the entire group becomes relevant to an account of each member's attitudes. Furthermore, the pattern of initial positions of other group members on an issue also becomes relevant to an explanation of individuals' equilibrium attitudes, because it is the net effect of the *content* of other group members' initial positions (transmitted directly and via intermediaries) that determines the content of each member's equilibrium position. Hence, social influence network theory leads to an elaborated form in which contextual effects are manifested (Friedkin 1990).

1.4.2 Explanations of Collective Outcomes

Groups and individuals also are integrated when the process of interpersonal influence produces collective (group-level) events or has collective properties or features that are characteristic of the group rather than of particular individuals. The theoretical problem of showing how individual actions or interpersonal interactions produce group-level phenomena is a classic problem in sociology – an aspect of the micro–macro problem (Alexander, Giesen, Munch, and Smelser 1987). Social influence network theory provides an explanation of particular forms of group-level outcomes in terms of the interpersonal influence process among group members. Coleman (1990) points out that specifying the micro-to-macro transition is a problem that is widely salient in the social sciences:

> This micro-to-macro problem is sometimes called by European sociologists the problem of transformation. In economics, it is (misleadingly) termed the problem of aggregation; in political science, a major instance of it is the problem of social choice. It is the process through which individual preferences become collective choices; the process through which dissatisfaction becomes revolution; through which simultaneous fear in members of a crowd turns into a mass panic; through which preferences, holdings of private goods, and the possibility of exchange create market prices and a redistribution of goods; through which individuals' task performance in an organization creates a social product; through which the reduction of usefulness of children to parents

leads families to disintegrate; through which interest cleavages
lead (or fail to lead) to overt social conflict. (Coleman 1990:
1321)

The same problem has intrigued and troubled researchers concerned with
the theoretical foundations of social psychology (Allison and Messick
1987). Some researchers have argued that our understanding of groups
and collective outcomes must be rooted in individuals' thoughts, feelings, and behaviors (Allport 1924, 1962; Homans 1964). However, the
theoretical approach to dealing with the emergence of collective social
psychological outcomes has remained elusive. Asch observed that

> We need a way of understanding group process that retains the
> prime reality of individual *and* group, the two permanent poles
> of all social processes. We need to see group forces arising out
> of the actions of individuals and individuals whose actions are
> a function of the group forces that they themselves (or others)
> have brought into existence. We must see group phenomena as
> both the *product and condition* of actions of individuals. (Asch
> 1952: 251)

Allport describes this issue as the "master problem" of social psychology:

> In spite of advances in many areas of social psychology and
> the social sciences, we are still faced, if we view the situa-
> tion candidly, with the realization that our theories of social
> causality, and of the relation of action at the "societal" level
> to what we recognize as the acts of individuals, are far from
> adequate.... We must try to discover some more satisfactory
> paradigm for "the group and the individual." Some way must
> be found to describe in general terms that layout of conditions
> surrounding and involving individuals which we have called "the
> group," and to formulate, in the precise yet *universal* manner of
> science, what actually goes on in the situation we call "collective"
> action. In this broader sense the problem of the individual and
> the group is really the "master problem" of social psychology.
> (Allport 1962: 7)

The micro-to-macro transition is not a problem for which there is a single theoretical solution. Different collective outcomes may arise from different social processes and, therefore, different theories may be involved.
The generic problem is a statement about the form of a theoretical account
of group-level outcomes, which may or may not also include an account of
how group-level conditions affect the individual-level outcomes. Lawler,
Ridgeway, and Markovsky (1993) have reviewed some of the work in
social psychology that has addressed the micro–macro problem.

Our theoretical contribution to the literature on the micro-to-macro transition is limited to the specification of the interpersonal influence process (1.1) that affects group members' attitudes on issues and explains particular group-level phenomena. The joint or aggregate interpersonal influences unfolding over time among the members of a group produce phenomena that are not characteristics of the individual but of the group as a social unit. The influence mechanism describes the individual-level integration of possibly diverse influential positions on an issue. The system of equations describes a network of endogenous interpersonal influences that, over time, generates flows of influence and emergent collective characteristics of the group.

These collective features include the emergence of a consensual position on an issue from an initial state of heterogeneity. Such an emergent consensus renders moot the problem of *social choice* concerned with formal procedures (voting schemes) by which a collective decision may be reached among disagreeing persons. Our readers' experiences in decision-making groups, where formal votes on issues are often dispensed with upon the emergence of an apparent informal consensus, are instances of this. An emergent consensus also may be internalized as a group-level norm that constrains future attitudes and behaviors. Sherif's (1936) experiment is the seminal demonstration that internalized norms may be generated in this fashion.

An emergent pattern of interpersonal disagreements also is an instance of a micro-to-macro transition, especially when group members' enter into an influence process on an issue with the expectation of reaching consensus. The influence process may transform group members' attitudes but not result in a consensus. For example, the process may reduce interpersonal disagreements and transform heterogeneous distributions of initial positions on an issue into bimodal or multimodal distributions consisting of emergent within-group factions that have distinct perspectives on an issue. In such a case, the resulting pattern of interpersonal disagreements also is an emergent group-level characteristic (an equilibrium faction structure) that sets the stage for the problem of social choice.

A group's matrix of total (direct and indirect) interpersonal influences V is a collective product of individual-level responses to interpersonal influences that unfold over time. It is a characteristic group-level construct that is not obtainable from any single individual or even from the aggregate of individuals' direct responses, because V depends on the structure of the network of direct interpersonal influences, W, and the process of interpersonal influence that unfolds in the network. The *realized* impact of group members on an issue is described by V. Thus, the network of total interpersonal influences has been employed as a basis for describing the power or influence structure of a group and the positions of individuals in the structure (Friedkin 1991).

In addition, as we will show, our approach may be employed to describe the transformation of group members' attitudes *about one another* and, via these interpersonal attitudes, to provide an account of emergent networks of direct endogenous interpersonal influences W. Sociologists have noted that social groups in field settings may form influence networks in which group members are consensually stratified in terms of the weight that each group member accords to others, i.e., networks in which the rows in W are identical or nearly so. From a state in which group members have heterogeneous profiles of accorded influence, we will present a formal perspective on the social process that generates homogeneous profiles of accorded influence.

Apart from social influence network theory, it is remarkable that work on the micro-to-macro linkage has not included sustained programs of research concerned with the development of formal theories on the formation of *attitudinal agreements and consensus.* Formal theories of collective behavior have not emphasized the *attitudes* that are likely to mediate the relationship between persons' circumstances and behavior; this weakness in the literature on behavioral outcomes exists because attitude change has not been explicitly incorporated into the social process that produces the collective or coordinated behavior of persons. Instead, these theories have focused on behavioral interactions (offers and decisions in bargaining in social exchange, adoption or rejection of innovations in social diffusion, membership and participation decisions in social movements and collective action) in which some persons' behaviors are direct triggers of other persons' behaviors. Such direct behavior-on-behavior triggers do exist but, we believe, have been overemphasized as a form of endogenous interpersonal influence that generates collective behaviors.

Sociological work in the symbolic interaction tradition supports the conclusion that social groups are constituted and maintained by the thoughts, feelings, and actions of individuals (Charon 2001; Hewitt 2000; Stryker 1981; Stryker and Statham 1985). Arguably, what we may view as stable and constraining social structures and norms are group-level phenomena that are continuously being negotiated and maintained by the persons who are situated in the group. Therefore, in principle, some of the variable collective properties of social groups might be explained on the basis of social processes involving interpersonal interactions and individual-level responses to more or less dynamic conditions. When group-level conditions are the outcomes of such social processes, group-level analyses may be reduced to accounts of the social processes within each group that have produced these group-level outcomes. In this light, the theoretical status of group-level explanations appears suspect, and it seems wiser to exhaust the ability of micro-level (individual and interpersonal) processes to account for collective outcomes than to develop group-level theories about such outcomes.

Hence, for example, we do not invoke the construct of a collective con-straining norm. In terms of our approach, any such norm enters into the process as an effect on individuals' *initial* positions on an issue. Given het-erogeneous initial positions on an issue, we do not assume that the mean of the distribution of these initial positions indicates a shared norm. Our approach begins with the positions that persons take on the issue, which may be more or less strongly held normatively constrained positions, and focuses on the influence process that may or may not transform any dis-agreements into a shared position. The emergent shared position may or may not be taken by group members as a correct, optimal, or normative collective position. Our approach bears on the emergence of shared norms (Friedkin 2001). We argue that it is worthwhile to explore the ability of this influence network process to account for consensual positions *with-out* the assumption that interpersonal influences produce conformance to a norm that is either (a) implicit in the distribution of group members' initial positions (i.e., the assumption of social categorization theory) or (b) invoked as a social choice procedure to reach a collective agreement (i.e., the assumption of social decision scheme theory).

1.4.3 Individuals in Groups

Much of the empirical analysis to be presented in this book will focus on the within-group influence process and its consequences for the collective outcomes (e.g., consensus) and collective process-features (e.g., efficiency) of small groups. However, our theoretical perspective also extends to an analysis of large populations of individuals. The individuals of such a population are embedded in a super–influence network, and this super-network may be partitioned into disjoint groups (as we have defined "group" above), such that the total interpersonal influences between the members of different groups are absent or negligible. We hold that most large-scale influence networks are "nearly decomposable systems" (Pattee 1973). The within-group dynamics that we are analyzing in small groups should also apply to groups of any size and does not imply convergence to shared issue positions within large-scale groups.

The dominant paradigm in sociology for investigating effects on atti-tudes involves probability samples of individuals drawn from a large pop-ulation. A *probability sample* of N individuals from a large population is likely to contain members of different groups. Sociologists acknowledge that each of the sampled individuals is embedded in various groups, and networks of relations, that may affect his or her attitudes. Social influ-ence network theory deals with the influence networks of these groups, but it also has implications for and applications to survey research. Rather than beginning with an individual-level model of effects on attitudes and extending it to analyze endogenous interpersonal influences, we begin with a model of endogenous interpersonal influences and apply it to a sample of independent individuals, drawn from different groups, who are not affected by one another's responses.

Assuming equilibrium for each such independent individual $i = 1, 2, \ldots, N$ in a probability sample, the scalar equilibrium equation of social influence network theory should hold:

$$y_i^{(\infty)} = a_{ii} \sum_{j=1}^{n_i} w_{ij} y_j^{(\infty)} + (1 - a_{ii}) y_i^{(1)}. \tag{1.6}$$

Here, each member i of the sample is embedded in a group of size n_i, in which the interpersonal influences on an issue have reached equilibrium, but only the equilibrium attitudes of those $j \neq i$ in i's group, who have some positive *direct* influence on i, are involved in the equation. The equation may be elaborated with $y_i^{(1)} = \sum_{k=1}^{K} \beta_k X_{ik}$, in which case the initial attitudes of the sample members may be treated as an unobserved variable,

$$y_i^{(\infty)} = a_{ii} \sum_{j=1}^{n_i} w_{ij} y_j^{(\infty)} + (1 - a_{ii}) \sum_{k=1}^{K} \beta_k X_{ik}. \tag{1.7}$$

In the final chapter of the book (Chapter 12), we develop the theoretical implications of this scalar-level viewpoint on the origins of persons' equilibrium attitudes.

1.5 Concluding Remarks

A potential contribution of social influence network theory will be realized if it contributes to a better theoretical integration of the array of phenomena that have been investigated in the field of group dynamics. The absence of integrative theoretical frameworks that constrain and link lines of inquiry has been repeatedly noted by reviewers and cited as a major reason for the decline of research on small groups in mainstream social psychology. Social influence network theory may be able to address this problem with its assertion that social influences on attitudes can be conceptualized in terms of three theoretical constructs: the network of interpersonal influences, persons' susceptibilities to these interpersonal influences, and persons' initial attitudes on an issue. These three constructs mediate the effects of other variables on attitudes. The domain of antecedent variables is large: personality characteristics, social identities, and task demands, among many other conditions, affect persons' susceptibilities to influence. Source attributes, recipient attributes, and message content, among many other conditions, affect the interpersonal influence of persons. Socioeconomic status, sociodemographic conditions, and norms, among many other variables, affect persons' initial attitudes on issues. We believe that all of these conditions affect attitudes through effects on susceptibility, interpersonal influence, and initial issue positions and that there is a single core social process by which persons integrate the content of influential attitudes.

Although our book is mainly addressed to sociologists, we hope to foster a fruitful exchange of ideas between sociologists and psychologists working in the area of group dynamics. Sociological and psychological contributions to the field of group dynamics have remained quite separate. The contributions of these two disciplines appear in separate journals, edited books rarely contain contributions from both disciplines, and there appears to be little evidence in the form of ideas and formal acknowledgments that any significant cross-fertilization has occurred. We believe that the increasingly weak intersection of studies in sociology and psychology concerned with group dynamics is artificial and theoretically limiting.

2

Formalization: Attitude Change
in Influence Networks

Persons' attitudes are typically formed in interpersonal environments in which influential positions on issues are in disagreement and liable to change. Our investigation focuses on the formation of attitudes, including shared attitudes and consensus, in groups whose members are communicating their positions on an issue. The communication of an attitude to others may occur in various ways, including spoken or written communication (via an expression of opinion, belief, or preference) and nonverbal communication (via overt behavior, a subtle gesture, or a facial expression). An influential communication, in which one person's attitude affects another's, is an endogenous interpersonal influence, whereas all other effects on attitudes are exogenous influences on the attitudes. The attitudes that are being shaped by these influences may deal with any object about which group members can express a positive or negative evaluation – particular issues, places, persons, events, institutions, symbols, or beliefs. When persons are modifying their attitudes in response to information about the attitudes of other group members, and these other members are doing the same thing, flows of interpersonal influence are generated that permit important indirect effects of members' attitudes on the attitudes of others via intermediaries. In this chapter, we formally present social influence network theory as a mathematical model of endogenous interpersonal influence on attitudes that takes into account the network of such influences.

Work on models that describe endogenous interpersonal influences on attitudes has been sporadic, scattered among various academic disciplines, and disconnected, in the sense of not being linked to other related work. Formal models of endogenous interpersonal influences on attitudes appear in the literatures of psychology, sociology, political science, statistics, mathematics, physics, and engineering. Within this broad literature, it is striking that a number of independent investigations have converged on the assumption that attitude change in influence networks might be described by a mechanism of *weighted averaging* of influential attitudes. Our own work over approximately two decades has been focused on the theoretical development and application of models based on this mechanism (Friedkin 1986, 1990, 1991, 1998, 1999, 2001; Friedkin and Cook 1990; Friedkin and Johnsen 1990, 1997, 1999, 2002, 2003). The model that we have come to focus on, which we refer to as our *standard model*, is specified by

$$y_i^{(t+1)} = a_{ii} \sum_{j=1}^{n} w_{ij} y_j^{(t)} + (1 - a_{ii}) y_i^{(1)}, \tag{2.1}$$

$i = 1, 2, \ldots, n$, where w_{ij} is the direct influence of j on i ($0 \leq w_{ij} \leq 1$ and $\sum_j w_{ij} = 1$ for all i); $a_{ii} = 1 - w_{ii}$ is the complement of i's self-weight, that is, the susceptibility or lack of resistance of i to interpersonal influence ($0 \leq a_{ii} \leq 1$); $y_i^{(1)}$ is the initial attitude of i; and $y_k^{(t)}$ is the attitude of k at time t. This model posits that the attitude of person i at time $t + 1$ forms as a weighted average of all the group members' attitudes at time t (including person i's own attitude at time t) and person i's initial attitude. This system of equations can be summarized in matrix form as follows:

$$\mathbf{y}^{(t+1)} = \mathbf{AW}\mathbf{y}^{(t)} + (\mathbf{I} - \mathbf{A})\mathbf{y}^{(1)}, \tag{2.2}$$

for $t = 1, 2, 3, \ldots$, where $\mathbf{W} = [w_{ij}]$ is the $n \times n$ matrix of endogenous interpersonal influences for a group with n members, $\mathbf{A} = \mathrm{diag}(a_{11}, a_{22}, \ldots, a_{nn})$ is the $n \times n$ diagonal matrix of group members' susceptibilities to endogenous interpersonal influence, and $\mathbf{y}^{(t)}$ is the $n \times 1$ vector of members' attitudes toward a particular issue or object at time period t. Thus, the model describes how the array of individual attitudes $\mathbf{y}^{(t)}$ is transformed into the array $\mathbf{y}^{(t+1)}$ at each $t = 1, 2, 3, \ldots$.

Our social influence network model (2.2) builds on French's formal model of social power (French 1956; Harary 1959) and DeGroot's consensus formation model (Berger 1981; Chatterjee and Seneta 1977; DeGroot 1974). It has a close formal relationship with the rational choice model of group decision-making proposed by Lehrer and Wagner (Lehrer and Wagner 1981; Wagner 1978, 1982), the model of group decision-making proposed by Graesser (1991), and Anderson's weighted averaging model of information integration (Anderson 1981; Anderson and Graesser 1976). Social influence network theory also has an intimate formal relationship with an interdisciplinary tradition in statistics that includes work in geography, political science, and sociology on models of the influences among persons and spatial units (Anselin 1988; Doreian 1981; Duncan and Duncan 1978; Duncan, Haller, and Portes 1968; Erbring and Young 1979; Marsden and Friedkin 1994; Ord 1975).

Here we trace the development of the theory and present an exegesis of our standard model. We assume that the reader is familiar with the notation and operations of matrix algebra. Our start point is French's (1956) formal theory of social power. We then turn to Harary's (1959) and DeGroot's (1974) generalizations of the model, and our further generalizations. The influence network construct $\mathbf{W}$ appears in all of these models. They differ in the constraints that are placed on $\mathbf{W}$ and in the role played by group members' initial attitudes $\mathbf{y}^{(1)}$ during the influence process. This theoretical movement has been toward a minimal set of formal constraints within the framework of a nonnegative row stochastic matrix representation of the influence network of a group $\mathbf{W} = [w_{ij}]$, where $0 \leq w_{ij} \leq 1$ for all i and j and $\sum_j w_{ij} = 1$ for all members i of the group. In this movement, the theoretical importance of group members' self-weights $w_{11}, w_{22}, \ldots, w_{nn}$ in $\mathbf{W}$ has grown, and they now appear to be a crucial component of influence networks. A group member i's self-weight is, of course, the complement of the aggregate interpersonal weight of others on i, $w_{ii} = 1 - \sum_{j \neq i}^n w_{ij}$, for all i. (To simplify the notation, here and elsewhere, summations of the form $\sum_{j \neq i}^n x_{ij}$ denote $\sum_{\substack{j=1 \\ j \neq i}}^n x_{ij}$.) In our standard model, we assume that a positive self-weight for i implies some degree of continuing attachment to (anchorage on) i's initial ($t = 1$) position on an issue. The allowance for such a continuing attachment or anchorage is a formal departure from the models entertained by French, Harary, and DeGroot. With it, we dramatically enlarge the theoretical domain of influence networks in which consensus may *not* be formed via the interpersonal influence process.

2.1 Development of Social Influence Network Theory

Social influence network theory has been under development since the 1950s, in successive generalizations, by mathematicians and social psychologists concerned with the question of how group members respond to endogenous interpersonal influences and form shared attitudes, including group consensus. In this section, we describe this line of theoretical development.

2.1.1 French's Formal Theory of Social Power

The network theory of social influence began with French (1956), who hypothesized that individuals balance tensions in the field of interpersonal influences that are acting upon them by repeatedly shifting their attitudes to the mean attitude of those persons who are influencing them. It was, and remains, a widely accepted baseline hypothesis among psychological social psychologists that pressures toward uniformity in groups cause group members' attitudes to converge to the mean of group members' initial attitudes. French introduced an influence network into this process and stipulated that group members will shift their attitudes to the mean attitude of the *subset* of the group's members who are directly influencing them.

Formally, French's model is

$$\mathbf{y}^{(t+1)} = \mathbf{W}\mathbf{y}^{(t)} \tag{2.3}$$

for $t = 1, 2, 3, \ldots$, where $\mathbf{y}^{(1)}$ is an $n \times 1$ vector of persons' initial attitudes on an issue, $\mathbf{y}^{(t)}$ is an $n \times 1$ vector of persons' attitudes at time t, and $\mathbf{W} = [w_{ij}]$ is an $n \times n$ matrix of interpersonal influences. French assumed a homogeneous field of interpersonal influences, i.e.,

$$w_{ij} = \frac{b_{ij}}{\sum\limits_{k=1}^{n} b_{ik}} \tag{2.4}$$

for all i, where $\mathbf{B} = [b_{ij}]$ is an $n \times n$ matrix in which $b_{ij} = 1$ if person j influences person i, $b_{ij} = 0$ otherwise, and each person is assumed to influence him- or herself ($b_{ii} = 1$ for all i). French refers to persons' self-weights, on the main diagonal of $\mathbf{W}$, as their *resistance*; i.e., w_{ii} is the influence of i's attitude at time t on his or her own attitude at time $t + 1$, which lessens the aggregate relative influence of others, $\sum_{j \neq i}^{n} w_{ij} = 1 - w_{ii}$.

French's model describes how group members *cognitively integrate* different attitudes, but the outcome of this process depends on the *social structure* in which the process occurs. Figure 2.1, reproduced from French's article, illustrates the hypothesized consequences of structural variation in influence networks. Although the five groups shown in Figure 2.1 have identical distributions of initial attitudes, there are dramatic differences in the eventual outcomes of the influence process, the beginnings of which are shown in Figure 2.1: some groups reach consensus, others do not; and the groups that reach consensus do so at different rates and settle on different outcomes. An implication of the introduction of social structure is that an emergent consensus does not necessarily form on the mean initial position of the group members.

The networks shown in Figure 2.1 are examples of four types of network connectivity that French argued were indicative of a group's level of structural cohesion; the complete network is a special case of a strongly connected network. The definitions of these four types are based on an analysis of the paths and semipaths of a digraph, i.e., directed network, N (Harary, Norman, and Cartwright 1965). In the following, all points are assumed to be in N.

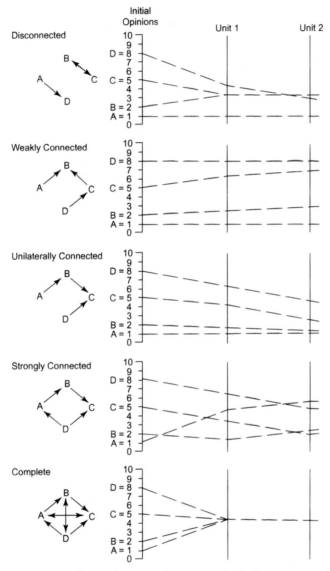

Figure 2.1 Effects of structural variation in influence networks upon attitudes. French (1956: 187) Units 1, 2,..., ∞ correspond to our time periods $t = 2, 3, ..., ∞$. Here the relation $j \to i$ means that j influences i based on i's according of influence to j.

For distinct points p_i and p_j, there exists a *path* in N from p_i to p_j if there is a sequence of distinct points $p_{k_0}, p_{k_1}, p_{k_2}, \ldots, p_{k_r}$ for $r \geq 1$, where $p_i \equiv p_{k_0}$ and $p_j \equiv p_{k_r}$, such that $p_{k_0} \rightarrow p_{k_1}, p_{k_1} \rightarrow p_{k_2}, p_{k_2} \rightarrow p_{k_3}, \ldots, p_{k_{r-1}} \rightarrow p_{k_r}$ are directed edges in N. There exists a *semipath* in N from p_i to p_j, $p_{k_0}, p_{k_1}, p_{k_2}, \ldots, p_{k_r}$ for $r \geq 1$, where $p_i \equiv p_{k_0}$ and $p_j \equiv p_{k_r}$, such that $p_{k_0} \rightarrow p_{k_1}$ or $p_{k_0} \leftarrow p_{k_1}$, $p_{k_1} \rightarrow p_{k_2}$ or $p_{k_1} \leftarrow p_{k_2}, \ldots p_{k_{r-1}} \rightarrow p_{k_r}$ or $p_{k_{r-1}} \leftarrow p_{k_r}$ are directed edges in N. If there is a path from p_i to p_j, then p_i is said to *reach* p_j. If there is a semipath from p_i to p_j (it is also a semipath from p_j to p_i), then p_i is said to be *joined* to p_j (and p_j is joined to p_i). A network N is *strongly connected* if p_i and p_j are mutually reachable for all p_i and p_j ($i \neq j$) in N. A network N is *unilaterally connected* if either p_i can reach p_j or p_j can reach p_i for all p_i and p_j ($i \neq j$) in N. A network N is *weakly connected* if there is a semipath in N joining p_i and p_j for all p_i and p_j ($i \neq j$) in N. A network N is *disconnected* if it is not weakly connected. Logically, if N is strongly connected, then it is also unilaterally and weakly connected, and if it is unilaterally connected, then it is also weakly connected.

The *connectivity category* of a network is its highest level of connectivity (3 = strong, 2 = unilateral, 1 = weak, or 0 = disconnected).

In French's illustration, Figure 2.1, the vector of initial attitudes is

$$\mathbf{y}^{(1)} = \begin{bmatrix} 1 \\ 2 \\ 5 \\ 8 \end{bmatrix}$$

and the influence networks are

1. Disconnected   2. Weakly Connected   3. Unilaterally Connected

$$\mathbf{W} = \begin{bmatrix} 1 & 0 & 0 & 0 \\ 0 & \frac{1}{2} & \frac{1}{2} & 0 \\ 0 & \frac{1}{2} & \frac{1}{2} & 0 \\ \frac{1}{2} & 0 & 0 & \frac{1}{2} \end{bmatrix} \quad \mathbf{W} = \begin{bmatrix} 1 & 0 & 0 & 0 \\ \frac{1}{3} & \frac{1}{3} & \frac{1}{3} & 0 \\ 0 & 0 & \frac{1}{2} & \frac{1}{2} \\ 0 & 0 & 0 & 1 \end{bmatrix} \quad \mathbf{W} = \begin{bmatrix} 1 & 0 & 0 & 0 \\ \frac{1}{2} & \frac{1}{2} & 0 & 0 \\ 0 & \frac{1}{2} & \frac{1}{2} & 0 \\ 0 & 0 & \frac{1}{2} & \frac{1}{2} \end{bmatrix}$$

4. Strongly Connected   5. Complete

$$\mathbf{W} = \begin{bmatrix} \frac{1}{2} & 0 & 0 & \frac{1}{2} \\ \frac{1}{2} & \frac{1}{2} & 0 & 0 \\ 0 & \frac{1}{2} & \frac{1}{2} & 0 \\ 0 & 0 & \frac{1}{2} & \frac{1}{2} \end{bmatrix} \quad \mathbf{W} = \begin{bmatrix} \frac{1}{4} & \frac{1}{4} & \frac{1}{4} & \frac{1}{4} \\ \frac{1}{4} & \frac{1}{4} & \frac{1}{4} & \frac{1}{4} \\ \frac{1}{4} & \frac{1}{4} & \frac{1}{4} & \frac{1}{4} \\ \frac{1}{4} & \frac{1}{4} & \frac{1}{4} & \frac{1}{4} \end{bmatrix}$$

where French's labels A, B, C, and D correspond to the rows and columns 1, 2, 3, and 4, respectively, in the above matrices. The attitudes that result from the process described by (2.3) can be found by substitution:

$$\begin{aligned}
\mathbf{y}^{(2)} &= \mathbf{W}\mathbf{y}^{(1)} \\
\mathbf{y}^{(3)} &= \mathbf{W}^2\mathbf{y}^{(1)} \\
\mathbf{y}^{(4)} &= \mathbf{W}^3\mathbf{y}^{(1)} \\
&\vdots \\
\mathbf{y}^{(\infty)} &= \mathbf{W}^\infty\mathbf{y}^{(1)},
\end{aligned} \qquad (2.5)$$

assuming equilibrium is attained. Hence, for each of the five influence networks described by French, the attitude changes are as follows:

1. Disconnected Network

$\mathbf{y}^{(1)}$	$\mathbf{y}^{(2)}$	$\mathbf{y}^{(3)}$	$\mathbf{y}^{(4)}$	...	$\mathbf{y}^{(\infty)}$
1	1	1	1	...	1
2	3.5	3.5	3.5	...	3.5
5	3.5	3.5	3.5	...	3.5
8	4.5	2.7	1.9	...	1

2. Weakly Connected Network

$\mathbf{y}^{(1)}$	$\mathbf{y}^{(2)}$	$\mathbf{y}^{(3)}$	$\mathbf{y}^{(4)}$	...	$\mathbf{y}^{(\infty)}$
1	1	1	1	...	1
2	2.7	3.4	3.9	...	4.5
5	6.5	7.2	7.6	...	8
8	8	8	8	...	8

3. Unilaterally Connected Network

$\mathbf{y}^{(1)}$	$\mathbf{y}^{(2)}$	$\mathbf{y}^{(3)}$	$\mathbf{y}^{(4)}$	...	$\mathbf{y}^{(\infty)}$
1	1	1	1	...	1
2	1.5	1.2	1.1	...	1
5	3.5	2.5	1.9	...	1
8	6.5	5	3.7	...	1

4. Strongly Connected Network

$\mathbf{y}^{(1)}$	$\mathbf{y}^{(2)}$	$\mathbf{y}^{(3)}$	$\mathbf{y}^{(4)}$	...	$\mathbf{y}^{(\infty)}$
1	4.5	5.5	5.2	...	4
2	1.5	3	4.2	...	4
5	3.5	2.5	2.7	...	4
8	6.5	5	3.7	...	4

	5. Complete Network				
$y^{(1)}$	$y^{(2)}$	$y^{(3)}$	$y^{(4)}$	...	$y^{(\infty)}$
1	4	4	4	...	4
2	4	4	4	...	4
5	4	4	4	...	4
8	4	4	4	...	4

French was interested not only in the structural conditions under which a consensus would form, but also in the effects of the distribution of initial attitudes. He applied his model to the classic conformity situation in which a deviate is faced with a different unanimous attitude of the other group members. His question was, "What happens to the attitude of a single deviate member?" Assuming a complete influence network, his answer was that the attitude change of a deviate i would be $y_i^{(\infty)} - y_i^{(1)} = \bar{y}^{(1)} - y_i^{(1)}$, where $\bar{y}^{(1)}$ is the mean of all group members' initial attitudes, because in such a network group members' attitudes converge to the mean of their initial attitudes.

French also applied his model to an analysis of leadership in a group. His measure of leadership is the total aggregated direct and indirect influences of a person on the other members of the group, i.e., the sum of the column entries for each person in $\mathbf{W}^\infty$, the matrix of endogenous interpersonal influences that transforms initial attitudes into equilibrium attitudes,

$$\mathbf{y}^{(\infty)} = \mathbf{W}^\infty \mathbf{y}^{(1)}. \tag{2.6}$$

He illustrated this measure with a weakly connected influence network for which the matrix of *direct* endogenous interpersonal influences is

$$\mathbf{W} = \begin{bmatrix} 1 & 0 & 0 & 0 \\ \frac{1}{2} & \frac{1}{2} & 0 & 0 \\ \frac{1}{2} & 0 & \frac{1}{2} & 0 \\ 0 & \frac{1}{3} & \frac{1}{3} & \frac{1}{3} \end{bmatrix}$$

and the matrix of *total* or net endogenous interpersonal influences is

$$\mathbf{W}^\infty = \begin{bmatrix} 1 & 0 & 0 & 0 \\ 1 & 0 & 0 & 0 \\ 1 & 0 & 0 & 0 \\ 1 & 0 & 0 & 0 \end{bmatrix}.$$

The aggregated total effects of each person are 4, 0, 0, 0 for persons 1, 2, 3, and 4, respectively. In this network, the leadership of the group is concentrated entirely on person 1 and the group members' attitudes converge to that person's initial attitude; they would do so for any distribution of initial attitudes in the group.

2.1.2 Harary and DeGroot's Generalization

Harary (1959) realized that the process described by French (1956) had algebraic properties similar to those of a discrete–time stationary Markov chain, and he relaxed French's assumption of an *even* distribution of interpersonal influences. Specifically, he allowed group members' self-weights (w_{ii}) to be different from the interpersonal weights of other members' attitudes, but he retained French's assumption that a group member accords *equal weight* to the attitudes of those other members who have some influence on him or her (Harary 1959: 181).

DeGroot (1974), evidently unaware of the earlier work of French and Harary, developed the same model of the attitude formation process. In DeGroot's model, the homogeneity assumptions of French and Harary are relaxed. The process has the form

$$\mathbf{y}^{(t+1)} = \mathbf{W}\mathbf{y}^{(t)}, \quad t = 1, 2, \ldots, \tag{2.7}$$

where $\mathbf{y}^{(t)}$ is an $n \times 1$ vector of attitudes and $\mathbf{W}$ is an $n \times n$ matrix of interpersonal influences with only the general constraints

$$0 \le w_{ij} \le 1$$

$$\sum_{k=1}^{n} w_{ik} = 1 \tag{2.8}$$

for all i and j; i.e., group members are not assumed to accord the same relative weight to each of the other members who has an influence upon them. DeGroot also pointed out that the model could be generalized to deal with m-dimensional attitudes on an issue $\mathbf{Y}^{(t)}$, i.e., an $n \times m$ matrix of the coordinates of each person's attitude in an m-dimensional space.

DeGroot's analysis focused on the structural conditions under which consensus would be reached, and subsequent technical work on DeGroot's model has been concerned with the same issue (Berger 1981; Chatterjee and Seneta 1977). DeGroot showed that if consensus is reached in a strongly connected group, then the matrix of total interpersonal influences has the form

$$\mathbf{W}^{\infty} = \begin{bmatrix} \pi_1 & \pi_2 & \cdots & \pi_n \\ \pi_1 & \pi_2 & \cdots & \pi_n \\ \vdots & \vdots & \vdots & \vdots \\ \pi_1 & \pi_2 & \cdots & \pi_n \end{bmatrix}, \tag{2.9}$$

where $0 \le \pi_i \le 1$ for all i and $\sum_{k=1}^{n} \pi_k = 1$. The vector $\boldsymbol{\pi} = (\pi_1, \pi_2, \ldots, \pi_n)$ is a left eigenvector of $\mathbf{W}$ that is associated with the eigenvalue 1 (i.e., $\boldsymbol{\pi} \mathbf{W} = \boldsymbol{\pi}$), the maximum real eigenvalue for $\mathbf{W}$. Hence, $\boldsymbol{\pi}$ gives the total relative effect (proportionate contribution) of each group member in determining the value (x) of the consensus position on an issue:

$$x = \pi_1 y_1^{(1)} + \pi_2 y_2^{(1)} + \cdots + \pi_n y_n^{(1)}.$$

These total interpersonal effects are strictly a function of the influence network, $\mathbf{W}$, and thus independent of the vector of initial attitudes. For a $\mathbf{W}$ that produces consensus, this eigenvector of total effects is equivalent to French's measure of leadership (we need only divide French's measure by n); hence π is a measure of the relative influence of each person in the group. Note that if the focus is shifted to the distribution of initial attitudes, and consensus is reached, then the relative impact of a particular initial position, which may be held by one or more persons, is simply the sum of the elements of π that are associated with that initial attitude position. Hence, we can easily shift between an analysis of interpersonal influence and an analysis of within-group factions with shared positions on an issue (Friedkin 1998).

It is important to recognize that the matrix of total influences $\mathbf{W}^\infty$ may not take the form described in (2.9) and that, when it does not, consensus may be reached in special cases of group members' initial positions on an issue. For example, for the weakly connected influence network of Figure 2.1,

$$\mathbf{W}^\infty = \begin{bmatrix} 1 & 0 & 0 & 0 \\ 0.5 & 0 & 0 & 0.5 \\ 0 & 0 & 0 & 1 \\ 0 & 0 & 0 & 1 \end{bmatrix}, \tag{2.10}$$

and for the initial positions described by French, $\mathbf{y}^{(1)} = [\,1\ 2\ 5\ 8\,]^{\mathrm{T}}$, a consensus is not formed, $\mathbf{y}^{(\infty)} = [\,1\ 4.5\ 8\ 8\,]^{\mathrm{T}}$. However, for a different $\mathbf{y}^{(1)} = [\,1\ 2\ 5\ 1\,]^{\mathrm{T}}$ in which persons 1 and 4 compose a faction that is in initial agreement, a consensus will be reached. Furthermore, for the unilaterally connected network in Figure 2.1, we have

$$\mathbf{W}^\infty = \begin{bmatrix} 1 & 0 & 0 & 0 \\ 1 & 0 & 0 & 0 \\ 1 & 0 & 0 & 0 \\ 1 & 0 & 0 & 0 \end{bmatrix}, \tag{2.11}$$

which illustrates that $\mathbf{W}^\infty$ may take the form described in (2.9) both in unilaterally connected and in strongly connected influence networks; consensus may be reached in such networks, regardless of group members' initial positions on an issue.

2.1.3 Friedkin and Johnsen's Generalizations

We proposed a further generalization of the model (Friedkin and Johnsen 1990) that allowed continuing influences of initial attitudes on the attitudes being formed during the social influence process:

$$\mathbf{y}^{(t+1)} = \alpha \mathbf{W} \mathbf{y}^{(t)} + (1 - \alpha) \mathbf{y}^{(1)}, \tag{2.12}$$

for $t = 1, 2, \ldots$, where $\mathbf{y}^{(t)}$ is an $n \times 1$ vector of attitudes at time t, and $0 \leq \alpha \leq 1$ is the proportionate effect, for all group members, of interpersonal influences relative to the influence of their initial positions. Subsequently, we further generalized the model (Friedkin 1998; Friedkin and Johnsen 1999), relaxing the constraint of a uniform effect of interpersonal influences on all group members:

$$\mathbf{y}^{(t+1)} = \mathbf{A} \mathbf{W} \mathbf{y}^{(t)} + (\mathbf{I} - \mathbf{A}) \mathbf{y}^{(1)}, \tag{2.13}$$

where

$$\mathbf{A} = \begin{bmatrix} a_{11} & 0 & \cdots & 0 \\ 0 & a_{22} & \cdots & 0 \\ \vdots & \vdots & \ddots & 0 \\ 0 & 0 & \cdots & a_{nn} \end{bmatrix}$$

and a_{ii} $(0 \leq a_{ii} \leq 1)$ describes i's susceptibility or lack of resistance to interpersonal influence for each i. Note that (2.12) is a special case of (2.13) in which $\mathbf{A} = \alpha \mathbf{I}$. The construct $\mathbf{W} = \begin{bmatrix} w_{ij} \end{bmatrix}$ is the general unconstrained-weight matrix that is defined by DeGroot; i.e., w_{ij} is the direct relative influence of j on i, with $0 \leq w_{ij} \leq 1$ for all i and j and $\sum_{k=1}^{n} w_{ik} = 1$ for all i. Also note that here we do not assume that $a_{ii} = 1 - w_{ii}$ for all i, as we do in our standard model.

For $\mathbf{A} = \mathbf{I}$, this model includes the French, Harary, and DeGroot models as special cases, and for $\mathbf{A} \neq \mathbf{I}$, it allows for a continuing direct influence of some members' initial attitudes. It is useful to allow (but not require) continuing influences of initial positions on attitudes. In this form, the model permits either equilibrium disagreements or consensus in a large domain of influence networks and, in so doing, addresses Abelson's (1964) general complaint that consensus appears as the ineluctable outcome of a broad class of social influence models.

The model (2.13) is easily generalized to m-dimensional attitudes:

$$\mathbf{Y}^{(t+1)} = \mathbf{A} \mathbf{W} \mathbf{Y}^{(t)} + (\mathbf{I} - \mathbf{A}) \mathbf{Y}^{(1)}, \tag{2.14}$$

where $\mathbf{Y}^{(t)} = \begin{bmatrix} y_{ik}^{(t)} \end{bmatrix}$ is an $n \times m$ matrix $(m \geq 1)$, i.e.,

$$\mathbf{Y}^{(t)} = \begin{bmatrix} \mathbf{y}_1^{(t)} & \mathbf{y}_2^{(t)} & \cdots & \mathbf{y}_m^{(t)} \end{bmatrix},$$

each column k of which is transformed over time,

$$\mathbf{y}_k^{(1)} = \begin{bmatrix} y_{1k}^{(1)} \\ y_{2k}^{(1)} \\ \vdots \\ y_{nk}^{(1)} \end{bmatrix}, \mathbf{y}_k^{(2)} = \begin{bmatrix} y_{1k}^{(2)} \\ y_{2k}^{(2)} \\ \vdots \\ y_{nk}^{(2)} \end{bmatrix}, \ldots, \mathbf{y}_k^{(t)} = \begin{bmatrix} y_{1k}^{(t)} \\ y_{2k}^{(t)} \\ \vdots \\ y_{nk}^{(t)} \end{bmatrix}, \ldots$$

according to

$$\mathbf{y}_k^{(t+1)} = \mathbf{A}\mathbf{W}\mathbf{y}_k^{(t)} + (\mathbf{I} - \mathbf{A})\mathbf{y}_k^{(1)}.$$

Thus, without loss of generality, the analysis of the m-dimensional model can be reduced to the analysis of the 1-dimensional model applied to each dimension. Chapter 3 describes several m-dimensional applications of the model that are involved in the present investigation of small groups.

In our 1990 article, we introduced several models with more relaxed constraints, including a model in which all of the constructs might vary over time:

$$\mathbf{Y}^{(t+1)} = \mathbf{A}^{(t)}\mathbf{W}^{(t)}\mathbf{Y}^{(t)} + \left(\mathbf{I} - \mathbf{A}^{(t)}\right)\mathbf{Y}^{(1)}. \qquad (2.15)$$

We will draw on this generalization in Chapter 11, where we link the model with expectation states theory and affect control theory.

We note that we might also relax the constraint of *nonnegative* weights in $\mathbf{W}$, for example, letting $-1 \leq w_{ij} \leq 1$ and $\sum_{k=1}^{n} |w_{ik}| = 1$, while still preserving some of the parsimony of the model. We have yet to explore the properties of such systems (and do not do so here), preferring to maintain the simpler assumption of nonnegative weights in this book.

Finally, we note that we might relax the deterministic assumptions of the model. French (1956) distinguished power and influence networks. The former describe relations of potential interpersonal influence. The latter are the possible realizations of influence networks that can arise under the constraints of a given power structure. For example, French treats each of the networks displayed in Figure 2.1 as a fully realized power structure in which all of the interpersonal influences that might occur do occur. Each of the displayed power structures implies a sample space of alternative influence networks. Friedkin (1986) formalized this distinction so that the outcomes of power structures might be described in terms of expected values. Our deterministic model of synchronistic interpersonal influences is a simplification. Here, again, our theoretical agenda is to probe the merits of the simple and analytically tractable formalization of the interpersonal influence process that is described by our standard model. Our commitment to this agenda rests on its fruitfulness to date.

2.2 Our Standard Model

The model (2.13), with $a_{ii} = 1 - w_{ii}$ for all i, is the model (1.1) that we introduced in Chapter 1 and the model (2.1) with which we opened the present chapter. Most of the analysis in this book will be concentrated on model (2.1) and, accordingly, we denote it as our *standard model*. In some of the mathematical analysis of model (2.13) and in all of its empirical applications, we invoke the assumption that a person's susceptibility to interpersonal influence is the complement of that person's self-weight, i.e., $a_{ii} = 1 - w_{ii}$ for all i. This assumption posits that the susceptibility of each group member i is equivalent to the aggregate relative weight of the direct interpersonal influences of other group members on i,

$$a_{ii} = 1 - w_{ii} = \sum_{j \neq i} w_{ij}, \qquad (2.16)$$

for all i. Hence, the greater the self-weight of a group member, the greater the relative weight of the group member's initial position in the determination of his or her attitude at each time t.

In applications of the standard model, we sometimes employ a construct $C = [c_{ij}]$, i.e.,

$$C = \begin{bmatrix} 0 & c_{12} & \cdots & c_{1n} \\ c_{21} & 0 & \cdots & c_{2n} \\ \vdots & \vdots & \ddots & \vdots \\ c_{n1} & c_{n2} & \cdots & 0 \end{bmatrix},$$

that describes the relative direct interpersonal influence of j on i where, for all i and j, $0 \leq c_{ij} \leq 1$, $c_{ii} = 0$, and $\sum_{k=1}^{n} c_{ik} = 1$ or 0. This construct may be viewed either as a fundamental construct or as a derivative of $\mathbf{W}$. Given $\mathbf{W}$,

$$c_{ij} = \frac{w_{ij}}{\sum_{k \neq i} w_{ik}} = \frac{w_{ij}}{1 - w_{ii}}, \quad j \neq i, \qquad (2.17)$$

for $w_{ii} < 1$. For $w_{ii} = 1$, where $w_{ij} = 0$ for all $j \neq i$, we define $c_{ij} = 0$ for all $j \neq i$ and set $a_{ii} = 0$ under the assumption that $a_{ii} = 1 - w_{ii}$. Given $\mathbf{A}$ and $\mathbf{C}$,

$$\mathbf{W} = \mathbf{AC} + \mathbf{I} - \mathbf{A}, \qquad (2.18)$$

under the assumption that $a_{ii} = 1 - w_{ii}$ for all i. Thus, given separate, suitably scaled, measures of $\mathbf{C}$ and $\mathbf{A}$, these measures may be combined to form $\mathbf{W}$.

2.2.1 The Cognitive Algebra of Weighted Averaging

The scalar equation of our standard model describes a mechanism by which persons weigh and integrate their own attitudes with the attitudes of other group members. The weights on the various influential attitudes sum to 1, i.e., $a_{ii} \sum_{j=1}^{n} w_{ij} + (1 - a_{ii}) = 1$, so that i's attitude at time $t + 1$ is formed as a weighted average of the attitudes of others at time t, i's own attitude at time t, and i's initial position. Weighted averaging has been widely postulated as the mechanism that is involved in an individual's integration of interpersonal influences. This mechanism is entailed in numerous formal models of the attitude formation process, including models of dyadic influence, where a person is combining his or her own prior attitude with the attitude of a single other source (Anderson and Hovland 1957; Fink, Kaplowitz, and Bauer 1983; Himmelfarb 1974; Hunter, Danes, and Cohen 1984, Chapter 3; Kaplowitz and Fink 1991; Kaplowitz, Fink, and Blake 1986; Saltiel and Woelfel 1975), and models of endogenous influence for larger groups, where the individual is integrating influences from multiple sources (Anderson and Graesser 1976; Graesser 1991).

As a general phenomenon, weighted averaging is consistent with Festinger's (1953) view of interpersonal influence as a finite distributed force:

> When a person or a group attempts to influence someone, does that person or group produce a totally new force acting on the person, one which had not been present prior to the attempted influence? Our answer is No – an attempted influence does not produce any new motivation or force. Rather, what an influence attempt involves is the redirection of psychological forces which already exist. (Festinger 1953: 237)

Even when it has not been explicitly described as part of a formal model, the idea of weighted averaging has been widely assumed. For instance, Turner et al. (1987) note the presence of this assumption in work on norm formation:

> That theories of social influence have been characterized by individualism is evidenced by numerous facts... but is illustrated perhaps most simply by an implicit assumption that social norms form through the averaging of individual positions as members exchange their separate and private stocks of information. (Turner et al. 1987: 25)

Similarly, Graesser (1991) has noted the widespread presence of the assumption in work on group decision-making:

> Any theory of group decision must have a representation for member compromises. A natural hypothesis is that the compromise is some kind of average, and various group theorists have referred to this kind of representation. For the most part, however, the averaging hypothesis has remained at an informal, often implicit level, and has not been developed adequately to provide a basis for group theory. (Graesser 1991: 1)

The merits of the assumption of weighted averaging in attitude formation has been most systematically investigated by Anderson and his collaborators as part of the development of information integration theory (Anderson 1981; 1991a; 1991b; 1996). Information integration theory is concerned with discovering the formal rules, or cognitive algebra, by which individuals combine different items of information (including prior attitudes and beliefs) to form a revised attitude or belief. During the more than 30 years in which evidence on this cognitive algebra has been accumulated, various plausible combinatorial models (integration rules) have been assessed. Anderson and his colleagues have concluded that a weighted averaging mechanism is consistent with the process of integration for many types of cognitive responses, including the integration of conflicting attitudes in group decision making (Anderson and Graesser 1976; Graesser 1991).

To more precisely situate our approach in the *intersection* of the analysis of social cognitions and the analysis of social structures, consider the following formal derivation. First, we postulate a *cognition mechanism* in which an individual i's attitude on an issue y_i is formed as a weighted average of k units of information $x_1, x_2, \ldots, x_k$,

$$y_i = \sum_{j=1}^{k} \bar{w}_{ij} x_j. \quad \left(0 < \bar{w}_{ij} < 1, \sum_{j=1}^{k} \bar{w}_{ij} = 1 \right). \qquad (2.19)$$

In cognitive science, this postulate is most closely associated with Anderson's (1981, 1991a, 1991b, 1996) information integration theory. Second, we *embody* $m \leq k$ of these units of information; i.e., the m units of information are positions of m different persons on the issue, $x_1 = y_1, x_2 = y_2, \ldots, x_m = y_m$, so that

$$y_i = \sum_{j=1}^{m} \bar{w}_{ij} y_j + \sum_{j=m+1}^{k} \bar{w}_{ij} x_j. \qquad (2.20)$$

Third, we allow for *change* over time in the embodied positions of the m persons:

$$y_i^{(t+1)} = \sum_{j=1}^{m} \bar{w}_{ij} y_j^{(t)} + \sum_{j=m+1}^{k} \bar{w}_{ij} x_j \quad (t = 1, 2, \ldots). \qquad (2.21)$$

Fourth, we *transform* the weights into relative weights within each of the dynamic $(\sum_{j=1}^{m} \bar{w}_{ij} y_j^{(t)})$ and fixed $(\sum_{j=m+1}^{k} \bar{w}_{ij} x_j)$ terms of this mechanism. For the moment, we take $0 < m < k$. The algebra is simple, but tedious:

$$
\begin{aligned}
y_i^{(t+1)} &= \left(\frac{\sum_{j=1}^{m} \bar{w}_{ij}}{\sum_{j=1}^{m} \bar{w}_{ij}} \right) \sum_{j=1}^{m} \bar{w}_{ij} y_j^{(t)} + \left(\frac{\sum_{j=m+1}^{k} \bar{w}_{ij}}{\sum_{j=m+1}^{k} \bar{w}_{ij}} \right) \sum_{j=m+1}^{k} \bar{w}_{ij} x_j \\
&= \left(\sum_{j=1}^{m} \bar{w}_{ij} \right) \sum_{j=1}^{m} \left(\bar{w}_{ij} \Big/ \sum_{j=1}^{m} \bar{w}_{ij} \right) y_j^{(t)} \\
&\quad + \left(\sum_{j=m+1}^{k} \bar{w}_{ij} \right) \sum_{j=k+1}^{k} \left(\bar{w}_{ij} \Big/ \sum_{j=m+1}^{k} \bar{w}_{ij} \right) x_j, \qquad (2.22)
\end{aligned}
$$

or, letting $a_i \equiv \sum_{j=1}^{m} \bar{w}_{ij}$, $w_{ij} \equiv \bar{w}_{ij} / \sum_{r=1}^{m} \bar{w}_{ir}$, and $y_i^{(1)} \equiv \sum_{j=m+1}^{k} (\bar{w}_{ij} / \sum_{r=m+1}^{k} \bar{w}_{ir}) x_j$, we obtain

$$y_i^{(t+1)} = a_i \sum_{j=1}^{m} w_{ij} y_j^{(t)} + (1 - a_i) y_i^{(1)} \quad (t = 1, 2, \ldots). \qquad (2.23)$$

When $m = 0$, $a_i = 0$, and when $m = k$, $a_i = 1$. To this point, the focus has been on the response of a single individual to informational units. Fifth, and finally, we *embed* the mechanism in a group with n members, $i = 1, 2, \ldots, n$, which is a closed set, which need not be maximal, with respect to inclusion of all persons who either accord or have been accorded positive weight on an issue. Each such group consists of one or more weakly connected components with respect to the relation of positive accorded weights. Now we have n individuals whose time $t + 1$ attitudes may be a change from their time t attitudes based on prior attitude changes of those group members, if any, to whom they have accorded positive weights. This embedding may introduce zero weights in those instances where an individual accords zero weight to particular other members of the group. The equation (2.23) is modified by setting $m = n$ and re-indexing the variables:

$$y_i^{(t+1)} = a_{ii} \sum_{j=1}^{n} w_{ij} y_j^{(t)} + (1 - a_{ii}) y_i^{(1)} \quad (i = 1, 2, \ldots, n; \ t = 1, 2, \ldots).$$

$$(2.24)$$

Thus, we arrive at the social cognition mechanism on which our influence network theory is based. Recall that we settled on this mechanism as a result of our formal and empirical investigations of the French–Harary–DeGroot model. The present derivation suggests deeper micro foundations for this formalization.

The mechanism of weighted averaging is formally consistent with the observed tendency for emergent attitudes and agreements to lie within the range of group members' initial attitudes (Friedkin and Johnsen 1999; Friedkin and Cook 1990) and with the observed spectrum of attitudinal distributions that appear as products of group members' endogenous interpersonal influences. Social psychological investigations of interpersonal influence have been oriented differently in psychology and sociology: psychologists have tended to assume that pressures toward accommodation result in movement toward the mean of the distribution of initial attitudes in a group, whereas sociologists have tended to assume that such pressures result in stratification or domination of certain persons and their initial positions over others. Both compromise (equality) and domination (inequality) are evident in the outcomes of small groups and, hence, a general model of social influence should allow for both. As we will show later in our findings on small groups, when a group forms an agreement, the agreement is sometimes on an initial attitude of one of the members and sometimes on a compromise position that may or may not be close to the mean of the group members' initial attitudes. Moreover, it cannot be realistically assumed that all groups reach consensus. Thus, Horowitz (1962: 182) argues that "any serious theory of agreements and decisions must at the same time be a theory of disagreements and the conditions under which decisions cannot be reached." The weighted averaging mechanism described by our standard model is formally consistent with a variety of attitudinal distributions that are observed as outcomes in small groups.

Not all formal models of interpersonal influence are consistent with the constraining framework of the range or convex hull of initial attitudes and with the spectrum of emergent agreements and disagreements in groups. Hubbell's (1965) model forces predicted equilibrium attitudes outside the range of a group's initial attitudes. The models of Galam and Moscovici (1991), Kelly (1981), and Taylor (1968) account for agreements that settle on a group member's initial attitude, but do not explain compromise agreements. Abelson's (1964) formal models account for agreements but do not explain disagreements, to his apparent consternation:

> Since universal ultimate agreement is an ubiquitous outcome of a very broad class of mathematical models, we are naturally led to inquire what on earth one must assume in order to generate the bimodal outcomes of community cleavage studies. (Abelson 1964: 153)

Abelson turned to computer simulations of the influence process in order to develop a model that might account for both consensus and a settled pattern of disagreement in a group, as have others (Nowak, Szamrej, and Latane 1990; Penrod and Hastie 1980; Stasser, Kerr, and Davis 1989; Tanford and Penrod 1984).

The available evidence reviewed and presented suggests that persons in groups may integrate conflicting interpersonal influences as weighted averages of influential attitudes. Currently, no other formal mechanism appears to possess the same desirable theoretical properties. Perhaps, as our knowledge of the functioning of the human brain increases, we may eventually derive the appropriate "cognitive algebra" from an understanding of biochemical or neurological mechanisms. It would be satisfying to discover that such fundamental mechanisms could support the weighted averaging mechanism that has been widely incorporated into models of social influence.

2.2.2 The Self–Other Balance

A remarkable number of lines of inquiry deal with persons' susceptibility to interpersonal influence. This literature includes (a) the fundamental dichotomies that have been proposed by Freud (Id vs. Superego), Mead (I vs. Me), and Reisman (inner-directed vs. other-directed), (b) the phenomenon of deindividualization stemming from Le Bon's treatise on crowds, (c) Milgram's concept of an agentic state, (d) cross-cultural work on individualism vs. collectivism, (e) experimental work on personality correlates of influenceability and other conditions affecting resistance to attitude change, and (f) group conditions affecting pressures towards uniformity. We believe that this literature bears on a single latent dimension, the "self–other" balance on which persons vary, that describes the extent to which a person is susceptible to interpersonal influences (versus being self-weighted or resistant) in forming his or her attitudes in particular issue domains.

Early developments of social influence network theory did not adequately deal with the self-weights ($w_{ii}, i = 1, 2, \ldots, n$) in $\mathbf{W}$. In French's (1956) seminal model, persons were assumed to place the same weight on their own attitudes and the attitudes of each person who influenced

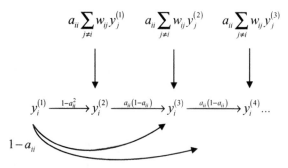

Figure 2.2 The influence process for each group member.

them. But French recognized that this assumption was potentially misleading when he wrote:

> Resistance... has not been treated separately or in detail in this model. In a further development it might be coordinated to such factors as "certainty of own opinion" or, as Kelman and Mausner call it, "prior reinforcement," and to various personality characteristics such as rigidity and authoritarianism. (French 1956: 560)

In the models of Harary (1959) and DeGroot (1974), self-weight determines the relative influence of a person's time t attitude $y_i^{(t)}$ in forming the person's time $t + 1$ attitude on an issue,

$$y_i^{(t+1)} = w_{ii} y_i^{(t)} + \sum_{j \neq i} w_{ij} y_j^{(t)}. \qquad (2.25)$$

That is, the self-weight is strictly on whatever the transformed position of the person happens to be at time t.

In our standard model, the above mechanism (2.25) is elaborated with a self-weight that also allows some degree of direct anchorage on the initial position of the person:

$$y_i^{(t+1)} = a_{ii} \left(w_{ii} y_i^{(t)} + \sum_{j \neq i} w_{ij} y_j^{(t)} \right) + (1 - a_{ii}) y_1^{(1)}, \qquad (2.26)$$

where $w_{ii} = 1 - a_{ii}$ is the person's resistance or lack of susceptibility to interpersonal influence. The theoretical motivation for this elaboration is to present an account, consistent with a weighted-averaging mechanism, that allows the emergence of settled patterns of interpersonal disagreements in strongly connected and unilaterally connected influence networks. With it, we enlarge the theoretical domain of influence networks in which interpersonal disagreements may not be resolved.

Figure 2.2 illustrates the influence process for each group member i at each time period. Persons' initial attitudes have a continuing influence on a person's time t attitudes. In the formation of i's $t = 2$ attitude, the influence of $y_i^{(1)}$ is $1 - a_{ii}^2$, because

$$y_i^{(2)} = a_{ii} w_{ii} y_i^{(1)} + a_{ii} \sum_{j \neq i} w_{ij} y_j^{(1)} + (1 - a_{ii}) y_i^{(1)} \qquad (2.27)$$

$$= \left(1 - a_{ii}^2\right) y_i^{(1)} + a_{ii} \sum_{j \neq i} w_{ij} y_j^{(1)}.$$

At subsequent $t > 2$, the direct influence of $y_i^{(1)}$ is $1 - a_{ii}$ and the influence of $y_i^{(t)}$ on $y_i^{(t+1)}$ is $a_{ii} (1 - a_{ii})$:

$$y_i^{(t+1)} = a_{ii} w_{ii} y_i^{(t)} + a_{ii} \sum_{j \neq i} w_{ij} y_j^{(t)} + (1 - a_{ii}) y_i^{(1)} \qquad (2.28)$$

$$= a_{ii} (1 - a_{ii}) y_i^{(t)} + a_{ii} \sum_{j \neq i} w_{ij} y_j^{(t)} + (1 - a_{ii}) y_i^{(1)}.$$

In this mechanism, the self–other balance appears with

$$(a_{ii} w_{ii} + 1 - a_{ii}) + \left(a_{ii} \sum_{j \neq i} w_{ij} \right) = \left(1 - a_{ii}^2\right) + \left(a_{ii}^2\right) = 1, \quad (2.29)$$

in which $1 - a_{ii}^2$ is a person's self-weight and a_{ii}^2 is the person's other-weight at each time t during the influence process. Thus, in terms of this approach, the greater the susceptibility $a_{ii} = \sum_{j \neq i} w_{ij}$ of person i, the more he or she is other-directed, deindividualized, and collectivistic in the influence process on a particular issue. In Freud's framework, acknowledging that we are stretching the substantive correspondence, the Id is reflected in i's initial position $y_i^{(1)}$, the Superego is reflected in i's $\sum_{j \neq i} w_{ij} y_j^{(t)}$, and the Ego regulates the two constructs via the value of a_{ii}. Here, the Id is only one factor among others that generate a person's initial disposition on an issue, and the Superego is constructed by a person's allocations of interpersonal influence to others. In George Herbert Mead's distinction between "Me" and "I,"

> He had in him all the attitudes of others, calling for a certain response; that was the "me" of that situation, and his response is the "I."

The "Me" for person i is the resultant of others' attitudes with some direct influence on person i, $a_{ii} \sum_{j \neq i} w_{ij} y_j^{(t)}$. This resultant may or may not be based on a *consensual* attitude among the others who directly influence i. Mead's "I" is person i's response $y_i^{(t+1)}$ at each point in time during the influence process, which also reflects i's self-weight. The contribution of "Me" depends on i's susceptibility or lack of resistance to interpersonal influence, and on how i distributes influence to particular others. The

"I" response depends on the weight i accords to self. Milgram's concept of an agentic state, in which a person is either obedient to authority or incompliant, formally corresponds to the binary states $a_{ii} = 1$ and $a_{ii} = 0$, respectively.

2.2.3 Total Interpersonal Influences

The implications of the social influence mechanism are manifested in the direct and indirect interpersonal influences among a group's members. Flows of interpersonal influence are produced by the repetitive responses of persons to changes in the attitudes of those persons who are directly influencing them. Our standard model assumes the occurrence of a sequence, $t = 1, 2, \ldots.$, of simultaneous responses in a stable social structure of interpersonal influences and initial positions. The process also may be viewed as state transitions of the attitude array. Here we define the matrix $\mathbf{V}^{(t)} = \left[v_{ij}^{(t)} \right]$ that includes all the interpersonal influences (direct and indirect) that arise from the process and that transform group members' initial positions on an issue into their time $t + 1$ positions,

$$
\begin{aligned}
\mathbf{y}^{(t+1)} &= \mathbf{A}\mathbf{W}\mathbf{y}^{(t)} + (\mathbf{I} - \mathbf{A})\,\mathbf{y}^{(1)} \\
&= \mathbf{V}^{(t)}\mathbf{y}^{(1)},
\end{aligned} \tag{2.30}
$$

for $t = 1, 2, \ldots$. In our standard model, $\mathbf{V}^{(t)}$ is strictly determined by $\mathbf{A}$ and $\mathbf{W}$; i.e., it is a resultant of the influence process, and its content is theoretically independent of the content of group members' positions on the issue. It is, in other words, a process-derived implication of the influence network of the group. Appendix B derives $\mathbf{V}^{(t)}$ and describes the conditions of equilibrium,

$$
\begin{aligned}
\mathbf{y}^{(\infty)} &= \mathbf{A}\mathbf{W}\mathbf{y}^{(\infty)} + (\mathbf{I} - \mathbf{A})\,\mathbf{y}^{(1)} \\
&= \mathbf{V}\mathbf{y}^{(1)},
\end{aligned} \tag{2.31}
$$

where $\mathbf{V}^{(\infty)} \equiv \mathbf{V}$. Below we present the key results for (2.30) and (2.31).

In general,

$$
\mathbf{y}^{(t+1)} = \mathbf{V}^{(t)}\mathbf{y}^{(1)} \quad (t = 1, 2, \ldots), \tag{2.32}
$$

where

$$
\begin{aligned}
\mathbf{V}^{(t)} &= \mathbf{A}\mathbf{W}\mathbf{V}^{(t-1)} + (\mathbf{I} - \mathbf{A}) \\
&= (\mathbf{A}\mathbf{W})^t + \left[\sum_{k=0}^{t-1} (\mathbf{A}\mathbf{W})^k \right] (\mathbf{I} - \mathbf{A}), \quad t = 1, 2, \ldots,
\end{aligned} \tag{2.33}
$$

where $\mathbf{V}^{(0)} \equiv \mathbf{I}$ and $(\mathbf{A}\mathbf{W})^0 = \mathbf{I}$. The scalar equation for (2.32) is

$$
y_i^{(t+1)} = v_{i1}^{(t)} y_1^{(1)} + v_{i2}^{(t)} y_2^{(1)} + \cdots + v_{in}^{(t)} y_n^{(1)} \tag{2.34}
$$

for all i. The coefficients in $\mathbf{V}^{(t)}$ are nonnegative ($0 \leq v_{ij}^{(t)} \leq 1$) and each row of $\mathbf{V}^{(t)}$ sums to unity ($\sum_{k=1}^{n} v_{ik}^{(t)} = 1$). Hence, at every point in time during the influence process, persons' attitudes are weighted averages of the group members' initial attitudes.

Assuming that the process reaches an equilibrium, which henceforth will mean that $\lim_{t \to \infty} \mathbf{V}^{(t)} = \mathbf{V}^{(\infty)} \equiv \mathbf{V}$ exists, by (2.32)

$$\mathbf{y}^{(\infty)} = \mathbf{V} \mathbf{y}^{(1)}. \tag{2.35}$$

Here, the scalar equation for (2.35) is

$$y_i^{(\infty)} = v_{i1} y_1^{(1)} + v_{i2} y_2^{(1)} + \cdots + v_{in} y_n^{(1)}. \tag{2.36}$$

Thus, $\mathbf{V}$ is the matrix of *total interpersonal* influences that transforms group members' initial attitudes into their final equilibrium attitudes. In practice (i.e., for any $\mathbf{AW}$), when $\mathbf{V} = \lim_{t \to \infty} \mathbf{V}^{(t)}$ exists, $\mathbf{V}$ may be computed from (2.33) using a sufficiently large value of t for which the entries in $\mathbf{V}^{(t)}$ change negligibly in passing to $\mathbf{V}^{(t+1)}$; for example, $\left| v_{ij}^{(t+1)} - v_{ij}^{(t)} \right| < 10^{-5}$ for all i and j. A direct determination of $\mathbf{V}$ is available when $\mathbf{I} - \mathbf{AW}$ is nonsingular, as follows. From (2.31), we obtain $(\mathbf{I} - \mathbf{AW}) \mathbf{y}^{(\infty)} = (\mathbf{I} - \mathbf{A}) \mathbf{y}^{(1)}$, which gives

$$\mathbf{y}^{(\infty)} = (\mathbf{I} - \mathbf{AW})^{-1} (\mathbf{I} - \mathbf{A}) \mathbf{y}^{(1)} \tag{2.37}$$

for a nonsingular $\mathbf{I} - \mathbf{AW}$. In this special case,

$$\mathbf{V} = (\mathbf{I} - \mathbf{AW})^{-1} (\mathbf{I} - \mathbf{A}), \tag{2.38}$$

with the caveat that an ill-conditioned $\mathbf{I} - \mathbf{AW}$ (with a determinant very close to 0) is a potential problem.

The equilibrium attitudes that are produced by the process may settle on the mean of group members' initial positions, on a compromise position that differs from the mean of initial attitudes and from any initial position, on an initial position of a group member, or on modified positions that are not in agreement. However, in all cases, the equilibrium positions will be in the range of the group members' initial positions.

2.3 Linking Functions

Throughout the book, we develop and employ *linking functions* between some constructs of the model and others, or between constructs of the model and constructs that are not of the model, or vice versa. The coupling assumption of the standard model, $a_{ii} = 1 - w_{ii}$, links a_{ii} to w_{ii} and vice versa, and $\mathbf{W} = \mathbf{AC} + \mathbf{I} - \mathbf{A}$ (which is based on the coupling assumption) links $\mathbf{W}$ to $\mathbf{A}$ and $\mathbf{C}$. Linking functions are also invoked whenever we assign a *measure* to one of the model's constructs. Coombs reminds us that "a measurement or scaling model is actually a theory about behavior [i.e., some specific construct], admittedly on a miniature level, but nevertheless theory" (1964: 5). Auxiliary linkages may extend the standard model and allow its application to a variety of problems that lie outside the domain of the attitude change process. In applications that draw on both the standard model and auxiliary linkage functions, the formal theoretical structure of the application is defined by all of the equations involved.

2.4 Concluding Remarks

The condition for an interpersonal influence process is established when attitudinal information is conveyed in the interactions of individuals on an issue. How individuals respond to such information is the fundamental focus of our theory. Social influence network theory presents (a) a formalization of individuals' attitudinal responses to complex interpersonal environments in which individuals are interacting with one or more others, who may not share the same attitudinal position on an issue, (b) a formalization of the social process of interpersonal influence that unfolds in a group on the basis of these responses, and (c) a formalization of the implications of the process as it unfolds in the influence network of the group. The formal tractability of the theory allows a variety of conclusions and predictions to be drawn on the basis of mathematical analysis. The theory encompasses a variety of special cases and substantive applications that arise from the consideration of particular types of attitudes, $y^{(t)}$, group sizes, n, network structures, W, group members' susceptibilities to interpersonal influence, A, and initial positions, $y^{(1)}$. For each substantive circumstance that is defined by these constructs, the process of interpersonal influence has implications for shifts of attitude on an issue and the formation of interpersonal agreements. We posit a common social process that plays out in different social structures and that has potentially different consequences because of the different contextual conditions in which the process occurs.

In this chapter, we have traced the development of the theory and described the basic features of the standard model upon which our work is concentrated. We have noted that this theory has been advanced, via successive generalizations, by mathematicians and social psychologists concerned with the question of how group members respond to interpersonal influences and form shared attitudes, including group consensus. The literature on interpersonal influence processes contains a variety of different formalizations, but it is difficult to locate a formalization that has sustained the interest of investigators in different disciplines for over half a century, as has social influence network theory since the publication of French's (1956) seminal formal model. With our standard model as the vehicle, we seek to further advance this line of formalization, to further draw out its implications, and to probe its merits.

In this chapter, we have described several implications of the theory for the production of flows of interpersonal influence and for the total influence of a group member on each other group member that arises from these flows. We will substantially enlarge the set of implications of this approach in the remaining chapters of the book, bring empirical evidence to bear on some of these implications, and employ the theory as a guiding framework for advancing particular lines of empirical research in the social psychology of small groups. Our main interest lies in probing the predictive merits of the formalization and exploring its usefulness as an integrative theoretical framework for the literature on small group dynamics.

3

Operationalization: Constructs and Measures

Social influence network theory is based on three constructs – persons' attitudes, susceptibilities, and interpersonal influences. In the previous chapter, we focused on the mechanism underlying attitude changes that result from endogenous interpersonal influences. Under the assumptions of our standard model, this mechanism is $\mathbf{y}^{(t+1)} = \mathbf{A}\mathbf{W}\mathbf{y}^{(t)} + (\mathbf{I} - \mathbf{A})\mathbf{y}^{(1)}$. Here we focus on the substantive foundations and operationalization of the constructs involved in this mechanism. Theories may be interesting, but to be useful they need to be operationalized. The domain of operationalization includes not only the possible substantive realizations of the theoretical constructs but also the measurement models for these substantive realizations. There is an intimate dance between theory and measurement, and we devote the present chapter to this *pas de deux*.

The first construct, $\mathbf{y}^{(t)}$, defines the substantive domain of our theory, i.e., the $n \times 1$ array of group members' attitudes on an issue at time t. We see the substantive domain of our theory as large. The theory deals with attitudes and their change, but it also encompasses other cognitions that are not easily subsumed by the conventional definition of attitudes as a positive or negative evaluation of an object. Here, we will describe the attitude construct in the general form in which we employ it, and provide several realizations of the construct that are consistent with our specification. The attention that we devote to this construct will highlight some nonobvious assumptions of our theory, and also serve to situate the present empirical investigation of relatively simple 1-dimensional realizations of the construct in a broader theoretical domain of potential m-dimensional realizations. We will deal with particular m-dimensional realizations of attitudes at various points in the book, where we analyze lines of extant work that involve them.

The second and third constructs, $\mathbf{A}$ and $\mathbf{W}$, define the influence network of a group that bears on $\mathbf{y}^{(t)}$. Operationalization of the theory requires

52

a measurement model for the self and interpersonal weights involved in these constructs. These measurement models are formally constrained by our theory and, hence, they share certain formal properties. However, it is important to recognize that the substantive basis of an influence network may vary for different issues that arise in the same group of persons, for the same issue that arises in different groups of persons, and for different persons within the same group on one issue.

In previous work, we have employed two different approaches to the operationalization of the influence network. In one, the weights are measured in terms of structural features of an observed network of interpersonal communications among group members (Friedkin 1998, 2001). In the other, the weights are based on self-reported cognitive relations of accorded influence (Friedkin 1999; Friedkin and Johnsen 1999). The latter approach stays close to the cognitive theoretical foundations of the theory, and we employ it in our analyses of small groups in experimental settings. Similarly, our work on the theoretical linkage of expectation states theory, affect control theory, and social influence theory draws on cognitive relations (i.e., the interpersonal attitudes of group members on semantic-differential dimensions of evaluation, potency, and activity) for an account of the formation of an influence network. The modeling issues are again nontrivial, and the attention that we devote to them in this chapter serves to situate the approach taken in our empirical investigation of small groups within a broader framework.

In this chapter, we also present an operationalization of the theory in which the group members' susceptibilities to interpersonal influence $\mathbf{A}$ are *derived* from measures of their initial and final attitudes on an issue, $\mathbf{y}^{(1)}$ and $\mathbf{y}^{(\infty)}$ respectively, and measures of their relative interpersonal influences, $\mathbf{C}$ (recall the definition of this construct in Chapter 2). This operationalization *fits* our standard model to the data. It allows us to compare the accuracy of the fitted model, based on derived susceptibilities, and the model that is entirely based on empirical measures of the constructs. It allows us to assess the correspondence of the standard model's derived susceptibilities with our empirical measure of their individual susceptibilities directly; assessing this correspondence is a probe of the validity of the model. It also provides a formal framework for the operationalization of the standard model in circumstances where direct measures of group members' susceptibilities are unavailable.

At the conclusion of this chapter, we present a schematic diagram of our general analytic framework. Our analysis defines and employs a number of constructs. The diagram displays the linkages between the empirical measures and the theoretical constructs that we will draw upon. The former may be empirical components that are combined to form a measure of the influence network $\mathbf{W}$. The latter may be derived or predicted constructs from the model and measures. We developed this schematic as an aid to ourselves and found it to be useful. We present it to the reader as a prelude to the analytic work in other chapters.

3.1 The Attitude Construct

Our theory deals with attitudes and their change, but it also encompasses other cognitions that are not easily subsumed by the conventional definition of attitudes. Most social psychologists define an attitude as a *positive* or *negative* evaluation of an object; hence, attitudes may be distinguished from other cognitions that do not involve such an evaluation. For instance, an opinion concerning the subjective probability of a particular event or the amount of resources to be allocated to a particular activity might not be considered an attitude. In light of this distinction, it is misleading to describe our theory as a "theory of attitude change" if such a designation implies a domain of application that is limited to positive or negative evaluations of objects. We emphasize that the $y^{(t)}$ in our standard model can involve *any* cognition that is susceptible to change as a result of interpersonal influence: such cognitions include attitudes, opinions, sentiments, beliefs, values, judgments, and preferences concerning objects, events, issues, problems, ideas, behaviors, feelings, oneself, and other persons. We employ the attitude construct as a rubric for the class of cognitive phenomena that are susceptible to interpersonal influence. A more fundamental reason for our emphasis on attitudes is that they may be implicated in all forms of cognition to the extent that persons automatically evaluate in positive or negative terms the objects that are visible to them (Bargh and Ferguson 2000).

Person i can only be influenced by an attitude of person j if it has been displayed and made visible in some fashion. The display may be explicit (verbal or written) or through body language, facial expression, or other behavior. The display also may occur when information is transmitted about the attitudes of another person through one or more intermediaries. Usually, there is a behavioral component, i.e., a display, for any attitude that is influential. However, attitudes also may be imputed or attributed to persons in the absence of any overt behavioral display; for instance, a stereotypical attitude may be imputed based on an observation of (information about) another person's group affiliation or personal attributes.

It is possible that a person i may incorrectly perceive or attribute an attitude to another person j, or a person j may display an attitude that is not his or her true attitude. The former error may occur when a person misinterprets a behavioral display; the latter error may occur when a socially desirable or convenient attitude is displayed that is not a person's true attitude toward an object. It is exceedingly difficult to ascertain whether a displayed attitude differs from the attitude that a person actually holds. Private attitudes that are not displayed cannot be influential for other persons and therefore are outside the scope of our theory. If some true attitudes in a group are private and the corresponding displayed attitudes are incongruent with these private attitudes, then that will very likely lead to predicted equilibrium attitudes at variance with the true equilibrium attitudes of the group. We assume a veridicality sufficient to ensure a consistent set of attitudes, so that for all *i* the displayed attitude of person *i* is the attitude that is involved in all of the interpersonal influences of *i* on other group members.

A simple form of social influence occurs when a group of persons are communicating and displaying their attitudes on a 1-dimensional issue. The issue might deal with the amount (or proportion) of available funds (or time) to allocate to a given activity; it might concern a judgment on the subjective probability of a particular event (for example, the guilt or innocence of a defendant); or it might involve an evaluation (positive or negative) of an object (a person, event, issue, etc.). On such issues, the position of person *i* at time *t* is simply $y_i^{(t)}$, measured on the appropriate scale (e.g., dollars, hours, probability), and the ordered set of such positions among *n* persons at time *t* is

$$
\mathbf{y}^{(t)} = \begin{bmatrix} y_1^{(t)} \\ y_2^{(t)} \\ \vdots \\ y_n^{(t)} \end{bmatrix}.
$$

The small groups of dyads, triads, and tetrads that we analyze in Chapters 4–9 involve issues of this form.

However, there are other (more complex or less obvious) types of cognitions that also fall within the scope of our theory. Three additional forms of the attitude construct arise in Chapters 8, 10, and 11. The first case concerns an issue in which the members of a group are *prioritizing* alternatives, *distributing* an amount of some resource over a set of alternatives, or *choosing* one alternative from a set of two or more alternatives. This realization of the attitude construct is implicated in our analysis of Asch's conformity studies (Chapter 8) and our analysis of social decision scheme research on jury outcomes (Chapter 10). The second concerns attitudes about *persons*. The third deals with multidimensional attitudes in which a particular attitude toward an object is defined in terms of two or more scale values. These latter two realizations of the attitude construct are conjoined in our analysis of expectation state theory and affect control theory (Chapter 11).

3.1.1 Weighted Alternatives

Consider persons who are prioritizing m alternatives or distributing an amount of some resource over m alternatives, where each person's attitude is represented by the *relative weight* that the person accords to a particular alternative or by the *proportion* of available resources (e.g., time, funds) that the person believes should be allocated to each of the k alternatives. Here, the issue $\mathbf{Y}^{(t)} = [y_{ik}^{(t)}]$ is an $n \times m$ weight matrix of the form $0 \le y_{ik}^{(t)} \le 1$ for each person $i = 1, 2, \ldots, n$ and each alternative $k = 1, 2, \ldots, m$, such that $\sum_{k=1}^{m} y_{ik}^{(t)} = 1$ for all i. For such a $\mathbf{Y}^{(t)}$, a nonobvious property of the influence process specified by our standard model is that the process preserves the form of the issue; i.e., the weights assigned by each person to the alternatives will sum to 1 at each time t. In general, from

$$\mathbf{Y}^{(t+1)} = \mathbf{V}^{(t)}\mathbf{Y}^{(1)} \tag{3.1}$$

$\mathbf{Y}^{(t+1)}$ must be row-stochastic if $\mathbf{Y}^{(1)}$ is row-stochastic. Let $\mathbf{j}_m$ denote an $m \times 1$ vector of ones. Multiplying both sides of this equation by $\mathbf{j}_m$ gives

$$\mathbf{Y}^{(t+1)}\mathbf{j}_m = \mathbf{V}^{(t)}\mathbf{Y}^{(1)}\mathbf{j}_m = \mathbf{V}^{(t)}\mathbf{j}_n = \mathbf{j}_n, \tag{3.2}$$

which shows that if $\mathbf{Y}^{(1)}$ is row-stochastic, then so is $\mathbf{Y}^{(t+1)}$ for $t = 1, 2, \ldots$.

Depending on the application, the quantitative attitudes $\mathbf{Y}^{(t)}$ may be periodically displayed as categorical choices via a threshold function. Let $\ddot{\mathbf{Y}}^{(t)} = [\ddot{y}_{ik}^{(t)}]$ be an $n \times m$ binary matrix of each group member's choices from among $m \ge 1$ alternative positions on an issue. The special categorical nature of this matrix is denoted by a "double-dotted" $\mathbf{Y}^{(t)}$. For example, persons may choose their most preferred alternatives,

$$\ddot{y}_{ik}^{(t)} = \begin{cases} 0 & \text{if} \quad y_{ik}^{(t)} < \max\left(y_{i1}^{(t)}, y_{i2}^{(t)}, \ldots, y_{im}^{(t)}\right) \\ 1 & \text{if} \quad y_{ik}^{(t)} = \max\left(y_{i1}^{(t)}, y_{i2}^{(t)}, \ldots, y_{im}^{(t)}\right), \end{cases} \tag{3.3}$$

for all i at each time $t = 1, 2, 3, \ldots$, where this maximum value may occur for more than one alternative. Or alternatives may be chosen based on whether they attain a criterion value ε,

$$\ddot{y}_{ik}^{(t)} = \begin{cases} 0 & \text{if} \quad y_{ik}^{(t)} < \varepsilon \\ 1 & \text{if} \quad y_{ik}^{(t)} \ge \varepsilon. \end{cases} \tag{3.4}$$

Here, each row of $\ddot{\mathbf{Y}}^{(t)}$ may contain up to m entries with a value of 1 (indicating the person's choices of particular alternatives) with any remaining entries having values of 0.

Consider a group of four persons who are discussing three alternatives and periodically displaying their most preferred alternative. Suppose that the initial positions of the persons on this issue are

$$
\mathbf{Y}^{(1)} = \begin{bmatrix} 0.20 & 0.20 & 0.60 \\ 0.50 & 0.25 & 0.25 \\ 0.25 & 0.60 & 0.15 \\ 0 & 0 & 1 \end{bmatrix} \qquad \ddot{\mathbf{Y}}^{(1)} = \begin{bmatrix} 0 & 0 & 1 \\ 1 & 0 & 0 \\ 0 & 1 & 0 \\ 0 & 0 & 1 \end{bmatrix}.
$$

Person 1 accords weight 0.20 to the first two alternatives and weight 0.60 to the third alternative; person 2 accords weight 0.50 to the first alternative and weight 0.25 to the second and third alternatives; person 3 accords weight 0.25 to the first alternative, weight 0.60 to the second alternative, and weight 0.15 to the third alternative; and person 4 views the third alternative as the only viable one, assigning it full weight. Interpersonal influences may alter these attitudes and, depending on the influence network, produce consensus. Suppose that each person is influenced most heavily by one other person in the group (person 1 by person 4, person 2 by person 4, person 3 by person 1, and person 4 by person 2) and that the influence network of the group is

$$
\mathbf{W} = \begin{bmatrix} 0.001 & 0.250 & 0.250 & 0.499 \\ 0.200 & 0.001 & 0.200 & 0.599 \\ 0.799 & 0.100 & 0.001 & 0.100 \\ 0.150 & 0.699 & 0.150 & 0.001 \end{bmatrix},
$$

where $a_{ii} = 1 - w_{ii}$ for all i. Hence, from $\mathbf{Y}^{(t+1)} = \mathbf{AWY}^{(t)} + (\mathbf{I} - \mathbf{A})\mathbf{Y}^{(1)}$,

$$
\mathbf{Y}^{(2)} = \begin{bmatrix} 0.188 & 0.212 & 0.600 \\ 0.091 & 0.160 & 0.749 \\ 0.210 & 0.186 & 0.604 \\ 0.417 & 0.294 & 0.289 \end{bmatrix} \qquad \ddot{\mathbf{Y}}^{(2)} = \begin{bmatrix} 0 & 0 & 1 \\ 0 & 0 & 1 \\ 0 & 0 & 1 \\ 1 & 0 & 0 \end{bmatrix}
$$

$$
\mathbf{Y}^{(3)} = \begin{bmatrix} 0.283 & 0.234 & 0.483 \\ 0.330 & 0.256 & 0.414 \\ 0.201 & 0.216 & 0.583 \\ 0.123 & 0.172 & 0.705 \end{bmatrix} \qquad \ddot{\mathbf{Y}}^{(3)} = \begin{bmatrix} 0 & 0 & 1 \\ 0 & 0 & 1 \\ 0 & 0 & 1 \\ 0 & 0 & 1 \end{bmatrix}
$$

$$
\vdots
$$

$$
\mathbf{Y}^{(\infty)} = \begin{bmatrix} 0.234 & 0.218 & 0.548 \\ 0.234 & 0.218 & 0.548 \\ 0.234 & 0.218 & 0.548 \\ 0.234 & 0.218 & 0.548 \end{bmatrix} \qquad \ddot{\mathbf{Y}}^{(\infty)} = \begin{bmatrix} 0 & 0 & 1 \\ 0 & 0 & 1 \\ 0 & 0 & 1 \\ 0 & 0 & 1 \end{bmatrix}.
$$

A virtual quantitative consensus is generated (the results have been rounded) in which the first two alternatives are assigned roughly equal weights and the third alternative is assigned a weight that is more than double that of each other alternative. A consensual qualitative choice is generated based on individuals' choices of their most preferred alternatives.

We note that, for a $\mathbf{Y}^{(1)}$ that is an $n \times m$ row-stochastic weight matrix on m alternatives, individuals' choices also may be treated as random responses and the equilibrium weights as the expected values of each alternative response for each group member. The sum of the expected values for each alternative, i.e., the column sums of $\mathbf{Y}^{(\infty)}$, would be the expected frequencies, based on the model, for the number of group members who choose each of the alternatives. Because $\mathbf{Y}^{(\infty)}$ is row-stochastic, these expected frequencies sum to n.

Obviously, a categorical choice threshold function also may be employed in the special case of a 1-dimensional attitude. If $\mathbf{y}^{(t)}$ involves an evaluative (negative–positive) attitude and $\varepsilon = 0$, then $\ddot{y}_i^{(t)} = 0 | y_i^{(t)} < \varepsilon$ indicates a negative object-related choice and $\ddot{y}_i^{(t)} = 1 | y_i^{(t)} \geq \varepsilon$ indicates a nonnegative object-related choice. If $\mathbf{y}^{(t)}$ are jurors' subjective probabilities of the guilt or innocence of a defendant, and ε is a burden-of-proof threshold, then the jurors' votes $\ddot{\mathbf{y}}^{(t)}$ are $\ddot{y}_i^{(t)} = 0 | y_i^{(t)} < \varepsilon$ and $\ddot{y}_i^{(t)} = 1 | y_i^{(t)} \geq \varepsilon$ for each juror i at each time t.

3.1.2 Attitudes about Persons

Attitudes about *individuals* constitute an exceedingly important special case of attitudes that are susceptible to social influence. These attitudes may deal with a single person (e.g., his or her reputation or competence) or a subset of persons in a group or social category. The application of our theory is straightforward for persons who are not members of the influence network. For instance, the attitude object might be a particular out-group about which stereotypical attitudes are being formed; in such a case $\mathbf{Y}^{(t)}$ would be an $n \times 1$ vector of evaluative (positive or negative) attitudinal scores about the out-group. The attitude object also might be a particular person, for instance, Thomas Jefferson, on the two dimensions of his personal character and public competence; in such a case, $\mathbf{Y}^{(t)}$ would be an $n \times 2$ matrix of evaluations on the two dimensions. The attitudinal objects might be a set of k candidates for a job or political office, in which case $\mathbf{Y}^{(t)}$ would be an $n \times k$ matrix of evaluative attitudinal scores for the k candidates or a prioritized weighting of the alternative candidates at time t, as described in a previous section.

Matters may become complex (but tractable) when the attitudinal objects are members of the influence network, i.e., when $\mathbf{Y}^{(t)}$ is an $n \times n$

matrix of the attitudes of group member i about group member j for all group members i and j. If a group member i's attitudes about other group members are influential, then these influences may affect the attitudes of others, including their attitudes about i; and i's attitudes may be affected by the attitudes of others, including i's attitude about him- or herself. These dual effects are played out in the flows of interpersonal influence that occur in the influence network.

Our standard model does not cover the situation in which the attitudes about other group members may transform the influence network that is shaping persons' attitudes:

$$\mathbf{W}^{(t)} = f\left\{\mathbf{Y}^{(t)}\right\} \tag{3.5}$$

and

$$\mathbf{Y}^{(t+1)} = \mathbf{A}^{(t)}\mathbf{W}^{(t)}\mathbf{Y}^{(t)} + \left(\mathbf{I} - \mathbf{A}^{(t)}\right)\mathbf{Y}^{(1)}. \tag{3.6}$$

In Chapter 11, we relax the assumptions of the standard model to cover this case. For the moment, we shall simplify matters and assume that the influence network is fixed. Here, $\mathbf{Y}^{(t)}$ is an $n \times n$ matrix of evaluative attitudes for the n members of the group, in which $y_{ii}^{(t)}$ is a person's attitude toward self, and the influence network is stable. For instance, if

$$\mathbf{W} = \begin{bmatrix} 0.000 & 0.323 & 0.274 & 0.402 \\ 0.244 & 0.000 & 0.286 & 0.470 \\ 0.132 & 0.279 & 0.000 & 0.588 \\ 0.272 & 0.233 & 0.495 & 0.000 \end{bmatrix}$$

is the influence network of a group whose members are assessing the merits of each person for a leadership position, and if the members' initial attitudes on this issue are

$$\mathbf{Y}^{(1)} = \begin{bmatrix} 0.001 & 0.763 & -0.377 & 1.483 \\ -0.653 & 0.483 & 0.627 & 0.402 \\ -3.296 & 2.238 & -0.234 & -0.140 \\ -0.527 & 0.075 & 0.382 & 0.990 \end{bmatrix},$$

then a consensus will form that will favor person 2 for the leadership position:

$$\mathbf{Y}^{(\infty)} = \begin{bmatrix} -1.221 & 0.879 & 0.129 & 0.642 \\ -1.221 & 0.879 & 0.129 & 0.642 \\ -1.221 & 0.879 & 0.129 & 0.642 \\ -1.221 & 0.879 & 0.129 & 0.642 \end{bmatrix}.$$

The matrix of total interpersonal influences indicates that person 4 is more influential than person 2 in determining the attitudes of group members on the merits of the various candidates:

$$V = \begin{bmatrix} 0.179 & 0.212 & 0.275 & 0.334 \\ 0.179 & 0.212 & 0.275 & 0.334 \\ 0.179 & 0.212 & 0.275 & 0.334 \\ 0.179 & 0.212 & 0.275 & 0.334 \end{bmatrix}.$$

Nonetheless, person 2 would be selected for the office if the members voted according to their most preferred candidate.

The class of attitudes about persons-as-objects has an important bearing on the phenomenon of *reflected appraisals* (Cooley [1902] 1983: 183; Mead 1934; Yeung and Martin 2003). The attitudes of group members toward themselves and others are shaped by interpersonal influences that, in turn, are affected by the attitudes of group members, and so on. The displayed attitudes of influential others toward person *i* describe a viewpoint on person *i*'s identity that may change *i*'s self-orientation depending on *i*'s susceptibility to interpersonal influence. Person *i*'s attitude toward self may be a *reflected appraisal* of the attitudes of others, but this interpersonal determination of *i*'s self-orientation is governed by his or her susceptibility to influence. Interpersonal influences on *i* may either support, lower, or heighten person *i*'s self-orientation, depending on whose attitudes are influential. In this process, person *i* is not only a potential recipient of influence; he or she also is a potential *source* of influence: person *i* is simultaneously a recipient and an agent of influence and these "roles" are determined, respectively, by *i*'s susceptibility to influence and by the amount of influence that is being accorded to *i* by others. Because person *i* may directly or indirectly influence those persons who have some influence on him or her, person *i* may shape the social environment in which he or she is situated so that the definition of the situation, as construed by *others*, more closely corresponds to person *i*'s own *initial* definition. Hence, the agents of influence are in competition with each other, whether or not they recognize it, in the determination of the definition of the situation for each person. This competition is especially clear when a consensual definition of the situation emerges from the process, because in that case each person's *initial* position (his or her initial fundamental attitude) makes a proportional contribution to the content of the consensual understanding of the group as a whole.

3.1.3 Multidimensional Attitudes

The object of a person's attitude may be multidimensional in the sense that multiple cognitive orientations are *required* to adequately represent the person's attitude. For such objects, the attitude of a person can be represented by $m \geq 2$ real numbers, each number describing the location of the person on a dimension of the attitude. If each person is conceptualized as occupying a position in an m-dimensional space that is determined by the $m \geq 2$ coordinates of the person's attitude, then the distance between two persons' attitudes may be described by the Euclidean weighted distance between their positions in this m-dimensional space,

$$
d_{ij}^{(t)} = \left[\sum_{k=1}^{m} q_k \left(y_{ik}^{(t)} - y_{jk}^{(t)} \right)^2 \right]^{1/2} , \tag{3.7}
$$

where $0 < q_k < 1$ is a weight for each dimension and $\sum_k q_k = 1$. If the weights are also subject to interpersonal influence (as in a prioritization issue discussed above), then (3.7) assumes that they are consensual weights. In the simplest case, the m attitudinal dimensions are equally weighted.

With our standard model, the influence process operates as if m separate attitudes are being modified.[1] Thus, it is meaningful to describe how the social influence process affects a particular dimension of an issue when there is some reason (substantive or theoretical) to focus on that dimension. For instance, it is meaningful to describe the effect of the social influence process on one dimension of employees' job satisfaction (e.g., an attitude about their degree of autonomy at work) when this dimension is one of several aspects of an employee's overall level of satisfaction with his or her job. This will be the case for our analysis of the semantic-differential EPA profile (evaluation, potency, and activity) involved in affect control theory. If persons' susceptibilities to interpersonal influence vary depending on the dimension, then a different $\mathbf{A}_k$ matrix could be specified for each dimension. If persons' interpersonal influences vary depending on the dimension, then a different $\mathbf{W}_k$ matrix could be specified for each dimension. We assume that attitudes on one dimension do not affect attitudes on other dimensions, and so each dimension may be treated separately.

3.1.4 Initial Attitudes

The construct of an initial attitude $\mathbf{y}^{(1)}$ warrants special attention. In our theory, an initial attitude describes the position of a person on an issue prior to any endogenous interpersonal influences. Temporally, it is the *predisposition* of a person on an issue, i.e., the first attitude in

---

[1] These m dimensions are associated through time, however, by virtue of their simultaneous transformation by $\mathbf{V}^{(t)}$.

the sequence of attitudes that a person may hold during the process of attitude change. When $a_{ii} = 0$, there are no interpersonal influences on i, and i's initial attitude is i's equilibrium attitude. At equilibrium, for all i,

$$\mathbf{y}^{(\infty)} = \mathbf{A}\mathbf{W}\mathbf{y}^{(\infty)}(\mathbf{I} - \mathbf{A})\mathbf{y}^{(1)}$$

or

$$(\mathbf{I} - \mathbf{A}\mathbf{W})\mathbf{y}^{(\infty)} = (\mathbf{I} - \mathbf{A})\mathbf{y}^{(1)}. \tag{3.8}$$

Assuming $a_{ii} < 1$ for all i, which means that $\mathbf{I} - \mathbf{A}$ is nonsingular, we have

$$(\mathbf{I} - \mathbf{A})^{-1}(\mathbf{I} - \mathbf{A}\mathbf{W})\mathbf{y}^{(\infty)} = \mathbf{y}^{(1)}. \tag{3.9}$$

It is evident that $\mathbf{y}^{(1)}$ describes the attitudes that group members would hold were it not for the interpersonal influences that may have modified them.

In our standard model, group members' initial attitudes on an issue are assumed to be a fixed position for each member. When $a_{ii} < 1$, person i's initial position has some influence on i's attitudes at *every* point in time during the influence process. The stability of initial attitudes depends on the stability of the antecedent conditions that have determined them,

$$\mathbf{y}^{(1)} = f(\mathbf{X}), \tag{3.10}$$

where $\mathbf{X}$ is a $n \times m$ matrix of these antecedent conditions. If $\mathbf{X}$ is in flux during the influence process, then group members may be modifying their attitudes on grounds other than the interpersonal influences described by $\mathbf{A}\mathbf{W}$, and $\mathbf{V}$ does not suffice to account for the transformation of group members' initial attitudes into their equilibrium attitudes.

The measurement of initial attitudes is most straightforward in experimental settings, where an issue is posed to group members and each member independently and privately records his or her position on it prior to any interaction with other members of the group. Such is the basis of the initial attitudes of the group members that we analyze in this book. The measurement of initial attitudes is far more complex in field settings. Persons' expressed attitudes may be their initial positions on issues with respect to social influence processes that have not yet begun, or they may be equilibrium positions that have been affected by a particular influence process, or they may be transitional positions (attitudes in formation) that are being modified by an influence process. The theoretical status of their reported attitudes (equilibrium, initial, or transitional) may be difficult to ascertain. Longitudinal data on individuals' attitudes will establish a time-ordering of attitudes, but such data do not clearly establish whether the first panel of attitudes may be treated as initial attitudes and the final panel of attitudes may be treated as equilibrium attitudes. Suppose that an influence process has begun and that data are gathered on the attitudes of group members at two points in time. If these two sets of attitudes are measures of the initial and equilibrium attitudes of the influence process, then $y^{(\infty)} = Vy^{(1)}$ and $y^{(1)} = V^{-1}y^{(\infty)}$ if V is non-singular. If the first measure is not in fact the initial attitudes of group members, then postmultiplying V by this measure is not a theoretically justified prediction of the second measure; and if the second measure is not in fact the equilibrium attitudes of group members, then postmultiplying V^{-1} by this measure is not a theoretically justified prediction of the first measure. With over-time data, the investigator must have a plausible basis for treating one attitude as an initial position and another as an equilibrium position with respect to the influence process that unfolds in a particular influence network W.

Initial attitudes are only "initial" with respect to a particular subsequent set of interpersonal influences, specified by A and W, that act upon the group members' attitudes, and they are assumed to be fixed for that set of influences. Thus, an initial attitude need not be an attitude on a *new* issue; it may be the outcome of a prior influence process on the issue. For example, consider a group that has adjourned at time t_1 with the expectation of revisiting the issue, and that does so:

$$y_1^{(t_1)} = V_1^{(t_1-1)}y_1^{(1)}$$
$$y_2^{(t_2)} = V_2^{(t_2-1)}y_2^{(1)}, \tag{3.11}$$

where the output of the first process is the input to the second process, i.e., $y_2^{(1)} = y_1^{(t_1)}$, and the output of the second process is $y_2^{(t_2)}$. Either or both of the times t_1 and t_2 may be the equilibrium time ∞. There will be no change in the group members' attitudes if $y_1^{(t_1)}$ is consensus (equilibrium or transitory), but there may be a change $y_2^{(t_2)} \neq y_2^{(1)}$ otherwise. Revisiting an issue on which consensus has not been reached, either with the same or a different influence network, may produce additional changes.

Clearly, the output–input perspective given in (3.11) may be generalized to more than two processes. Furthermore, in (3.11) the outcome of the first influence process $y_1^{(t_1)}$ becomes the input of the second influence process, which assumes that $y_1^{(t_1)}$ is the only determinant of group members' initial positions on the issue when it is revisited. A more general viewpoint on group members' initial positions on issues that are periodically revisited by a group is that the outcomes of prior considerations of the issue become personal precedents for each group member that are factored into determination of their initial positions on the issue when it arises again, along with other altered antecedent variables that are salient in this determination. For instance,

$$\begin{aligned}
\mathbf{y}_1^{(1)} &= f_1(\mathbf{X}_1) \\
\mathbf{y}_1^{(t_1)} &= \mathbf{V}_1^{(t_1-1)}\mathbf{y}_1^{(1)} \\
\mathbf{y}_2^{(1)} &= f_2(\mathbf{X}_2, \mathbf{y}_1^{(t_1)}) \\
\mathbf{y}_2^{(t_2)} &= \mathbf{V}_2^{(t_2-1)}\mathbf{y}_2^{(1)}
\end{aligned}$$ (3.12)

describes a situation in which there are (a) an array of antecedent conditions $\mathbf{X}_1$ that determine group members' initial attitudes on an issue and (b) an incorporation of the previous group outcome $\mathbf{y}_1^{(t_1)}$ into an array of conditions $\mathbf{X}_2$, which may differ from $\mathbf{X}_1$, when the issue is revisited.

Considerable potential complexity is eliminated when the interpersonal influence process is investigated in an experimental setting that provides measures of group members' independent positions on an issue prior to the visibility of other group members' positions on the issue. The empirical findings that we report in this book are based on such a setting. It is not our viewpoint that investigating group dynamics in field settings is a hopeless endeavor. Friedkin (1998, 2001) has employed structural proxies for group members' initial positions in a multidimensional social space defined by their network of social relations; i.e., $\mathbf{Y}^{(1)} = \mathbf{X}$, where $\mathbf{X}$ is an $n \times m$ matrix of group members' coordinates in such an m dimensional social space. With such an operationalization, the influence process alters the positions of the group members in the social space by modifying the columns of coordinates in $\mathbf{X}$. An alternative operationalization, consistent with this approach, would estimate expected initial positions based on groups members' fixed individual-level sociodemographic characteristics (their age, gender, education, income, etc.). That is, for example, with the specification $\mathbf{y}^{(1)} = \mathbf{X}\boldsymbol{\beta} + \mathbf{u}$, we have $\mathbf{y}^{(\infty)} = \mathbf{A}\mathbf{W}\mathbf{y}^{(\infty)} + (\mathbf{I} - \mathbf{A})(\mathbf{X}\boldsymbol{\beta} + \mathbf{u})$, which casts an investigation of interpersonal influence into the tractable domain of a mixed regressive–autoregressive analysis (Anselin 1988; Ord 1975). Such operationalizations are not matters that we address in this book.

3.2 The Influence Network Construct

The influence network of a group is the collection of weights that a group's members accord to their own attitudes, and those of other group members, on issues that arise in the group. The network is defined by two constructs: the matrix of group members' susceptibilities to interpersonal influence,

$$
\mathbf{A} = \begin{bmatrix} a_{11} & 0 & \dots & 0 \\ 0 & a_{22} & \dots & 0 \\ \vdots & \vdots & \ddots & \vdots \\ 0 & 0 & \dots & a_{nn} \end{bmatrix},
$$

and the matrix of relative weights that group members place on their time t attitudes, in forming their time $t + 1$ attitudes,

$$
\mathbf{W} = \begin{bmatrix} w_{11} & w_{12} & \dots & w_{1n} \\ w_{21} & w_{22} & \dots & w_{2n} \\ \vdots & \vdots & \ddots & \vdots \\ w_{n1} & w_{n2} & \dots & w_{nn} \end{bmatrix}.
$$

With the assumption $a_{ii} = 1 - w_{ii}$ for all i, the two constructs $\mathbf{A}$ and $\mathbf{W}$ are coupled, and $\mathbf{W}$ suffices to describe $\mathbf{A}$.

Our standard model assumes that $\mathbf{W}$ is fixed. One of the remarkable early discoveries about social groups is that often they rather quickly develop stable structures of interpersonal relations (Bales 1950; Fisek and Ofshe 1970; Newcomb 1961). A large cumulative body of field studies support the prevalence of stable patterns of social relations in groups (Ridgeway 2001). We would be discounting a central empirical contribution of sociological analysis if we did not expect and posit that distinctive patterns of social relations, including relations of interpersonal influence, are maintained in many social groups over some period of time and that these structures serve as stable social contexts in which various social processes unfold.

Even so, treating an influence network as a fixed context in which an issue unfolds is a strong assumption. An alternative assumption is that the influence network on a particular issue forms quickly and changes more slowly than do the attitudes of group members on the issue, so that, relative to the attitude change process on the issue, the influence network may be treated as fixed. We develop the argument below that influence networks are quickly formed and stabilized on the basis of group members' attitudes about themselves and other group members as issue-contextualized attitudinal objects. The assumption of a fixed $\mathbf{W}$ affords considerable analytical tractability. More importantly, it guides and disciplines our empirical analysis by imposing a formal constraint on predictions and explanations. We believe that it is worthwhile to thoroughly address the merits and limitations of a parsimonious set of strong assumptions, before relaxing them and entering into a more complex and less constrained realm of formalization.

3.2.1 The Attitudinal Basis of Influence Networks

Lee and Ofshe (1981) argue that persons accord influence based on their unconscious conditioned responses to other persons' displays of deferential (uncertain and unassertive) and nondeferential (confident and assertive) behaviors during interpersonal interaction. Lee and Ofshe also suggest that persons' evaluations of the content of displayed issue positions are rationalizations of interpersonal influences that have already been accorded. In other words, influence may be accorded to persons on bases that precede and are independent of persons' specific arguments on an issue (Zajonc 1980). Consistent with this viewpoint, expectation states theorists (Berger, Wagner, and Zelditch 1985) argue that influence networks arise and stabilize rapidly in task-oriented groups when interpersonal influences are governed by widely held normatively conditioned attitudes about the relative competence of persons who vary in their visible status characteristics (such as age, race, gender). We argue, more generally, that networks of interpersonal influence may rapidly emerge and stabilize in social groups because persons immediately respond to other persons as *attitudinal objects* upon receipt of information about them. These attitudes about self and others take the form of positive and negative evaluations on the multiple dimensions of the information that they already possess and are receiving about the person-as-object: physical appearance, socioeconomic characteristics, life-course experiences, and present behavior and attitudes. Affect control theorists (Heise 2002) argue that these inward attitudinal responses resolve into three broad dimensions of normatively conditioned evaluation (good vs. bad), potency (weak vs. strong), and activity (passive vs. active), according to which many specific attitudes may be represented.

Attitudes toward other persons-as-objects may arise on the basis of *any and all* information that is available, including the merits of their arguments. However, in this pool of information, we posit that persons' initial attitudes (i.e., their "first impressions") are the major basis of the interpersonal influences that are accorded. According to this postulate, deeming a person to be a sage or an idiot, or to be respected or discounted, occurs rapidly (automatically) in persons' minds, and this evaluative assessment of the person and accord of influence occurs prior to the assessment of the merits of the person's expressed thoughts on a particular issue. Perceived power bases (formal authority, expertise, control of rewards and punishments, and possession or control of other valued resources), obvious physical attributes (skin color, physical attractiveness, age, gender), manner of speaking and general demeanor are categories of information about particular persons that may be processed rapidly and generate an automatic response. The initial evaluative attitudes toward persons-as-objects are the filter through which the salience of other persons' expressed attitudes on issues is processed. Some psychologists have posited that more *meaningful* forms of interpersonal influence occur when there is "central processing" of the content of arguments (Petty and Cacioppo 1986b). This may or may not be true, depending on the definition of meaningful influence. What we are arguing is that once an influence relation has been established on "peripheral" bases, the merits of a person's argument may or may not be clearly assessed and affect the weight that is accorded to it.

The studies of persuasion theorists indicate that a large number of factors may affect persons' susceptibilities and interpersonal influences (Hovland, Janis, and Kelley 1953; Mackie and Skelly 1994; Perloff 1993; Petty and Cacioppo 1986a; Shavitt and Brock 1994), as do studies in which conditions are varied in the context of a unified experimental paradigm (Asch 1956; Milgram 1974). Moreover, Sherif's (1936) classic study on attitude formation demonstrates that persons will draw on expressed attitudes of others in forming their own attitudes on an issue, without supporting argumentation and readily applicable norms. It seems that interpersonal influence (the relative weight of self vs. others and the distribution of interpersonal weights) may arise on the basis of virtually any type of relevant information that is available to persons (Ridgeway 2001). Festinger (1950, 1954) hypothesizes that tensions of uncertainty on the correctness of issue positions are reduced primarily by the formation of interpersonal agreements. This hypothesis remains the best single explanation for why persons will draw on various relevant discriminating characteristics of others for the social comparisons that generate "locomotion" toward agreement.

There is a long tradition of work on *normative* social influence in which persons are responding to attributes of other persons on the basis of norms and stereotypes that are applied to persons-as-objects, as opposed to the informational value of their arguments (Deutsch and Gerard 1955; Turner 1991). Expectation state theorists (Berger, Conner, and Fisek 1974; Berger, Wagner, and Zelditch 1985) have suggested that status characteristics differentiate persons-as-objects who ought to be accorded some influence in a given domain of issues. Similarly, self-categorization theorists (Abrams and Hogg 1990a; Hogg and Tindale 2001; Turner 1991; Turner and Oakes 1989) suggest that interpersonal influences are accorded to persons who occupy prototypical (normative) positions in distributions of attitudes held by in-group and out-group members, and that influence is not accorded to out-group members. Affect control theorists (Heise 2002; Smith-Lovin and Heise 1988) also emphasize the normative foundations of interpersonal influence. Our argument draws on this normative tradition, but we broaden the conditioning of immediate responses to include individual differences in the conditioning of these responses. Hence, persons with shared norms may vary in their immediate conditioned responses to persons-as-objects and in their profiles of accorded influence.

These attitudinal foundations of interpersonal influence explain why interpersonal influences may be subsequently maintained across issues and independent of the content of persons' arguments: the arguments of positively signed persons are positively valued, whereas the arguments of negatively signed persons are either ignored or negatively valued. The conditioned initial (first impression or automatic) attitudinal foundations of interpersonal influence are consistent with the rapid emergence of a structure of interpersonal influence, and if these initial foundations are stable, then the influence network also will be relatively stable. Such emergence may be more or less issue-contextualized. Whether substantially different or similar influence networks operate across a domain of issues will depend on whether different or similar profiles of initial conditioned responses occur on each issue in a particular domain. Our argument allows for stability across different issues predicated on a powerful (dominating) subset of factors that have constrained group members' attitudes about each other and themselves.

Finally, to more completely formalize the above argument, we will specify the process of influence network stabilization. If persons' initial attitudes toward other group members (including themselves) are consensual, then the influence network based on such attitudes is immediately stable. If persons' initial attitudes toward other group members are in disagreement and not susceptible to interpersonal influence, then the influence network based on such attitudes also is immediately stable. Otherwise, the influence network that is based on group members' initial attitudes may modify these attitudes and their profiles of accorded influence until a stable matrix of interpersonal attitudes about group members and a stable network of interpersonal influences are formed. The equilibrium network may or may not entail a consensual set of individual profiles of accorded influence. If the network evolution process is sufficiently slow, then the influence network existing at a particular time may be treated as the stable context within which the issue-specific attitude change process unfolds. We describe a model of this network evolution process later in the book, which dovetails social influence theory with expectation states theory and affect control theory.

3.2.2 Measurement Models for Influence Networks

Our general perspective on W is that the weights accorded by person i to self and others $(w_{i1}, w_{i2}, \ldots, w_{in}$, with $a_{ii} = 1 - w_{ii})$ depend on the *salience* of i's initial $(y_i^{(1)})$ attitude for i and the interpersonal visibility and salience of group members' time t attitudes for i $(y_1^{(t)}, y_2^{(t)}, \ldots, y_n^{(t)})$, which include i's time t attitude $(y_i^{(t)})$. Person j's attitude $(j \neq i)$ cannot directly influence person i's attitude unless j's attitude is both visible and salient for person i. Interpersonal influence is absent or precluded if person j's attitude on the issue is visible but irrelevant for i, or if it is unknown to i (e.g., undisclosed). The distinction between visibility and salience allows for situations in which a person j, whose attitude on an issue might or would be accorded some nonzero weight by i, cannot be accorded such weight, because j's attitude is unknown or undisclosed to i. Clearly, for example, the existence *per se* of persons with bases of influence that might be acknowledged (e.g., experts or authorities) does not imply that their potential interpersonal influence is realized. Thus, information flows about persons' attitudes on an issue (minimally, their visibility) are potentially important in the formation of the influence network on a particular issue.

Our measurement models for $\mathbf{W}$ assume that a measure is available for the *realized* basis of influence,

$$
\mathbf{B} = \begin{bmatrix} b_{11} & b_{12} & \ldots & b_{1n} \\ b_{21} & b_{22} & \ldots & b_{2n} \\ \vdots & \vdots & \ddots & \vdots \\ b_{n1} & b_{n2} & \ldots & b_{nn} \end{bmatrix}, \tag{3.13}
$$

where $b_{ij} \geq 0$ and $b_{ij} > 0 \Leftrightarrow a_{ii} w_{ij} > 0$. Hence, $b_{ij} = 0 \Leftrightarrow a_{ii} w_{ij} = 0$ for all i and j. The joint correspondence $b_{ij} > 0 \Leftrightarrow a_{ii} w_{ij} > 0$ is our criterion for a realized basis of influence in the following sense: we assume that $\mathbf{B}$ is related, in some specified way, to group members' susceptibilities in $\mathbf{A}$ and interpersonal influences $\mathbf{W}$.

Let

$$
\mathbf{R} = \begin{bmatrix} r_{11} & r_{12} & \ldots & r_{1n} \\ r_{21} & r_{22} & \ldots & r_{2n} \\ \vdots & \vdots & \ddots & \vdots \\ r_{n1} & r_{n2} & \ldots & r_{nn} \end{bmatrix}, \tag{3.14}
$$

where $r_{ij} = b_{ij} / \sum_{k=1}^{n} b_{ik}$ for all i and j, under the assumption there is at least *one* attitude that is visible and salient to each group member, i.e., $\sum_{k=1}^{n} b_{ik} > 0$ for all i, which might be i's *own* attitude on the issue. Because $\mathbf{R}$ is row-stochastic, it is a possible and natural operationalization of $\mathbf{W}$. However, in specific applications, this direct equivalence $\mathbf{W} = \mathbf{R}$ may not be entirely suitable. The standard methodological concerns about validity and reliability, here the taking of $\mathbf{R}$ as a direct measure of the construct $\mathbf{W}$, apply.

For every suitable **B** we also may obtain a measure of the matrix of relative interpersonal influences **C**,

$$\mathbf{C} = \begin{bmatrix} 0 & c_{12} & \dots & c_{1n} \\ c_{21} & 0 & \dots. & c_{2n} \\ \vdots & \vdots & \ddots & \vdots \\ c_{n1} & \dots. & c_{n,n-1} & 0 \end{bmatrix}, \tag{3.15}$$

with $c_{ii} = 0$ for all i and

$$c_{ij} = \frac{b_{ij}}{\sum\limits_{k \neq i} b_{ik}} \quad (i \neq j) \tag{3.16}$$

for $\sum_{k \neq i} b_{ik} > 0$. When $\sum_{k \neq i} b_{ik} > 0$, the susceptibility of i might be any value $0 < a_{ii} \leq 1$, because the indication of some interpersonal influence implies a susceptibility value $a_{ii} > 0$. When $\sum_{k \neq i} b_{ik} = 0$, there is no indication of any interpersonal influence on i, and we have $a_{ii} \sum_{k \neq i} w_{ik} = a_{ii}^2 = 0$. In this case, $1 - w_{ii} = a_{ii} = 0$, so that $w_{ii} = 1$, and we set $c_{ij} = 0$ for all $1 \leq j \leq n$. With a suitable **B**, the relative weights in **C** will correspond to the relative *interpersonal* weights in **W**. When $a_{ii} = \sum_{k \neq i} w_{ik} = 0$, then every $w_{ik} = 0$ and $w_{ii} = 1$, so $c_{ij} = 0$ for all j. When $a_{ii} = \sum_{k \neq i} w_{ik} > 0$,

$$c_{ij} = \frac{w_{ij}}{\sum\limits_{k \neq i} w_{ik}} = \frac{w_{ij}}{a_{ii}} \quad (i \neq j). \tag{3.17}$$

It follows that $w_{ij} = a_{ii} c_{ij}$ for $i \neq j$ when $\sum_{k \neq i} w_{ik} > 0$ (or equivalently when $\sum_{k \neq i} c_{ik} = 1$) and that

$$\mathbf{W} = \mathbf{AC} + \mathbf{I} - \mathbf{A}. \tag{3.18}$$

There are various situations in which (3.18) is useful. They include situations in which only strictly *interpersonal* measures are available and a separate measure of self-weights (or susceptibilities) is incorporated into the operationalization of **W**. In other words, in the absence of a global measure of **W**, *separate* measurement models for **A** and **C** may be developed and employed to operationalize **W**.

With only a measure of **C**, a measure of **A** might be based on information in **B**. For example, the measure of **A** might be based on the row or column *sums* of **B**, other measures of i's structural centrality in **B**, or other features of the network structure in which i is situated. If **B** is based on a network of interpersonal contacts, then **A** might also be based on that contact network; e.g., see Friedkin (1998, 2001). If **B** is based on information about group members' positions in the distribution of initial positions on an issue, then **A** also might be based on that distribution.

But the measure of **A** need not be linked to **B**. The number of plausible measurement models for **W** is large, and an analysis of the merits of alternative measurement models is unexplored terrain.

3.2.3 Our Measurement Model

We noted, above, that in specific applications, a direct equivalence $W = R$ may not be entirely suitable. We believe that we are dealing with such a case in the present investigation, where the operationalization of **W** is based on persons' *subjective* reports of their self-weights and the relative weights (direct influences) of others on their positions on an issue. Here, the reported *interpersonal* subjective weights of the matrix **R** are likely to reflect the *net direct impact* of a person j on i, namely, the combination $a_{ii}w_{ij}$ $(i \neq j)$.

Hence, with such data, our measurement model for the relationship between **R** and **W** builds on the assumption that

$$a_{ii}w_{ij} = r_{ij} \quad (i \neq j). \tag{3.19}$$

Clearly, under this assumption,

$$c_{ij} = \frac{r_{ij}}{\sum_{k \neq i} r_{ik}} \quad (i \neq j).$$

Moreover, from our standard model of the influence process, with $a_{ii} = 1 - w_{ii}$, it follows that

$$a_{ii} = 1 - w_{ii} = \sqrt{1 - r_{ii}} \tag{3.20}$$

because $1 = r_{ii} + \sum_{k \neq i} r_{ik} = r_{ii} + \sum_{k \neq i} a_{ii}w_{ik} = r_{ii} + a_{ii}^2$. Thus, with **A** and **C** in hand, we can obtain **W** as in (3.18).

Because

$$1 = a_{ii}w_{ii} + a_{ii} \sum_{k \neq i} w_{ik} + (1 - a_{ii}) = a_{ii}w_{ii} + a_{ii}^2 + (1 - a_{ii}), \tag{3.21}$$

and $r_{ii} = 1 - a_{ii}^2$, we have $r_{ii} = a_{ii}w_{ii} + 1 - a_{ii}$. Hence, $R = AW + I - A$, where $AW + I - A = V^{(1)}$. In short, we take the position that the matrix of subjects' self-reported (subjective) weights is $R = V^{(1)}$. This approach warrants empirical scrutiny, and we evaluate its merits in the next chapter.

To illustrate this approach, let

$$R = \begin{bmatrix} 0.80 & 0.20 & 0 & 0 \\ 0.40 & 0.10 & 0.20 & 0.30 \\ 0 & 0.80 & 0.20 & 0 \\ 0 & 0.20 & 0.05 & 0.75 \end{bmatrix}$$

be the reported matrix $\mathbf{R}$ of group members' subjective reports of their self-weights, and the interpersonal influences upon them, in their discussion of an issue. Then

$$\mathbf{C} = \begin{bmatrix} 0 & 1 & 0 & 0 \\ 0.44\bar{4} & 0 & 0.22\bar{2} & 0.33\bar{3} \\ 0 & 1 & 0 & 0 \\ 0 & 0.800 & 0.200 & 0 \end{bmatrix}$$

and, from (3.20) and (3.18),

$$\mathbf{A} = \begin{bmatrix} 0.447 & 0 & 0 & 0 \\ 0 & 0.949 & 0 & 0 \\ 0 & 0 & 0.894 & 0 \\ 0 & 0 & 0 & 0.500 \end{bmatrix}$$

and

$$\mathbf{W} = \begin{bmatrix} 0.553 & 0.447 & 0 & 0 \\ 0.422 & 0.051 & 0.211 & 0.316 \\ 0 & 0.894 & 0.106 & 0 \\ 0 & 0.400 & 0.100 & 0.500 \end{bmatrix}$$

for the group's influence network.

The employment of subjective weights is a particularly attractive approach for specifying $\mathbf{W}$. Subjective weights have been widely employed in operationalizations of formal models of individual decision making (Abelson and Levi 1985: 240). It eliminates the condition of visibility, when it is made implicit in the report of the subjective weights in $\mathbf{R}$. It simultaneously provides direct measures of persons' self-weights and interpersonal influences. It stays close to the attitudinal foundations of interpersonal influence discussed earlier in this chapter.

French and Raven's (1959) widely employed typology of the bases of interpersonal influence emphasizes the subjective foundations of these bases (*perceived* expertise, *perceived* authority, *perceived* power to reward or punish, etc.), and in work on the foundations of persuasion (Hovland, Janis, and Kelley 1953), the influence-source's *credibility* in the mind of the influence-target appears as a key construct. The idea that interpersonal influence might be accurately measured via persons' reports of the influences upon them has been widely adopted. Hunter's (1953) seminal analysis of community power structures, for example, relies on a measure of "reputational" influence. Similarly, Simon (1953) states that

> If we accept the proposition we have just been urging, that expectations of consequences are a major determinant of behavior, then we can use such expectations, so long as the situation remains stable, to estimate where power lies... we ask the participants what the power structure is. (Simon 1953: 508)

We believe that the advantages of the allocation-model measure are compelling, and we employ it in the experimental investigations to be reported. The distinctive feature of this measurement model is not its reliance on a subjective measure of interpersonal influence, but its extension of the subjective measure to include a report of self-weights.

3.3 Fitted Susceptibilities

Our standard model also may be operationalized with *fitted* susceptibilities. In this section, we show how group members' susceptibility values **A** and the main diagonal of **W**, assuming $w_{ii} = 1 - a_{ii}$ for all i, may be derived from the standard model of the influence process, given measures of their initial and final attitudes on an issue, $\mathbf{y}^{(1)}$ and $\mathbf{y}^{(\infty)}$ respectively, and measures of their relative interpersonal influence, **C**. This operationalization *fits* our standard model to the data. It allows us to compare the accuracy of the predictions of the fitted model, based on derived susceptibilities, and the predictions of a model that is entirely based on empirical measures of its constructs. It also allows us to directly assess the correspondence of the standard model's derived susceptibility value for an individual and the individual's subjective report of his or her susceptibility, which is the complement of the reported self-weight obtained from **R**. It further provides a formal framework for operationalizing the standard model in circumstances where direct measures of group members' susceptibilities are unavailable.

With $\mathbf{W} = \mathbf{AC} + \mathbf{I} - \mathbf{A}$ and

$$\begin{aligned} \mathbf{y}^{(\infty)} &= \mathbf{AW}\mathbf{y}^{(\infty)} + (\mathbf{I} - \mathbf{A})\mathbf{y}^{(1)} \\ &= \mathbf{A}(\mathbf{AC} + \mathbf{I} - \mathbf{A})\mathbf{y}^{(\infty)} + (\mathbf{I} - \mathbf{A})\mathbf{y}^{(1)}, \end{aligned} \tag{3.22}$$

the resulting scalar equation is

$$y_i^{(\infty)} = a_{ii}(1 - a_{ii})y_i^{(\infty)} + a_{ii}^2 \sum_{k \neq i} c_{ik} y_k^{(\infty)} + (1 - a_{ii})y_i^{(1)} \tag{3.23}$$

for all i. It follows that

$$y_i^{(\infty)} - y_i^{(1)} = a_{ii}(y_i^{(\infty)} - y_i^{(1)}) + a_{ii}^2 \left(\sum_{k \neq i} c_{ik} y_k^{(\infty)} - y_i^{(\infty)} \right) \tag{3.24}$$

and

$$(1 - a_{ii})(y_i^{(\infty)} - y_i^{(1)}) = a_{ii}^2 \left(\sum_{k \neq i} c_{ik} y_k^{(\infty)} - y_i^{(\infty)} \right). \tag{3.25}$$

Hence,

$$\frac{a_{ii}^2}{1 - a_{ii}} = \frac{y_i^{(\infty)} - y_i^{(1)}}{\sum_{k \neq i} c_{ik} y_k^{(\infty)} - y_i^{(\infty)}} \tag{3.26}$$

for $\sum_{k \neq i} c_{ik} y_k^{(\infty)} - y_i^{(\infty)} \neq 0$. In this case, letting

$$\Delta_i \equiv \frac{y_i^{(\infty)} - y_i^{(1)}}{\sum_{k \neq i} c_{ik} y_k^{(\infty)} - y_i^{(\infty)}}, \tag{3.27}$$

we have $a_{ii}^2 = \Delta_i (1 - a_{ii})$ or $a_{ii}^2 + \Delta_i a_{ii} - \Delta_i = 0$, which has the solutions

$$a_{ii} = \frac{-\Delta_i \pm \sqrt{\Delta_i^2 + 4\Delta_i}}{2}. \tag{3.28}$$

The a_{ii} computed from (3.28) is a complex number for $-4 < \Delta_i < 0$, greater than one for $\Delta_i \leq -4$, and less than one for $0 \leq \Delta_i$:

	$a_{ii} = \dfrac{-\Delta_i + \sqrt{\Delta_i^2 + 4\Delta_i}}{2}$	$a_{ii} = \dfrac{-\Delta_i - \sqrt{\Delta_i^2 + 4\Delta_i}}{2}$
$\Delta_i \leq -4$	$a_{ii} \geq 2$	$1 < a_{ii} \leq 2$
$-4 < \Delta_i < 0$	Complex number	Complex number
$\Delta_i \geq 0$	$0 \leq a_{ii} < 1$	$a_{ii} \leq 0$

But the assumptions $w_{ii} = 1 - a_{ii}$ and $0 \leq w_{ii} \leq 1$ imply that $0 \leq a_{ii} \leq 1$. Hence, for each real-valued Δ_i, the estimate of a_{ii} is selected to be the real number in the legitimate range $[0, 1]$ that is numerically the closest (in the complex plane) to either of the two a_{ii} values computed from (3.28).

Thus, the resulting solution for $\sum_{k \neq i} c_{ik} y_k^{(\infty)} - y_i^{(\infty)} \neq 0$ is

$$a_{ii} = \begin{cases} 1 & \text{if } \Delta_i \leq -2 \\ \dfrac{-\Delta_i}{2} & \text{if } -2 < \Delta_i < 0 \\ \dfrac{-\Delta_i + \sqrt{\Delta_i^2 + 4\Delta_i}}{2} & \text{if } \Delta_i \geq 0, \end{cases} \tag{3.29}$$

and for $\sum_{k \neq i} c_{ik} y_k^{(\infty)} - y_i^{(\infty)} = 0$, we set

$$a_{ii} = \begin{cases} 1 & \text{if } y_i^{(\infty)} - y_i^{(1)} \neq 0 \\ 0 & \text{if } y_i^{(\infty)} - y_i^{(1)} = 0. \end{cases} \tag{3.30}$$

When $\sum_{k \neq i} c_{ik} y_k^{(\infty)} - y_i^{(\infty)} = 0$ and $y_i^{(\infty)} - y_i^{(1)} \neq 0$, it follows from (3.25) that $a_{ii} = 1$.

Special consideration is required when $\sum_{k \neq i} c_{ik} y_k^{(\infty)} - y_i^{(\infty)} = 0$ and $y_i^{(\infty)} - y_i^{(1)} = 0$, because here mathematically a_{ii} might have any value. Person i's attitude has not changed either because person i was not susceptible to interpersonal influence, or because he or she was susceptible to such influence but (a) remained in the same position as a result of exactly balancing cross pressures or (b) returned to that position after departing from it. The absence of susceptibility ($a_{ii} = 0$) is more likely than the other alternatives and, in any case, is most consonant with the observed outcome for i in the influence process. Thus, we set $a_{ii} = 0$, with the understanding that this assumption is a potential source of error in the model. Finally, we recall that $a_{ii} = 0$ by definition when in C there is no indication of any interpersonal influences on i. Here, if i's attitude has changed, the change cannot be attributed to interpersonal influences.

For an illustration of the derivation of A consider

$$
C = \begin{bmatrix} 0 & 0.600 & 0.200 & 0.200 \\ 0.267 & 0 & 0.467 & 0.267 \\ 0 & 0 & 0 & 0 \\ 0.235 & 0.412 & 0.353 & 0 \end{bmatrix}, \quad y^{(1)} = \begin{bmatrix} 20 \\ 50 \\ 40 \\ 20 \end{bmatrix}, \quad y^{(\infty)} = \begin{bmatrix} 40 \\ 40 \\ 40 \\ 40 \end{bmatrix}.
$$

It follows from (3.27) and (3.28) that

$$
A = \begin{bmatrix} 1 & 0 & 0 & 0 \\ 0 & 1 & 0 & 0 \\ 0 & 0 & 0 & 0 \\ 0 & 0 & 0 & 1 \end{bmatrix}
$$

and from $W = AC + I - A$ that

$$
W = \begin{bmatrix} 0 & 0.600 & 0.200 & 0.200 \\ 0.267 & 0 & 0.467 & 0.267 \\ 0 & 0 & 1 & 0 \\ 0.235 & 0.412 & 0.353 & 0 \end{bmatrix}.
$$

3.4 An Overview of the Analytic Framework

Figure 3.1 is a schematic representation of our general analytic framework. Our analysis defines and involves a number of constructs that are employed in various places in the book. The figure displays the linkages between the empirical measures and theoretical constructs that we draw upon. The former may be empirical components that are combined to form a measure of the influence network W. The latter may be derived or predicted constructs from the model and measures. We developed this

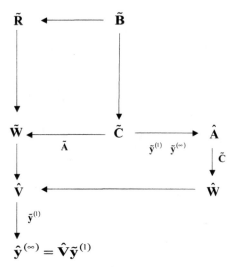

Figure 3.1 Analytic framework for accounts and predictions.

schematic as an aid to ourselves, and found it to be useful. Below we explicate the analytic pathways displayed in Figure 3.1.

3.4.1 Notation

As the preceding sections have shown, the formal architecture of our standard model is operationalized in terms of empirical (measured) or of derived or predicted values of the constructs. Empirical values of a subset of the constructs of the standard model sometimes allow the derivation or prediction of values for other constructs in terms of the model. We denote *empirical* values of the standard model's constructs with a tilde ($\tilde{\mathbf{y}}^{(1)}, \tilde{\mathbf{y}}^{(2)}, \ldots, \tilde{\mathbf{y}}^{(\infty)}, \tilde{\mathbf{A}}, \tilde{\mathbf{C}}$, and $\tilde{\mathbf{W}}$) and *derived* or *predicted* values of these constructs with a circumflex ($\hat{\mathbf{y}}^{(1)}, \hat{\mathbf{y}}^{(2)}, \ldots, \hat{\mathbf{y}}^{(\infty)}, \hat{\mathbf{A}}, \hat{\mathbf{C}}, \hat{\mathbf{W}}$, and $\hat{\mathbf{V}}$).

3.4.2 Fundamental Equations

The equilibrium equation of the standard model can be expressed in either of two forms,

$$\mathbf{y}^{(\infty)} = \mathbf{A}\mathbf{W}\mathbf{y}^{(\infty)} + (\mathbf{I} - \mathbf{A})\mathbf{y}^{(1)} \qquad (3.31)$$

or

$$\mathbf{y}^{(\infty)} = \mathbf{V}\mathbf{y}^{(1)}, \qquad (3.32)$$

where $\mathbf{V} \equiv \mathbf{V}^{(\infty)}$ is

$$\mathbf{V} = (\mathbf{I} - \mathbf{AW})^{-1}(\mathbf{I} - \mathbf{A})$$

when $\mathbf{I} - \mathbf{AW}$ is nonsingular, or more generally is estimated by

$$\mathbf{V} \approx \mathbf{V}^{(t)} = (\mathbf{AW})^t + \left[\sum_{k=0}^{t-1} (\mathbf{AW})^k \right] (\mathbf{I} - \mathbf{A}), \qquad (3.33)$$

for a sufficiently large t when $\mathbf{V} = \lim_{t \to \infty} \mathbf{V}^{(t)}$ exists. As (3.33) shows, $\mathbf{V}$ is determined by $\mathbf{A}$ and $\mathbf{W}$. With $a_{ii} = 1 - w_{ii}$ for all i, $\mathbf{V}$ is determined by $\mathbf{W}$ or by $\mathbf{W} = \mathbf{AC} + \mathbf{I} - \mathbf{A}$. Thus, given a measure $\tilde{\mathbf{y}}^{(1)}$, we may determine $\hat{\mathbf{y}}^{(\infty)}$ either (a) from $\tilde{\mathbf{W}}$, or (b) from $\tilde{\mathbf{A}}$ and $\tilde{\mathbf{C}}$, or (c) from $\hat{\mathbf{A}}$ and $\tilde{\mathbf{C}}$, where $\hat{\mathbf{A}}$ is derived from the model in terms of $\tilde{\mathbf{y}}^{(1)}$, $\tilde{\mathbf{y}}^{(\infty)}$, and $\tilde{\mathbf{C}}$. In the first two alternatives, $\hat{\mathbf{y}}^{(\infty)}$ *predicts* $\tilde{\mathbf{y}}^{(\infty)}$, and in the third, it explains (fits) $\tilde{\mathbf{y}}^{(\infty)}$.

3.4.3 Three Analytic Pathways

Three pathways of analysis are described in Figure 3.1. We employ all three pathways in the analysis presented in the next chapter.

In one pathway, a row-normalized $\tilde{\mathbf{R}}$ (3.14) is formed from the basis $\tilde{\mathbf{B}}$ (3.13), and $\tilde{\mathbf{W}}$ is obtained, for example, from our measurement model (3.19) and (3.20). Another pathway to $\tilde{\mathbf{W}}$ is based on a $\tilde{\mathbf{B}}$ in which the main-diagonal values are missing or ignored: i.e., only $\tilde{\mathbf{C}}$ is formed from the available data in $\tilde{\mathbf{B}}$, and $\tilde{\mathbf{A}}$ is obtained either from $\tilde{\mathbf{B}}$ (e.g., the structural centralities of persons), or from *other* data or assumptions. In both of these pathways, $\mathbf{A}$ and $\mathbf{W}$ are operationalized with empirical measures, then $\hat{\mathbf{V}}$ is derived, and, in turn, the group members' equilibrium attitudes are predicted. Here, $\hat{\mathbf{y}}^{(\infty)} = \hat{\mathbf{V}}\tilde{\mathbf{y}}^{(1)}$ and the errors of prediction are $\mathbf{e} = \tilde{\mathbf{y}}^{(\infty)} - \hat{\mathbf{y}}^{(\infty)}$.

The third pathway draws on *fitted* susceptibilities; i.e., $\tilde{\mathbf{C}}$ is formed from $\tilde{\mathbf{B}}$, and $\hat{\mathbf{A}}$ is derived from (3.28), taking into account group members' observed initial and equilibrium attitudes. Here, $\hat{\mathbf{W}} = \hat{\mathbf{A}}\tilde{\mathbf{C}} + \mathbf{I} - \hat{\mathbf{A}}$, $\hat{\mathbf{y}}^{(\infty)} = \hat{\mathbf{V}}\tilde{\mathbf{y}}^{(1)}$, where $\hat{\mathbf{V}}$ is obtained from $\hat{\mathbf{A}}$ and $\hat{\mathbf{W}}$, and the errors of prediction are $\mathbf{e} = \tilde{\mathbf{y}}^{(\infty)} - \hat{\mathbf{y}}^{(\infty)}$.

We note that constructs other than group members' susceptibilities may be derived or predicted with the standard model. We do not draw on these other potential derivations or predictions. The standard model allows the derivation of group members' *initial positions* from empirical measures of group members' susceptibilities $\tilde{\mathbf{A}}$, influence network $\tilde{\mathbf{W}}$ or $\tilde{\mathbf{C}}$ ($\tilde{\mathbf{W}} = \tilde{\mathbf{A}}\tilde{\mathbf{C}} + \mathbf{I} - \tilde{\mathbf{A}}$), and their equilibrium positions $\tilde{\mathbf{y}}^{(\infty)}$; i.e., $\hat{\mathbf{y}}^{(1)} = (\mathbf{I} - \tilde{\mathbf{A}})^{-1}(\mathbf{I} - \tilde{\mathbf{A}}\tilde{\mathbf{W}})\tilde{\mathbf{y}}^{(\infty)}$ for a nonsingular $(\mathbf{I} - \tilde{\mathbf{A}})$. However, the derivation of $\hat{\mathbf{y}}^{(1)}$ should not be based on an ill-conditioned $\mathbf{I} - \tilde{\mathbf{A}}$. The matrix $\mathbf{I} - \tilde{\mathbf{A}}$ will be ill-conditioned if it contains any $\tilde{a}_{ii}$ that is close to 1. Moreover, in very special cases (e.g., in dyads), group members' interpersonal influences ($\hat{\mathbf{W}}$ or $\hat{\mathbf{A}}\hat{\mathbf{W}}$) may be derived from measures of $\tilde{\mathbf{y}}^{(\infty)}$ and $\tilde{\mathbf{y}}^{(1)}$; see Chapter 6.

3.5 Concluding Remarks

We have devoted a considerable amount of attention to the underlying conceptualization and operationalization of the constructs of our standard model. Detailed attention to such matters is warranted. The range of applications of the model is large not only because the model pertains to the theoretically fundamental process of endogenous interpersonal influences, but also because the domain of realizations of the attitude and influence network constructs is large. Different types of attitudes and different substantive bases for group members' self-weights and interpersonal weights may be analyzed within the formal framework of the standard model.

Moreover, our attention to operationalization is warranted by the multiple analytic foci that may be addressed with the model. We may and do focus on the question of consistency. To what extent is the formal model able to explain (account for) group members' observed final positions on an issue and any changes of their initial positions that occurred during the group discussion? We may and do focus on the question of prediction. To what extent is the formal model able to predict such outcomes without a fitting or optimization of the values of the model's constructs? We may and do employ the model as a theoretical foundation for *deriving* group members' susceptibilities in order to analyze the empirical correspondence of the derived values and group members' subjective (self-reported) self-weights. When interest is focused on susceptibility per se, the model may be employed to derive individual susceptibilities that are then taken as the values of the dependent variable of an analysis. Thus, the domain of operationalization includes analytical foci that are addressed to the merits of the model as well as those addressed to the model's employment.

Our standard model of the influence system is deterministic. Our analytic framework generates $\hat{\mathbf{y}}^{(\infty)} = \hat{\mathbf{V}}\tilde{\mathbf{y}}^{(1)}$ with errors $\mathbf{e} = \tilde{\mathbf{y}}^{(\infty)} - \hat{\mathbf{y}}^{(\infty)}$. We will show that with fitted susceptibilities, exact fits may be achieved. With models without fitted susceptibilities, the modeling errors are often larger than those obtained with fitted susceptibilities, which is neither a surprise nor a problem per se. When $\mathbf{e} \neq 0$, it is a matter of judgment whether the errors are sufficiently egregious to warrant concern. Formal models entail simplifying assumptions, which usually generate errors that may be acceptable. Measures of theoretical constructs are imperfect, but their errors also may be acceptable. There are no fixed or easy rules that can be marshaled for the evaluation of this, or any, model except one. If the predictions of a model are rarely useful, and if the explanations based on the model do not sufficiently advance our understanding, including the theoretical integration of different lines of work, then the model should be discarded in favor of one that is more useful or one that more significantly advances our understanding, or both.

4

Assessing the Model

In this chapter, we evaluate social influence network theory with data from a series of experiments on small groups: dyads, triads, and tetrads. First, we evaluate whether certain general implications of the standard model, which do not depend on the merits of our measures of A and W, are consistent with the spectrum of observed group outcomes of the attitude change and consensus formation process in groups. Second, we evaluate the accuracy of the model, drawing on subjects' reports of their initial and final (end-of-trial) attitudes on issues, and their allocation of subjective weights to themselves and others in forming their final attitudes. On each issue, we compare the accuracy of this model with the accuracy of a baseline model that predicts the convergence of attitudes to the mean of group member's initial attitudes on an issue. Third, we assess the performance of an optimized model in which group members' susceptibilities are fitted to the data that group members provided about their attitudes and interpersonal influences; and we evaluate the correspondence between the fitted susceptibilities and group members' reported subjective self-weights. Our examination of the latter correspondence is a probe of the phenomenological validity of the model via its derived susceptibility values. Other predictions and applications of the model will be presented in subsequent chapters.

4.1 Three Experiments

We begin with a description of the experiments on dyads, triads, and tetrads that we employ to assess the model. These data provide a basis for describing the influence systems of small groups in which discussions are occurring on issues and members are attempting to reconcile their disagreements to reach consensus. The form of each experiment is roughly the same. Each member of a group privately recorded his or her initial

Table 4.1 *Three experiments*

Experiments	Groups	Issues	Trials
Tetrads	50	5	250
Triads	32	3	96
Dyads	52	2	104

position on an issue. A discussion of the issue ensued. After some specified time, or upon reaching group consensus or a deadlock, group members privately recorded their final positions on the issue and provided estimates of the relative interpersonal influences of the other group members upon their final positions. Table 4.1 describes the number of different groups and issues involved in these experiments.

4.1.1 Tetrads Experiment

The tetrads experiment involved 50 four-person groups of college students: 25 all-female groups and 25 all-male groups. Group members were asked to attempt to resolve their initial differences of attitude on various issues. Subjects were randomly assigned to positions in one of five different communication networks. These networks are the star, kite, circle, slash, and complete networks displayed in Figure 4.1.[1] During the experiment, neither the structure of the communication network nor individuals' positions in the network were altered.

Each group member occupied a private room and was given an issue to consider in isolation from the other three group members. Each person was asked to record an initial attitude on the issue. Group members then discussed their attitudes using a simple telephone system. Each subject's telephone displayed the names of persons with whom direct communication was possible. Only dyadic communication was permitted and (depending on the network) only certain communication channels could be activated by each subject. Group members were instructed that they could communicate with other members of the group as frequently as they liked, but that they must communicate at least once with each person whose name was listed on their telephones.

Group members were given up to 20 minutes to discuss the assigned issue. Each group was instructed that attaining consensus was feasible and desirable:

> Your goal is to reach consensus. If it seems difficult to reach consensus, remember that most groups are able to come to some

[1] Along with the chain (1–2–3–4), which was not involved in the experiments, these five networks include all the nonisomorphic connected graphs that can occur in a four-person group.

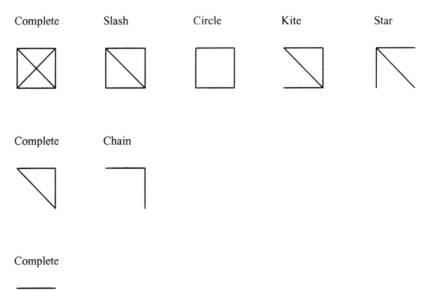

Figure 4.1 Communication networks in tetrads, triads, and dyads.

decision if those who disagree will restate their reasons and if the problem is reread carefully.

Upon reaching group consensus or a deadlock, group members were asked to record their final attitudes on the issue.

Each group dealt with five issues in sequence. To eliminate crossover effects, the order of the issues was systematically varied among the groups. Three discussion issues were choice dilemmas: the "Sports," "School," and "Surgery" issues (described below). Two other issues involved making a judgment about an appropriate monetary reward: the "Asbestos" and "Disaster" issues (also described below). Individuals' attitudes on these issues were represented by real numbers: subjective probabilities on the "risky shift" issues or dollars on the monetary issues.

4.1.2 Triads Experiment

The triads experiment involved 32 three-person groups: 16 all-male groups and 16 all-female groups. Each group dealt with the three choice dilemmas (Sports, School, and Surgery) in either the complete or chain communication network shown in Figure 4.1. One-half of the triads operated under a "high"-pressure condition, and one-half operated under a "low"-pressure condition. In the high-pressure condition, subjects were instructed that attaining consensus was feasible and desirable:

We would like you to reach an agreement. If at the end of 20 minutes there are remaining differences that you believe might be reconciled, you may have an additional 10 minutes for discussion. You may terminate the session at any time if you believe that the remaining differences of opinion cannot be reconciled. However, it has been our experience that most discussion groups are able to reach an agreement within the 20- (plus optional 10-) minute time frame.

Under the low-pressure condition, subjects were instructed that any outcome was acceptable:

When the buzzer sounds a second time it is the signal for you to begin telephone communication with the other person(s). Now is the time to reconsider your choice. Discuss the situation with the other person(s). The conversation that you will have may or may not lead you to alter your first opinion, and you may or may not come to an agreement. Any of these outcomes are OK with us. You will have 20 minutes in which to discuss the issue. You may have an additional 10 minutes if you want them.

4.1.3 Dyads Experiment

The dyads experiment involved 52 two-person groups: 20 all-male groups and 32 all-female groups. Dyads were given up to 30 minutes to discuss an issue. Twenty-six of the dyads were placed under the high-pressure condition described in the triads experiment, and 26 dyads were placed under the low-pressure condition. Each dyad dealt with two discussion issues in sequence: the Surgery and School choice dilemmas.

4.1.4 Discussion Issues

We drew three of the discussion issues from the literature on choice shifts and group polarization; see Chapter 9 for a review and analysis of this literature. Prior findings on choice shifts and group polarization have been based mainly on issues in which subjects assess an acceptable level of risk in adopting a particular course of action. Three of the discussion issues we used involve questions that have been used by other investigators and on which there has been some evidence of group polarization. On these three choice dilemmas (Sports, School, and Surgery), subjects were instructed to choose between two alternative courses of action:

One alternative involves greater risk than the other, while also offering a greater potential reward. Consider the alternatives. Then indicate what probability of success would be necessary for you to choose the alternative which is potentially more rewarding, but which also carries a greater degree of risk.

The Sports issue involved a choice between alternative plays in a game between two college teams (one play would tie the game; the other play could win it or lose it):

> *Sports.* You are a captain of a college team. You are playing in the crucial contest against your team's traditional rival. The Game has been an intense struggle and now, in the final seconds of the game, your team is slightly behind. Fortunately, you are in a good position to successfully complete a play that will almost certainly produce a tie score. You are also in a position to attempt a play that is much riskier. If successful, it would result in a victory for your team; if unsuccessful, your team's defeat.

The School issue involved a choice between two Ph.D. programs (one program has a low failure rate; the other program has a higher failure rate but a much better academic reputation):

> *School.* You are a college senior planning to go on for the Ph.D. For the Ph.D., you may enter Quality University. Because of Quality's rigorous standards, only a fraction of the graduate students manage to receive the Ph.D. you desire. You may also make a different choice, to enter O.K. University. O.K. has a much poorer reputation than Quality. At O.K. almost every student receives a Ph.D.

The Surgery issue involved a choice between two courses of medical treatment (one treatment entails little risk but a drastic curtailment of lifestyle; the riskier treatment might bring about a complete cure):

> *Surgery.* You have just completed a visit to your family doctor, and then to a cardiac specialist. You have been told that you have a severe heart ailment. Due to your heart disease, you must drastically curtail your customary way of life. There is an alternative. There is a medical operation available that has the potential to bring about a complete cure of your heart ailment. However, the operation could prove fatal.

The subjects' responses (attitudes) were restricted to one of 20 probability values: 0.05, 0.10, 0.15, ..., 0.95, 1. Previous research indicates that subjects have heterogeneous initial attitudes on these issues and take them seriously. We use percentage values (5–100) of these scores in our reports and analyses.

The experiments also included two issues of monetary reward, involving compensation for asbestos removal and court damages for a chemical spill:

> *Asbestos.* The Elmwood Unified School District has some older buildings with asbestos ceiling tiles which must be removed. The job is dirty and tedious. Unskilled labor might be hired at the minimum wage of 5.50 per hour; however, some members of the school board believe that the job calls for greater remuneration than 5.50 per hour in view of the potential hazards in dealing with asbestos. How much ought the personnel who are going to do this work be paid on an hourly basis?

> *Disaster.* The 37th District Federal Court is hearing a case where plaintiffs in India have filed a class action suit against the Consolidated Chemical Company of Hunnicutt, Maryland. One hundred employees suffered irreversible lung damage as a consequence of an accident at company's plant in India and are no longer able to work at their former jobs at the plant. The average income for these workers was 375 U.S. dollars per year (in a country where the average per capita annual income in 1977 was 150 dollars). Lawyers for the injured workers are seeking two million dollars per plaintiff: for the lost wages they would have earned and for punitive damages. Lawyers for the company argue that if the company is forced to pay 200 million dollars, it could not afford to maintain the plant, which has been marginally profitable. And while the 100 plaintiffs may gain in wealth, the remaining 3500 workers who depend on the plant for their livelihood will find themselves out of a job. The lawyers for the company emphasize that while the company was not at fault in the accident, it is willing to work out some reasonable form of compensation. What is the dollar amount that would be just compensation for each of the plaintiffs?

The range of awards on the Disaster issue was substantial, and we employ the natural logarithm of the awards in our analyses.

4.1.5 Initial and End-of-Trial Attitudes

Subjects' attitudes on an issue were measured at the beginning and at the end of each experimental trial, and we denote these attitudes as $\tilde{y}^{(1)}$ and $\tilde{y}^{(\infty)}$, respectively: the initial attitudes are persons' self-reports of their positions on an issue prior to interpersonal communication on the issue among group members, and the end-of-trial attitudes are persons' self-reports of their positions on an issue after a sustained period of interpersonal communication on the issue among group members.

4.1.6 Interpersonal Influences and Self-Weights

After recording their final attitudes on an issue, subjects were asked to estimate the extent to which each group member influenced their final attitude:

> You have been given a total of 20 chips. Each chip represents influence upon your final opinion. Divide the chips into two piles, *Pile A* and *Pile B*. *Pile A* will represent the extent to which the conversations you had with the other persons influenced your final opinion. *Pile B* will represent the extent to which the conversations you had with the other persons did not influence your final opinion. Now consider the extent to which you feel each member of the group influenced the group's final opinion. Divide the chips in *Pile A* into piles for each person according to how much they influenced your final opinion.

The task of allocating chips is a "physical model" of the assumption that interpersonal influence is a finite distributed resource. We denote the resulting matrix of weights, as $\tilde{\mathbf{R}} = [\tilde{r}_{ij}]$, where $\tilde{r}_{ij}$ is the number of chips that person i accords to person j divided by the total number of chips (20 chips). Note that $\tilde{r}_{ii}$ is person i's self-assessment of the extent to which the conversations with the other persons did *not* influence i's final attitude (i.e., the relative size of *Pile B*).

4.2 A Spectrum of Group Outcomes

In this section, we evaluate whether several general implications of the standard model are consistent with the spectrum of observed group outcomes of the attitude change and consensus formation process in groups. We describe various types of outcomes that may arise from a group's discussion of an issue, and we document that each of these outcomes occurs with a noteworthy relative frequency in our data. A general formal model of the influence process should be able to account for each of these types of outcome. Models that are scope-restricted with respect to the types of outcome that they are able to predict bypass the explanation of outcomes that do not satisfy their scope restrictions.

Table 4.2 describes a simple typology of group outcomes: (a) end-of-trial consensus versus disagreement, (b) in the case of consensus, whether the agreement that is reached is a new, i.e., compromise, attitude or one of the initial attitudes of group members, and (c) in the case of a consensus

Table 4.2 *A spectrum of group outcomes*

	Count	%
Tetrads:		
Consensus on a boundary initial position	31	12.4
Consensus on an internal initial position	73	29.2
Consensus on a new internal position	106	42.4
Disagreement in the range of initial positions	39	15.6
Consensus outside the range of initial positions	0	0.0
Disagreement outside the range of initial positions	1	0.4
TOTAL TETRADS	250	100
Triads:		
Consensus on a boundary initial position	18	18.8
Consensus on an internal initial position	13	13.5
Consensus on a new internal position	20	20.8
Disagreement in the range of initial positions	44	45.8
Consensus outside the range of initial positions	0	0.0
Disagreement outside the range of initial positions	1	1.0
TOTAL TRIADS	96	100
Dyads:		
Consensus on a boundary initial position	23	22.1
Consensus on an internal initial position	—	—
Consensus on a new internal position	28	26.9
Disagreement in the range of initial positions	35	33.7
Consensus outside the range of initial positions	10	9.6
Disagreement outside the range of initial positions	8	7.7
TOTAL DYADS	104	100
TOTAL GROUP-ISSUE TRIALS	450	

on one of the members' initial attitudes, whether the initial attitude is one of the two boundary, i.e., most extreme, attitudes in the group or not. If the consensus is a boundary attitude, the case is described as an instance of "consensus on a boundary initial position." If the consensus is an initial attitude that is *not* one of the two boundary attitudes, the case is described as an instance of "consensus on an internal initial position." If the consensus is an attitude that is not one of the group members' initial attitudes, the case is described as an instance of "consensus on a new position." Finally, we also have categorized group outcomes with respect to whether any of the group members' final attitudes are higher than the maximum, or lower than the minimum, value of the group members' initial attitudes on an issue. We refer to instances of such outlying final attitudes as breaches of the convex hull or the range of initial positions. A prediction of the theory is that there should be no breaching of the convex hull of initial positions. *The distribution of observed collective (end-of-trial) outcomes among the categories of this typology shows that group outcomes take a variety of forms and that no particular form is dominant.*

There are three immediate implications for a formal theory of inter-personal influence. First, it cannot be assumed that groups always reach consensus; whether or not they do depends on the felt pressure to reach consensus, among other conditions, as we will show in subsequent chapters. A network theory of interpersonal influence on attitudes should be formally consistent both with the emergence of consensus in a group and with changes of attitudes that do not result in consensus. Second, it cannot be assumed that groups tend to form a consensus either on new positions (which are not one of the initial positions of any member) or on existing alternative positions (given by the members' initial attitudes); they do both with substantial frequency. Third, consensus is frequently formed on a boundary initial position. A network theory of interpersonal influence should be formally consistent with all of these outcomes.

Social psychological investigations of interpersonal influence have been split between psychological investigations, which have tended to assume that pressures toward uniformity result in convergence to the mean of initial attitudes, and sociological investigations, which have tended to assume that inequalities of interpersonal influence, including interpersonal domination, are a characteristic feature of a group's influence network. Both symmetrical and asymmetrical interpersonal influence may exist in small groups and, hence, any general model of social influence should allow for both. A convergence to the mean of initial attitudes may be treated as a special case of influence process outcomes and, as such, accounted for by a general model that allows other outcomes.

4.3 Convex Hull of Initial Positions

Our theory implies that revised attitudes are convex combinations of initial attitudes. This result has two further implications. First, an initial consensus should be maintained, and at the same issue-position value. Second, all revised attitudes, whether at equilibrium or during the influence process, should be in the *range* of the initial attitudes on a 1-dimensional issue, and this generalizes to the result that the revised vectors of m-dimensional attitudes should be in the convex hull of the m-dimensional initial attitudes. We employ the term convex hull because it precisely defines the geometric form of the constraint for m-dimensional issues $(m \geq 2)$.[2] For a 1-dimensional issue, it simply refers to the interval

[2] On a multidimensional issue, every time t outcome for a group member lies within the range of initial attitudes of all the group members on each dimension. This outcome is a convex linear combination of all the initial attitude vectors of the group. The set of all convex linear combinations of the $1 \times m$ row vectors of $Y^{(1)}$ forms a geometric object in m-dimensional real space called the *convex hull* of the row vectors of $Y^{(1)}$. Thus, our employment of the term "convex hull" precisely describes a geometric implication of our model. In the case of a 1-dimensional issue, the convex hull becomes the range.

[minimum, maximum] of initial attitudes in a group, and the constraint may be referred to interchangeably as the range or the convex hull of initial attitudes.

There is strong support in the literature for the theory's prediction that an initial consensus will be maintained (Barnlund 1959; Thorndike 1938). Barnlund reported that, in small groups assembled to solve problems of logic, an initial consensus was not questioned (the group moved on to the next problem), regardless of whether the consensus was correct or incorrect. Similarly, Thorndike (1938: 351) found that an initial consensus was rarely modified regardless of whether the consensus was correct or incorrect; in his results, an initial consensus was modified in only 3 of 725 group problem-solving trials in which the group's judgment was correct, and in 1 of 263 trials in which the group's judgment was incorrect. Consensus is assumed to be either correct (whether or not it is) or satisfactory; in either case, it is deemed conclusive. Our data on dyads, triads, and tetrads provided only ten cases of initial consensus, and eight of these cases occurred among the dyads. In three cases (all dyads) the consensus was modified, resulting in an automatic breach of the convex hull of initial attitudes, to a new consensus.

The findings in Table 4.2 support the theory's prediction that the social influence process is unlikely to result in attitudes that breach the convex hull of initial positions. But these findings also indicate that this constraint is less reliable in dyads than in triads and tetrads.[3] One or more members of a group breached the convex hull of initial attitudes of their group in 20 issue-trials, and 18 of these cases occurred in dyads. Breaches were rare in triads and tetrads, but in dyads they occurred in 17.3% of the trials. The breaches occurred in a variety of ways. Among the dyads, a consensus was formed in 10 of the 18 groups where a breach occurred; i.e., both persons moved outside the convex hull. In 3 of these 10 cases there was an initial consensus. In the other 8 cases of the 18, where no consensus was formed, either one member remained inside the convex hull while the other member moved *away* from the initial position of the other (5 cases), or one member remained inside the convex hull while the other member leapfrogged over the initial position of the other (2 cases), or both members moved outside the convex hull in the same direction without forming a consensus (1 case). Among the triads and tetrads, where only two breaches occurred, neither group formed a consensus: in one case a person who occupied a boundary position moved outside the

---

[3] Sniezek and Henry (1989, 1990) report the occurrence of frequent breaches of the convex hull in their experiments on triads. However, as they are careful to note, their studies solicit subjective confidence intervals from subjects. It is not evident that the observed breaches were outside the range of the minimum lower bound and maximum upper bound of group members' set of confidence intervals.

convex hull, and in the other case a person leapfrogged over a boundary position.

Clearly, breaching is associated with the size of the group, being more probable in dyads than in triads and tetrads, where the probability of breaching is negligible. Although over 80% of the dyads conformed to our expectation of no breaching, the frequency of breaching among dyads is sufficiently substantial to motivate concern, and a detailed analysis is presented in Chapter 6. As a result of that analysis, we have come to understand that the relatively high incidence of breaches among dyads is associated with the special properties of the *group dynamics* that occur when both members of the dyad are supersusceptible to interpersonal influence with respect to one another's positions on an issue.

The convex hull of initial attitudes is a nontrivial constraint on small group outcomes. Figure 4.2 displays the intervals defined by the minimum and maximum values of initial attitudes for each group and issue and the locations of group members' final attitudes on these intervals. In this figure, the intervals are represented as vertical line segments, initial consensus with pluses, and the locations of group members' final attitudes as solid dots. When consensus is reached, there will be one dot on the line segment; when consensus is not reached, there will be two or more dots; and when a breach of the convex hull has occurred, there will be one or more dots that do not lie on the line segment.

Note that in some groups the interval of initial attitudes covers a substantial part of the maximum possible interval, e.g., [5,100] for the risky-shift attitudes; hence, in those groups it is unimpressive that the end-of-trial attitudes of group members are within the convex hull of the initial attitudes in their group. However, in other groups, the interval of initial attitudes is far more limited in its range; the intervals are sometimes in the lower part of the domain of the attitude scale of an issue and sometimes in the upper part of the domain. Our interest focuses on the intervals with limited ranges. Our evidence suggests that the convex hull of initial positions is a nontrivial constraint on settled attitudes and that any postulated mechanism for a social influence process should be formally consistent with this constraint.

The constraint of the convex hull of initial attitudes has important implications for the evaluation of any theoretical model of the social influence process. With sufficiently small groups, any model that generates predicted equilibrium attitudes that are in the convex hull of initial attitudes of each group is likely to do better than a model that generates predictions outside the convex hull. Within the class of models that constrain predictions to the convex hull, and in the special case of a predicted consensus, the predicted value could be the mean or median of initial attitudes, or a *randomly selected value* within the convex hull of a particular group's initial attitudes; any of those values are likely to be

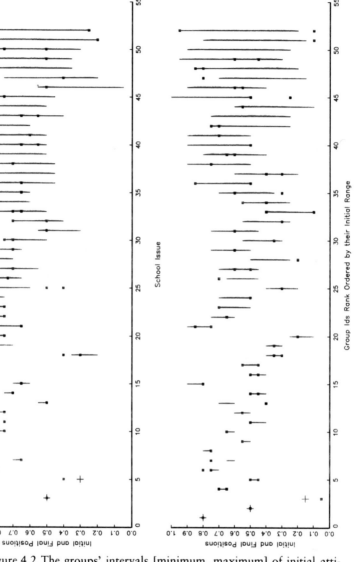

Figure 4.2 The groups' intervals [minimum, maximum] of initial attitudes and the locations of group members' final attitudes. Vertical line segments are the ranges of initial positions. Dots are the final positions. Pluses are the positions of initial consensus.

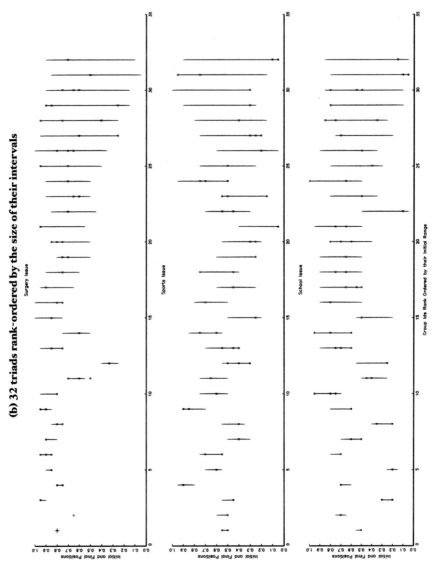

Figure 4.2 (*Continued*)

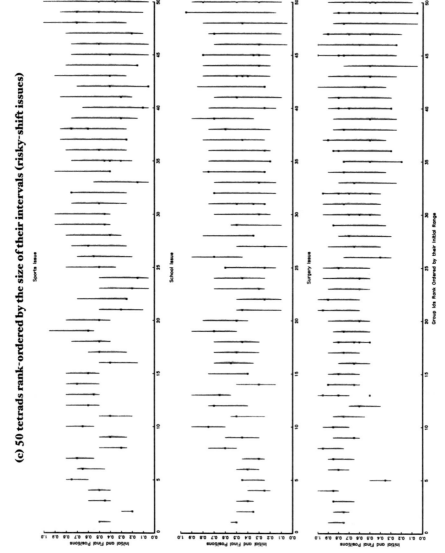

Figure 4.2 *(Continued)*

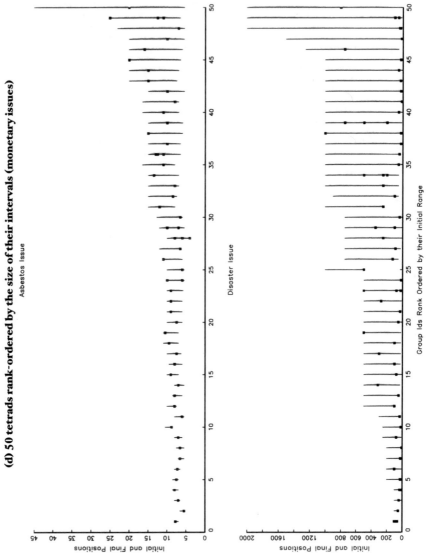

Figure 4.2 (*Continued*)

Table 4.3 *Increasing mean size of the initial range of attitudes with group size*

	Mean size of initial range	Std. dev.	N
School issue			
Dyads	26.539	20.449	52
Triads	37.500	20.868	32
Tetrads	44.500	16.880	50
$F(2,131) = 11.192, p < 0.001$			
Surgery issue			
Dyads	25.346	19.901	52
Triads	32.813	25.651	32
Tetrads	45.700	22.737	50
$F(2,131) = 12.090, p < 0.001$			
Sports issue			
Dyads	—	—	—
Triads	36.094	20.428	32
Tetrads	45.500	18.578	50
$F(1,80) = 4.627, p < 0.034$			

statistically significant predictors of observed consensus values in a sample of small groups. Thus, information about persons' initial attitudes can be used without any other assumptions (or on the basis of models with seriously flawed assumptions) about the influence process. Small ranges of group members' initial attitudes are more likely to be observed in small groups than in large groups whose members have been randomly drawn from a population with heterogeneous initial attitudes on an issue. Two of our issues (Surgery and School) were dealt with in all three group sizes (dyads, triads, and tetrads); one issue (Sports) was dealt with in two group sizes (triads and tetrads). In all cases, the mean size of the initial range increases with group size; see Table 4.3. When small initial ranges occur in groups, any two values within such ranges (e.g., an observed and predicted attitude) will be strongly correlated across the groups.

More generally, consider a population of persons with initial attitudes that are normally distributed, $N(0, 1)$, from which persons are drawn randomly to form K groups of size n. Let $MAXY1_k$ and $MINY1_k$ be the maximum and minimum initial attitudes of the members of group $k = 1, 2, \ldots, K$. Now define, and obtain as follows, two values in the convex hull of group k, which we shall designate as the mean observed ($OBSYE_k$) and predicted ($PREYE_k$) end-of-trial attitudes for group k:

$$OBSYE_k = \omega_1 MAXY1_k + (1 - \omega_1) MINY1_k$$
$$PREYE_k = \omega_2 MAXY1_k + (1 - \omega_2) MINY1_k,$$

where ω_1 and ω_2 are random numbers drawn independently for each group from the uniform distribution over $[0, 1]$. Doing this for each

Table 4.4 *Monte Carlo cumulative distributions of the correlation (r) of two randomly selected values in the convex hull of initial attitudes of groups of different sizes (n)*

r	$n = 2$	$n = 3$	$n = 4$	$n = 6$	$n = 8$	$n = 12$
1.000	0.000	0.000	0.000	0.000	0.000	0.000
0.950	0.000	0.000	0.000	0.000	0.000	0.000
0.900	0.000	0.000	0.000	0.000	0.000	0.000
0.850	0.034	0.000	0.000	0.000	0.000	0.000
0.800	0.217	0.000	0.000	0.000	0.000	0.000
0.750	0.535	0.002	0.000	0.000	0.000	0.000
0.700	0.797	0.022	0.000	0.000	0.000	0.000
0.650	0.931	0.092	0.003	0.000	0.000	0.000
0.600	0.980	0.265	0.020	0.000	0.000	0.000
0.550	0.995	0.480	0.075	0.003	0.000	0.000
0.500	0.999	0.697	0.200	0.014	0.002	0.000
0.450	1.000	0.852	0.373	0.048	0.009	0.002
0.400	1.000	0.940	0.579	0.129	0.037	0.009
0.350	1.000	0.979	0.758	0.265	0.103	0.030
0.300	1.000	0.995	0.881	0.440	0.223	0.082
0.250	1.000	0.999	0.948	0.626	0.386	0.184
0.200	1.000	1.000	0.980	0.781	0.576	0.337
0.150	1.000	1.000	0.994	0.891	0.740	0.518
0.100	1.000	1.000	0.998	0.955	0.866	0.692
0.050	1.000	1.000	1.000	0.984	0.941	0.830
0.000	1.000	1.000	1.000	0.995	0.978	0.922

Note: These cumulative distributions describe the proportion of correlations among 10,000 Monte Carlo trials with a value greater than or equal to r.

of the K groups generates a $K \times 2$ matrix of random values that, for each group, are in the convex hull of the group's initial attitudes. The correlation (r) of these values, $OBSYE_k$ and $PREYE_k$ $(k = 1, K)$, can be substantial. Table 4.4 shows the cumulative distributions of 10,000 correlations obtained in this way, based on 100 groups $(K = 100)$ of different sizes $(n = 2, 3, 4, 6, 8,$ and $12)$. Note, for example, that the proportion of correlations greater than or equal to 0.5 is 0.999 for $n = 2$, 0.697 for $n = 3$, 0.200 for $n = 4$, 0.014 for $n = 6$, 0.002 for $n = 8$, and 0.000 for $n = 12$. Not surprisingly, the effect of the constraint diminishes as group size increases, but clearly it can be substantial in sufficiently small groups. We suspect that this effect is enhanced for attitudes measured on bounded scales, such as subjective probability scales or scales with constrained options.

For sufficiently small groups, it appears that any theory is likely to provide a powerful and statistically significant prediction of groups' mean end-of-trial attitude on an issue (e.g., their consensus attitude), so long as the prediction falls in the convex hull of the group members' initial attitudes. Hence, as part of the assessment of our theory presented in the following sections, we take the convex hull of initial attitudes into account. We do so by controlling for the mean of group members' initial attitudes as follows:

$$\bar{\tilde{y}}_k^{(\infty)} = \beta_0 + \beta_1 \bar{\hat{y}}_k^{(\infty)} + \beta_2 \bar{\tilde{y}}_k^{(1)} + e, \tag{4.1}$$

where $\bar{\tilde{y}}_k^{(\infty)}$ is the mean observed end-of-trial attitude for group k, $\bar{\hat{y}}_k^{(\infty)}$ is the network model's predicted mean end-of-trial attitude for group k, and $\bar{\tilde{y}}_k^{(1)}$ is the mean observed initial attitude for group k. An end-of-trial consensus was reached in 71.6% of the issue-trials among the dyads, triads, and tetrads (Table 4.2); in those cases of consensus, the mean observed end-of-trial attitude is the consensus value. Further note that

$$\begin{aligned} \bar{\tilde{y}}_k^{(\infty)} &= \beta_0' + \beta_1' \left(\bar{\hat{y}}_k^{(\infty)} - \bar{\tilde{y}}_k^{(1)} \right) + \beta_2' \bar{\tilde{y}}_k^{(1)} + e \\ &= \beta_0' + \beta_1' \bar{\hat{y}}_k^{(\infty)} + \left(\beta_2' - \beta_1' \right) \bar{\tilde{y}}_k^{(1)} + e, \end{aligned} \tag{4.2}$$

so that $\beta_1 = \beta_1'$ can be interpreted not only as the independent effect of the network model, but also as an indicator of whether the network model is predicting the location of the mean observed end-of-trial attitude relative to the baseline mean of observed initial attitudes; the coefficient for the network model's prediction should be positive. Our findings to be presented, on the independent effects of the network model, indicate that the network model contributes an account that does not entirely rest on constraining predictions to the convex hull of initial attitudes, and that it is predicting the direction and distance of group members' mean end-of-trial attitudes from their mean initial attitudes on an issue.

4.4 Allocation of Subjective Weights

In this section, we evaluate the measurement model for **A** and **W** described in Chapter 3, which is based on subjects' allocation of subjective weights to themselves and others in forming their attitudes on an issue. The start point is an $n \times n$ matrix $\tilde{\mathbf{R}} = [\tilde{r}_{ij}]$ of group members' allocations of subjective weights, where $0 \leq \tilde{r}_{ij} \leq 1$ for all i and j, and $\sum_k \tilde{r}_{ik} = 1$ for all i. With the data gathered from the experiments on dyads, triads, and tetrads, we operationalize $\tilde{\mathbf{R}}$ with the pile-sort measure described earlier in the chapter, repeated here for convenience:

> You have been given a total of 20 chips. Each chip represents influence upon your final opinion. Divide the chips into two piles, *Pile A* and *Pile B*. *Pile A* will represent the extent to which the conversations you had with the other persons influenced your

final opinion. *Pile B* will represent the extent to which the conversations you had with the other persons did not influence your final opinion. Now consider the extent to which you feel each member of the group influenced the group's final opinion. Divide the chips in *Pile A* into piles for each person according to how much they influenced your final opinion.

The relative sizes of these allocations, for each group member, provide the measure of $\tilde{\mathbf{R}}$. The assumptions of our measurement model (Section 3.2.3) are $a_{ii}w_{ij} = \tilde{r}_{ij}$ for all $i \neq j$ (3.19), and $a_{ii} = 1 - w_{ii} = \sqrt{1 - r_{ii}}$ (3.20) for all i. Hence, we obtain a measure of $\tilde{\mathbf{A}}$, $\tilde{\mathbf{W}}$ (3.18), and $\hat{\mathbf{V}}$ (2.38) or (2.33) and a prediction of group members' equilibrium attitudes, $\hat{\mathbf{y}}^{(\infty)} = \hat{\mathbf{V}}\tilde{\mathbf{y}}^{(1)}$.

Here we assess the assumption $\tilde{r}_{ij} = a_{ii}w_{ij}$ ($i \neq j$) of our measurement model against two alternative interpretations of the relative weights in $\tilde{\mathbf{R}}$. One alternative takes $\tilde{\mathbf{R}}$ as a direct measure of $\mathbf{W}$, and the other takes it as a direct measure of $\mathbf{V}$. We assess the differences between these models with the values of their maximum percentage relative errors of prediction. The models generate a percentage relative error PRE_i for each group member,

$$PRE_i = \frac{\left| \tilde{y}_i^{(\infty)} - \hat{y}_i^{(\infty)} \right|}{\tilde{y}_i^{(\infty)}} \times 100, \tag{4.3}$$

for $\tilde{y}_i^{(\infty)} \neq 0$. We denote the maximum PRE_i among a group's members for a particular issue as the model's MPRE for that group and issue. We refer to an MPRE greater than 100% as a *gross* error.

4.4.1 Direct Relative Weights

If $\tilde{\mathbf{R}}$ is interpreted as a measure of $\mathbf{W}$, $\tilde{\mathbf{W}} = \tilde{\mathbf{R}}$, $\tilde{r}_{ij} = w_{ij}$, and $\tilde{r}_{ii} = w_{ii} = 1 - a_{ii}$, so that $a_{ii} = 1 - \tilde{r}_{ii}$. In contrast, in our preferred model, group members' subjective interpersonal weights reflect *both* the degree of susceptibility to interpersonal influence and the relative weight accorded to another group member; i.e., $\tilde{r}_{ij} = a_{ii}w_{ij}$ and hence $a_{ii} = \sqrt{1 - \tilde{r}_{ii}}$. The two models are identical when $\tilde{\mathbf{A}} = \mathbf{I}$, i.e., $\tilde{r}_{ij} = a_{ii}w_{ij} = w_{ij}$ for all i and j, and $\tilde{r}_{ii} = w_{ii} = 0$ for all i.

We find that the predicted equilibrium attitudes, $\hat{\mathbf{y}}^{(\infty)} = \hat{\mathbf{V}}\tilde{\mathbf{y}}^{(1)}$, with $\hat{\mathbf{V}}$ based on our preferred assumption, are more accurate than the predictions with $\hat{\mathbf{V}}$ based on the alternative assumption ($\tilde{\mathbf{W}} = \tilde{\mathbf{R}}$). Comparing the MPRE of the predictions for each group–issue trial, the MPREs are equivalent in 46 (10.2%) of the group–issue trials and, among the 404 trials on which they differ, the MPRE for our preferred assumption is less than that for $\tilde{\mathbf{W}} = \tilde{\mathbf{R}}$ in 86.4% of these trials. The mean MPREs are

19.76 and 24.95 for the preferred and alternative models, respectively ($t = -12.126$, $df = 449$, $p < 0.001$, two-tailed, paired comparison). The evidence favors $\tilde{r}_{ij} = a_{ii} w_{ij}$ over $\tilde{r}_{ij} = w_{ij}$.

4.4.2 Total Relative Weights

We might also interpret $\tilde{R}$ as V, i.e., the row-stochastic equilibrium total (direct and indirect) influence of each group member. Our preferred interpretation implies that $\tilde{R} = V^{(1)} = AW + I - A$. However, with $\tilde{R} = V$, the alternative assumption is that subjects are evaluating the equilibrium total (direct and indirect) relative influences on them. Although this interpretation of $\tilde{R}$ is implausible in a group with a complexly configured influence network, it may hold in small groups where members might be better able to monitor all the attitude changes that are arising from the interpersonal influences amongst them.

We find that the predicted equilibrium attitudes based on our preferred measurement model are more accurate than the predictions of the alternative measurement model in which $\tilde{R}$ is taken as a direct measure of V. Comparing the MPRE for the two predictions for each group–issue trial, the MPREs are equivalent in 75 (16.7%) of the group–issue trials, and among the 375 trials on which they differ, the MPRE for our preferred assumption is less than that for $\tilde{R} = V^{(\infty)}$ in 60.0% of these trials. The mean MPREs are 19.76 and 21.77 for the preferred and alternative models, respectively ($t = -4.477$, $df = 449$, $p < 0.001$ two-tailed, paired comparison). Hence, we conclude that the evidence favors $\tilde{r}_{ij} = a_{ii} w_{ij}$ over $\tilde{r}_{ij} = v_{ij}$.

4.5 Accuracy of the Standard Model

In this section, we compare the performance of our model against the baseline model that predicts a convergence of attitudes to the mean of group member's initial attitudes on an issue. Our measurement model for the influence network of a group allows for *inequalities* of interpersonal influences and self-weights, whereas the baseline model is silent on this matter. If such inequalities are prevalent and important, then a measurement model for W that allows for such inequalities should outperform a model that does not take them into account. For the matrix of relative weights $\tilde{R}$, our measurement model for W is $\tilde{r}_{ii} = 1 - a_{ii}^2$ and $\tilde{r}_{ij} = a_{ii} w_{ij}$.

Table 4.5 presents the correlations for the predicted mean equilibrium attitude for a group k, $\bar{\tilde{y}}_k^{(\infty)}$, and the observed mean end-of-trial attitude for the same group, $\bar{\bar{y}}_k^{(\infty)}$. These correlations are strong and statistically

Table 4.5 *Regressions of groups' mean observed attitudes on their mean predicted end-of-trial attitudes and mean observed initial attitudes (unfitted susceptibilities)*

	β_0	$\beta_1 \bar{\bar{y}}^{(\infty)}$	$\beta_2 \bar{\bar{y}}^{(1)}$	r	N
Dyads surgery issue	16.896	0.773***		0.914	52
	13.655***	0.641***	0.178†	0.920	
Dyads school issue	2.543	0.964***		0.883	52
	1.291	0.906***	0.079	0.884	
Triads surgery issue	19.796***	0.739***		0.894	32
	12.891*	0.473***	0.369**	0.922	
Triads sports issue	−2.540	1.030***		0.961	32
	−5.921	0.922***	0.288	0.963	
Triads school issue	1.286	0.971***		0.986	32
	−2.303	0.840***	0.196*	0.988	
Tetrads sports issue	−1.703	1.012***		0.933	50
	−1.259	1.032***	−0.028	0.933	
Tetrads asbestos issue	0.764†	0.906***		0.961	50
	1.051†	0.953***	−0.083	0.961	
Tetrads school issue	−1.246	1.021***		0.839	50
	0.025	1.069***	−0.074	0.840	
Tetrads disaster issue	0.449	0.873***		0.765	50
	0.175	0.753***	0.175	0.769	
Tetrads surgery issue	0.571	0.989***		0.918	50
	−1.203	0.874***	0.143	0.920	

Notes: All correlations r are significant at the $p < 0.001$ level. $\bar{\bar{y}}^{(\infty)}$ is the mean predicted final attitude for a group; $\bar{\bar{y}}^{(1)}$ is the mean observed initial attitude for a group.
***$p < 0.001$; **$p < 0.01$; *$p < 0.05$; $^\dagger p < 0.10$.

significant. Table 4.5 also presents the results of a linear regression of the observed end-of-trial mean $\bar{\bar{y}}_k^{(\infty)}$ on our model's prediction $\bar{\bar{y}}_k^{(\infty)}$, controlling for the observed mean initial attitude $\bar{\bar{y}}_k^{(1)}$ of a group k. The network model is capturing information about the influence process that is not accounted for by the baseline model. As we previously noted (4.2), a significant coefficient for the predicted values $\bar{\bar{y}}_k^{(\infty)}$, controlling for $\bar{\bar{y}}_k^{(1)}$, indicates the independent effect of the network model and whether the network model is predicting the *location* of the mean observed end-of-trial attitude *relative to the baseline mean of initial attitudes*. Thus, it appears unlikely that the strength of this account can be entirely attributed to the mere placement of the model's prediction within the convex hull of a group's initial attitudes. If such mere placement were the main contribution of the network model, then the mean initial attitude of a group would be the "best guess" prediction.

Table 4.6 describes the maximum percentage relative errors of our network model for the groups. The mean error is less than 20%. The model's accuracy does not significantly differ for dyads, triads, and tetrads; nor does its accuracy significantly differ in the prediction of the various types

Table 4.6 *Analysis of maximum percentage relative errors of prediction*

(a) Group size

	n	Mean MPRE	Std. error	95% confidence bounds Lower	Upper
Dyads	104	15.837	2.12757	11.617	20.056
Triads	96	19.156	2.44695	14.298	24.014
Tetrads	250	21.632	1.33547	19.002	24.262
TOTAL	450	19.764	1.03545	17.730	21.799

	Sum of squares	df	Mean square	F	Sig.
Between	2,512.010	2	1256.005	2.622	0.074
Within	214,117.021	447	479.009		
TOTAL	216,629.031	449			

(b) Type of group outcome

	n	Mean MPRE	Std. error	95% confidence bounds Lower	Upper
Consensus (Boundary Initial)	72	16.667	3.041	10.604	22.730
Consensus (Internal Initial)	86	19.942	2.552	14.868	25.016
Consensus (Compromise)	154	17.071	1.187	14.726	19.417
Disagreement	118	20.958	1.979	17.039	24.876
TOTAL	430*	18.644	0.998	16.684	20.605

	Sum of squares	df	Mean square	F	Sig.
Between	1,438.849	3	479.616	1.122	0.340
Within	182,133.712	426	427.544		
TOTAL	183,572.560	429			

Note: *The mean MPRE for groups with at least one breaching attitude are significantly higher than those for groups without such breaches. The mean MPRE for groups with a breaching consensus (10 groups) is 44.0 (s.d. 34.0), and for groups with a breaching disagreement (10 groups) it is 43.7 (s.d. 34.2). Eighteen of these 20 groups are dyads.

of nonbreaching group outcomes described in the typology of Table 4.2. Not surprisingly, for the 20 groups (mostly dyads) in which a breach of the convex hull of initial attitudes occurred, the mean error is substantially greater than for all other types of outcomes. For this model, the mean error of 18.644 for the nonbreaching group outcomes is significantly less than the mean error of 22.963 for the baseline model on the same groups ($t = -4.573$, $df = 429$, $p < 0.001$).

Finally, in Table 4.7, we evaluate the correspondence of the observed and predicted ranges of end-of-trial attitudes within each group. The predicted range of group members' equilibrium attitudes is $\max(\hat{y}_k^{(\infty)}) - \min(\hat{y}_k^{(\infty)})$ for group k. The observed range of the end-of-trial

Table 4.7 *Regressing the range size of a group's observed end-of-trial attitudes,* $\max(\tilde{y}_k^{(\infty)}) - \min(\tilde{y}_k^{(\infty)})$, *on the predicted equilibrium range size for the group,* $\max(\hat{y}_k^{(\infty)}) - \min(\hat{y}_k^{(\infty)})$, *for group k (OLS regression coefficients and standard errors in parentheses)*

	β_0	β_1	r	N
Dyads surgery issue	0.785 (1.814)	0.963*** (0.132)	0.719	52
Dyads school issue	−1.945 (1.305)	1.275*** (0.115)	0.842	52
Triads surgery issue	−0.240 (2.532)	0.817*** (0.141)	0.726	32
Triads sports issue	−3.026 (2.022)	0.836*** (0.135)	0.750	32
Triads school issue	−3.131 (2.107)	1.079*** (0.143)	0.809	32
Tetrads sports issue	−1.844 (1.571)	0.422** (0.144)	0.389	50
Tetrads asbestos issue	−0.225 (0.3440)	0.518*** (0.518)	0.465	50
Tetrads school issue	−7.376*** (2.068)	1.043*** (0.143)	0.725	50
Tetrads disaster issue	−0.409** (0.123)	0.934*** (0.131)	0.717	50
Tetrads surgery issue	−5.637* (2.442)	1.305*** (0.126)	0.830	50

***$p < 0.001$; **$p < 0.01$; *$p < 0.05$; †$p < 0.10$.

attitudes, i.e., $\max(\tilde{y}_k^{(\infty)}) - \min(\tilde{y}_k^{(\infty)})$, should be positively associated with the predicted range. When the predicted size of the range is zero (i.e., a predicted consensus) the observed range size should be zero or near zero, and when the predicted range size is not zero (i.e., a predicted disagreement) the observed range size should be correspondingly large. Obviously, the predicted range size of the baseline model (i.e., its prediction of a consensus on the mean of initial attitudes) is always zero, and we do not consider it here. The findings are consistent with our theoretical expectations. In subsequent chapters we evaluate additional predictions of the standard model on group-level outcomes. We also will analyze these data at the individual level in the development of a theoretical perspective on individuals embedded in groups.

4.6 Fitted Susceptibilities

In this section, we present an optimized account of the observed transformation of group members' attitudes via interpersonal influences. In this account, group members' susceptibilities are *fitted* to the data that group members provided about their attitudes and interpersonal influences. This analysis demonstrates how our standard model may be operationalized in the absence of a measure of group members' self-weights. It also evaluates the accuracy of such an optimized account. We further evaluate whether the model's *derived* susceptibility values are consistent with group members' empirical susceptibilities (obtained from their *reported* self-weights), or whether they are values without a demonstrated construct validity. The derived susceptibilities are obtained independent of the data for the subjective self-weights. If the model's formalization is accurate and the measures of initial and final attitudes, and relative interpersonal influences, are accurate, then we should expect an empirical correspondence between the formally derived susceptibilities and the available measures of our subjects' self-reported susceptibilities.

4.6.1 Assessing the Performance of the Model with Fitted Susceptibilities

To obtain fitted susceptibilities, we again employ the pile-sort measure $\tilde{R}$, but now we ignore the main-diagonal values of $\tilde{R}$ to form a matrix of relative *interpersonal* influences $\tilde{C}$. Given $\tilde{C}$ and the measures of group members' initial and end-of-trial attitudes on an issue, fitted susceptibility values $\hat{A}$ may be derived from (3.27), (3.29), and (3.30). In essence, for this analysis we obtain an $\hat{A}$ that is most consistent with our model. The open empirical issue is the accuracy of this fitted account.

Table 4.8 reports findings on the association between the predicted mean equilibrium attitude for a group k, $\bar{\hat{y}}_k^{(\infty)}$, and the observed mean end-of-trial attitude for the same group, $\bar{\tilde{y}}_k^{(\infty)}$. In regressions of $\bar{\tilde{y}}_k^{(\infty)}$ on $\bar{\hat{y}}_k^{(\infty)}$, controlling for the mean initial attitude $\bar{\tilde{y}}_k^{(1)}$, the effects of the network model's predicted values are positive and significant, while the effects of the groups' mean initial attitudes are generally insignificant.

Table 4.9 describes the maximum percentage relative errors for the groups. The mean error is 7.7%. The model's accuracy significantly differs for dyads, triads, and tetrads. The mean error is substantially higher among dyads than other groups. The model's accuracy also significantly differs in the prediction of the various types of nonbreaching group outcomes described in the typology of Table 4.2. The fitted account is rarely in error for consensus outcomes on an initial position. Errors are more substantial among groups that reached a compromise consensus on a position that is not one of the group members' initial positions, and it also is more substantial among groups that failed to reach consensus. Not surprisingly, for the groups (mostly dyads) in which a breach of the convex hull of initial attitudes occurred, the mean error is substantially greater than for all other types of outcomes. Comparing the mean

Table 4.8 *Regressions of groups' mean observed attitudes on their mean predicted end-of-trial attitudes and mean observed initial attitudes (fitted susceptibilities)*

	β_0	$\beta_1 \bar{\bar{y}}^{(\infty)}$	$\beta_2 \bar{\bar{y}}^{(1)}$	r	N
Dyads surgery issue	11.657**	0.849***		0.892	52
	12.562*	1.077***	−0.241	0.896	
Dyads school issue	−1.649	1.016***		0.850	52
	−0.945	1.108***	−0.105	0.851	
Triads surgery issue	10.075**	0.875***		0.957	32
	10.546**	0.939***	−0.072	0.957	
Triads sports issue	−0.396	0.999***		0.988	32
	0.532	1.025***	−0.042	0.988	
Triads school issue	−1.253	1.023***		0.996	30
	−1.402	1.016***	0.009	0.996	
Tetrads sports issue	−0.130	0.963***		0.947	49
	−0.958	1.011***	−0.068	0.947	
Tetrads asbestos issue	0.437	0.961***		0.972	50
	0.886†	1.043***	−0.135	0.973	
Tetrads school issue	−1.284	1.025***		0.948	50
	−1.898	1.013***	0.025	0.948	
Tetrads disaster issue	0.149	0.951***		0.843	50
	−0.129	0.863***	0.145	0.846	
Tetrads surgery issue	3.820	0.945***		0.930	50
	3.875	0.948***	−0.004	0.930	

Notes: $\bar{\bar{y}}^{(\infty)}$ is the mean predicted attitude for a group; $\bar{\bar{y}}^{(1)}$ is the mean observed initial attitude for a group.
***$p < 0.001$; **$p < 0.01$; *$p < 0.05$; †$p < 0.10$.

percentage errors in Tables 4.6 and 4.9, there is a substantial overall improvement in the accuracy of the model when fitted susceptibilities are employed (7.7% vs. 19.8%). The improvement is modest for dyads.

Our approach with no fitting provides strikingly similar findings to those obtained with fitting on the contributions of the influence network; compare Tables 4.5 and 4.8. The main difference between these two sets of predictions is disclosed by the mean MPRE values, which indicate (not surprisingly) an improvement in accuracy for the optimized model; compare Tables 4.6 and 4.9.

4.6.2 Construct Validity of Fitted Susceptibilities

Below we assess whether the fitted susceptibilities are valid measures of the theoretical construct for which they have been derived. The empirical question is whether the model's derived susceptibility values are consistent with the group members' reported subjective susceptibilities (obtained from their subjective self-weights), or whether they are values without any demonstrated construct validity. To address this question, we analyze

Table 4.9 *Analysis of maximum percentage relative errors of prediction with fitted susceptibilities*

(a) Group size

	n	Mean MPRE	Std. error	95% confidence bounds Lower	Upper
Dyads	104	11.4231	2.28458	6.8921	15.9540
Triads	96	3.8854	1.12915	1.6438	6.1271
Tetrads	250	7.6000	0.93498	5.7585	9.4415
TOTAL	450	7.6911	0.78591	6.1466	9.2356

	Sum of squares	df	Mean square	F	Sig.
Between	2,840.940	2	1,420.470	5.206	0.006
Within	121,955.124	447	272.830		
TOTAL	124,796.064	449			

(b) Type of group outcome

	N	Mean MPRE	Std. error	95% confidence bounds Lower	Upper
Consensus (boundary initial)	72	0.0833	0.08333	−0.0828	0.2495
Consensus (internal initial)	86	0.3605	0.29815	−0.2323	0.9533
Consensus (compromise)	154	12.5844	1.13160	10.3488	14.8200
Disagreement	118	4.8814	1.45307	2.0036	7.7591
TOTAL	430*	5.9326	0.62511	4.7039	7.1612

	Sum of squares	df	Mean square	F	Sig.
Between	12,077.977	3	4,025.992	28.581	0.000
Within	60,007.067	426	140.862		
TOTAL	72,085.044	429			

Note: *The mean MPRE for groups with at least one breaching attitude are significantly higher than those for groups without such breaches. The mean MPRE for groups with a breaching consensus (10 groups) is 48.4 (s.d. 36.8), and for groups with a breaching disagreement (10 groups) it is 42.6 (s.d. 34.0). Eighteen of these 20 groups are dyads.

the association of the derived susceptibility values $(\hat{a}_{ii})$ and the empirical susceptibility values $(\tilde{a}_{ii} = \sqrt{1 - \tilde{r}_{ii}})$ that are based on subjects' reported self-weights. The 1,496 derived susceptibilities $(\hat{a}_{ii})$ do not involve $\tilde{r}_{ii}$ in their derivation. However, the two susceptibilities, $\hat{a}_{ii}$ and $\tilde{a}_{ii}$, should be positively related under our assumptions, and they are, with $r = 0.630$ ($p < 0.001$). A closer examination of this association follows.

Ideally, the assumptions invoked for the derived and empirical suscep- tibility values should generate a commensurate correspondence between the two sets of values. The derived values should not be systematically

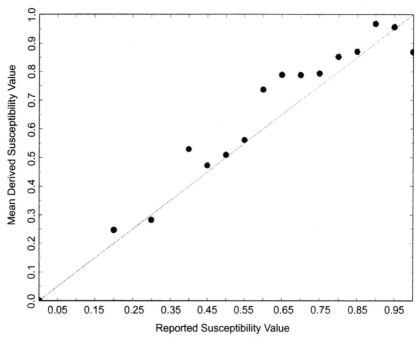

Figure 4.3 Derived and reported susceptibilities.

higher or lower than the empirical values based on our subjects' reports of the influences that have affected their attitudes. We find that when the reported susceptibility $\tilde{a}_{ii}$ is 0 or 1, the mean derived susceptibility $\hat{a}_{ii}$ also is near the corresponding extreme. The empirical susceptibilities are $\tilde{a}_{ii} = 0$ in 131 cases and $\tilde{a}_{ii} = 1$ in 36 cases. The means of the derived susceptibilities $(\hat{a}_{ii})$ for these two subsets of cases are 0.000 and 0.870, respectively. Regressing all of the 1,496 fitted susceptibilities $(\hat{a}_{ii})$ on their corresponding empirical susceptibilities $(\tilde{a}_{ii})$,

$$\hat{a}_{ii} = \beta_0 + \beta_1 \tilde{a}_{ii} + e_{ii}, \tag{4.4}$$

where $\beta_0 = 0.037$ (s.e. 0.023, $p = 0.110$) and $\beta_1 = 1.003$ (s.e. 0.032, $p = 0.000$). Figure 4.3 plots the means of the derived susceptibility values for each empirical susceptibility value (rounded to intervals of 0.05). The line on this plot is for $\beta_0 = 0$ and $\beta_1 = 1$. This plot of conditional means suggests that the correspondence between derived and empirical susceptibility values is modestly weaker for higher values of susceptibility than for lower values.

Figure 4.4 displays the histograms of the derived values by group size. The derived susceptibilities (i.e., susceptibilities that are most consistent with our model and the data) are *markedly* bimodal, with the modes being

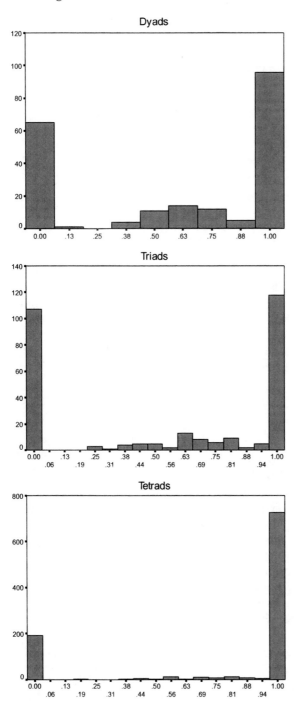

Figure 4.4 Histograms of derived susceptibility values in dyads, triads, and tetrads.

Table 4.10 *The distribution of derived susceptibility values for groups under low and high pressure to reach consensus*

	Pressure to consensus		
Susceptibility values	Low	High	TOTAL
$\hat{a}_{ii} = 0$	41.9%	20.8%	24.3%
	(104)	(260)	(364)
$0 < \hat{a}_{ii} < 1$	33.5%	9.0%	13.0%
	(83)	(112)	(195)
$\hat{a}_{ii} = 1$	24.6%	70.2%	62.6%
	(61)	(876)	(937)
TOTAL	100%	100%	100%
	(248)	(1248)	(1496)

Note: $\chi^2 = 201.754$, $df = 2$, $p < 0.001$.

exactly 0 and 1.[4] The higher the reported $\tilde{a}_{ii}$, the greater the probability of a derived $\hat{a}_{ii} = 1$ in the influence process that determined i's equilibrium attitude. The empirical support for this association is obtained from a logistic regression of *derived* susceptibility values on the *reported* susceptibility values $\tilde{a}_{ii}$. Setting all derived susceptibility values above 0.50 to 1, and those equal to or below 0.50 to 0 (which is a reasonable cut point for the observed distributions), the estimated logistic coefficients are

$$\ln\left(\frac{\Pr(\hat{a}_{ii} > 0.50)}{1 - \Pr(\hat{a}_{ii} > 0.50)}\right) = \beta_0 + \beta_1 \tilde{a}_{ii} = -2.892 + 5.977\tilde{a}_{ii}.$$

The *estimated probabilities* $\Pr(\hat{a}_{ii} > 0.50)$ are strongly correlated ($r = 0.992$) with the reported $\tilde{a}_{ii}$.

The above analysis has focused on the correspondence of the derived and empirical susceptibility values. The concurrent validity of the derived susceptibility values is further buttressed by the findings presented in Table 4.10. Under high pressure to reach group consensus, which was among the manipulated experimental conditions, 91.0% of the derived susceptibilities are 0 or 1; under low pressure 66.5% are either 0 or 1. Zero susceptibility is more likely under low pressure than high pressure to reach group consensus (41.9% versus 20.8%). Supersusceptibility ($\hat{a}_{ii} = 1$) is less likely under low than under high pressure to reach consensus (24.6% versus 70.2%). A susceptibility value that is not 0 or

---

[4]   In the derivation of a group's susceptibilities, when V does not exist, we set $\hat{a}_{ii} = 1$ to $\hat{a}_{ii} = 0.999$ to obtain the equilibrium V. This occurred in 38 group–issue trials, 35 of which are dyads. In the present analysis of the distribution of susceptibilities, the $\hat{a}_{ii} = 0.999$ are treated as $\hat{a}_{ii} = 1$.

1 $(0 < \hat{a}_{ii} < 1)$ is more likely under low pressure than under high pressure (33.5% versus 9.0%). Among these $0 < \hat{a}_{ii} < 1$ susceptibility values, the median and mean values are 0.686 and 0.657, respectively, under the high-pressure condition, and 0.618 and 0.634, respectively, under the low-pressure condition. In sum, the derived susceptibilities tend to be either 0 or 1; they are more likely to be 1 under high pressure than under low pressure; and when they are neither 0 nor 1, they are on average closer to 1 than 0 under both high and low pressure to reach consensus.

4.6.3 Self-Weight: Agentic State or Quantitative Dimension?

The above findings raise an important question concerning the fundamental nature of persons' susceptibilities to interpersonal influence. Milgram (1974) posited that susceptibility to interpersonal influence is an "agentic" state, which a person is either in (reflecting the attitudes of others) or not in (representing one's self).

> Moved into the agentic state, the person becomes something different from his former self, with new properties not easily traceable to his usual personality. (Milgram 1974: 143)

In terms of social influence network theory, $w_{ii} = 1 - a_{ii} = 0$ indicates that person i is in this state, and $w_{ii} = 1 - a_{ii} = 1$ indicates that person i is not in this state. Our evidence on the distribution of derived susceptibility values indicates that in most instances susceptibility is either absent or complete and that, when it is neither absent nor complete, it tends to be high. Moreover, for groups under pressure to reach consensus, it appears that the baseline condition of group members is "agentic" on most issues.

Persons who are embedded in social groups may depart from the "agentic" state for reasons of conscience, strong belief, or practical exigency; but we posit that a regular pronounced departure from this state (i.e., the occurrence of high self-weight across issues that arise in the group) is likely to occur only for persons who are *accorded* unusually large amounts of influence on most issues by group members. In this view, a high level of self-weight across issues is a *social construction* of the group based on group members' evaluative attitudes toward one another. This viewpoint is consistent with the mechanism of reflected appraisals through which group members come to view themselves as influential to the extent that others view them so, and become more self-weighted the more they view themselves as influential. More generally, it is consistent with the idea that, relative to a high baseline level of susceptibility, a disproportionate structural centrality in the group's social structure increases self-weight and lowers susceptibility. Friedkin (1998, 2001) employs this idea to obtain a structural measure of self-weight.

4.7 Concluding Remarks

We have described the process of attitude change in a group as one in which each member of a group weighs his or her own and other members' attitudes on an issue, and repetitively modifies his or her attitude until a settled attitude on the issue is formed. This perspective reconciles the psychologists' viewpoint on interpersonal influence as a strain toward the mean of persons' initial attitudes and the sociologists' viewpoint on such influence as a source of inequality and domination. These outcomes – convergence on the mean of initial attitudes and convergence on the initial attitude of a particular person or subgroup – are special cases of consensus in our theory. The outcomes of groups vary: attitudes may settle on the mean of group members' initial attitudes; they may settle on a compromise attitude that is different from any of the initial attitudes and the mean of initial attitudes; they may settle on an initial attitude of a group member that is not the mean of group members' initial attitudes; and they may settle on more or less altered attitudes which do not form a consensus. Because all of these types of outcomes are frequent, a general model of social influence must encompass them all. The formal applicability of the present theory to all these situations is a component of its appeal for us.

In this chapter, we have analyzed evidence from three experiments on issue-resolution episodes in dyads, triads, and tetrads. We have shown that the model predicts the mean and range size of end-of-trial attitudes of group members with a substantial degree of accuracy. We also have shown how the model's fit may be optimized with derived susceptibilities. The surprise in these data is the number of end-of-trial attitudes in dyads that appeared outside the convex hull of group members' initial attitudes: the mechanism of social influence that we have postulated is not consistent with movements of attitude outside the range of a group's initial attitudes. Although over 80% of the dyads conformed to our expectation of no breaching, and although those breaches that did occur are numerically near the convex hull of the group members' initial attitudes, the frequency of breaching among dyads is sufficiently substantial to warrant either a caveat concerning the application of the model to dyads, or a scope restriction to larger groups. We delve into this matter in Chapter 6, where we present and support a hypothesis about why dyads are more prone to breaches than larger groups. We show that the dynamics of dyadic influence systems, i.e., dynamics predicted by our model, provides a basis for understanding this anomaly.

Our findings suggest that a network model of social influence contributes to an account of attitude changes via interpersonal influences beyond the account afforded by classical psychological models that assume a convergence to the mean of initial attitudes. If attitudes tend to converge to the mean of initial attitudes, then there would be little call for the development of a more refined network approach to attitude change. But we have seen that the baseline model (i.e., the mean of group members' initial attitudes) often fails to make an independent contribution to the prediction of the mean of group members' end-of-trial attitudes, whereas the network model consistently does so in its account of these attitudes. Even so, in this or any assessment of a social influence model, there are compelling grounds for including the baseline mean of a group's initial attitudes as a control, especially in studies of small groups. A strong baseline correlation between observed and predicted group-mean attitudes may exist simply because of the tendency for group members' settled attitudes to lie within the convex hull of their initial attitudes.

Formal models of social processes are based on simplifying assumptions that are a potential source of prediction error, even when measurement errors can be discounted. It is difficult to disentangle the contributions of measurement error and formal errors of model specification, and we do not attempt to do so. Our standard model can only be operationalized when it is *combined* with measurement models of its constructs. It is this combination that is subject to evaluation. Theoretical advancements may occur when the assumptions of the standard model are discarded or modified. Measurement advancements occur when particular measurement models are discarded or modified. The entire implemented edifice is subject to scrutiny, given the intimate interplay between theory and measures.

We see the interplay of theory and measures in various places in the findings that we have presented. For example, our standard model stipulates that group members' susceptibilities are $0 \leq a_{ii} \leq 1$ for all i, and when the derived susceptibility values, based on the available measures of the model's constructs, fall outside their permissible range, for example, $\hat{a}_{ii} < 0$ or $\hat{a}_{ii} > 1$, we constrain them, in this example, setting $\hat{a}_{ii} < 0$ to 0 and $\hat{a}_{ii} > 1$ to 1. An important question is whether the appearance of theoretically anomalous derived susceptibility values call for a relaxation of the model's assumptions. Our tentative position on this question is that they do not, although extensions of the model might be developed to address them. An assessment of the usefulness of any model is made more difficult when the model involves assumptions that may limit its general applicability. For example, our standard model assumes a fixed influence network and fixed initial attitudes. In various places in the book, we relax some of the assumptions of the standard model. But the impulse to relax assumptions must be weighed against the potentially marginal payoffs obtained from the extension. These and other kindred issues and questions are involved in the present assessment of our network theory of interpersonal influences on attitudes.

We conclude with a note on the employment of derived susceptibilities and optimized accounts of observed attitudes that are based on fitted susceptibilities. There are various circumstances under which derived susceptibility values are useful. They allow a comparison of the accuracy of a fitted model, based on derived susceptibilities, and a model that is entirely based on empirical measures of the constructs. They allow a direct assessment of the correspondence of the standard model's fitted susceptibilities and an empirical measure of individual susceptibilities. They may be employed to operationalize the standard model in circumstances where an empirical measure of group members' susceptibilities is unavailable. They may be employed as the dependent variables in an investigation concerned with the antecedents of susceptibility. However, with respect to the operationalization of our standard model, our preference and intent is to base an operationalization on empirical measures of *all* model constructs, including the susceptibility construct. With such an operationalization, the model presents a prediction in which the total direct contribution of interpersonal influences to an individual's observed attitudes is equivalent to the measure of that individual's susceptibility.

Part II

Influence Network Perspective on Small Groups

5

Consensus Formation and Efficiency

This chapter begins with a formal analysis of the conditions of consensus formation, based on our standard model. We include a formal analysis of the important special case of influence networks with binary susceptibilities in which each group member's susceptibility is strictly either 0, i.e., the person's initial position on an issue is not influenced by other group members, or 1, i.e., the person attaches no weight to his or her own initial position. Our theory and empirical evidence suggest that binary susceptibilities may be the rule, not the exception, in the formation of consensus through interpersonal influences. In the previous chapter, we noted that Milgram (1974) raised the fundamental empirical question of the nature of susceptibility in the context of his studies on obedience. Individuals appeared to be either in the cognitive state of an "agent" whose actions conformed to the preferences of an authority, or not in such a state. Our analysis suggests a broader hypothesis in which reaching consensus in a group, with members who are in initial disagreement on an issue, depends on the existence of members who accord no weight to their own initial positions on an issue. Such members shift their positions on an issue to a personal subjective norm, which is a weighted average of the time-t positions of other group members, at each time t during the influence process, and in so doing become the "agents" of that subjective norm even as the norm changes during the course of the influence process.

The remaining sections of the chapter describe three substantive applications of social influence network theory. We develop an influence network perspective on Sherif's (1936) findings on norm formation. We then turn to our data on dyads, triads, and tetrads and report empirical findings on (a) the conditions affecting the formation of consensus and (b) the efficiency with which consensus is reached. Our findings on the conditions of consensus formation report effects of particular contextual conditions on the formation of consensus, e.g., group size, pressure on group members to reach consensus, and their range of initial positions

115

on an issue. We demonstrate that our standard model contributes to the prediction of consensus independent of these contextual conditions. Our analysis of the efficiency of the consensus formation process is theoretically oriented. We are not interested in efficiency per se. However, the rapidity with which initial disagreements are reduced to a consensus may be predicted by our standard model in terms of the number of iterations (time periods $t = 1, 2, 3, \ldots$) that are required to reach a consensual equilibrium under the empirical conditions of a group's members' influence network $(\tilde{A}, \tilde{W})$ and initial positions on an issue $\tilde{y}^{(1)}$. An empirical correspondence between observed and predicted times to reach consensus suggests that our standard model is capturing meaningful process features of the group discussion. Again, we pursue the agenda of this book by building on classic foundations, in this case Sherif (1936) and Milgram (1974), with analyses and findings that emphasize the theoretical importance of the influence network construct and our formalization of the influence process that unfolds in it.

5.1 Conditions of Consensus Formation

There are some influence networks $\mathbf{AW}$ that will generate consensus for all possible arrays of initial attitudes, and in this section we will describe the structural characteristics of such networks. There also are influence networks that will generate consensus for particular, but not all, arrays of initial attitudes. We restrict our formal analysis to the necessary and sufficient conditions for the production of an *exact* consensus in a group, independent of group members' initial attitudes, i.e., for all possible $\mathbf{y}^{(1)}$. We conclude this section with an example of a network in which the generation of consensus depends on the array of initial attitudes.

Groups may reach a near (nonexact) consensus under a broader set of conditions than those we will describe below for an exact consensus. Whether or not a particular influence network $\mathbf{AW}$ is consistent with the production of an exact or near-equilibrium consensus, independent of initial attitudes, may be ascertained from our standard model

$$\mathbf{y}^{(t+1)} = \mathbf{AW}\mathbf{y}^{(t)} + (\mathbf{I} - \mathbf{A})\mathbf{y}^{(1)} \tag{5.1}$$

by (a) selecting arbitrary values for $\mathbf{y}^{(1)}$ and (b) examining whether the range of the values in $\mathbf{y}^{(t+1)}$ declines to a threshold range near zero at some time t and is maintained there over subsequent time periods. A network's capacity to produce an equilibrium consensus also may be ascertained from the total influence matrix $\mathbf{V}$ that is obtained either analytically from

$$\mathbf{V} = (\mathbf{I} - \mathbf{AW})^{-1}(\mathbf{I} - \mathbf{A})$$

for a nonsingular $\mathbf{I} - \mathbf{AW}$, or numerically from

$$\mathbf{V}^{(t)} = (\mathbf{AW})^t + \left[\sum_{k=0}^{t-1} (\mathbf{AW})^k \right] (\mathbf{I} - \mathbf{A})$$

when $\lim_{t \to \infty} \mathbf{V}^{(t)}$ exists. If $\mathbf{I} - \mathbf{AW}$ is nonsingular, then $\lim_{t \to \infty} \mathbf{V}^{(t)}$ exists, but $\lim_{t \to \infty} \mathbf{V}^{(t)}$ may exist when $\mathbf{I} - \mathbf{AW}$ is singular. In general, the existence of $\mathbf{V}^{(\infty)}$ with *identical rows* is a necessary and sufficient condition for an exact equilibrium consensus that does not depend on the initial attitudes of a group on an issue.

The existence of $\mathbf{V}^{(\infty)}$ with *identical rows* is consistent with only two forms of A. If an equilibrium consensus is formed in a group, i.e.,

$$y_*^{(\infty)} \equiv y_1^{(\infty)} = y_2^{(\infty)} \ldots = y_n^{(\infty)},$$

then from the equilibrium scalar equation

$$y_i^{(\infty)} = a_{ii} \sum_{j=1}^{n} w_{ij} y_j^{(\infty)} + (1 - a_{ii}) y_i^{(1)}, \tag{5.2}$$

it follows that

$$(1 - a_{ii}) \left[y_*^{(\infty)} - y_i^{(1)} \right] = 0. \tag{5.3}$$

Hence, if $y_*^{(\infty)} \neq y_i^{(1)}$, then $a_{ii} = 1$ and, equivalently, if $a_{ii} < 1$, then $y_*^{(\infty)} = y_i^{(1)}$. If $y_*^{(\infty)} - y_i^{(1)} = 0$, then the value of a_{ii} remains undetermined (it may be any value), and if $a_{ii} = 1$, then the amount of attitude change $y_*^{(\infty)} - y_i^{(1)}$ remains undetermined. For an exact equilibrium consensus that does not depend on initial attitudes, there cannot be more than *one* member of the group with $y_*^{(\infty)} = y_i^{(1)}$, because with two or more such members consensus is *restricted* to a constrained $\mathbf{y}^{(1)}$ in which there are shared initial attitudes. There cannot be more than one member with $a_{ii} < 1$, because the initial attitudes of two or more members with $a_{ii} < 1$ would have to be identical for an exact equilibrium consensus. Hence, for the group as a whole, an exact equilibrium consensus that does not depend on group members' initial attitudes is only consistent with either $\mathbf{A} = \mathbf{I}$ or an $\mathbf{A}$ with one member i for whom $a_{ii} < 1$ and $n - 1$ members $j \neq i$ with $a_{jj} = 1$.

Finally, only $\mathbf{AW}$s with a particular form of network structure are consistent with the existence of $\mathbf{V}^{(\infty)}$ with identical rows. The $\mathbf{AW}$ must contain a unique strong component of k members (containing at most one member with $a_{ii} < 1$) whose members influence, directly or indirectly, all other $n - k$ members of the group, for whom $a_{jj} = 1$. In the special case of a network with one person for whom $a_{ii} = 0$, the unique strong component is trivially that person ($k = 1$). Such $\mathbf{AW}$ are necessary, but not sufficient, to produce $V^{(\infty)}$ with identical rows and an exact consensus that is independent of group members' initial attitudes. An additional necessary condition is that $V^{(\infty)}$ exists, and it may not exist in unusual special cases of cyclic systems. We provide examples of cyclic systems in the following section.

It should be clear that, although some influence networks will produce consensus regardless of initial attitudes, there are faction structures (other than an initial consensus) that *enable* the production of consensus. Faction structures also are important because they enable the aggregation of interpersonal influences in support of particular initial positions. Thus, with respect to an analysis of consensus production in groups, the collective outcomes of the interpersonal influence process among group members on issues depend on the co-joined social structure defined by AW and $y^{(1)}$.

5.2 Binary Resistances and Conformities

In this section we define, illustrate, and discuss an important special case of the standard model, which we refer to as the binary susceptibility model. In the binary susceptibility model, each group member's susceptibility is either 0 or 1, or near these values. Our empirical findings on dyads, triads, and tetrads suggest that susceptibilities are often either 0 or 1, or near these extremes, for the influence networks that form on particular issues when group members are under pressure to reach consensus.

One realization of the binary susceptibility model is an interpersonal influence system in which group members' attitudes converge to the mean of their initial attitudes on an issue. Whether or not it suffices to posit that group members' attitudes converge to the mean of their initial attitudes is a matter on which the theoretical approaches of sociologists and psychologists differ in their perspectives. The sociological perspective emphasizes that interpersonal influences in groups are often markedly stratified and, therefore, inconsistent with the assumption of a ubiquitous convergence of attitudes to the mean of group members' initial attitudes. The psychological perspective tends to discount inequalities of interpersonal influence and emphasizes, instead, that interpersonal influences in small groups tend to draw group members to a position that minimizes the average distance that group members must shift their attitudes in order to reach consensus. This emphasis is evident in the ongoing assertion among some prominent psychologists that the process of interpersonal influence entails a simple (as opposed to a weighted) averaging of group members' attitudes (McGarty, Turner, Hogg, David, and Wetherell 1992; Turner and Oakes 1989). This assertion underlies the work on group polarization

(Isenberg 1986; Lamm and Myers 1978), in which it is assumed that the formation of a group consensus that is *not* the mean of group members' initial attitudes is indicative of a process that is *different* from the process of social influence postulated by Asch (1951), Sherif (1936), and other classical investigators in the group dynamics tradition. It also underlies the work on social categorization theory in which a convergence of attitudes to a prototypical attitudinal position that is *not* the mean of group members' initial attitudes is viewed as indicative of a process that is different from the process of social influence postulated in the classical tradition of group dynamics. Obviously, a weighted averaging mechanism is consistent with a consensus that lies anywhere in the range or convex hull of a group's initial attitudes.

5.2.1 Superconformity Systems

When $\mathbf{A} = \mathbf{I}$, our standard model simplifies to $\mathbf{y}^{(t+1)} = \mathbf{W}\mathbf{y}^{(t)}$ for $t = 1, 2, \ldots$. No direct weight is attached to a group member's own attitude $w_{ii} = 0$ for all i, and each group member moves his or her attitude to a weighted average of other group members' attitudes at each time t:

$$y_i^{(t+1)} = \sum_{j \neq i}^{n} w_{ij} y_j^{(t)} \tag{5.4}$$

for all i. Each group member is maximally conforming, although it is important to recognize that what they are conforming to is determined by the weights accorded to the particular positions held by other group members.

The simplest baseline superconformity model is one in which all group members' attitudes are visible and equally salient for each i. For instance,

$$\mathbf{A} = \begin{bmatrix} 1 & 0 & 0 & 0 \\ 0 & 1 & 0 & 0 \\ 0 & 0 & 1 & 0 \\ 0 & 0 & 0 & 1 \end{bmatrix}, \quad \mathbf{W} = \begin{bmatrix} 0 & 0.\overline{3} & 0.\overline{3} & 0.\overline{3} \\ 0.\overline{3} & 0 & 0.\overline{3} & 0.\overline{3} \\ 0.\overline{3} & 0.\overline{3} & 0 & 0.\overline{3} \\ 0.\overline{3} & 0.\overline{3} & 0.\overline{3} & 0 \end{bmatrix}$$

where $0.\overline{3} = 0.333\ldots = 1/3$, and

$$\mathbf{V} = \begin{bmatrix} 0.25 & 0.25 & 0.25 & 0.25 \\ 0.25 & 0.25 & 0.25 & 0.25 \\ 0.25 & 0.25 & 0.25 & 0.25 \\ 0.25 & 0.25 & 0.25 & 0.25 \end{bmatrix}.$$

The result is a consensus, $\hat{\mathbf{y}}^{(\infty)} = \mathbf{V}\mathbf{y}^{(1)}$, on the mean initial attitude of group members regardless of their initial attitudes.

However, in the special case of a dyad with $\mathbf{A} = \mathbf{I}$, we have

$$\mathbf{A} = \begin{bmatrix} 1 & 0 \\ 0 & 1 \end{bmatrix} \quad \text{and} \quad \mathbf{W} = \begin{bmatrix} 0 & 1 \\ 1 & 0 \end{bmatrix}.$$

Here the result is a cyclic influence system for which there are no equilibrium attitudes, except in the case of an initial consensus. Letting $\mathbf{A} \neq \mathbf{I}$, but maintaining the assumption of supersusceptibilities, with $a_{11} = a_{22}$ near 1, the result is a virtual consensus that is near the mean of the initial attitudes of the two members. With their supersusceptibilities, both persons place negligible weight on their own initial positions on an issue, and they abandon their positions at each time t to accommodate one another; but each person finds that the other is attempting to accommodate him or her. In such a situation, the equilibrium is a consensus that reflects both members' initial positions. Getting to that equilibrium is an exceedingly inefficient process when the initial discrepancy of attitudes is large.

In the superconformity model, for $n > 2$, the assumption of a complete matrix of homogeneous interpersonal influences may be relaxed. If the interpersonal weights in one or more of the rows of $\mathbf{W}$ are heterogeneous, then a group consensus may or may not be formed, and a consensus (if formed) may or may not be the mean of group members' initial attitudes. With this generalization of the superconformity model, a cyclic influence system may occur in $n > 2$ groups. For example, a decentralized "circle" network such as

$$\mathbf{C} = \begin{bmatrix} 0 & 1 & 0 & 0 \\ 0 & 0 & 1 & 0 \\ 0 & 0 & 0 & 1 \\ 1 & 0 & 0 & 0 \end{bmatrix}, \quad \mathbf{A} = \begin{bmatrix} 1 & 0 & 0 & 0 \\ 0 & 1 & 0 & 0 \\ 0 & 0 & 1 & 0 \\ 0 & 0 & 0 & 1 \end{bmatrix},$$

and

$$\mathbf{W} = \mathbf{AC} + \mathbf{I} - \mathbf{A} = \begin{bmatrix} 0 & 1 & 0 & 0 \\ 0 & 0 & 1 & 0 \\ 0 & 0 & 0 & 1 \\ 1 & 0 & 0 & 0 \end{bmatrix}$$

has no equilibrium. For the same $\mathbf{C}$, letting $\mathbf{A} \neq \mathbf{I}$, but maintaining the assumption of equivalent supersusceptibilities, e.g.,

$$\mathbf{A} = \begin{bmatrix} 0.99 & 0 & 0 & 0 \\ 0 & 0.99 & 0 & 0 \\ 0 & 0 & 0.99 & 0 \\ 0 & 0 & 0 & 0.99 \end{bmatrix}$$

and

$$W = AC + I - A = \begin{bmatrix} 0.01 & 0.99 & 0 & 0 \\ 0 & 0.01 & 0.99 & 0 \\ 0 & 0 & 0.01 & 0.99 \\ 0.99 & 0 & 0 & 0.01 \end{bmatrix},$$

we obtain an equilibrium V that, when rounded to two decimal places, is

$$V = \begin{bmatrix} 0.25 & 0.25 & 0.25 & 0.25 \\ 0.25 & 0.25 & 0.25 & 0.25 \\ 0.25 & 0.25 & 0.25 & 0.25 \\ 0.25 & 0.25 & 0.25 & 0.25 \end{bmatrix}$$

Here, as in the case of the dyad, the result is a virtual consensus that is near the mean of the initial attitudes of the group's members. And, as in the dyad, depending on the amount of initial disagreement, when all group members are superconformists, the process of consensus formation may be exceedingly inefficient.

A perhaps surprising implication of superconformity occurs in centralized influence networks such as

$$A = \begin{bmatrix} 1 & 0 & 0 & 0 \\ 0 & 1 & 0 & 0 \\ 0 & 0 & 1 & 0 \\ 0 & 0 & 0 & 1 \end{bmatrix} \quad \text{and} \quad W = \begin{bmatrix} 0 & 0.\overline{3} & 0.\overline{3} & 0.\overline{3} \\ 1 & 0 & 0 & 0 \\ 1 & 0 & 0 & 0 \\ 1 & 0 & 0 & 0 \end{bmatrix}.$$

Here one member, person 1, is accorded maximum influence by each of the other members, and person 1 accords equal weight to each of the other group members. The result is an endless cycling between

$$V^{(t)} = \begin{bmatrix} 1 & 0 & 0 & 0 \\ 0 & 0.\overline{3} & 0.\overline{3} & 0.\overline{3} \\ 0 & 0.\overline{3} & 0.\overline{3} & 0.\overline{3} \\ 0 & 0.\overline{3} & 0.\overline{3} & 0.\overline{3} \end{bmatrix} \quad \text{and} \quad V^{(t+1)} = \begin{bmatrix} 0 & 0.\overline{3} & 0.\overline{3} & 0.\overline{3} \\ 1 & 0 & 0 & 0 \\ 1 & 0 & 0 & 0 \\ 1 & 0 & 0 & 0 \end{bmatrix}$$

for $t = 2, 3, \ldots$. In the first stage, the three noncentral members adopt the initial position of the central member, whereas the central member adopts the mean of the initial positions of the three other members. In the second stage, the central member holds his or her initial position on the issue, whereas the other members adopt the mean of their three initial positions. Letting $A \neq I$, but maintaining the assumption of equivalent supersusceptibilities, e.g.,

$$A = \begin{bmatrix} 0.99 & 0 & 0 & 0 \\ 0 & 0.99 & 0 & 0 \\ 0 & 0 & 0.99 & 0 \\ 0 & 0 & 0 & 0.99 \end{bmatrix}, \quad C = \begin{bmatrix} 0 & 0.\overline{3} & 0.\overline{3} & 0.\overline{3} \\ 1 & 0 & 0 & 0 \\ 1 & 0 & 0 & 0 \\ 1 & 0 & 0 & 0 \end{bmatrix},$$

we obtain

$$W = AC + I - A = \begin{bmatrix} 0.01 & 0.33 & 0.33 & 0.33 \\ 0.99 & 0.01 & 0 & 0 \\ 0.99 & 0 & 0.01 & 0 \\ 0.99 & 0 & 0 & 0.01 \end{bmatrix}$$

and

$$V = \begin{bmatrix} 0.503 & 0.166 & 0.166 & 0.166 \\ 0.497 & 0.174 & 0.164 & 0.164 \\ 0.497 & 0.164 & 0.174 & 0.164 \\ 0.497 & 0.164 & 0.164 & 0.174 \end{bmatrix}.$$

The result is an equilibrium that is a near consensus in which the initial position of the structurally central member is disproportionately influential.

All of these illustrations of superconformity systems involve strongly connected influence networks. Whether or not consensus is attainable in a superconformity system with heterogeneous interpersonal influences depends on the structure of the interpersonal network and the initial attitudes of the group's members. In general, when all group members are superconformists and V exists, consensus will be reached in a strongly connected influence network or within the strong components of the network. However, consensus also may be attained in unilateral, weak, and disconnected networks depending on the pattern of initial agreements among the group's members.

5.2.2 Mixed Binary-State Systems

Given initial disagreement among a group's members, *all* binary susceptibility systems (regardless of the structure of interpersonal influences) are consistent with the formation of consensus, when they have one or more (but not all) members who are superresistant to interpersonal influences.[1] A classic special case of a mixed binary-state system is a group with $n - 1$ members who have a fixed identical attitude on an issue and another member whose attitude is susceptible to the influence of at least one of the $n - 1$ other members. In this case, the prediction of the binary susceptibility model is exceedingly simple: the minority member will adopt the initial position of the majority. Another classic special case is a group with a minority of one who has a fixed position on an issue and $n - 1$ other susceptible members who are influenced directly or indirectly by the minority member. In essence, the attainment of consensus is held

---

[1] Such systems do not necessarily form a consensus. For a given structure of interpersonal influences, whether they do or not depends on the initial positions of the group members on an issue.

hostage to the adoption of the minority position. Again, the prediction of the binary susceptibility model is exceedingly simple: the members of the group will over time reach a consensus on the initial position of the minority member. The above classic cases are instances of groups with one superresistant faction of size k and $n - k$ other members who are supersusceptible. We will examine these and other special cases in subsequent chapters of the book, as part of a more general treatment of susceptibilities that are not constrained to binary values.

5.3 Revisiting Sherif's Findings

Sherif's (1936) evidence is the classic demonstration that interpersonal influences based on the mere visibility of attitudes on an issue may result in a convergence of individuals' attitudes to a consensus. In Sherif's experiments, group members repetitively voiced their attitudes about an ambiguous phenomenon, the perceived amount of movement of a point of light associated with an autokinetic effect. Sherif observed that subjects' attitudes altered over time and converged. But the exact mechanism by which subjects combined their own and others' attitudes, and were able to achieve a near consensus based on this process, remains unclear. No formal procedure was invoked to achieve consensus, there was no preexisting normative attitude, and there was no rational calculation, e.g., objective measurement of the light's movement. Consensus was formed on the basis of the mere visibility of group members' attitudes. Sherif further demonstrated, and others have confirmed, that the consensus formed in this fashion was preserved over some period in the minds of the subjects. When individuals were asked to provide a judgment at a later date (a day later, 28 days later, one year later!), their attitude on the issue closely corresponded to the manifest position they had reached previously via the interpersonal influences on their attitudes (Bovard 1948; Rohrer, Baron, Hoffman, and Swander 1954).

Here we examine some of the details revealed in Sherif's (1936) profiles of the convergence of subjects' judgments on the autokinetic effect. We reproduce his display of findings in Figure 5.1. Sherif's experimental design involved eight dyads and eight triads that met over a period of 4 days (Sessions I–IV). The over-time profile of each subject is based on the subject's median judgment in a session on the amount of movement of the light. Four of the eight dyads began as individuals who formed their judgments independently in Session I and then formed judgments as a dyad in Sessions II–IV. Four of the eight dyads began as a group in Session I, continued as a group in Sessions II and III, and then formed their judgments independently in Session IV. An analogous design was implemented for the eight triads.

124   *Social Influence Network Theory*

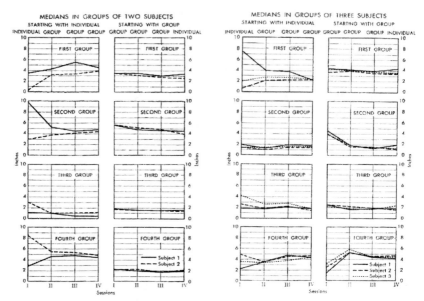

Figure 5.1 Sherif's (1936) findings.

Individuals who formed their judgments independently in Session I varied in their initial median values. Subsequently, during Sessions II–IV, their median values converged. Within each session, we think that the most plausible mechanism underlying the convergence of subjects' judgments is a "cognitive algebra" of weighted averaging. Clearly, some subjects modified their judgments more than others. Inequalities of interpersonal influence may have occurred on the basis of subjects' associating the voiced judgments of others with the persons who were voicing them and, in turn, the visible characteristics of these persons, including qualities of their pronouncements (loudness, confidence, etc.). Inequalities also may have occurred based on individual differences in resistance, so that the less resistant (less self-weighted) members' judgments gravitated over time toward the positions of the more resistant (more heavily self-weighted) members' position on the issue. Subjects who formed their judgments in a *group* in Session I varied considerably less in their initial median values than subjects who formed their judgments independently in Session I. The only reasonable conclusion is that substantial convergence of positions occurred during Session I. Subsequently, during Sessions II–IV, the convergence was maintained.

An interesting feature of these data is that the value of an achieved near-consensus sometimes "drifted" across sessions. Our theory does not explain this phenomenon. We offer an explanation of how consensus may be formed, but not how an *achieved consensus* in a group changes. Our model is formally consistent with a "transitory" consensus that occurs during the process of interpersonal influence *prior* to the equilibrium consensus of a group. It also is formally consistent with the occurrence of additional attitude changes, when the equilibrium attitudes of a group on an issue are *revisited* and are factored into the initial attitudes of *another* influence process on the issue:

$$
\begin{aligned}
\mathbf{y}_1^{(\infty)} &= \mathbf{V}_1^{(\infty)} \mathbf{y}_1^{(1)} \\
\mathbf{y}_2^{(\infty)} &= \mathbf{V}_2^{(\infty)} \left[\mathbf{y}_1^{(\infty)} + \mathbf{u}_2 \right] \\
\mathbf{y}_3^{(\infty)} &= \mathbf{V}_3^{(\infty)} \left[\mathbf{y}_2^{(\infty)} + \mathbf{u}_3 \right]
\end{aligned}
\tag{5.5}
$$

$$\vdots$$

A special case of such a sequence of influence processes is $\mathbf{V}_1^{(\infty)} = \mathbf{V}_2^{(\infty)} = \mathbf{V}_3^{(\infty)} = \dots$ and $\mathbf{u}_2 = \mathbf{u}_3 = \dots = 0$. If an equilibrium consensus is achieved, then its content should be maintained, unless it is disturbed by conditions ($\mathbf{u}_k \neq 0$) other than interpersonal influences. The drifting consensus that occurs in some of Sherif's groups might be explained by modest (perhaps random) departures of group members from their median positions of the previous session. However, note that the "drift" of an achieved near-consensus across sessions is dramatic in the second and fourth groups of triads that formed their judgments as a group in Session I.

Consensus is frequently accounted for by *postulating* the existence of shared norms. If a shared norm importantly constrains persons' positions on an issue, then group members' initial attitudes on an issue should be consensual and interpersonal influences will operate minimally (if at all) to reinforce that initial consensus. However, social norms are usually not the sole determinants of attitudes, and persons may differ in their initial attitudes on an issue even while they have a shared normative orientation. When norms are ambiguous, persons may interpret or weigh them differently. For these reasons, the observation that shared normative orientations enter into the formation of persons' attitudes does not carry us very far toward a theoretical understanding of how the members of a group settle on their attitudes and reach consensus.

We reverse the common assumption that shared norms generate consensus and argue, instead, that consensus produced through interpersonal influences generates norms, which in turn become factors (among many factors) that may influence persons' future positions on issues. This perspective is consistent with Lewin (1958), Sherif (1936), and Festinger (1950, 1954), among others, who view the process of interpersonal influence as the main mechanism in the formation of shared norms. For instance, Rosenberg (1968: 60) writes:

> It is a sociological axiom that when people become group members, they tend to interact with other group members; this interaction leads to group norms – characteristic attitudes, values, practices, conceptions or right and wrong, etc. Even if they originally entered the group with these norms, the group interaction tends to solidify, crystallize, and stabilize the norms.

The experiments of Sherif (1936), Bovard (1948), and Rohrer, Baron, Hoffman, and Swander (1954) present the clearest demonstration of the formation of norms via interpersonal interaction. Our contribution to this line of inquiry on norm formation is a formal model that shows how consensus is formed through interpersonal influences. Our linkage to norm formation is based on the assumption that consensus *validates* the consensually held attitude, giving it normative content; see Friedkin (2001) for a field setting application of this approach. The conditions under which agreements, formed through interpersonal influence, take on normative content, or do not take on such content, are an important question that we cannot answer with the present data.

5.4 Findings on Conditions of Consensus Formation

Our substantive focus here is on *emergent* consensus from initial disagreement. Our analysis draws on 440 of the 450 group–issue trials among the dyads, triads, and tetrads on which there was an initial disagreement among the members.[2] Among the experimentally manipulated conditions, group size and pressure to reach consensus affect the probability that a consensus is achieved. The other manipulated experimental conditions have no effect on the probability of consensus formation. The sex composition of the groups (all male vs. all female) has no effect, nor does the structure of the telephonic communication network, nor does the issue considered by the groups (with the exception of the Disaster issue, for which consensus was significantly less likely than for the other issues considered by the tetrads), nor does the position of an issue in the sequence of trials in which the issues were considered by the group. We find some limited evidence for an effect of the size of the initial range of positions on the probability of achieved consensus. Below we present the findings on group size, pressure to reach consensus, and range of initial

---

[2]   An emergent consensus was achieved in 73.2% of the groups, i.e., 322 of the 440 groups with an initial disagreement. The 10 eliminated trials with an initial consensus involved 8 dyads and 2 triads.

positions. Then, controlling for these contextual conditions, we show that the smaller the standard model's *predicted range of equilibrium positions*, the more likely there is an observed end-of-trial consensus. The influence network of the group, which transforms initial positions via our standard model, provides a purchase on the occurrence of an emergent consensus.

5.4.1 Group Size and Pressure to Reach Consensus

Table 5.1 presents findings on the effects of group size and pressure to reach consensus. All the tetrads were under high pressure to reach consensus. Controlling for group size, consensus is more likely to be formed under high pressure than under low pressure in dyads and triads. Controlling for the pressure to reach consensus, consensus is more likely in dyads than triads under low pressure, and unrelated to group size under high pressure. The probability of consensus is similar for the triads and tetrads under high pressure.

5.4.2 Range of Initial Positions on an Issue

Binary logistic regressions of consensus (0 = no consensus, 1 = consensus) on the range of initial positions (Table 5.2) indicate mixed effects of the initial range on consensus formation. A decrease in the probability of consensus as the range of initial positions increases appears only among tetrads on the risk-assessment issues (Sports, School, and Surgery) and among dyads under low pressure to reach consensus. Pressure to reach consensus was not manipulated in the experiment on tetrads: all of the tetrads were encouraged to reach consensus. Triads considered the same set of risk-assessment issues as the tetrads, and a subset of the triads did so under high pressure. There is no effect of the initial range on consensus formation among triads under high pressure or, for that matter, under low pressure. Hence, the effect of the range of initial positions does not appear to be robust across social contexts.

The null findings for dyads and triads indicate, counter to intuition, that reaching consensus is no more likely when the initial range of positions on an issue is narrow than when the initial range of positions is wide. In an additional analysis for the pooled issues among dyads and triads ($N = 190$), the estimated effects obtained from a binary logistic regression of consensus on a group's initial range of positions and pressure to reach consensus are $\exp(B) = 0.986$ and $\exp(B) = 7.405$, with 95% confidence intervals of $[0.970, 1.001]$ and $[3.846, 14.259]$, respectively, for the initial range and pressure to reach consensus variables. Hence, we can only conclude that an effect of the range of initial positions may appear on some issues among the largest of the three group sizes that we have dealt with. In contrast to the pressure to reach consensus, which manifested

Table 5.1 *Effects of pressure and group size on consensus formation*

(a) Effect of pressure on consensus formation, controlling for size

Size	Consensus	Pressure	
		Low	High
Dyads			
	No	58.8%	28.9%
	Yes	41.2%	71.1%
	TOTAL	100%	100%
		(51)	(45)
Triads			
	No	78.7%	17.0%
	Yes	21.3%	83.0%
	TOTAL	100%	100%
		(47)	(47)
Tetrads			
	No		16.0%
	Yes		84.0%
	TOTAL		100%
			(250)

Dyads ($\chi^2 = 8.663$, $df = 1$, $p = 0.003$)
Triads ($\chi^2 = 35.852$, $df = 1$, $p < 0.001$)

(b) Effect of group size on consensus formation, controlling for pressure

Pressure	Consensus	Size		
		Dyads	Triads	Tetrads
Low				
	No	58.8%	78.7%	
	Yes	41.2%	21.3%	
		100%	100%	
		(51)	(47)	
High				
	No	28.9%	17.0%	16.0%
	Yes	71.1%	83.0%	84.0%
		100%	100%	100%
		(45)	(47)	(250)

Low pressure: $\chi^2 = 4.479$, $df = 1$, $p = 0.034$
High pressure: $\chi^2 = 1.834$, $df = 1$, $p = 0.175$ (excluding tetrads)

consistent significant effects on the probability of consensus in dyads and triads (with or without a control for the range of initial positions), it seems clear that the initial range of positions is not a general factor in determining consensus outcomes. The importance of the initial range is the constraint on the *location* of the achieved consensus within the convex hull of initial positions and not its effects on the probability of a consensus being formed.

Table 5.2 Probability of achieved consensus as a function of the range of initial positions, controlling for group size and pressure to reach consensus (standard errors in parentheses)

	Pooled risk-assessment issues (Sports, School, Surgery)					Asbestos	Disaster
	Dyads LPress 1	Dyads HPress 2	Triads LPress 3	Triads HPress 4	Tetrads HPress 5	Tetrads HPress 6	Tetrads HPress 7
Range of initial positions	-0.035*	0.004	0.001	-0.026	-0.069***	-0.040	0.231
	(0.017)	(0.018)	(0.016)	(0.017)	(0.016)	(0.058)	(0.337)
Constant	0.599	0.801	-1.361	2.599**	5.185***	2.499***	2.470*
	(0.529)	(0.576)	(0.703)	(0.843)	(0.955)	(0.677)	(1.015)
-2LL	64.195	54.060	48.646	40.634	110.846	32.098	48.597
N	51	45	47	47	150	50	50

Notes: The analysis is based on the 440 groups that dealt with the risk assessment issues, and it excludes 10 groups with an initial consensus.

$^{†}p < 0.10$; $^{*}p < 0.05$; $^{**}p < 0.01$; $^{***}p < 0.001$ (2-tailed).

5.4.3 Contribution of the Standard Model

Table 5.3 shows that the narrower the network model's *predicted* range of equilibrium attitudes, the more likely the group members' report of an end-of-trial consensus, controlling for their range of initial positions, group size, pressure to reach consensus, and issue type (risk-assessment and monetary issues). Equilibrium predictions are available for all 450 group trials. For the predicted equilibrium attitudes $\hat{y}^{(\infty)} = [\hat{y}_i^{(\infty)}]$, $i = 1, 2, \ldots, n$, the *predicted range of equilibrium attitudes* in a group is $\max\{\hat{y}_1^{(\infty)}, \hat{y}_2^{(\infty)}, \ldots, \hat{y}_n^{(\infty)}\} - \min\{\hat{y}_1^{(\infty)}, \hat{y}_2^{(\infty)}, \ldots, \hat{y}_n^{(\infty)}\}$. The effect holds for each group size, high and low pressure to reach consensus, and issue type (risk-assessment and monetary issues). The nonsignificant (two-tailed) effect for triads under high pressure on the risk-assessment issues is significant ($p = 0.054$, two-tailed; $p = 0.027$, one-tailed) when the nonsignificant ($p = 0.979$) initial-range variable is trimmed from the model.

The initial conditions under which an influence network is formed on an issue include group size, the array of group members' initial positions on the issue, and the pressure on group members to reach consensus. These initial conditions may affect the connectivity category of the influence network that is formed in the group and the susceptibilities of group members to interpersonal influence.[3] In turn, the *realized* social structure of the group, i.e., the *joint condition* of group members' initial positions, susceptibilities, and interpersonal influences, determine the predicted range of equilibrium attitudes produced by the process and the predicted time to reach this equilibrium. This social structure is *in the influence process* and its implications are *realized through the process*.

5.5 Findings on Efficiency of Consensus Formation

In this section, we assess the ability of our standard model to predict the observed time to end of trial. We are not interested in efficiency per se, but we address it as a probe into the merits of our formalization of the group-discussion process. The rapidity with which initial disagreements are reduced to a consensus, or a settled state of disagreement, may be

---

[3] An influence network may be strong, unilateral, weak, or disconnected. These connectivity categories (defined in Chapter 1) are based on the network **N** corresponding to $S = [s_{ij}]$, where $s_{ij} = 1$ if $a_{ii}w_{ij} > 0$ and $s_{ij} = 0$ if $a_{ii}w_{ij} = 0$, for all i, j. The main-diagonal values in S do not enter into the definition of the connectively category of **AW**. However, a network in which there is at least one member i with $a_{ii} = 0$ cannot be strongly connected, and a network with at least two members i and j with $a_{ii} = a_{jj} = 0$ cannot be unilaterally connected. Among the 450 networks that were formed on the issue trials, 100 involved one or more members with zero susceptibility (69 unilateral, 18 weak, and 13 disconnected networks) and 350 had no member with zero susceptibility (340 strong and 10 unilateral networks).

Table 5.3 *Probability of achieved consensus as a function of the network model's predicted range of equilibrium positions, controlling for range of initial positions, group size, and pressure to reach consensus (standard errors in parentheses)*

	Pooled risk-assessment issues (Sports, School, Surgery)					Asbestos	Disaster
	Dyads LPress	Dyads HPress	Triads LPress	Triads HPress	Tetrads HPress	Tetrads HPress	Tetrads HPress
	1	2	3	4	5	6	7
Predicted range of positions	−0.607**	−0.203*	−0.251*	−0.076	−0.242***	−2.623*	−2.679*
	(0.207)	(0.095)	(0.113)	(0.051)	(0.053)	(1.081)	(1.134)
Range of initial positions	−0.011	0.063	0.023	0.001	−0.015	0.749*	0.231
	(0.023)	(0.033)	(0.018)	(0.025)	(0.24)	(0.331)	(0.337)
Constant	2.449**	0.654	0.114	2.487**	5.933***	2.492**	2.717*
	(0.914)	(0.618)	(0.885)	(0.872)	(1.265)	(0.823)	(1.123)
−2LL	39.429	43.692	37.126	36.988	65.069	18.123	38.393
N	51	45	47	47	150	50	50

Notes: The analysis is based on the 440 groups that dealt with the risk assessment issues, and it excludes 10 groups with an initial consensus.
$^{t}p < 0.10$; $^{*}p < 0.05$; $^{**}p < 0.01$; $^{***}p < 0.001$ (2-tailed).

predicted by our standard model in terms of the number of iterations (time periods $t = 1, 2, 3, \ldots$) that are required to reach an equilibrium under the empirical conditions of a group's members influence network $\tilde{W}$ and initial positions on an issue $\tilde{y}^{(1)}$. A correspondence between observed and predicted times to reach consensus or stalemate would indicate that our standard model is capturing meaningful processual features of the group discussion.

5.5.1 Observed and Predicted Efficiency

Our measure of efficiency is

$$E = \frac{1}{1 + T}, \tag{5.6}$$

where T is either the *observed* time $\tilde{T}$ to end of trial for a group measured in minutes or the *predicted* number of time periods (i.e., the state transitions $t = 1, 2, 3, \ldots$ of our standard model) $\hat{T}$ required to reach an equilibrium. Here, this equilibrium is defined as $\max\{|\hat{y}_1^{(t+1)} - \hat{y}_1^{(t)}|,$ $|\hat{y}_2^{(t+1)} - \hat{y}_2^{(t)}|, \ldots |\hat{y}_n^{(t+1)} - \hat{y}_n^{(t)}|\} \leq 10^{-5}$ under the empirical conditions of a group's members' influence network $\tilde{W}$ and initial positions on an issue $\tilde{y}^{(1)}$. With this measure $0 < E \leq 1$, perfect efficiency $E = 1$ occurs for $T = 0$, e.g., when a group that is in initial consensus on an issue immediately takes that initial consensus as the group decision. The measure declines with T and approaches $E = 0$ in the limit with sufficiently large values of T.

Table 5.4 presents the frequency distributions for the observed times to end of trial $\tilde{T}$ for each group size. In the experimental trials, an issue trial was deemed concluded either at the end of the allotted time for the trial or, before that time, when all of the subjects privately recorded their final positions on the issue and provided them to the experimenter. Dyads and triads were given up to 30 minutes to discuss an issue; tetrads were given up to 20 minutes. For the dyads and triads, observed times to end of trial are (with one exception) strictly within the 30-minute time frame; i.e., all but one trial was completed in 26 minutes or less. All of the tetrads were placed under strong pressure to reach consensus. Note that all but 8 of the 210 tetrads that reached consensus did so prior to the 20-minute deadline, and that 28 of the 40 tetrads that failed to reach consensus reported their failure at the end of the 20-minute deadline. Clearly, the experimental design for the tetrads generated a distinctly different profile of observed times to end of trial than the experimental designs for the dyads and triads. Given the deadlines for the trials, we treat $\tilde{T}$ as a right-censored variable on the values 20 for tetrads and 30 for dyads and triads. Hence, $\tilde{E}$ is a left-censored variable on the values $1/(1 + 19.5) = 0.049$ for tetrads

Table 5.4 *Frequency distributions of observed times (minutes) to end of trial*

(a) Dyads				(b) Triads				(c) Tetrads			
	Consensus				Consensus				Consensus		
Time	No	Yes	Total	Time	No	Yes	Total	Time	No	Yes	Total
				2	0	1	1	2	0	4	4
1	0	2	2	3	0	3	3	3	0	14	14
2	4	4	8	4	1	4	5	4	0	17	17
3	3	13	16	5	2	3	5	5	0	18	18
4	3	15	18	6	3	4	7	6	1	19	20
5	6	4	10	7	3	3	6	7	0	19	19
6	4	7	11	8	3	6	9	8	0	24	24
7	5	2	7	9	3	6	9	9	1	11	12
8	1	4	5	10	2	0	2	10	0	11	11
9	1	1	2	11	3	3	6	11	1	11	12
10	3	1	4	12	1	3	4	12	1	16	17
11	5	1	6	13	3	1	4	13	1	8	9
12	1	1	2	14	3	2	5	14	0	6	6
13	1	1	2	15	2	2	4	15	1	7	8
14	1	0	1	16	3	2	5	16	0	6	6
15	1	0	1	17	1	2	3	17	2	5	7
16	1	0	1	18	0	1	1	18	2	4	6
17	0	1	1	19	5	1	6	19	2	2	4
18	1	0	1	20	3	1	4	20	28	8	36
20	0	2	2	21	3	0	3				
21	1	0	1	24	0	2	2				
24	0	2	2	26	0	1	1				
26	1	0	1	30	1	0	1				
TOTAL	43	61	104	TOTAL	45	51	96	TOTAL	40	210	250

Note: Dyads and triads were given up to 30 minutes to discuss an issue; tetrads were given up to 20 minutes.

and $1/(1 + 29.5) = 0.033$ for dyads and triads. From Table 5.4, note that there are 0 censored observations for dyads, 1 such observation for triads, and 36 such observations for tetrads.

Table 5.5 presents the results of a Tobit regression in which observed efficiency $\bar{E}$ is regressed on predicted efficiency $\hat{E}$, controlling for the predicted range of end-of-trial positions. We expect these efficiency measures to be positively associated. We control for the predicted end-of-trial range to address the inflation of observed times to end of trial that may arise as group members attempt to resolve intractable disagreements; the group may have reached an equilibrium state of disagreement relatively rapidly, as predicted by the model, but delayed the report of such a stalemate in a fruitless effort to resolve it. Hence, we also hypothesize a negative association for observed efficiency and the predicted end-of-trial range of positions; i.e., the larger the predicted end-of-trial range, the lower

Table 5.5 *Tobit regression of observed efficiency on predicted efficiency, controlling for the predicted range of end-of-trial positions (standard errors in parentheses)*

(a) Tetrads		
Predicted efficiency	1.615**	(0.5031)
Predicted range of positions	−0.003***	(0.0004)
Constant	0.091***	(0.0088)
Log likelihood = 249.817; 250 observations; 36 left-censored, 214 uncensored, and 0 right-censored observations for $\tilde{E}$.		
(b) Triads		
Predicted efficiency	0.202***	(0.0527)
Predicted range of positions	−0.001*	(0.0004)
Constant	0.097***	(0.0067)
Log likelihood = 146.246; 96 observations; 1 left-censored, 95 uncensored, and 0 right-censored observations for $\tilde{E}$.		
(c) Dyads: all trials		
Predicted efficiency	0.106†	(0.0555)
Predicted range of positions	−0.001*	(0.0006)
Constant	0.171***	(0.0109)
Log likelihood = 106.026; 104 observations; 0 left-censored, 104 uncensored, and 0 right-censored observations for $\tilde{E}$.		
(c) Dyads: excluding breaching trials		
Predicted efficiency	0.140*	(0.0634)
Predicted range of positions	−0.002**	(0.0008)
Constant	0.171***	(0.0121)
Log likelihood = 87.301; 86 observations; 0 left-censored, 86 uncensored, and 0 right-censored observations for $\tilde{E}$.		

†$p < 0.10$; *$p < 0.05$; **$p < 0.01$; ***$p < 0.001$ (2-tailed).

the observed efficiency of the group. These expectations are supported in Table 5.5 for the tetrads and triads. Again, the dyads appear exceptional, and the exception appears to be linked with the occurrence of anomalous observed breaches of the convex hull of initial positions. The expected associations are more strongly in evidence when the analysis of dyads is restricted to trials without such observed breaches than without this restriction.

5.5.2 Concurrent Validity of Predicted Efficiency

If some variable X of the empirical influence networks of groups is associated with the observed efficiency of the groups, then the variable X also should be commensurately associated with the predicted efficiency of the groups. Specifically, given a significant association of the *observed* efficiency with some measured variable X that is a group-level characteristic, a commensurate (same-sign) significant association should exist for the *predicted* efficiency and the variable X. For example, the *observed*

Table 5.6 *Commensurate associations of predicted and observed efficiencies*

	Consensus trials (N = 322)		All trials (N = 450)	
Correlates	$\hat{E}$	$\tilde{E}$	$\hat{E}$	$\tilde{E}$
Predicted efficiency (Pearson)		0.307***		0.245***
Strong connectivity category vs. not (phi)	−0.380***	−0.193***	−0.359***	−0.067
Density of nonzero interpersonal influences in the network (pearson)	−0.490***	−0.261***	−0.511***	−0.106*
High pressure vs. not (phi)	−0.138*	−0.200***	0.096*	−0.065
Mean within-group susceptibility (pearson)	−0.503***	−0.356***	−0.510***	−0.163***
Maximum susceptibility (pearson)	−0.496***	−0.388***	−0.549***	−0.219***
Minimum susceptibility (pearson)	−0.329***	−0.218***	−0.329***	−0.063
Range of initial attitudes (pearson)	−0.202***	−0.256***	−0.150**	−0.278***
Range of predicted equilibrium attitudes (pearson)	0.006	0.070	0.073	−0.217***

†$p < 0.10$; *$p < 0.05$; **$p < 0.01$; ***$p < 0.001$ (2-tailed).

efficiency of groups under high pressure to reach consensus is lower than the observed efficiency of groups under low pressure to reach consensus; we should find a commensurate significant negative association for the *predicted* efficiency and pressure variables.

The array of findings presented in Table 5.6 support the concurrent process validity of the network model's predicted times to equilibrium. We present findings based on all 450 group trials and findings for those group trials with achieved consensus. Achieved consensus occurred in 322 of the 450 issue trials. The substantive rationale for the restricted analysis is that groups whose members have achieved consensus are more likely to *immediately* report that outcome than will groups whose members have "struggled on" in an unsuccessful attempt to break a stalemate. The restriction removes this inflation effect on the observed times to end of trials that is coupled with the failure to reach consensus. Our confidence *must* be eroded in the process validity of the network model if we do not observe commensurate associations for the group trials with achieved consensus.

5.6 Concluding Remarks

In this chapter, we have analyzed the implications of influence networks for reaching consensus in groups. We have marshaled findings that bear on two predictions of the network model – the predicted range of equilibrium attitudes and the predicted time to equilibrium among dyads, triads, and tetrads considering various issues. Our findings, in the main, support the model. We have shown that the predicted range of equilibrium attitudes contributes to the prediction of the observed end-of-trial range of attitudes, controlling for the observed range of initial attitudes, for different issues (risk assessment and monetary), for groups of different sizes (dyads, triads, and tetrads), and for groups under different pressures to reach consensus (high and low pressure). We also have supported the predicted time to equilibrium of the model as a meaningful indicator of the efficiency of the influence process that occurs during the group discussion of an issue.

Our revisiting of Sherif (1936) suggests that the convergence to consensus has an intimate linkage with the formation of norms that constrain the future responses of individuals to the issues on which an initial heterogeneity of responses was reduced via interpersonal influences. The bases of interpersonal influence in Sherif's experimental setting rested on the interpersonal visibility of group members' responses; however, other bases cannot be discounted, because group members' responses were embodied by persons with potentially different visible individual (e.g., vocal) characteristics. Was there an unmeasured influence network at work in Sherif's experiments in which persons differed in their self-weights and the weights they accorded to particular other members of the group? We believe so. We have noted the striking formal correspondence of French's (1956) expository display of the reduction of initial opinion differences (our Figure 2.1) and Sherif's empirical display of the same (our Figure 5.1). Sherif did not detail the mechanism of this reduction; we suggest that it is akin to the mechanism formalized by French or the more general form of that mechanism specified by our standard model.

A social structure of interpersonal influence may exist prior to the discussion of a particular issue and be activated by the issue. In Sherif's experiments, any such prior structure might only be formed and manifested in the emergent responses of the subjects to one another as attitudinal objects and their displayed positions on the particular issue. The social structure of the group is *in the process*. We introduced this idea when we defined the influence network of a group as composed of the matrix of weights that group members' accord to their own and others' attitudes on an issue. Our standard model assumes that this influence network, once formed, is a fixed construct during the course of the influence process that unfolds in the group. Our standard model also assumes that group members' initial positions on an issue are fixed during the course of the influence process. The implications of the conjoined social structure – the group's influence network and its initial positions – are generated by the influence process. This is so even when the social structure of the group is fixed *prior* to emergence of an issue. The implications of such *a priori* social structures are realized by the influence process that is activated by the issue; such social structures only become meaningful when they enter into the influence process.

Social structure constrains the influence process but does not directly produce interpersonal agreements from an initial state of disagreement. Hence, both social structure and process are dually important. Our theoretical emphasis on social process is just that – our emphasis. A direct effect of social structure without an influence process might occur if the outcome of the process were a foregone conclusion. Such a circumstance occurs when there is an initial consensus on an issue, but it also may arise in other forms of social structure. An initial position on an issue that is shared by the overwhelming majority of group members may short circuit an interpersonal influence process if the attitude changes that might feasibly occur from such a process are seen as exceedingly unlikely to alter the group outcome. Similarly, in groups whose members have dealt with many issues as a group, the influence-process implications of the social structure of the group may be well understood by group members.

6

The Smallest Group

In this chapter, we analyze the process of interpersonal influence on attitudes in isolated dyads. Dyadic relationships are usually part of larger networks of interpersonal relationships. Although most relationships are not isolated, there are instances of dyads whose members are isolated on *particular issues* that do not involve the influences of other persons. Here, our theoretical focus is on the influence systems of such isolated dyads, the smallest groups in which interpersonal influence may occur.

Simmel (1950) argued that social processes in isolated dyads are qualitatively different from those in triads and larger groups. He suggested that the presence of a third party (e.g., a "tertius gaudens") importantly modifies the interaction between two persons. His ideas are not rigorously described but they are, nonetheless, important in sensitizing us to the possibility that certain social processes may occur in isolated dyads that do not occur in embedded dyads. Other investigators also have suggested that dyads are different from larger groups, that they may not simply be a special case of a group with n persons, but entail distinctive mechanisms (Levine and Moreland 1990: 586). For instance, Levine and Moreland (1998: 417) write,

Most social psychologists view dyads as groups, noting broad similarities between social behavior in dyads and larger groups. But several important differences have been noted as well (Moreland, Hogg, and Hains 1994). For example, some of the phenomena (e.g., socialization, majority–minority relations) that occur in larger groups cannot occur in dyads, and a few of the phenomena that occur in both settings (e.g., conflict, bargaining) take different forms. These differences suggest that a qualitative shift may occur when dyads become triads (see Mills (1958)).

Our approach to the dyad is based on our standard model for the influence process,

$$y^{(t+1)} = AWy^{(t)} + (I - A)y^{(1)} \qquad t = 1, 2, 3 \ldots, \qquad (6.1)$$

with $a_{ii} = 1 - w_{ii}$ for all i. For an isolated dyad,

$$W = \begin{bmatrix} w_{11} & w_{12} \\ w_{21} & w_{22} \end{bmatrix} = \begin{bmatrix} 1 - a_{11} & a_{11} \\ a_{22} & 1 - a_{22} \end{bmatrix}. \qquad (6.2)$$

Note that each member's susceptibility *is* the other member's relative interpersonal influence; i.e., $a_{11} = w_{12}$ and $a_{22} = w_{21}$ As a result of our studies of the application of social influence network theory to such dyads, a perspective on dyadic influence systems has emerged that has led us to set such systems aside for special scrutiny.

The first finding, which led us to this special treatment of the dyad, is that breaches of the convex hull of initial attitudes are relatively more frequent in dyads than in triads and tetrads. For the issues discussed by the dyads, triads, and tetrads, a breach occurs when one or more of the group members' end-of-trial attitudes is outside the range of their initial attitudes on an issue. Eighteen of the 20 observed breaches occurred in dyads. Although over 80% of the dyads conformed to our expectation of no breaching, and although those breaches that did occur were near the convex hulls of group members' initial attitudes, the substantially greater proportion of breaching in dyads relative to larger groups cannot be ignored.

The second finding that has led us to this perspective is the implication of our model that in dyads an exact consensus cannot be reached when both members of the group are maximally susceptible to interpersonal influence, i.e., when $a_{11} = a_{22} = 1$, because in such a case

$$W = \begin{bmatrix} 0 & 1 \\ 1 & 0 \end{bmatrix} \Rightarrow V^{(1)} = W = \begin{bmatrix} 0 & 1 \\ 1 & 0 \end{bmatrix} \Rightarrow y^{(2)} = \begin{bmatrix} y_2^{(1)} \\ y_1^{(1)} \end{bmatrix} \qquad (6.3)$$

$$\Rightarrow V^{(2)} = W^2 = \begin{bmatrix} 1 & 0 \\ 0 & 1 \end{bmatrix} \Rightarrow y^{(3)} = \begin{bmatrix} y_1^{(1)} \\ y_2^{(1)} \end{bmatrix}$$

$$\Rightarrow V^{(3)} = W^3 = \begin{bmatrix} 0 & 1 \\ 1 & 0 \end{bmatrix} \Rightarrow y^{(4)} = \begin{bmatrix} y_2^{(1)} \\ y_1^{(1)} \end{bmatrix}$$

$$\vdots$$

etc.

There is no equilibrium when $a_{11} = a_{22} = 1$ except in the trivial case of an initial consensus. When $y_1^{(1)} \neq y_2^{(1)}$, maximal accommodation in a dyad

($\mathbf{A} = \mathbf{I}$) produces a "frustration" sequence in which no progress is made toward a consensus, or even an equilibrium, as the two persons simultaneously and continuously leapfrog past one another. We will show that a strongly connected influence network in combination with sufficiently high susceptibilities generates *extreme* levels of inefficiency in the dyad.[1] However, strong connectivity in combination with high susceptibilities, including the special case of $\mathbf{A} = \mathbf{I}$, does not generally imply such inefficiency in larger groups.

The occurrence of mutually high levels of interpersonal influence in dyads (including, as an extreme, the cyclic influence system described above) creates social dilemmas that are not as frequently faced by members of larger groups. Efficient consensus formation is at odds with equality of interpersonal influence in the dyad. Inequality of interpersonal influence in a dyad fosters efficiency, but such inequality may be more difficult to establish in the intimate context of dyadic interaction than in larger groups, where asymmetry, leadership, and dominance may be fostered by the more complex interpersonal task-environment in which the subject is placed. We suspect that breaching behavior stems, in part, from the social dilemma experienced by two persons who are attempting to reach rapid agreement on the basis of mutually high levels of interpersonal influence. Both the theory and the evidence that we will present suggest that the anomalous breaches observed among the dyads may be a side effect of this social dilemma.

In addition, dyads are of theoretical interest as a special case of an influence system in which the influence network may be derived from observations of the initial and end-of-trial positions of the members on an issue. Moreover, the total interpersonal influences in the dyad that transform initial attitudes into equilibrium attitudes, $y^{(\infty)} = \mathbf{V}y^{(1)}$, may be determined as follows:

$$v_{12} = \left(y_1^{(\infty)} - y_1^{(1)}\right) \Big/ \left(y_2^{(1)} - y_1^{(1)}\right)$$
$$v_{21} = \left(y_2^{(\infty)} - y_2^{(1)}\right) \Big/ \left(y_1^{(1)} - y_2^{(1)}\right),$$

(6.4)

given an initial difference of positions on an issue. Hence, the *change* in person i's attitude is a proportion of the discrepancy between person i's and person j's initial attitudes, and this proportion is equal to the *total* influence of person j upon person i: $y_i^{(\infty)} - y_i^{(1)} = v_{ij}\left(y_j^{(1)} - y_i^{(1)}\right)$. With this approach, our standard model includes, as a special case, the linear discrepancy model that has been employed in experimental work on target-source influence. If person 2 is the source and person 1 the target, then the total impact of the source on the target is $v_{12} = \left(y_1^{(\infty)} - y_1^{(1)}\right) / \left(y_2^{(1)} - y_1^{(1)}\right)$.

---

[1]   An influence network $\mathbf{AW}$ is strongly connected if i directly or indirectly influences j for all i and j.

Finally, we focus on the dyad because it presents a simple setting in which to assess whether the size of an initial difference of positions on an issue has an effect on interpersonal influence. Findings on the relationship between the distance between initial attitudes and the amount of attitude change have been inconsistent (Aronson, Turner, and Carlsmith 1963; Hovland 1959; Hovland and Pritzker 1957). Some studies indicate that the relationship is negative, some that it is positive, and others that it is curvilinear (∩ shaped), with interpersonal influence less likely for small or large distances than for intermediate distances. [2] We address this literature in dyads where both members may modify their attitudes, as opposed to the situation in which one member is taken by design as a source, with a fixed position on an issue, who may or may not influence a target.

6.1 Anchored and Unanchored Influence Systems

A detailed formal analysis of dyadic systems is presented in Appendix C. Here, we distinguish and focus on two substantively important types of dyadic influence networks, which we refer to as *anchored* and *unanchored* influence systems. Within the class of noncyclic influence networks in which at most one person is completely susceptible to interpersonal influence ($a_{ii} < 1$ and $a_{jj} \leq 1$), there are two important special cases. The first case arises when one member is not susceptible ($a_{ii} = 0$ and $a_{jj} \leq 1$). The second arises when both members are susceptible ($0 < a_{ii} < 1$ and $0 < a_{jj} \leq 1$). The former case includes the linear discrepancy model with a fixed source-position on an issue and a target that may be influenced by the source. The latter case pertains to a dyadic discussion of an issue in which neither member's position is fixed.

6.1.1 Anchored Systems

We define an anchored dyad as one in which $a_{ii} = 0$ and $a_{jj} \leq 1$. In the experimental literature on persuasion, stemming from the path-breaking work of Hovland et al. (1953), a common experimental design holds *constant* the initial attitude of one person (the source) and examines conditions under which the other person (the target) is influenced by the

---

[2] This literature includes negative relationships (Aronson, Turner, & Carlsmith 1963; Bochner & Insko 1966; Cohen 1959; Fisher & Lubin 1958; Hovland, Harvey, & Sherif 1957); positive relationships (Bergin 1967; Cohen 1959; Goldberg 1954; Greenwald 1966; Hovland & Pritzker 1957; Zimbardo 1960); and curvilinear relationships (Aronson, Turner, and Carlsmith 1963; Bochner and Insko 1966; Festinger 1954; Festinger and Aronson 1968; Hovland, Harvey, and Sherif 1957; Hovland, Janis, and Kelley 1953; Insko, Murashima, and Saiyadain 1966; Sherif, Sherif, and Nebergall 1965)

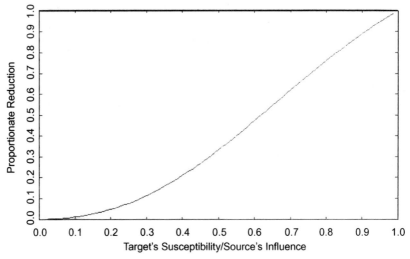

Figure 6.1 Reduction of attitude discrepancy in the linear discrepancy model.

source. Letting person 1 be the target of influence, the influence network that corresponds to this design is

$$\mathbf{W} = \begin{bmatrix} w_{11} & w_{12} \\ 0 & 1 \end{bmatrix} = \begin{bmatrix} 1 - a_{11} & a_{11} \\ 0 & 1 \end{bmatrix}$$

for $a_{11} < 1$. By design, person 1 has no influence on person 2, and the initial attitude of person 2 is fixed. What is problematic is the extent to which the target (person 1) moves toward the fixed position of the source (person 2). The equilibrium model for the transformation of the target's attitude on an issue is

$$y_1^{(\infty)} - y_1^{(1)} = v_{12} \left(y_2^{(1)} - y_1^{(1)} \right) \tag{6.5}$$

and, in the special case of a *fixed* attitude for the source, we can derive from (2.31)

$$v_{12} = \frac{a_{11} w_{12}}{1 - a_{11} w_{11}} = \frac{a_{11}^2}{1 - a_{11} + a_{11}^2}. \tag{6.6}$$

The change in the target's attitude is a proportion of the discrepancy between the initial positions of the target and the source, and here the value of the proportionate reduction is strictly a function of the susceptibility of the target.

Figure 6.1 plots the value of the proportionate reduction of the attitude discrepancy (6.6) as a function of the susceptibility of the target or the direct interpersonal weight of the source; they are identical values in the

dyad ($a_{ii} = 1 - w_{ii} = w_{ij}$). In accord with the linear discrepancy model
of attitude change, experimentally induced effects on the target's susceptibility, or the influence of the source, will be manifested by an approximately linear increase in the total influence of the source on the target,
above a baseline susceptibility of 0.30, and a corresponding reduction of
the initial attitudinal difference between the source and target (Chaiken,
Wood, and Eagly 1996; Mackie and Skelly 1994; Perloff 1993; Petty
and Cacioppo 1986a; Petty and Wegener 1997; Shavitt and Brock 1994).
Based on observed initial and equilibrium attitudes of the target, the susceptibility of person 1 (and interpersonal influence of person 2) may be
derived, as we have shown in Chapter 3.

6.1.2 Unanchored Systems

We define an unanchored dyad as a noncyclic system in which both members are susceptible to interpersonal influence, i.e., $0 < a_{ii} < 1$ and $0 <
a_{jj} \le 1$. The influence process for these systems includes cases in which
one person is moving toward the relatively fixed position of the other
member of a dyad (whose susceptibility is near zero). However, the
microdynamics of these systems also includes processes of greater complexity. A series of examples will illustrate the potential array of alternative ways in which equilibrium is attained in these systems. These
examples also illustrate that dyadic influence systems present some surprising features. In what follows, we denote the distance between the two
persons' positions on an issue at time t as $\delta^{(t)} = \left|y_2^{(t)} - y_1^{(t)}\right|$ for $t \ge 1$.

EXAMPLE 6.1. Not surprisingly, attitude differences are substantially
reduced when both a_{11} and a_{22} are high. For instance, when $a_{11} = 0.75$
and $a_{22} = 0.95$, i.e.,

$$\mathbf{W} = \begin{bmatrix} 0.25 & 0.75 \\ 0.95 & 0.05 \end{bmatrix},$$

there is fairly rapid convergence toward approximate agreement:

	$t=1$	$t=2$	$t=3$	$t=4$	$t=5$	$t=6$	$t=7$	$t=8$	...	$t=\infty$
$y_1^{(t)}$	0	0.563	0.160	0.346	0.189	0.245	0.180	0.193	...	0.106
$y_2^{(t)}$	1	0.098	0.562	0.221	0.373	0.239	0.283	0.226	...	0.153
$\delta^{(t)}$	1	0.465	0.402	0.125	0.184	0.006	0.103	0.033	...	0.047

Note: $a_{11} = 0.75$, $a_{22} = 0.95$, $\delta^{(t)} = |y_2^{(t)} - y_1^{(t)}|$.

Note that there are points during this process where the divergence of attitude has almost been eliminated (such as at $t = 6$) only to widen again.
The two attitudes are closer at $t = 6$ than they are at equilibrium, and the
equilibrium attitudes are substantially different from those that would be

Social Influence Network Theory

formed if the process were terminated at $t = 6$. If the dyadic interaction proceeded only to a point at which near agreement was reached, then such agreement would most likely be around 0.24. Also, note the "leapfrogging" of attitudes at the start of the process. When both susceptibilities are sufficiently large, the characteristic feature of the influence process in the dyad is a "leapfrogging" of attitudes in the early stages. However, it can be shown that if $y_i^{(1)} > y_j^{(1)}$, then $y_i^{(\infty)} > y_j^{(\infty)}$.

EXAMPLE 6.2. When both persons are near the maximum susceptibility, for example,

$$W = \begin{bmatrix} 0.01 & 0.99 \\ 0.99 & 0.01 \end{bmatrix},$$

the process will bring the positions of the persons into virtual agreement, but the convergence to equilibrium is slow, and the "leapfrogging" of attitudes occurs over extended time periods:

	$t=1$	$t=2$	$t=3$	$t=4$	$t=5$	$t=6$	$t=7$	$t=8$	$\ldots$	$t=\infty$
$y_1^{(t)}$	0	0.980	0.029	0.952	0.057	0.925	0.083	0.900	$\ldots$	0.497
$y_2^{(t)}$	1	0.020	0.971	0.048	0.943	0.075	0.917	0.100	$\ldots$	0.503
$\delta^{(t)}$	1	0.960	0.942	0.904	0.886	0.850	0.834	0.800	$\ldots$	0.006

Note: $a_{11} = 0.99$, $a_{22} = 0.99$, $\delta^{(t)} = |y_2^{(t)} - y_1^{(t)}|$.

EXAMPLE 6.3. Not surprisingly, if both susceptibilities are low ($a_{ii} << 1$), then the initial attitude difference will not be substantially reduced. For instance, when $a_{11} = a_{22} = 0.2$, i.e.,

$$W = \begin{bmatrix} 0.8 & 0.2 \\ 0.2 & 0.8 \end{bmatrix},$$

there is little change in the persons' attitudes:

	$t=1$	$t=2$	$t=3$	$t=4$	$t=5$	$t=6$	$t=7$	$t=8$	$\ldots$	$t=\infty$
$y_1^{(t)}$	0	0.040	0.045	0.045	0.045	0.045	0.045	0.045	$\ldots$	0.045
$y_2^{(t)}$	1	0.960	0.955	0.955	0.955	0.955	0.955	0.955	$\ldots$	0.955
$\delta^{(t)}$	1	0.920	0.910	0.910	0.910	0.910	0.910	0.910	$\ldots$	0.910

Note: $a_{11} = 0.20$, $a_{22} = 0.20$, $\delta^{(t)} = \left|y_2^{(t)} - y_1^{(t)}\right|$.

EXAMPLE 6.4. If each person accords equal weight to his or her own and the other's attitudes, then there is *immediate* convergence to a *nonconsensual* equilibrium with some movement of each person toward the other:

$$W = \begin{bmatrix} 0.5 & 0.5 \\ 0.5 & 0.5 \end{bmatrix}$$

gives

	$t=1$	$t=2$	$t=3$	$t=4$	$t=5$	$t=6$	$t=7$	$t=8$	...	$t=\infty$
$y_1^{(t)}$	0	0.250	0.250	0.250	0.250	0.250	0.250	0.250	...	0.250
$y_2^{(t)}$	1	0.750	0.750	0.750	0.750	0.750	0.750	0.750	...	0.750
$\delta^{(t)}$	1	0.500	0.500	0.500	0.500	0.500	0.500	0.500	...	0.500

Note: $a_{11} = 0.50$, $a_{22} = 0.50$, $\delta^{(t)} = \left| y_2^{(t)} - y_1^{(t)} \right|$.

EXAMPLE 6.5. Movement to equilibrium will be rapid when there is a sufficiently large *imbalance* in persons' susceptibilities to interpersonal influence. If there is one, and only one, person whose interpersonal influence is near its maximum value, then "leapfrogging" attitudes will not occur and there will be a rapid convergence of attitudes to an equilibrium that is close to the initial attitude of the heavily self-weighted person. For example, when $a_{11} = 0.90$, $a_{22} = 0.10$, and

$$\mathbf{W} = \begin{bmatrix} 0.10 & 0.90 \\ 0.10 & 0.90 \end{bmatrix},$$

we have

	$t=1$	$t=2$	$t=3$	$t=4$	$t=5$	$t=6$	$t=7$	$t=8$	...	$t=\infty$
$y_1^{(t)}$	0	0.810	0.875	0.886	0.889	0.889	0.889	0.889	...	0.889
$y_2^{(t)}$	1	0.990	0.997	0.998	0.999	0.999	0.999	0.999	...	0.999
$\delta^{(t)}$	1	0.180	0.122	0.112	0.110	0.110	0.110	0.110	...	0.110

Note: $a_{11} = 0.90$, $a_{22} = 0.10$, $\delta^{(t)} = \left| y_2^{(t)} - y_1^{(t)} \right|$.

In the class of noncyclic unanchored systems, consensus is approached when *either* of the two susceptibilities is near 1. That is, consensus is approached for *all* susceptibilities $0 < a_{ii} < 1$ of one member of the dyad if the susceptibility of the other member j is sufficiently close to 1. One highly accommodative member is required.

6.1.3 Two Special Cases of Unanchored Influence Systems

There are two special cases of unanchored systems that warrant attention because they are often treated in the literature on dyads. The first is a *peer system* in which the interpersonal influences are equal (Examples 6.2–6.4), and the second is a *status order* in which there is "agreement" on the relative influence of each member (Example 6.5).

Peer System. In a peer system each person attaches the same direct interpersonal influence to the other:

$$\mathbf{W} = \begin{bmatrix} 1-\alpha & \alpha \\ \alpha & 1-\alpha \end{bmatrix},$$

where $\alpha \equiv a_{11} = a_{22}$ with $0 \leq \alpha < 1$. The susceptibilities are homogenous, $\mathbf{W}$ is doubly stochastic, and the total interpersonal influences are equal:

$$v_{12} = v_{21} = \frac{\alpha^2}{1 - \alpha + 2\alpha^2}. \tag{6.7}$$

Hence, as $\alpha \to 1$, $v_{ij} \to 0.5$ and the influence process becomes one that produces consensus at the mean of the two persons' initial attitudes. Compare Examples 6.2–6.4 above.

Status Order. A status order is a special type of influence network in which each member accords the same rank order of influence to all the members of the group. Here we describe a homogeneous status order for the dyad, where each column of $\mathbf{W}$ is uniform:

$$\mathbf{W} = \begin{bmatrix} 1 - \alpha & \alpha \\ 1 - \alpha & \alpha \end{bmatrix},$$

where $\alpha \neq 0.5$ (Example 6.5). Here, the *interpersonal* influences (w_{12} and w_{21}) also are linked ($w_{21} = 1 - w_{12}$). The total interpersonal influences of the two members are

$$v_{12} = \frac{\alpha^3}{(1 - \alpha)^2 + \alpha^2}, \qquad v_{21} = \frac{(1 - \alpha)^3}{(1 - \alpha)^2 + \alpha^2}. \tag{6.8}$$

Surprisingly, $v_{12} \neq 1 - v_{21}$, which says that a homogeneous status order in $\mathbf{W}$ does not produce a homogeneous status order in $\mathbf{V}$, except in the extreme cases where α is 0 or 1.

6.1.4 Structural Dilemma in the Dyad

Here we compare dyads with larger systems that are comparable to the dyad in having *two* discrete initial positions on an issue. Figure 6.2 compares the predicted transformation of attitudes in dyads, triads, and tetrads in which there are only two initial positions that are shared by one or more persons; the number of persons in each position is indicated in the figure. For this comparison, we also assume that the susceptibilities and interpersonal influences of the members of each group are homogeneous:

$$\mathbf{W} = \begin{bmatrix} 1 - \alpha & \alpha \\ \alpha & 1 - \alpha \end{bmatrix} \quad \mathbf{W} = \begin{bmatrix} 1 - \alpha & \alpha/2 & \alpha/2 \\ \alpha/2 & 1 - \alpha & \alpha/2 \\ \alpha/2 & \alpha/2 & 1 - \alpha \end{bmatrix}$$

$$\mathbf{W} = \begin{bmatrix} 1 - \alpha & \alpha/3 & \alpha/3 & \alpha/3 \\ \alpha/3 & 1 - \alpha & \alpha/3 & \alpha/3 \\ \alpha/3 & \alpha/3 & 1 - \alpha & \alpha/3 \\ \alpha/3 & \alpha/3 & \alpha/3 & 1 - \alpha \end{bmatrix}.$$

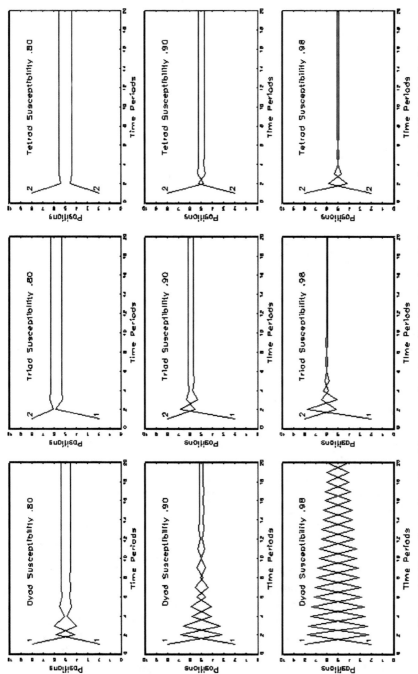

Figure 6.2 Transformation of positions over time in egalitarian dyads, triads, and tetrads with different levels of susceptibility to interpersonal influence.

147

For these networks, the separate graphs describe the transformation of the members' initial positions for different levels of susceptibility ($A = \alpha I$, $0 < \alpha < 1$ for α values of 0.80, 0.90, and 0.98).

Consensus is approached as the level of susceptibility increases, and it is attained relatively rapidly when group members' level of susceptibility is near its maximum, *except in the case of the dyad.* In a dyad with susceptibilities near 1, the distribution of influence in V is highly sensitive to small differences in the susceptibilities of the two members. Ironically, high mutual interpersonal influences are structural foundations for an inefficient chaotic resolution of disagreement. We suspect that this circumstance triggers frustration–aggression side effects (Berkowitz 1989). There is a rough reverse analogy with the Prisoner's Dilemma, where rational self-interest (lack of cooperation) produces difficulties. In the influence system of the dyad, high mutual accommodation (cooperation) produces difficulties. Rapid consensus in the dyad occurs to the extent that the interpersonal influences are substantially *different.* In the case of perfect dominance, $a_{ii} = 1$ and $a_{jj} = 0$, consensus is immediate. In groups larger than the dyad, high susceptibilities also may produce an inefficient process, but such inefficiency is not a *characteristic* feature of strongly connected (including complete) influence networks with high susceptibilities.

6.2 Findings on the Dyad

In this section, we present empirical findings on the sample dyads involved in the experiments. We have previously established (Tables 4.5–4.7) that our standard model predicts both the mean observed end-of-trial positions and the observed range of end-of-trial positions in dyads; moreover, we showed that the model's predictions of individual end-of-trial positions is relatively accurate, with a maximum percentage relative error of 11.4% on average. Here, we parse the predictions of the standard model. We probe the effects of initial attitude discrepancies on interpersonal influences and outcomes in dyads. We also probe effects of the dyad's influence network on the relative probabilities of different types of group outcomes. Finally, we probe features related to the efficiency of the influence process in dyads and the bearing of these features on the probability of outcomes that breach the convex hull of initial positions. In short, in all of the above, we employ the standard model as a theoretical guide to generate empirical analyses, which serve to shed light on the dyad as an influence system and to test specific predictions of our formalization. Note that in the dyad, with $a_{ii} = 1 - w_{ii}$, the relative direct influence of member j on i is perfectly confounded with i's susceptibility to influence, i.e., $a_{11} = w_{12}$ and $a_{22} = w_{21}$. Thus, in the findings to be presented, our empirical measure of a dyad's influence network is

$$\mathbf{W} = \begin{bmatrix} 1 - \tilde{a}_{11} & \tilde{a}_{11} \\ \tilde{a}_{22} & 1 - \tilde{a}_{22} \end{bmatrix},$$

where $\tilde{a}_{ii} = \sqrt{1 - \tilde{r}_{ii}}$ and $\tilde{r}_{ii}$ is the subjective self-weight that is reported by subject i on an issue trial.

6.2.1 Initial Attitude Differences and Interpersonal Influences

We have shown that for $\mathbf{A} \neq \mathbf{I}$ in the dyad, the *change* in person i's attitude is a proportion of the discrepancy between person i and person j's initial attitudes,

$$y_i^{(\infty)} - y_i^{(1)} = v_{ij} \left(y_j^{(1)} - y_i^{(1)} \right), \tag{6.9}$$

and that this proportion is equivalent to the total influence v_{ij} of j on i. In the dyad, $\mathbf{V}$ is strictly a function of the susceptibilities of the two members (a_{ii}, a_{jj}). Thus, from our theory, there is no reason to expect that v_{ij} need be the same as v_{ji}, and no reason to expect that a universal constant $0 < c < 1$ exists that governs attitude changes as follows $y_i^{(\infty)} - y_i^{(1)} = c(y_j^{(1)} - y_i^{(1)})$.

However, a relationship may exist between the initial *distance* between two persons' attitudes $\delta^{(1)} = \left| y_1^{(1)} - y_2^{(1)} \right|$ and their joint susceptibilities to interpersonal influence. In the dyad, two routes for the effect of $\delta^{(1)}$ are possible: it may affect the influence of j on i, i.e., w_{ij}, or the susceptibility of i, i.e., a_{ii}. But $a_{ii} = w_{ij}$ in the dyad; hence, the effect of $\delta^{(1)}$ will be the same by either route. Moreover, since $\delta^{(1)}$ is a contextual variable (i.e., a shared condition), it can only produce *different* levels of susceptibility for the two members of the dyad if it is responded to differently by each member. We examine the possibility that the initial distance $\delta^{(1)}$ has a main effect on $\mathbf{A}$, the members' susceptibilities, or equivalently, $\mathbf{W}$, the influence network, in dyads.

Among the 104 issue trials, 96 trials began with an initial difference of position on an issue. These are cases in which the initial position of one member is not fixed by design: both members' initial positions may change, neither members' initial positions may change, or only one member's initial position may change. The susceptibilities of the two members govern the outcomes. We find no significant correlation r of $\delta^{(1)}$ with either the mean, maximum, minimum, or absolute difference of the two members' susceptibilities (the r values are 0.030, 0.088, −0.022, and 0.082, respectively). These findings suggest that the influence networks constructed in dyads are independent of initial-position differences.

150   *Social Influence Network Theory*

Table 6.1 *Binary logistic regression of achieved consensus on maximum susceptibility and range of initial positions in a dyad (standard errors in parentheses)*

Variables	Coefficients	
	LPress	HPress
$\max(\tilde{a}_{11}, \tilde{a}_{22})$	10.181**	6.264*
	(3.762)	(2.759)
$\delta^{(1)} = \left| \tilde{y}_1^{(1)} - \tilde{y}_2^{(1)} \right|$	−0.070**	−0.001
	(0.025)	(0.020)
Constant	−6.381*	−3.693†
	(2.668)	(2.210)
−2LL	50.306	42.679
N	51	45

Notes: In these models, the addition of a quadratic term, $[\delta^{(1)}]^2 = \left| \tilde{y}_1^{(1)} - \tilde{y}_2^{(1)} \right|^2$, provides a marginal ($p < 0.10$) indication of a curvilinear association under the low-pressure condition and no indication of such an association under the high-pressure condition. This analysis is based on 96 issue trials, which excludes 8 dyads with an initial consensus.
†$p < 0.10$; *$p < 0.05$; **$p < 0.01$; ***$p < 0.001$.

6.2.2 Consensus Formation

Given an initial attitude discrepancy, reaching consensus is theoretically consistent only with $\max(a_{11}, a_{22})$ near 1. Table 6.1 elaborates the analysis of dyads presented in Table 5.2. The probability of achieved consensus increases with $\max(a_{11}, a_{22})$ among dyads, controlling for the range of initial positions on an issue $\delta^{(1)}$, under conditions of both high and low pressure to reach consensus. As in Table 5.2, $\delta^{(1)}$ is negatively associated with achieved consensus under low pressure to achieve consensus and not associated with achieved consensus under high pressure. Some influence network emerges on the issue, and to the extent that the maximum accorded influence is high in this network, the formation of a consensus becomes more likely.

The asymmetry of accorded influence within each dyad should be associated with the likelihood of reaching consensus on one of the *initial* attitudes of the two persons, versus a compromise consensus, breaching consensus, or unsettled disagreement. The logistic regression in Table 6.2 shows this association, controlling for the range of initial positions. The dependent variable is achieved consensus on an initial position or not, and the independent variable is the absolute difference between the subjects' accorded interpersonal influence, i.e., $|a_{11} - a_{22}| = |w_{12} - w_{21}|$. Because this measure of asymmetry may vary from 0 to 1, the findings indicate that the probability of achieved consensus on an initial position

Table 6.2 *Binary logistic regression of achieved consensus on an initial position in a dyad on the absolute difference between subjects' accorded interpersonal influences and range of initial positions (standard errors in parentheses)*

	Coefficients	
Variables	LPress	HPress
$\lvert \bar{a}_{11} - \bar{a}_{22} \rvert$	3.768*	7.323**
	(1.872)	(2.455)
$\delta^{(1)} = \left\lvert \bar{y}_1^{(1)} - \bar{y}_2^{(1)} \right\rvert$	−0.153**	−0.111*
	(0.055)	(0.053)
Constant	0.032	−2.986*
	(0.875)	(1.345)
−2LL	32.220	−17.089
N	51	45

Notes: In the dyad, $\lvert \bar{a}_{11} - \bar{a}_{22} \rvert = \lvert \bar{w}_{12} - \bar{w}_{21} \rvert$. In these models, the addition of a quadratic term, $[\delta^{(1)}]^2 = \lvert \bar{y}_1^{(1)} - \bar{y}_2^{(1)} \rvert^2$, provides a marginal ($p < 0.10$) indication of a curvilinear association under the low-pressure condition and no indication of such an association under the high-pressure condition. This analysis is based on 96 issue trials, which excludes 8 dyads with an initial consensus. $^{\dagger}p < 0.10$; $^*p < 0.05$; $^{**}p < 0.01$; $^{***}p < 0.001$.

is increased dramatically from a condition of perfect symmetry to a condition of perfect asymmetry. Here, controlling for a feature of the influence network, the greater the initial distance between two persons, the lower the odds of achieved consensus on an initial position under both low and high pressure to achieve consensus.

Table 6.3 restricts the analysis to 46 issue trials in which a nonbreaching consensus was achieved. Twenty-eight of these dyads achieved consensus on a compromise position and 18 on an initial position. Table 6.3 shows that the odds of achieved consensus on a compromise position relative to the odds of achieved consensus on an initial position increases with the extent of the initial attitude discrepancy. Reaching consensus is theoretically consistent only with max (a_{11}, a_{22}) near 1, and reaching consensus on an *initial* position is most consistent with asymmetrical influence $\lvert a_{11} - a_{22} \rvert$. Thus, the occurrence of achieved consensus on an initial position should be negatively associated with min (a_{11}, a_{22}) and positively associated with $\lvert a_{11} - a_{22} \rvert$. Table 6.3 shows that is the case. The two susceptibility measures, min (a_{11}, a_{22}) and $\lvert a_{11} - a_{22} \rvert$, are strongly correlated ($r = -0.908, p < 0.001$) and are analyzed separately. The range of initial positions is not associated with either susceptibility measure: $r = 0.210$ ($p = 0.162$) and $r = 0.003$ ($p = 0.985$) for min (a_{11}, a_{22}) and

Table 6.3 *Binary logistic regressions of achieved consensus on an initial position versus achieved consensus on a compromise position in a dyad on the range of initial positions, minimum susceptibility, and range of susceptibilities (standard errors in parentheses)*

	Coefficients		
Variables	Model 1	Model 2	Model 3
$\delta^{(1)} = \left| \tilde{y}_1^{(1)} - \tilde{y}_2^{(1)} \right|$	−0.099***	−0.203**	−0.321**
	(0.031)	(0.090)	(0.125)
$\min (\tilde{a}_{11}, \tilde{a}_{22})$		−15.087**	
		(7.858)	
$\left| a_{11} - a_{22} \right|$			14.787***
			(5.645)
Constant	1.657*	10.877**	0.199
	(0.671)	(4.048)	(1.070)
−2LL	44.388	16.381	16.131

Notes: This analysis is based on 46 issue trials on nonbreaching consensus and excludes dyads with an initial consensus. Twenty-eight of these dyads achieved consensus on a compromise position and 18 on an initial position. *p < 0.05; **p < 0.01; ***p < 0.001.

abs $(a_{11} - a_{22})$, respectively. We also find that, controlling for features of the influence network, the greater the initial distance between two persons, the lower the odds of achieved consensus on an initial position, and the larger the odds of a compromise consensus.

Figure 6.3 displays a bar chart of the distribution of distances of achieved consensus values from the mean initial positions for the 28 dyads that reached consensus on a compromise attitude that was within the range of their initial attitudes. Our formal analysis of the dyad (Appendix C) shows that for unanchored influence systems, consensus can only be approached, and the approach for $\mathbf{A} \to \mathbf{I}$ is to a weighted mean of the members' initial attitudes. We also show that if the susceptibilities of the two members are equal, $a_{11} = a_{22}$, then for $\mathbf{A} \to \mathbf{I}$ the approach will be to a consensus that is the mean initial position on an issue,

$$\mathbf{V} \approx \begin{bmatrix} 0.5 & 0.5 \\ 0.5 & 0.5 \end{bmatrix} \Rightarrow \mathbf{y}^{(\infty)} \approx \begin{bmatrix} \dfrac{\left(y_1^{(1)} + y_2^{(1)} \right)}{2} \\ \dfrac{\left(y_1^{(1)} + y_2^{(1)} \right)}{2} \end{bmatrix}, \qquad (6.10)$$

and that the maximum distance that either member has to travel to reach consensus is minimized. However, the travel time may be lengthy. The bar chart indicates that when a compromise consensus is reached, the

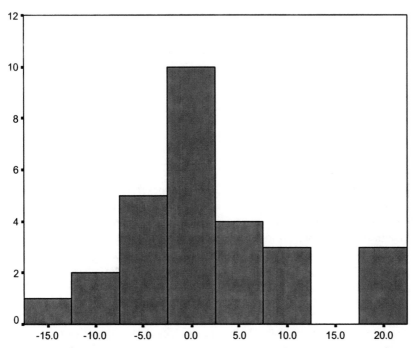

Figure 6.3 Distribution of the distance of achieved consensus values from the mean initial positions among dyads that reached consensus on a compromise position within the range of their initial positions.

achieved consensus value is within ±5 of the mean initial position of the group members for 19 of the 28 groups. The particular compromise consensus value that was achieved in a dyad is significantly correlated with the mean initial attitude of the two members ($r = 0.890, p < 0.001$). Regressing the achieved consensus value on the mean initial position, the estimated regression line has an estimated intercept that does not significantly differ from 0 ($p = 0.314$) and a slope of 0.916 ($p < 0.001$), for which the 95% confidence interval [0.727, 1.104] is consistent with the theory.

6.2.3 Efficiency of the Influence Process

Table 6.4 reports the mean observed times the dyads required to reach a consensus or irreconcilable disagreement on the issues. The observed time to end of trial is significantly less for achieved consensus within the range of initial positions than for the other outcomes ($t = -2.223$, $df = 102$, $p = 0.028$, two-tailed). Based on our formal analysis of the dyad, in the production of consensus we expect dominance structures (evidenced by one person adopting the initial position of the other person) to be more

Table 6.4 *Mean observed times (minutes) to end of trial in dyads*

	N	Mean	Std. dev.
Consensus on boundary initial position	23	4.57	2.97
Consensus on new internal position	28	6.96	6.45
Disagreement within range of initials	35	8.29	5.65
Consensus outside range of initials	10	7.70	4.57
Disagreement outside range of initials	8	8.13	3.64
TOTAL	104	7.04	5.30

efficient than compromise structures (evidenced by the joint movement of the two members to a new position in the range of initial positions). Consistent with this expectation, we find that the production of consensus is significantly more rapid in the cases where it involves a settlement on a boundary initial attitude than in the cases where it involves a settlement on a compromise within the range of initial attitudes on an issue ($t = -1.754$, $df = 39.47$, $p = 0.044$, one-tailed test with unequal variances). Our theory suggests that achieving a compromise consensus in the dyad may be a slow (frustrating) process. Indeed, we find that the mean time to reach compromise consensus does not significantly differ from the mean time to acknowledge an *irreconcilable disagreement* within the range of initial attitudes ($t = -0.865$, $df = 61$, $p = 0.390$, two-tailed). The same findings are obtained with a regression of the observed time to end of trial on two dummy variables, indicating the occurrence of consensus on a boundary position and a compromise position within the range of initial positions. Relative to the baseline (disagreeing and breaching groups) issue resolution is significantly more rapid among dyads whose members settle on a boundary initial position; groups that reach a compromise consensus do not significantly differ from the baseline.[3]

6.2.4 High Susceptibilities and Breaches

We have argued that high mutual susceptibilities in the dyad create a social dilemma—a tradeoff between an efficient formation of consensus,

---

[3] With respect to the 28 dyads that achieved consensus on a compromise position (Figure 6.3), it might be hypothesized that compromises different from the mean initial position take longer to reach than do compromises that settle on this value. However, such a hypothesis is based on slight differences in a_{11} and a_{22} near 1. It would be surprising to find an association between the observed time to end of trial and the distance of the consensus attitude from the mean initial position, and we found none. Although our theory is formally consistent with a compromise consensus that is not the mean of the members' initial attitudes, it does not provide a detailed account of the variation in time to end of trial with which such compromises are reached. What we can conclude with some confidence is that compromise consensus is less efficiently reached than consensus on an initial position.

Table 6.5 *Binary logistic regression of the occurrence of breaches in dyads on minimum susceptibility (standard errors in parentheses)*

Variables	Consensus pressure	
	High	Low
min $(\tilde{a}_{11}, \tilde{a}_{22})$	10.595**	−1.412
	(3.933)	(1.542)
Constant	−7.456**	−1.413*
	(2.591)	(0.595)
−2LL	34.331	40.216
N	52	52

Notes: This analysis is based on 104 issue-trials.
*$p < 0.05$; **$p < 0.01$; ***$p < 0.001$.

based on an asymmetrical influence network that is likely to take one of the initial positions of the two members as the consensus of the group, and an inefficient formation of consensus, based on a mutual accommodation that is likely to produce a compromise agreement. This dilemma should be especially pronounced when group members value the achievement of consensus. In the absence of such a value, the group may resolve the dilemma with an end-of-trial disagreement. Table 6.5 shows that the probability of breaching the convex hull of initial positions on an issue increases with the minimum susceptibility min (a_{11}, a_{22}) of dyads under high pressure to reach consensus and is unrelated to the min (a_{11}, a_{22}) of dyads under low pressure to reach consensus. The findings suggest that the probability of such breaches is affected by features of the influence process unfolding in dyads with two superaccommodative members. Our standard model of this influence process points to the unusual features of an influence process in dyads with such members.

6.2.5 Derived susceptibilities in the dyad

We conclude our findings with a consideration of derived susceptibility values that, in turn, completely specify a derived influence network in the dyad. Given an observed equilibrium (end-of-trial) disagreement in a dyad, $\tilde{y}_i^{(\infty)} \neq \tilde{y}_j^{(\infty)}$, we can formally derive A on the basis of (C.8)

$$\frac{a_{ii}^2}{1 - a_{ii}} = \frac{y_i^{(\infty)} - y_i^{(1)}}{y_j^{(\infty)} - y_i^{(\infty)}}.$$

In dyads, these derived susceptibilities provide an optimal and strictly *behavioral* measure of the influence network consistent with our model,

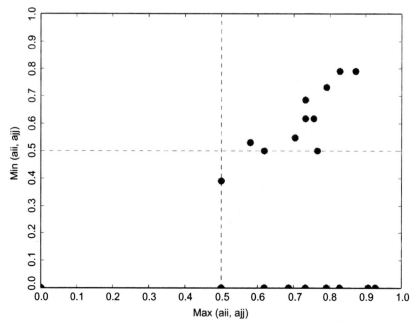

Figure 6.4 Derived susceptibilities for dyads with end-of-trial disagreement.

since the susceptibilities for the dyad are based exclusively on the observed initial and final attitudes of the two members. Figure 6.4 displays the derived susceptibilities $\hat{\mathbf{A}}$ for the 35 issue trials among dyads on which the outcome is an end-of-trial disagreement within the range of two persons' initial attitudes. Each point represents one or more group trials in which consensus was not reached; the x-axis is the max $(\hat{a}_{ii}, \hat{a}_{jj})$ in the dyad, and the y-axis is the min $(\hat{a}_{ii}, \hat{a}_{jj})$ in the dyad.

The influence networks of these 35 dyads break neatly into three types. First, there are 9 networks in which neither member was susceptible to the influence of the other and, therefore, no change of attitude occurred:

$$\hat{\mathbf{W}} = \begin{bmatrix} 1 & 0 \\ 0 & 1 \end{bmatrix}.$$

Second, there are 13 networks in which one member was not susceptible to influence and the other was, with susceptibilities ranging from 0.5 to 0.928. In these networks, there was some movement of the susceptible member toward the fixed position of the unsusceptible member:

$$\hat{\mathbf{W}} = \begin{bmatrix} 1 - \hat{a}_{11} & 0.500 \leq \hat{a}_{11} \leq 0.928 \\ 0 & 1 \end{bmatrix}.$$

Third, there are 13 networks in which both members are susceptible to influence, with the maximum susceptibilities ranging from 0.5 to 0.873 and the minimum susceptibilities ranging from 0.39 to 0.791. In no case are the two susceptibilities equal; hence, in every case there was some movement of the more susceptible member toward the position of the less susceptible member:

$$\hat{\mathbf{W}} = \begin{bmatrix} 1 - \hat{a}_{11} & 0.500 \le \hat{a}_{11} \le 0.873 \\ 0.390 \le \hat{a}_{22} \le 0.791 & 1 - \hat{a}_{22} \end{bmatrix}.$$

Where both persons are susceptible, the difference between the two persons' susceptibilities is, with one exception, less than 0.155: in four networks $0.037 \le |\hat{a}_{11} - \hat{a}_{22}| \le 0.059$, in seven networks $0.082 \le |\hat{a}_{11} - \hat{a}_{22}| \le 0.118$, and in the other two networks the difference is 0.154 and 0.266. The two members' susceptibilities tend to increase together toward the limit of $\mathbf{A} = \mathbf{I}$. If persons are susceptible, then they are moderately to strongly susceptible to interpersonal influence, and their susceptibilities are reciprocated in the sense of being approximately comparable in level. Since attitudes were measured in units of 0.05, these results are affected by that scaling, which may account for the clumping of the $|\hat{a}_{11} - \hat{a}_{22}|$ values around 0.05 and 0.10.

Our subjects either were not susceptible to influence or were susceptible at moderate to high levels. The choice to accommodate another having been made, the level of susceptibility may vary for reasons that we do not address here. Once the conditions for an interpersonal influence process have been established (i.e., some susceptibility), inequality of influence is a characteristic feature of the influence system. The main distinguishing feature between the influence structure of these equilibrium-disagreement dyads, versus those in which consensus was reached, is that the $\max(a_{ii}, a_{jj})$ susceptibility in the dyad is not near 1. A $\max(a_{ii}, a_{jj})$ value near 1 is a condition for an approximate consensus in the dyad.

6.3 Concluding Remarks

We have noted that in dyads, unlike our larger groups, there is a noteworthy frequency of "breaching" behavior, in which one or both group members settle on a position that is more extreme than either of the initial positions of the two members. We think that these occurrences arise in part from "frustration–aggression" sequences in dyads, produced by high mutual interpersonal influences, in which each person is over-accommodating the other and both are involved in an enervating effort to form an agreement. When two persons "leapfrog" past one another, they have abandoned their positions only to discover that they need not have done so. But having abandoned their positions, they may find it awkward to resume them and, hence, the circumstance in which they find themselves may cause frustration. Because only two persons are involved in the influence system, a field of uncertainty is generated in which there are no legitimate (socially supported) initial attitudes, and the inefficiency of high symmetrical interpersonal influences is likely to generate strains as time drags on without substantial progress toward an agreement. In the dyad, there is no comforting rationale for such difficulties. In larger groups, any difficulties encountered may be attributed to the "complexity of the situation" in which three or more different positions on an issue are being adjudicated. Our argument is that the influence process is the *same* in dyads as in larger groups, and it generates internal dilemmas and strains in the dyad that are not as often found in larger groups.

This analysis of the dyad bears on Newcomb's (1953) A–B–X system, consisting of two persons (A and B) who have favorable (+) or unfavorable (–) attitudes toward an object (X), which could be an event, person, object, or issue, and who also have positive (+) or negative (–) attractions toward each other. Following Heider (1946), Newcomb argues that there is a "strain toward symmetry" or balance in such systems and that a change in any of the four relations, if it disrupts balance, lead to changes in one or more of the other relations in order to restore balance. Given a disagreement on X, Newcomb describes various resolutions that include changes of attitude, interpersonal attraction, and distortions of these attitudes and attractions:

> As a result of repeatedly facing and "solving" problems of co-orientation with regard to a given B and a given X, a relatively stable equilibrium is established. If A is free either to continue or not to continue his association with B, one of two eventual outcomes is likely: (a) he achieves an equilibrium characterized by relatively great attraction toward B and by relatively high perceived symmetry [agreement], and the association is continued; or (b) he achieves an equilibrium characterized by relatively little attraction toward B and by relatively low perceived symmetry, and the association is discontinued.

Thus, Newcomb's perspective describes two equilibrium states for dyads in face-to-face interaction: (1) a positive mutual orientation and agreement or (2) a negative mutual orientation and disagreement.

Newcomb's balance perspective does not comfortably accommodate *stable* positive interpersonal relationships in which there are ongoing disagreements, of which some are resolved by the achievement of agreement and others remain unresolved. Disagreements are ongoing in stable interpersonal relationships, and persons cope with them in various ways. Newcomb's perspective also does not comfortably accommodate markedly asymmetrical interpersonal influences. One person may be dominant in a dyad, in which case all disputes will be resolved in favor of that person, or domination may switch depending on the issue. A stable asymmetry may be based on a person A who has a strong positive orientation toward a person B, and B with a neutral (or even negative) orientation toward A. An influential need not respect, like, or be attracted to the persons he or she influences.

In closing, we emphasize that our analysis of the dynamics of isolated dyadic influence systems is not applicable to dyads embedded in larger ($n > 2$) networks of interpersonal influences. It suffices to note that the occurrence of flows of interpersonal influence in $n > 2$ systems can make the relationship between observed attitude changes and interpersonal influence complex. In larger groups it cannot be assumed that the similarity of two persons' equilibrium attitudes is indicative of a strong interpersonal influence between them, because such similarity could have been produced by the influence of other persons. For instance, in the simple triadic influence system where

$$\mathbf{W} = \begin{bmatrix} 0 & 0.20 & 0.80 \\ 0.20 & 0 & 0.80 \\ 0 & 0 & 1 \end{bmatrix} \quad \text{and} \quad \mathbf{y}^{(1)} = \begin{bmatrix} 0 \\ 0.5 \\ 1 \end{bmatrix},$$

the predicted development of settled attitudes is

	$t=2$	$t=3$	$t=4$	$t=5$	...	$t=\infty$
$y_1^{(t)}$	0.900	0.960	0.996	0.998	...	1
$y_2^{(t)}$	0.800	0.980	0.992	0.999	...	1
$y_3^{(t)}$	1	1	1	1	...	1

Persons 1 and 2, who are not responding strongly to one another, both come to hold the attitude of person 3. The interpersonal effects of all persons who influence two persons must be taken into account in order to obtain confident conclusions about the origins of two persons' interpersonal agreement.

7

Social Comparison Theory

We have seen that the smallest group – the dyad – presents nontrivial features of the influence process when both members of the dyad are influencing each other. The special case of a dyad with a source, who holds a fixed position on an issue, and a target, who may be influenced by the source, is a simple special case within a larger theoretical domain of possible influence networks that may occur in the dyad. When a group is enlarged by one member – the triad – the theoretical domain of possible influence networks also is enlarged. Now three persons may be mutually influencing one another on an issue, the interpersonal influences on each member may not be identical, and the susceptibilities of each member to attitude change also may not be identical. Festinger's (1954) theory of social comparison processes is a seminal attempt to develop a theory about the influence networks of groups that is applicable to the triad and larger influence systems.

Festinger's theory focused on the effects of the distribution of group members' initial attitudes, and members' positions in those distributions, upon the network of interpersonal influences among group members. The theory triggered a large and still unsettled literature. Despite the classic status of social comparison theory, most of the empirical work on the theory has not directly dealt with Festinger's key propositions concerning the effects of group members' initial positions on an issue (Goethals and Darley 1977; Latané 1966; Suls and Miller 1977; Suls, Martin, and Wheeler 2000; Suls and Wills 1991; Wood 1989). Roughly ten years after the theory was proposed, Singer (1966: 104) wrote:

> The fate of social comparison theory has been grimly depicted and in one sense unfairly so. For while there have been no direct studies stemming from the theory, several investigators have extended the theory and productively explored the extensions. . . . Yet despite the work it invigorated, social comparison

160

theory has not been well documented nor have its tenets been placed on a firm footing.

Twenty years after this assessment, Jones (1985: 69) concluded that still little progress had been made:

> The theory certainly spawned research, yet many of its postulates and propositions have proved relatively intractable or exceedingly difficult to confirm. The issues raised by social comparison theory will be with us for a long time, but progress toward their solutions seems sporadic and generally indirect.

The situation remains the same today. In this chapter we describe social comparison theory and examine the merits of two formal models (Davis 1996; McGarty et al. 1992) that, in line with social comparison theory, draw exclusively on group members' arrays of initial attitudes to predict the consensus positions that emerge from an initial disagreement. We find that neither model presents a contribution to the prediction of the consensus positions of groups that is superior to the baseline prediction of a consensus on the mean of the group members' initial positions.

Based on this and additional analysis presented in this chapter, we conclude that influence networks are not, in general, strongly constrained by the initial positions of group members on an issue. Numerous factors enter into the formation of the influence networks in which the attitude change process unfolds, which make any emphasis on initial positions theoretically problematic. To be sure, there are special cases of initial attitude distributions that do importantly constrain a group's influence network and the outcomes of the group's influence process. However, within a broad spectrum of initial distributions of positions on issues, most initial distributions of positions do not constrain the influence networks of the groups. In groups with members who value the achievement of consensus, susceptibilities to interpersonal influence may be elevated independent of the distribution of initial attitudes; an implication of such independence is that the initial distances between group members may only weakly constrain the movements of group members' attitudes toward particular consensus positions. Our conclusion is that explanations of the attitudinal outcomes of issue discussions in small groups are substantially advanced with the employment of direct measures of groups' influence networks.

7.1 Social Comparison Hypotheses

The idea that persons' initial positions on issues affect their susceptibilities and interpersonal influences appears in a literature that is surprisingly large. Besides Festinger's seminal analysis of this idea, it has been addressed in persuasion research on dyadic influence systems (Anderson and Hovland 1957; French 1956; Hovland and Pritzker 1957) and in the literature on conformity, where a person is faced with a fixed unanimous attitude of others that is some distance from his or her own initial attitude (Asch 1951). It appears in social judgment theory (Sherif et al. 1965; Sherif and Hovland 1961), where persons who hold sufficiently extreme attitudes in the distribution of initial attitudes in a group are hypothesized to be less susceptible to interpersonal influence and more influential than persons who hold moderate attitudes on an issue. It appears in self-categorization theory (Turner 1991; Turner and Oakes 1989), where it is hypothesized that persons are influential to the extent that their positions are central or "prototypical" in the distribution of initial attitudes. It is the foundation of social decision scheme theory (Davis 1973; Stasser et al. 1989), where the initial distribution of attitudes (in combination with a rule for combining these attitudes) determines the group's decision on an issue, and Davis's (1996) extension of this approach. More broadly, the idea has been incorporated into formal work on interpersonal influence processes, for instance, in Abelson (1964: 143). We see all of this literature as falling into the domain of hypotheses described by Festinger's (1954) social comparison theory.

7.1.1 Distance between Attitudinal Positions

Festinger (1954) presented the following hypotheses about who a person will select for comparison:

> The tendency to compare oneself with some other specific person decreases as the difference between his attitude... and one's own increases. (p. 120)

> Given a range of possible persons for comparison, someone close to one's own... opinion will be chosen for comparison. (p. 121)

> If the only comparison available is a very divergent one, the person will not be able to make a subjectively precise evaluation of his [own] opinion.... (p. 121)

> When a discrepancy exists with respect to opinions... there will be tendencies to cease comparing oneself with those in the group who are very different from oneself. (p. 126)

We assume that comparison is based on the visibility of another's attitude and the according of some weight to it. Thus, the basic hypothesis is that as the difference between two persons' attitudes increases, the amount of direct influence $(a_{ii}w_{ij})$ of one attitude upon the other declines. It is unclear whether the proposed effect of distance is on susceptibility (a_{ii}), or the relative influence of one person on another (w_{ij}), or both ($a_{ii}w_{ij}$). It also is unclear whether an inability "to make a subjectively precise evaluation" fosters low or high self-weight ($w_{ii} = 1 - a_{ii}$). Festinger's hypothesis on modal positions and extremity (below) suggests that such inability fosters susceptibility.

7.1.2 Modal, Central, and Extreme Attitudinal Positions

A closely related set of hypotheses posits that persons with modal or central positions on an issue are more self-weighted and more influential than persons who hold less supported or extreme (peripheral) positions. Typically, the relative location of an issue-position (its modality or extremity) is defined in terms of the distribution of initial attitudes in a group, although it could be based on the distribution of initial attitudes in the larger population or on an absolute scale of possible attitudes. We review and discuss work related to the effects of modal, central, and extreme positions with respect to an issue on persons' susceptibilities and interpersonal influences.

Modal Positions. Festinger (1954) hypothesizes that persons who occupy modal positions are more resistant to change and more influential than persons who occupy less supported positions. Modal positions may or may not be near the mean of initial attitudes in a group, and they may or may not be "moderate" positions. We take Festinger's term *mode* to be the unique value of a distribution with the highest frequency, providing such a value exists. Not all distributions have a mode under this definition. In a triad, the mode is the shared position of two persons or all three. In large groups, there may be multiple shared positions, one of which may be the mode. It is probably important to distinguish between the effect of a modal position, and of a shared position that is not modal, on the occupants' and nonoccupants' susceptibilities and influences. Presumably, modal positions are emphasized by Festinger because such positions are validated by their occupants' agreement to a greater degree than a uniquely occupied position, or other shared positions, or a mean position that is unoccupied by group members.

Festinger proposes that persons who are close to the *modal* attitude of their group will differ from persons who are far from the modal attitude in terms of their influence on others and their susceptibility to attitude change:

> Specifically, those close to the mode of the group will have stronger tendencies to change the positions of others, relatively weaker tendencies to narrow the range of comparison and much weaker tendencies to change their own position compared to those who are distant from the mode of the group. (pp. 134–5)

The idea appears to be that persons who are close to the mode are more influential, more self-weighted, and more likely to assess a wider range of attitudes (although presumably according them low weight) than persons who are distant from the mode. Festinger's hypothesis also leaves open the question of how populated (in absolute or relative numbers) a modal position has to be in order to have effects. Confidence in one's attitude and resistance to change are increased given the belief or discovery that the attitude is shared by others (Brodbeck, 1956; Goethals, 1972; Goethals and Nelson, 1973; Gordon, 1966; Johnson, 1940; Kelley, 1955; Kelley and Volkart, 1952; Luus and Wells, 1994; Radloff, 1961). A shared position per se, whether it is modal or not, also might serve to validate the occupants' initial positions and increase their self-weight.

Festinger's hypothesis suggests that persons who are distant from the mode of the group are less influential, more likely to restrict their accord of influence to neighboring positions, and more susceptible to interpersonal influence than persons who are near the mode. However, if the distance between a peripheral position and its "nearest neighbor" is sufficiently large, then the influence of the "nearest neighbor" on the peripheral position should be low, and vice versa. But Festinger's hypothesis suggests that the inability "to make a subjectively precise evaluation" fosters a susceptibility to interpersonal influence that tends to be restricted to neighboring positions regardless of the distance separating them.

Festinger's hypothesis about the strength of modal positions appears in social decision scheme theory (Davis, 1973; Stasser et al., 1989) in the form of a "strength in numbers" hypothesis. In social decision scheme theory, the probability and direction of attitude changes are based on the relative sizes of the factions in a group, where each faction is composed of the adherents to a particular attitude position in the distribution of initial attitudes. Kerr (1992: 90) finds that a majority faction (i.e., the modal attitude) is more likely to persuade a minority faction when the distance between the two factions is small rather than large. Latané's (1981) social impact theory also emphasizes that *ceteris paribus* the strength of interpersonal influence is positively related to the number of persons sharing a particular position on an issue and negatively related to the distance between different positions.

Central Positions. Recently, in a variant of social decision scheme theory, Davis (1996) has hypothesized that the relative influence of a group member depends on the centrality of that person's initial position in the distribution of initial attitudes. Self-categorization theory (Turner et al. 1987; Turner and Oakes 1989) also proposes that central positions are more influential than peripheral positions:

> The prototypicality of in-group members is defined by means
> of the *meta-contrast principle* (Turner, 1985): the less a person

differs from in-group members and the more he or she differs from out-group members, the more representative is he or she of the in-group. Thus the prototype is the position which best defines what the group has in common *in contrast to other relevant out-groups.* ... The most consensual, normative position is understood both as a defining categorical property of the group prior to interaction and as the position on which members converge through social interaction. (McGarty et al. 1992: 3)

The out-group positions on an issue that enter into the definition of the prototypical in-group position are all those discrete initial positions on the attitude scale for the issue that are endorsed by some member of the out-group. It is the distribution of initial attitudes of both the in-group and out-group that determines which attitude is the most prototypical in the in-group:

The direction of effective influence within the group (who successfully influences whom) is a function of the relative persuasiveness of the members, which is based on the degree to which their response (their arguments, position, attributes, experience, role, etc.) is perceived as prototypical of the initial distribution of responses of the group as a whole, i.e., the degree of relative consensual support for a member. (Turner et al. 1987: 74)

Hence, self-categorization theory permits the central (prototypical or normative) attitude to be *any* position in the range of the in-group members' initial attitudes, depending on the out-group frame of reference; e.g., a prototypical position could be a modal attitude (as Festinger's hypothesis stipulates), or the mean initial attitude of the members of the in-group, or it could be one of the more *extreme* attitudes of the in-group.

Extreme Positions. According to social comparison theory, persons who occupy positions distant from the modal position of their group are *less* influential and *more* susceptible to interpersonal influence than persons who occupy positions near the group's modal position. But other investigators have argued that persons who hold extreme positions are likely to be more *resistant* to attitude change than persons who hold moderate positions because extremity implies a greater independence of thought, greater confidence, or greater attitude strength.[1] Baron et al. (1996) argue that when persons voice an extreme position, they recognize that their attitude could be the focus of scrutiny, criticism and even ridicule; hence,

[1] For independence of thought see (Abelson, 1964; Ferguson, 1971; Kelley and Kerr, 1992; Levinger and Schneider, 1969; Marquis, 1962; Sherif and Hovland, 1961; Tannenbaum, 1956), for confidence see (Allport and Hartman, 1925; Johnson, 1940; Kelley and Lamb, 1957; Suchman, 1950), and for attitude strength see (Cantril 1946a; Cantril 1946b; Hutchinson 1949; Riland 1959; Weksel and Hennes 1965).

they voice such a position only if they are committed to it.[2] Thus, moderate positions are more likely to be voiced than extreme positions when persons are uncertain or indifferent. A moderate position on an issue need not be the modal position of the group, but when it is, the members of a moderate modal position may be, contrary to Festinger's hypothesis, *less* resistant to attitude change than the members of more extreme positions.

Also contrary to Festinger's hypothesis, it has been argued that the holders of extreme positions are not only more resistant but also *more* influential than the holders of moderate positions (Baron et al. 1996). If moderate attitudes are based on uncertainty or indifference, then persons in moderate modal positions are more likely to accommodate persons who have strongly held extreme positions. Moreover, if there is a strong pressure to reach consensus and, despite this pressure, the holder of an extreme position is resistant to attitude change, then the more moderate members of the group (who are uncertain or indifferent) are likely to accommodate an extreme position. Festinger argues (see below) that pressures to uniformity do the opposite – inhibit the potential influence of extreme positions.

7.2 Contingencies, Interactions, and Scope Conditions

Festinger and others have postulated that the *relationship* between attitude discrepancies and interpersonal influence is affected by variables that are *not* features of the distribution of initial attitudes on an issue. Variables that affect the strength or sign of the relationship may be viewed as detailing the scope conditions of social comparison theory. We describe here some of contingencies that have been raised thus far.

7.2.1 Pressures toward Uniformity

Festinger hypothesizes that comparisons are more likely to be restricted to persons with similar attitudes as *pressures toward uniformity* in a group increase:

> As the pressure toward uniformity increases there should be observed an increase in the tendency to cease comparison with those who are too different from oneself. Specifically, this would mean that the range within which appreciable comparison with others is made should contract as the pressure toward uniformity increases. (p. 131)

---

[2] However, confidence is not always related to interpersonal influence. Persons can be resistant to attitude change without being influential.

Pressures toward uniformity are likely to encourage a person's efforts to resolve disagreements through changing either, others' attitudes or their own attitudes on an issue. However, Festinger's hypothesis about such pressures is that they tend to restrict interpersonal influence to persons with similar attitudes: the occupants of modal positions will be less likely to consider the range of attitudes of other group members, and the occupants of peripheral positions will be less likely to consider the position of the modal members. In effect, pressures toward uniformity may operate to increase the *perceived* distance between persons, so that persons' influences are restricted to smaller sets of group members.

Festinger's hypothesis springs from studies on the rejection of extreme deviates. Interpersonal influences and attitude changes increase as pressures toward uniformity increase (Back 1951; Gerard 1954; Schachter 1951). The rejection of perceived "deviates" also increases as pressures toward uniformity increase (Festinger et al. 1950; Festinger et al. 1952; Schachter 1951). Thus, under sufficiently strong pressures, the prediction is that individuals look mainly to those persons in their group whose attitudes are closest to their own. Group members are more likely to weigh a greater range of alternative attitudes under weak pressure than under strong pressure to reach consensus but, according to this hypothesis, they are less likely to be influenced by the extreme positions in this range when pressures toward uniformity are strong than when such pressures are weak.

The opposite hypothesis also is plausible. To produce consensus, group members may be more likely to accord influence to a greater range of alternative positions on an issue under the condition of strong pressure to reach consensus than under weak pressure. Festinger's hypothesis has been criticized by Singer (1965: 108) on these grounds:

> As long as social reality – the precursor of social comparison – was employed in the setting of pressures to uniformity (Festinger, Gerard, Hymovitch, Kelley, and Raven, 1952), the notion of rejection as psychological redefinition of the group made intuitive sense. One could get uniformity by excluding discrepant others. But if one is looking for gross evaluation, rejection makes no sense. If a person is seeking information as to whether an opinion is wrong or right, people who tell him he is wrong provide such information, and logically, despite any dissimilarities to him, they should not be rejected.

According little weight to "discrepant others" does not erode the possibility of reaching agreement in a group, if the pressure toward uniformity under which the group is operating diminishes the self-weight of persons whose positions differ markedly from those of the mass of the group. But if a divergent (minority) position is strongly held, then by the same mechanism (the demand for consensus diminishing self-weight), the other members of the group may be influenced by it.

7.2.2 Homophily

Festinger also hypothesizes that comparisons are more likely to be restricted to persons with similar attitudes as the similarity in their sociodemographic attributes increases or, in other words, persons are less likely to compare their attitudes with persons who have dissimilar attitudes as the sociodemographic dissimilarity between them increases:

> If persons who are very divergent from one's own opinion . . . are perceived as different from oneself on attributes consistent with the divergence, the tendency to narrow the range of comparability becomes stronger. (p. 133)

This hypothesis was subsequently elaborated as follows:

> When a person is confronted with an opinion contrary to his own which is held by people like himself, he experiences dissonance. . . . the magnitude of the dissonance thus introduced will depend upon (a) the importance of the person or group that voices the disagreement and (b) the importance and relevance to the individual of the issue concerning which the disagreement exists. (Festinger and Aronson 1968: 130)

Festinger's hypothesis concerning the importance of sociodemographic similarity/dissimilarity has appeared in a very strong form in self-categorization theory. Self-categorization theorists (Turner 1991; Turner et al. 1987) assert that a necessary condition for the interpersonal influence of person j on person i is that person i must categorize person j as similar to himself or herself on dimensions relevant to the issue. Hence, David and Turner (1996: 182) state that "Any evidence that psychological out-group membership can produce influence is contrary to the theory." The evidence on this assertion is mixed and, not surprisingly, problems have been encountered concerning the appropriate definition of in-group and out-group status (Martin and Hewstone 2001). Nonetheless, the basic idea is similar to Festinger's hypothesis that social comparison between discrepant positions on an issue is more likely to occur between persons who are similar in their sociodemographic characteristics than between persons who are dissimilar.

In sociology, positive associations of sociodemographic similarity with the occurrence and strength of interpersonal relations, including interpersonal influence, have been repeatedly indicated, and the assumption of such associations, i.e., the principle of homophily, has become a fundamental building block of sociological theory (Blau 1977; McPherson, Smith-Lovin, and Cook 2001; Merton 1968). In this tradition, social groups are conceptualized as being differentiated in a multidimensional space in which persons' positions are defined by their coordinates on various sociodemographic dimensions. A common finding is a *negative* association between two persons' distance in this social space and the probability and strength of their interpersonal relationship, including interpersonal visibility, contact, and influence. Indeed, on the basis of these findings, some sociologists, most notably Burt (1987), have reached the same conclusion as self-categorization theorists that the primary (i.e., necessary and sufficient) basis of persons' responses to other persons' attitudes and behaviors is close proximity in sociodemographic space.

However, the homophily principle is misleading when it entirely discounts the occurrence and importance of interpersonal influences among sociodemographically *dissimilar* persons.[3] Blau (1977) argued that homophily on one sociodemographic dimension usually involves an interaction between two persons who are different on numerous other dimensions. Reference group theory (Merton 1968) is consistent with the hypothesis that persons may be influenced by other persons who are dissimilar to themselves on certain salient dimensions. The influence of elites, leaders, and authorities may bridge large social distances in sociodemographic space (Bourgeois and Friedkin 2001). Singer (1965: 108) argued that "a person may not compare with a similar other but with an extreme other" when the extreme other has valuable information related to the issue. More generally, Goethals and Darley (1977) have argued that confidence and certainty in an attitude are increased when there is initial agreement with a dissimilar other and decreased when there is initial disagreement with a similar other; and they argue that confidence in an attitude will be unaffected by agreement with a similar other or disagreement with a dissimilar other.

In this broader perspective, interpersonal influence is not necessarily eroded by sociodemographic dissimilarity if the influence is secured by power bases such as identification, authority, or expertise. Indeed, network relations are affected by the distribution of bases of power (i.e., distance-spanning relations are formed and maintained) so that persons who are located in disparate regions of a social space may monitor the attitudes and behaviors, gain access to, and be influenced by (and perhaps influence) those members of the group who possess resources of interest to them. Moreover, violations of homophily, i.e., improbable, weak,

---

[3] We concentrate the discussion of this feature of the homophily principle, although we also believe that the principle overemphasizes the extent of interpersonal agreement in contacts among sociodemographically *similar* persons and misleadingly discounts the importance of endogenous interpersonal influences.

distance-spanning interpersonal relations and influence, may be consequential (Granovetter 1973). The principle of homophily is grounded on
a large number of studies, and it represents a statement of a tendency,
but it does not imply either the absence or unimportance of boundary-
spanning interpersonal influences.

7.2.3 Content of Initial Issue Positions

The distribution of initial attitudes on an issue may invest particular positions in the distribution with meaning. For example, if a modal position
lowers the susceptibilities and increases the interpersonal influences of
the occupants of the modal position, it may be because a modal position
is taken as credible or representative of the "collective will" of the group,
or as a relatively fixed position that must be accommodated regardless
of its merits. However, the content or meaning of certain positions also
may be affected by other conditions that are unrelated to the distribution
of initial attitudes. Persons' susceptibilities and interpersonal influences
may vary on the basis of a "rhetorical advantage" or attraction that stems
from a broader cultural or social structure in which the issue is situated.
For instance, jurors who favor acquittal in criminal cases tend to be more
influential than jurors who favor conviction (MacCoun and Kerr 1988;
Stasser, Kerr, and Bray 1982) as a result of criteria to establish guilt (e.g.,
guilt beyond a reasonable doubt) that govern such jury decisions. When
issue positions can be linked to evidential, moral, or ideological considerations, effects of the formal properties of a distribution of initial positions
on persons' susceptibilities and influences may be disrupted. More generally, individual differences in persons' responses to the positions taken
by others on an issue may disrupt any linkage between the distribution
of initial positions among persons and their distribution of interpersonal
influence.

7.2.4 Overview

An hypothesis can withstand the discovery of a few scope conditions that
describe limitations on its generalizability. However, an hypothesis usually cannot withstand the discovery of a complex array of contingencies,
interactions, and scope conditions: the loss of theoretical parsimony and
the lack of any single robust tendency means that it becomes difficult
to use the hypothesized relationship as a building block in the construction of larger integrative theoretical structures. Currently, it is an open
question whether the distribution of initial attitudes is a reliable basis on
which to predict the influence network of a group, or whether the relationship between these two constructs is so complex that it cannot serve
as a reliable basis for such theoretical structures.

7.3 Findings on Two Formal Models

There have been several attempts to develop formal models of Festinger's social comparison theory that draw exclusively on group members' initial positions on an issue to predict attitude changes and group outcomes. Two prominent recent models are Davis's (1996) consensus model, which stems from social decision scheme theory (SDS), and McGarty et al.'s (1992) meta-contrast ratio model (MCR), which stems from self-categorization theory. Both models draw on the distances between group members' initial attitudes on an issue for a prediction of the consensus position of a group that emerges from a group's discussion of an issue. In this section, we evaluate these two models.

Social influence network theory also presents a prediction of consensus positions. In Table 4.5 we showed that our standard model significantly contributes to the prediction of a group's mean end-of-trial position on an issue, controlling for the group's mean initial position on the issue. Here we restrict the analysis to groups with a consensus end-of-trial position in order to compare the predictions of the three models. We find that neither the SDS nor the MCR model reliably contributes to the prediction of groups' consensus positions, controlling for groups' mean initial positions.

7.3.1 Davis's Consensus Model

Davis (1996) hypothesized that the relative influence of each person in determining the content of a group's consensus on an issue depends on the *centrality* of each person's initial position relative to others in the distribution of initial attitudes on the issue. Group member j is self-weighted and influential the closer j's initial position is to the initial positions of others. Davis's model is

$$G = c_1 y_1^{(1)} + c_2 y_2^{(1)} + \cdots + c_n y_n^{(1)}, \qquad (7.1)$$

where G is the consensus position of a group, $0 \le c_j \le 1$ ($\sum_{j=1}^{n} c_j = 1$) is the relative contribution of j's initial (prediscussion) position on an issue to G, and c_j is a function of the distances between group members' initial positions,

$$c_j = \frac{\sum_{\substack{k \neq j}}^{n} \exp\left(-\left|y_j^{(1)} - y_k^{(1)}\right|\right)}{\sum_{i=1}^{n} \sum_{\substack{k \neq i}}^{n} \exp\left(-\left|y_i^{(1)} - y_k^{(1)}\right|\right)}, \qquad (7.2)$$

for each j. This model, from our perspective, deals with the total influence of each person in determining the content of the group consensus;

however, here the total influence is determined strictly in terms of the distances among group members' initial positions.

7.3.2 Self-Categorization Theory's Meta-contrast Ratio

McGarty et al. (1992) hypothesize that a consensus position is produced via group members' conformity to a shared in-group norm that is most prototypical of the group:

> The prototypicality of in-group members is defined by means of the *meta-contrast principle* (Turner, 1985): the less a person differs from the in-group members and the more he or she differs from out-group members, the more representative is he or she of the in-group. Thus the prototype is the position which best defines what the group has in common *in contrast to other relevant* out-groups. The person with the highest *meta-contrast ratio* (obtained by dividing a person's average difference from out-group members by his or her average difference from in-group members) holds the most consensual position. (McGarty et al. 1992: 3).

McGarty et al. propose that this approach may be applied even when measures are unavailable for the issue positions of manifest out-groups. They suggest that out-group positions are "implicit in the response scale employed to measure subjects' attitudes" (p. 4). Specifically, the out-group positions are taken to be those positions on the attitude scale that are *not* chosen by any of the in-group members, and it is assumed that equal numbers of the imputed out-group members occupy these positions.

McGarty et al. obtain a meta-contrast ratio (MCR_k) for each in-group member k as follows:

$$MCR_k = \frac{\frac{1}{n}\left(\sum_{i=1}^{n}|I_k - O_i|\right)}{\frac{1}{m-1}\left(\sum_{i=1}^{m-1}|I_k - I_i|\right)}, \tag{7.3}$$

where I_k is the initial position of in-group member k on the issue for an in-group with m members, and O_i $(i = 1, 2, \ldots, n)$ are the initial positions on the attitude scale that are not chosen by any of the in-group members. The predicted consensus position of the in-group is the initial position chosen by one or more of the in-group members with the highest MCR, i.e., $\max(MCR_1, MCR_2, \ldots, MCR_m)$. For example, given an integer attitude scale that runs from -4 to $+4$ and an in-group with three members, two of whom select -4 and one -3 on the scale, -4 is the prototypical (and predicted consensus) position of the in-group:

−4	−3	−2	−1	0	1	2	3	4	MCR_k
I_1									$MCR_1 = 10$
I_2									$MCR_2 = 10$
		I_3							$MCR_3 = 4$
			O_1	O_2	O_3	O_4	O_5	O_6	O_7

It appears that their formalization is not scope-restricted to contiguous in-group positions, as in the above example; they are mute on this matter. Although it appears to be scope-restricted to discrete scales with a finite number of positions, it is not scope-restricted to scales with a certain number of such positions. Clearly, the formalization involves important assumptions about the distribution of the imputed out-group members and the meaningfulness of the positions that are not selected by the in-group members. A variety of modeling questions are raised by this formalization, including whether a unique maximum MCR must exist, whether some constraint should be placed on the number of positions that may be taken by the imputed out-group members, whether the model should be scope-restricted to in-groups with fully contiguous positions on an issue, and whether the imputation of meaningful out-group positions is even possible given only information on the positions of the in-group.

7.3.3 Findings

Table 7.1 presents our findings on these models for each issue considered by the dyads, triads, and tetrads in our experiments. Because the SDS and MCR models are scope-restricted to the prediction of consensus, we restrict our analysis to those group-issue trials in which consensus was generated from an initial disagreement. We include the two monetary issues (Asbestos and Disaster) that involve continuous scales for which Davis's consensus model presents predictions, but the MCR does not. We also present the predictions of our standard model, i.e., the mean predicted equilibrium positions based on group members' reported influence networks.

Table 7.1a reports the correlations between groups' observed consensus positions and the predictions of the SDS consensus model, the self-categorization MCR model, the social influence network theory model (SINT), and the baseline initial mean model (BASE). The correlations of the BASE prediction exceed those of the SDS and MCR models; the correlations of SINT exceed those of BASE. Table 7.1b reports the regression coefficients for the predictions of each model, controlling for the baseline prediction. The MCR model does not fare well relative to the predictions of the other two models. The SDS consensus model does not reliably

Table 7.1 *Predicting the observed consensus position of a group (dyads, triads, and tetrads): Social decision scheme theory's consensus model (Davis 1996), self-categorization theory's meta-contrast ratio (McGarty et al. 1992), and social influence network theory's standard model*

(a) Correlations of the models' predictions with observed consensus positions

Issues	Base	SDS	MCR	SINT	N
Sports	0.800***	0.683***	0.192	0.939***	63
Asbestos	0.703***	0.312*	—	0.963***	45
School	0.733***	0.709***	0.070	0.894***	88
Disaster	0.667***	0.626***	—	0.778***	40
Surgery	0.835***	0.800***	0.330**	0.929***	76

(b) Regression coefficients, controlling for mean initial position

Models and issues	Predicted consensus position β_1	Mean initial position β_2	constant β_0	R^2
Sports issue				
SDS	0.022	0.977***	−5.632	0.641
MCR	2.177*	1.004***	−11.107*	0.676
SINT	1.060***	−0.035	−1.994	0.881
Asbestos issue				
SDS	0.102	1.085***	−1.030	0.631
MCR	—	—	—	—
SINT	0.976***	−0.145	1.420*	0.930
School issue				
SDS	0.341**	0.633***	0.605	0.572
MCR	−0.023	0.998***	−0.949	0.538
SINT	1.045***	−0.071	1.443	0.801
Disaster issue				
SDS	0.116	0.774†	0.192	0.446
MCR	—	—	—	—
SINT	0.872***	0.080	0.056	0.606
Surgery issue				
SDS	0.288**	0.588***	9.425*	0.726
MCR	−0.303	0.911***	8.581†	0.700
SINT	0.726***	0.182*	6.702*	0.872

Notes: This analysis is based on group-issue trials with initial disagreement among group members and end-of-trial consensus.
***$p < 0.001$; **$p < 0.01$; *$p < 0.05$; †$p < 0.10$.

contribute to the account of consensus positions beyond the account afforded by the baseline prediction. Controlling for the baseline prediction, a reliable independent contribution to the prediction of groups' consensus positions is only obtained with an approach that incorporates a direct measure of the realized influence networks of groups.

If there is a global model of **W**, which is strictly determined by the distances between group members' initial positions on an issue, and which outperforms the baseline prediction of the mean initial attitudes of group members, then it remains to be discovered. Social comparison theory, as we have seen, involves a set of hypotheses in which interpersonal differences of attitudes on an issue do not have a simple relationship with interpersonal influence. If the nuances of social comparison theory are important, then the failure of the SDS consensus model and the self-categorization MCR model might be attributed to not taking these nuances into account. SINT bypasses the complex conditions that form influence networks. It works directly with the realized influence networks of groups, presents a formalization of the *social process* that unfolds in these networks, and generates predictions of the outcomes of this process.

7.4 A Theoretical Perspective on Initial Distances

In this section, we draw on our theory to develop a formal perspective on the general implications of initial distances of attitudinal positions on an issue among a group's members. Our analysis highlights the theoretical importance of a person's initial deviance from the person's weighted average of other group members initial positions, i.e., $\sum_{j \neq i} c_{ij} y_j^{(1)} - y_i^{(1)}$, and the person's *response* to this deviance. We begin with a formal analysis and then present our findings.

7.4.1 Formal Analysis

From our standard model, we have

$$y_i^{(t+1)} = a_{ii} \sum_{j=1}^{n} w_{ij} y_j^{(t)} + (1 - a_{ii}) y_i^{(1)} \qquad (7.4)$$

$$= a_{ii}^2 \sum_{j \neq i}^{n} c_{ij} y_j^{(t)} + a_{ii}(1 - a_{ii}) y_i^{(t)} + (1 - a_{ii}) y_i^{(1)},$$

where $\mathbf{C} = [c_{ij}]$ is the matrix of relative interpersonal influences defined in Chapter 2. The time 2 response of member i to the initial positions of group members is

$$y_i^{(2)} = a_{ii}^2 \sum_{j \neq i} c_{ij} y_j^{(1)} + a_{ii}(1 - a_{ii}) y_i^{(1)} + (1 - a_{ii}) y_i^{(1)} \qquad (7.5)$$

$$= a_{ii}^2 \sum_{j \neq i} c_{ij} y_j^{(1)} + (1 - a_{ii}^2) y_i^{(1)}$$

$$= a_{ii}^2 \left(\sum_{j \neq i} c_{ij} y_j^{(1)} - y_i^{(1)} \right) + y_i^{(1)}.$$

The attitude change of member i is

$$y_i^{(2)} - y_i^{(1)} = a_{ii}^2 \left(\sum_{j \neq i} c_{ij} y_j^{(1)} - y_i^{(1)} \right). \tag{7.6}$$

Hence, the time 2 *response* of each group member i to his or her initial deviance (if any), i.e., $\sum_{j \neq i} c_{ij} y_j^{(1)} - y_i^{(1)}$, is governed by i's susceptibility on the issue. The initial deviance depends on a "normative" position $\sum_{j \neq i} c_{ij} y_j^{(1)}$ that is established *by* each i upon i's accord of influence to particular other positions, and that may differ from one group member to another depending on the interpersonal influence that they accord. This "normative" position will be identical to i's initial position only if i accords weight to others who were in initial agreement with him or her or, given disagreement among the group members who directly influence member i, if this "normative" position happens to be the same as i's initial position. Thus, the "normative" initial position for i can differ from i's initial position only if he or she accords weight to the attitudes of persons whose initial positions *differ* from his or her own. It is by according weight to persons with whom they are in initial disagreement that group members may find themselves at some distance from the "norms" that they, themselves, have generated on the basis of the interpersonal influences they have accorded to others. From this agent-based perspective, the deviance that triggers attitude change is self-constructed.

From (7.5), if $\sum_{j \neq i} c_{ij} y_j^{(1)} - y_i^{(1)} = 0$, then there is no initial deviance and hence no "normative" pressure for an attitude change. If $\sum_{j \neq i} c_{ij} y_j^{(1)} - y_i^{(1)} \neq 0$, then i may be motivated to reduce this initial deviance. If the attitude change is $y_i^{(2)} - y_i^{(1)} = \sum_{j \neq i} c_{ij} y_j^{(1)} - y_i^{(1)}$, then i's attitude moves to the initial "norm"; such movement requires complete susceptibility, $a_{ii} = 1$. Lesser movements toward this "norm" correspond to lower susceptibility values. Recall that whereas $\sum_j c_{ij} = 0$ implies $a_{ii} = 0$, $\sum_j c_{ij} = 1$ does not imply $a_{ii} = 1$, because the *relative* amount of interpersonal influence that i accords to other group members does not constrain $a_{ii} = 1 - w_{ii} = \sum_{j \neq i} w_{ij}$. A key empirical issue, relevant to social comparison theory, is whether there is a relationship between a person's initial deviance and his or her susceptibility.

7.4.2 Initial Deviance and Susceptibility

If group members' susceptibilities are unrelated to their initial deviances, then the $y_i^{(2)} - y_i^{(1)}$ attitude changes for all i may vary dramatically, depending on conditions affecting group members' susceptibilities that are unrelated to their initial deviances. If strong pressure to achieve agreement sufficiently elevates a group member's susceptibility, then *any*

Table 7.2 *Proportion of derived $\hat{a}_{ii} > 0$ in categories of deviance values*

Low-pressure condition			High-pressure condition		
Deviance category k	Proportion of N_k with $\hat{a}_{ii} > 0$	No. cases N_k	Deviance category k	Proportion of N_k with $\hat{a}_{ii} > 0$	No. cases N_k
0.00	0.200	10	0.00	0.434	76
0.05	0.400	40	0.05	0.608	125
0.10	0.529	34	0.10	0.736	110
0.15	0.571	21	0.15	0.790	100
0.20	0.583	24	0.20	0.862	94
0.25	0.600	15	0.25	0.901	81
0.30	—	1	0.30	—	1
0.35	—	1	0.35	—	1
0.40.	—	1	0.40	—	1
0.45	—	1	0.45	—	1
0.50	—	1	0.50	—	1
0.55	—	1	0.55	—	1
0.60	—	1	0.60	—	1
0.65	0.800	5	0.65	0.909	11
0.70	0.600	5	0.70	0.333	3
0.75	—	1	0.75	—	1
0.80	—	1	0.80	—	1
0.85	—	1	0.85	—	1
0.90	—	1	0.90	—	1
0.95	—	1	0.95	—	1

Note: The analysis is restricted to the "Risky-Shift" issues on which subjects reported their attitudes in units of 5 (0, 5, 10,..., 100). The deviance categories are determined by rounding the deviance level to the nearest 0.05.

deviance of the group member may be substantially reduced, *regardless of the size of the deviance.* Across individuals, susceptibilities may increase or decrease with their individual deviances, or there may be a curvilinear relationship between the two variables. For example, susceptibility may increase with increasing deviance, or it may increase and then decline for a deviance that is larger than some threshold value.

Here we work with derived susceptibility values. These susceptibilities, if they are not zero, tend to be high; we established this in Chapter 4. Table 7.2 shows that the proportion of group members' derived susceptibilities $\hat{a}_{ii} > 0$ increases with the observed initial deviance value $|\sum_{j \neq i} \tilde{c}_{ij} \tilde{y}_j^{(1)} - \tilde{y}_i^{(1)}|$ for i. The larger i's initial deviance, the more likely the occurrence of some susceptibility and attitude change. Table 7.2 also shows that, for the same deviance value, the likelihood of a positive susceptibility ($\hat{a}_{ii} > 0$) is more elevated among persons in groups that were placed under a high-pressure condition, which encouraged reaching consensus, than among persons in groups that were placed under a low-pressure condition, which did not explicitly encourage the achievement of consensus. The likelihood of positive susceptibility tends to increase with the deviance value, and this tendency is especially pronounced when groups are under explicit pressure to reach consensus. However, our data, which contain few instances of extreme initial deviance, do not allow a full assessment of this association.

We lack data on individuals' attitude changes $\left(\tilde{y}_i^{(2)} - \tilde{y}_i^{(1)}\right)$. The $y^{(2)}$ responses of group members potentially create a *new* normative situation in which particular group members may again find themselves at some distance from the normative time $t = 2$ attitudes of the persons to whom they accord influence. If the time $t = 2$ deviance is small, then an additional response may be moot, but if it is large, then additional movements of attitudes may occur that reduce the discrepancy, and so on at each time t. It does not appear plausible in general that group members immediately shift their attitudes to positions that are consonant with the equilibrium implications of an attitude process that is played out in a network. Thus, group members do not leap to equilibrium; they muddle their way to it, as it were, via repetitive responses to their deviance from the normative attitudes of their influential others.

7.5 Social Comparision in Triads

We now focus on triadic influence systems as a strategic site for analyzing social comparison hypotheses. We are especially interested in the behavior of triads in which two of the group members hold an identical initial attitude on an issue that differs from the attitude of the third member. In such triads, the shared position is both the modal and majority position of the group, and the two discrete initial positions in the triad are separated by a distance that may be small or large. Social comparison theory makes predictions about the behavior of persons in such a circumstance. When the modal initial position is also that of the majority, we have a clear instance of a potentially meaningful normative position, based strictly on initial positions, that may affect the susceptibilities of the members who hold it and of those who do not. If there are effects of distance, then the effects should also be observable in this setting. Unlike the dyad, the triad is the smallest group in which we can have both a unique mode and a single positive distance.

In triads there are three possible patterns of initial attitudes. (1) All members share the same initial position, in which case there would be an initial consensus and no change of attitude according to our theory. (2) Two of the members share an initial position, with the third member being located at some distance from that shared position. (3) All three members have different initial positions on the issue. Among the 96 issue

Table 7.3 *Group outcomes by type of distribution of initial positions on issues in triads*

	One position*		Two positions		Three positions		
	#	%	#	%	#	%	Totals
End-of-trial outcomes							
Consensus on boundary initial position	2	100	10**	37.0	6	9.1	18
Consensus on internal initial position	—	—	—	—	13	19.7	13
Consensus on new internal position	—	—	5	18.5	15	22.7	20
Disagreement in range of initial positions	—	—	12***	44.4	32	48.5	44
TOTALS	2	100%	27	100%	66	100%	95

The header spanning Two positions and Three positions: *Initial pattern of attitudes*.

* Cases of initial consensus.
*** In 8 of these 10 cases, the consensus was on the majority position.
*** In these 12 disagreements, the majority held fixed positions in 7 cases, the majority shifted to a new shared position in 2 cases, and the majority position was broken in 3 cases. In these 12 disagreements, the minority member shifted his or her position in 6 cases.
— Logically impossible cases.

trials in triads, there were 2 cases of the first type, 27 cases of the second type, 66 cases of the third type, and 1 case in which there was a breach of the convex hull of initial attitudes. The breaching case is set aside for the present analysis. Table 7.3 shows how the remaining 95 cases are distributed among the patterns of equilibrium outcomes.

In the special case of a triad with a modal position occupied by two of the three members, social comparison predicts that influence will decline with the distance between the two initial positions and that the occupants of the modal position will be less susceptible and more influential that the other member. Hence, we expect the probability of achieved consensus to decrease with the initial distance between the two discrete positions and, in cases where consensus is reached, we expect the consensus to be closer to the initial position advocated by the modal members than to the initial position of the other member. Furthermore, we expect that the attitudes of the occupants of the modal position are more likely to remain fixed than is the attitude of the other member of the triad. We evaluate these social-comparison hypotheses below.

7.5.1 Triads with a Majority Position and a Minority of One

In the 27 triads with a majority position of two members, the shared position is confounded with the modal position. This confound is useful in eliminating the potential complexity of effects that may arise when there are one or more modal positions or shared positions that are not

Table 7.4 *No finding of an association between the occurrence of a fixed majority position and group consensus in triads*

		Fixed majority position		
		Yes	No	Totals
Consensus	Yes	8	7	15
	No	7	5	12
	TOTALS	15	12	27

Note: Fisher's exact test p-value = 1; χ^2 p-value = 0.80.

modal. This confound may not occur in larger groups, where there may be multiple shared positions, not all of which are modal positions. Most of the issue trials among triads (81.5%) either produced consensus on one of the two *initial* positions or ended in disagreement, and the remainder (18.5%) produced a compromise consensus between the two initial positions. In 24 of the 27 triads, the two persons who were in initial agreement were also in agreement at equilibrium, and in 3 of the 27 cases, the initial agreement was broken and the triad ended in a state of disagreement. The initial agreement observed in the 24 cases was maintained in different ways: in 8 cases, the minority member joined the majority to form a consensus; in another 7 cases, the majority held to their initial position and the minority member did not join them (in these cases, the initial attitude of the minority member remained fixed in 4 cases and moved toward the majority in 3 cases); in 5 cases the majority and majority settled on a compromise position (i.e., both shifted their positions); in 2 cases a consensus was formed on the initial position of the minority member; and in 2 cases the majority shifted toward the minority position without consensus being reached.

Given these observations, the two main questions are whether the distance between the two initial positions of the group members affects the likelihood of a shift in the initial position of the majority (it remained fixed in 15 cases and did not remain fixed in 12 cases), and whether it affects the likelihood of reaching consensus (consensus was attained in 15 cases and not attained in 12 cases. In the present sample, these two variables are statistically independent (Table 7.4). In binary logistic regressions, there are no significant effects of the *distance* separating the two discrete initial positions on either the probability that the modal attitude remains fixed ($\exp(B) = 0.996$; $p = 0.848$) or the probability of reaching consensus in the group ($\exp(B) = 0.988$; $p = 0.555$). In those 15 of the 27 cases in which a consensus was reached, the modal position was fixed in 8 cases and shifted in 7 cases (2 of these shifts were to the other member's initial position and 5 were to a compromise position).

The small number of cases of compromise consensus (5 cases) does not allow us to assess the question of whether such shifts were to a consensus that was nearer on average to the initial modal position than the initial position of the other member.

Social comparison effects in triads with a majority and a minority position appear to boil down to the following. If two members of the triad are in initial agreement, they are unlikely to move to a state of equilibrium disagreement (they did so in 3/27 cases). If a consensus is formed, it is rarely a consensus on the initial position of the minority member (2/15 cases of consensus). According to social comparison theory, group members seek to validate their attitudes by comparing their attitudes with those of other group members and by forming interpersonal agreements. In a triad, with an initial majority position, the attitude of the majority is immediately validated; hence, a consensus is unlikely to form on the minority position. When the members of the majority position shift their position, they tend to do so as "fellow travelers." We suspect that when the majority alter their position, they do so as an accommodation to the minority member in an effort to reach the goal of group consensus. In effect, the minority may hold the achievement of consensus hostage to some accommodation of its position on the issue. This supposition is more plausible than one (often emphasized in the literature on minority–majority influence) in which the common shift in the majority position is viewed as the result of substantively grounded arguments advanced by the minority member. The effect of such a resistant minority on a majority position is a form of interpersonal influence; i.e., it is based on the *coercive power* of the minority to prevent consensus.

Hence, consistent with Festinger's theoretical viewpoint on group dynamics, we interpret these results as indicative of a basic drive toward tension reduction in the group that is achieved by the formation of interpersonal agreements. But these interpersonal agreements reduce tension in at least two different and not necessarily commensurate ways: (a) they reduce uncertainty and validate the equilibrium positions adopted by group members, and (b) they move the group toward the realization of a consensual outcome that is viewed as a more desirable and less awkward collective outcome than disagreement. These two pathways to tension reduction are not necessarily commensurate when the attitudes of *some* members of the group have been validated by a shared position on an issue, but a group consensus has not been reached. In such a case, the members who occupy a shared position must weigh whether the agreement that validates their position is more or less important than the attainment of group consensus: if it is viewed as more important, then they will not alter it; if it is viewed as less important, then they will be inclined to shift their position. At the same time, the minority of one is confronted by mutually reinforcing pressures: there is no social support for his or her position and a group consensus can be reached by accommodating to the majority position. Resistance to such accommodation can only be justified on the basis of a firmly held personal conviction that is independent of the lack of social validation. Where the possible bases of such independent personal convictions are weak (i.e., where issue positions are not strongly affected by ideology, values, knowledge, past personal experiences, or interpersonal animosities), then a minority of one is likely to accommodate the majority.

7.5.2 Triads with Three Different Initial Positions

In triads with members who have three different initial positions on an issue, there is no validation of any initial position based on occupation of a shared position, although the initial positions may receive differential support depending on initial distances between them. For example, when the two boundary attitudes are far apart, the intermediate position may be located nearer to one of them than the other, and these distances may serve to support one boundary attitude more than the other. Social comparison theory suggests that the relative positions of group members in this circumstance are important; although there is no modal position, there is a "nearest neighbor" for each occupant of the two boundary positions (i.e., the occupant of the position between them).

In triads with three different initial positions on an issue, 48.5% of the triads failed to reach consensus, which is not significantly different from the 44.4% of the majority–minority triads considered above. When consensus was reached, it was more likely (in 28/34 cases) to settle either on the intermediate position or on a new compromise position (with approximately equal likelihood) than to settle on one of the two boundary positions of the system. Again, the main finding may reside in the gross pattern of the outcomes rather than in the variation of distances among the positions.

As the range of group members' initial positions on an issue increases, the probability of consensus should decline. But a binary logistic regression of the occurrence of consensus on the size of the range of group members' initial positions does not support such an association ($N = 66$, $\exp(B) = 0.988$, $p = 0.325$). Focusing on the distance between the two "nearest neighboring" positions in the group, as the distance separating these two positions declines, one might expect the probability to increase that both of their equilibrium attitudes (including the consensus of the group, if such occurs) will fall into the range of these two initial positions, but it does not ($N = 66$, $\exp(B) = 1.014$, $p = 0.670$), with cases of equidistant neighbors set to missing). The distances separating the initial positions of the triads' members do not appear to affect either the occurrence of consensus or the equilibrium locations of their attitudes.

7.6 Concluding Remarks

We are inclined to conclude only that the distances between the initial issue positions that group members adopt are important (a) in framing the domain of feasible changes of attitude, (b) in creating "fellow travelers" who are apt to respond similarly to others' attitudes by virtue of their identical initial position on an issue, and (c) in raising the susceptibility of a minority of one. With respect to the latter two effects, distance is best viewed as a qualitative variable indicating a status that rests on the nominal identity and difference between positions. The quantitative variation of distance among attitudes does not appear to affect the relative interpersonal influences of group members importantly.

Our evidence also suggests that, to the extent that persons are motivated to form interpersonal agreements, they will reduce their deviance from the "normative" positions of their influential others, regardless of the amount of the deviance. Although persons may reject the influence of some persons whose attitudes are highly discrepant from their own, such effects do not imply that persons are only influenced by persons with whom they are in close initial agreement. Interpersonal influences occur between persons in substantial disagreement; thus, a "normative" deviance is generated by persons themselves. This self-generated tension is encouraged when the achievement of interpersonal agreement is viewed as a desirable outcome for the group.

Were there strong effects of *quantitative* variation of the distances among initial positions on issues taken by group members, the decades of research on social comparison effects would surely have discovered them. We have noted that the literature on these effects presents no robust set of findings across studies even for highly constrained experimental designs. The surprising rarity of direct tests of Festinger's (1954) social comparison hypotheses may not be indicative of a lack of interest in them, but instead of unpublished failures of inquiries to confirm them. Although the basic precepts of social comparison theory are attractive (and our evidence suggests that group members act to reduce the discrepancy between their positions and the "normative" positions of their influential others), networks of interpersonal influence do not appear to be powerfully affected by the initial distances among the members on issues. We believe that the value placed on reaching consensus (a value that was central to Festinger's theory) erodes the salience of the initial distances between group members. Persons attempt to deal with whatever distances there may be and their failure to reach consensus has little to do with the initial distances separating them.

At the level of Festinger's most basic precepts, we are in full accord with social comparison theory. Persons often do compare their positions on an issue with the positions of others; persons differ in the weights that they accord to particular other positions on an issues, and in their resistances/susceptibilities to interpersonal influence. Our theory specifies the influence process that unfolds in whatever influence network happens to arise and serve as a context for the influence process. It adds *social process* to a social comparison perspective that has not, heretofore, dealt with the manner in which the interpersonal influences in a social group combine to generate attitude changes on an issue. We do not believe that the influence network implicated in such changes is, as a general rule, strongly constrained by group members' initial differences of positions on an issue. Explanations of the attitudinal outcomes of issue discussions in small groups may be substantially improved by direct measures of groups' influence networks.

8

Minority and Majority Factions

Few studies on social influence have had the enduring impact of Asch's (1951; 1952; 1956) experiments on the conformity responses of individuals to a fixed unanimous majority. Asch's seminal investigation stimulated numerous studies, including work on the reverse situation – responses of a majority to a fixed minority position on an issue.

> A common theme in social influence research has been the power of large versus small factions (though for counterexamples, see Moscovici, 1976; Nemeth, 1986). Many recent models of social influence, such as social impact theory (Latané, 1981; Latané and Wolfe, 1981), the other–total ratio (Mullen, 1983), and the social influence model (Tanford & Penrod, 1984) all use faction size as the central component. Research specifically focused on influence in small groups has demonstrated the power of larger versus smaller factions (e.g., Tindale, Davis, Vollrath, Nagao, & Hinsz, 1990), and majority/plurality and related faction-size models have often been found to provide excellent fits to empirical data (e.g., Davis, 1982; Hastie, Penrod, & Pennington, 1983; Tindale & Davis, 1983, 1985). . . . Thus, for many small decision-making groups, a majority or faction-size model of social influence in groups should provide a good baseline prediction (Tindale, et al. 1996: 81–2).

It is now widely recognized that minority factions, including a minority of one confronting a unanimous faction of $n - 1$ others, may be influential. In particular, the work of Moscovici and his colleagues (Moscovici 1985; Moscovici and Mugny 1983; Mugny 1982; Nemeth 1986) on small factions, although controversial, has driven home the point that the influence of persons who are not members of the majority faction also must be considered in any broad theory of group processes.

185

In this chapter, we focus on the class of *groups with factions*, i.e., groups with a distribution of initial positions on an issue that includes one or more shared positions, as opposed to groups in which every member has a different initial position on an issue. Our theoretical contribution is to situate both the Asch and reverse-Asch experimental designs as special cases of the influence networks that may form in groups with factions. In the Asch design, the members of the majority faction are confederates of the experimenter with susceptibilities that are constrained to zero; in the reverse-Asch design, the member(s) of the minority faction are confederates of the experimenter with zero susceptibility. In both designs, the subjects with unconstrained susceptibilities may or may not be influenced by the confederates who hold a fixed position on an issue.

Such situations are special cases, based on experimental constraints, in a large domain of possible influence networks that may occur in groups with factions. This domain includes networks in which *all* members are being influenced. We develop a formal perspective on factions in the influence process and present a general measure of the influence of factions on the other members of the group. With respect to the Asch constraints, we show that Goldberg's (1954) index of conformity (a measure of the interpersonal influence on a person in conformity situations) can be derived from social influence network theory. We also develop a formal account of the conditions under which those faction members who are being influenced will maintain their agreement with each other when they shift their positions on an issue.

Our theoretical perspective on the attitude changes that occur in groups with factions is built directly on the logic of our standard model. The influence of a faction depends on the influence of the individuals who share a particular initial position and, thus, we base the analysis of groups with factions on the *aggregation* of the interpersonal influences of faction members. We contribute an approach to the study of factions that directly attends to the interpersonal influences among group members. The size of factions contributes to the influence of their members' position on an issue when faction members' direct interpersonal influences *aggregate* and produce total influences that are greater than the total influence of any one member of the faction. Our theoretical interest is focused on factions *in the interpersonal influence process* that may be modifying members' positions on an issue. In this chapter, we develop this approach and provide a theoretically grounded basis for studying the aggregation effects of factions.

Finally, in this chapter, we report empirical findings on naturally occurring factions. We introduced this subject in Chapter 7 as part of our analysis of social comparison effects in triads. Festinger's (1954) hypothesized that a person's distance from the largest faction (the mode of a group) affects the person's susceptibility and interpersonal influences.

Our analysis supported the idea that persons' susceptibilities to interpersonal influence are triggered by deviance of their positions on issues from the "normative" position of the persons who are influencing them, based on a weighted average of those positions, and that persons who alter their attitudes tend to do so in order to reduce this deviance. Thus, in a triad with an initial faction of two members, the third member's position often shifted toward that of the faction. We observed a tendency for persons to remain in agreement with the members of their faction during the influence process. Changes of modal attitude are consistent with the influence of a minority of one in triads, but we found that modal factions in triads rarely *adopted* the position of the minority of one. The influence of the minority member was manifested in most cases by shifts of the modal faction to a new position between the two initial positions of the group members. Festinger's hypothesis on the effect of modal positions does not specify whether the effect depends on the number of occupants in such positions, on whether this number constitutes a majority or not, or on the presence of multiple sources of dissent. In this chapter, we focus our empirical study on tetrads in which there may be two factions, or a modal majority faction, or a single faction and two different dissenting positions on an issue.

8.1 Formal Analysis

Faction-size effects may be negligible in naturally occurring nontransitory groups, where group members are likely to possess detailed information on the arguments and status characteristics of other members, and when formal votes are eschewed in favor of reaching consensus. There is no doubt that faction size has effects; but the conditions under which such effects occur may be very restricted. The occurrence of multiple sources of dissent from a majority position is more likely than the occurrence of a minority of one; and detailed information on the arguments and status characteristics of various group members is more likely than a disembodied display of attitudes. The literature on the Asch design indicates that the effect of a majority position, when it is based strictly on its numerical superiority, is substantially attenuated in the presence of multiple sources of disagreement. Moreover, the literature stemming from the work of Bales (1950), reinforced by sociological literature on groups in field settings, suggests that inequalities of interpersonal influence, and stratified patterns of such influence, are likely to appear *whenever* there is some basis for assessing the status characteristics, trustworthiness, credibility, power bases, and resources of other group members. Such inequalities may disrupt faction-size effects in situations where reaching consensus is more important than simply attaining a majority, and make any assertion of a faction-size effect on susceptibilities and interpersonal influences, based only on numerical differences between factions, highly problematic. We think factions mainly influence group outcomes on the basis of an *aggregation* of the interpersonal influences of a faction's members on members of their own faction as well as on other members of the group.

In this section, we analyze the systemic implications of factions in the influence process. Our analysis is focused on the case of two factions, but it is easily generalized to any number of factions. In the literature on majority and minority influence, one of two factions is intransigent. However, a general theory of the interpersonal influence process in the presence of factions must allow for attitude changes among and between the members of all factions. In this more general theoretical framework, the Asch (majority influence) and reverse-Asch (minority influence) designs are special cases of a circumstance in which a group is divided into two or more internally consensual factions that may vary in their relative size and degree of susceptibility to influence of their members.

8.1.1 Relative Total Influences of Two Factions

To illustrate, consider a group of n persons, where persons 1 and 2 advocate one position, $\left\{ y_1^{(1)} = y_2^{(1)} \right\}$, and persons 3 through n advocate another position, $\left\{ y_3^{(1)} = y_4^{(1)} = \ldots = y_n^{(1)} \right\}$. In terms of the two initial positions, this group would be partitioned as follows:

$$
\mathbf{W} = \begin{bmatrix} w_{11} & w_{12} & w_{13} & \cdots & w_{1n} \\ w_{21} & w_{22} & w_{23} & \cdots & w_{2n} \\ \hline w_{31} & w_{32} & w_{33} & \cdots & w_{3n} \\ \vdots & \vdots & \vdots & \ddots & \vdots \\ w_{n1} & w_{n2} & w_{n3} & \cdots & w_{nn} \end{bmatrix} \quad \mathbf{y}^{(1)} = \begin{bmatrix} y_1^{(1)} \\ y_2^{(1)} \\ \hline y_3^{(1)} \\ \vdots \\ y_n^{(1)} \end{bmatrix}.
$$

To describe the implications of this influence system for the equilibrium attitudes of the group's members, including the formation of a consensus, we need to consider the matrix of total influences that is based on the direct and indirect flows of interpersonal influence in the network:

$$
\mathbf{V} = \begin{bmatrix} v_{11} & v_{12} & v_{13} & \cdots & v_{1n} \\ v_{21} & v_{22} & v_{23} & \cdots & v_{2n} \\ \hline v_{31} & v_{32} & v_{33} & \cdots & v_{3n} \\ \vdots & \vdots & \vdots & \ddots & \vdots \\ v_{n1} & v_{n2} & v_{n3} & \cdots & v_{nn} \end{bmatrix}.
$$

The matrix of total effects, **V**, describes the relative contribution of each group member's initial attitude to determining the content of his or her own and other group members' equilibrium attitudes:

$$y_i^{(\infty)} = \sum_{j=1}^{n} v_{ij} y_j^{(1)}. \tag{8.1}$$

In terms of the observed attitude change of person i, the aggregated total influence of other persons on person i is

$$\sum_{j \neq i}^{n} v_{ij} = 1 - v_{ii} = \frac{y_i^{(\infty)} - y_i^{(1)}}{\bar{y}_i^{(1)} - y_i^{(1)}}, \tag{8.2}$$

where

$$\bar{y}_i^{(1)} = \sum_{j \neq i}^{n} \left(\frac{v_{ij}}{1 - v_{ii}} \right) y_j^{(1)} \tag{8.3}$$

for $v_{ii} \neq 1$. A *large* total influence of others on person i may be manifested by either a large or a *small* attitude change. The size of the attitude change depends on the distance between the initial attitude of person i and the weighted average of initial attitudes of the other members.

The total aggregated influence of a *faction* on person i is the sum of the individual total influences on person i from the persons in the faction. Thus, when some persons share the same initial attitude on an issue (i.e., when they form a faction), it is possible to assess the relative effect of that faction on the content of persons' equilibrium attitudes. In the present application, where there are two initial positions on the issue (i.e., two factions), the relative influence of each faction to person i is obtained by aggregating the influences associated with each faction, e.g.,

$$y_i^{(\infty)} = \dot{y}^{(1)} \left(\sum_{j=1}^{2} v_{ij} \right) + \ddot{y}^{(1)} \left(\sum_{j=3}^{n} v_{ij} \right), \tag{8.4}$$

where $\dot{y}^{(1)} = y_1^{(1)} = y_2^{(1)}$ and $\ddot{y}^{(1)} = y_3^{(1)} = \cdots = y_n^{(1)}$. Note that a particular faction may have a different impact on different persons, but all persons' equilibrium attitudes are weighted averages of the initial positions of the two factions. Obviously, this approach can be generalized to include more factions of different sizes.

A further simplification of (8.4) occurs if the $\mathbf{V}$ that is generated by $\mathbf{W}$ has homogeneous column entries,

$$
\mathbf{V} = \begin{bmatrix}
v_{11} & v_{22} & v_{33} & \cdots & v_{nn} \\
v_{11} & v_{22} & v_{33} & \cdots & v_{nn} \\
v_{11} & v_{22} & v_{33} & \cdots & v_{nn} \\
\vdots & \vdots & \vdots & \ddots & \vdots \\
v_{11} & v_{22} & v_{33} & \cdots & v_{nn}
\end{bmatrix}.
$$

In this case, an equilibrium consensus is attained in the group and the relative total influence of a particular faction on person i is the same for all i. Because a consensus is formed, the aggregated total influences described in (8.4) are the proportional contributions of each faction to the content (numerical value) of the group's consensus. Hence, when a consensus is reached, we can focus either on an individual-level analysis, in which the effects on group members' attitudes are described in terms of their individual susceptibilities and interpersonal influences, or (with a shift in our frame of reference) on a faction-level analysis, in which the effects on group consensus are described in terms of the total influences of the various factions in the group.

Although the influence network of a group determines the effects of its factions, so that small or large factions may be influential, there are influence networks in which the size of factions is strongly associated with their relative influence. For instance, in an influence network in which all members are equally influential on others, i.e., $\mathbf{A} = \alpha\mathbf{I}$ $(0 < \alpha \leq 1)$, $w_{ii} = 1 - \alpha$ for all i, and $w_{ij} = \alpha/(n-1)$ for all $i \neq j$, the aggregated total impact of factions depends strictly on their relative sizes. Hence, there are theoretical grounds for positing a substantial baseline effect of faction size independent of any effects of the factions per se on the influence network of a group.

Figures 8.1 and 8.2 illustrate the effects of various faction sizes (2, 3, and 4). Each group contains two initial positions (0.20 and 0.80), which are either a faction's shared position or the position of a minority of one. For simplicity, we assume that the susceptibilities and interpersonal influences of the members of each group are homogeneous; i.e., $w_{ij} = a_{ii}/(n-1)$ for all $i \neq j$. The separate graphs describe the transformation of the members' initial positions for different levels of susceptibility (0.50, 0.90, and 0.98). Consensus is approached as the level of susceptibility increases. Figure 8.1 describes a situation consisting of a minority of one against majorities of 2, 3, and 4 persons in groups of sizes 3, 4, and 5. As the size of the majority faction increases, the equilibrium positions of the members become closer to the initial positions of the majority faction; the larger the faction, the more influential is its position. Figure 8.2 describes a situation consisting of opposing factions of *equal* size in

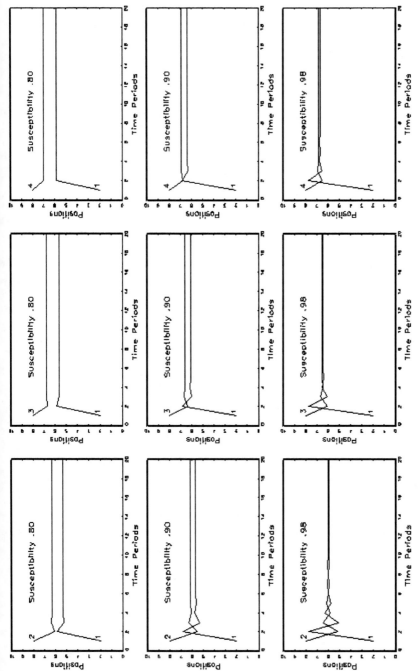

Figure 8.1 Transformation of positions over time in an egalitarian group with one member holding a minority position and an opposing majority position of two, three, or four persons.

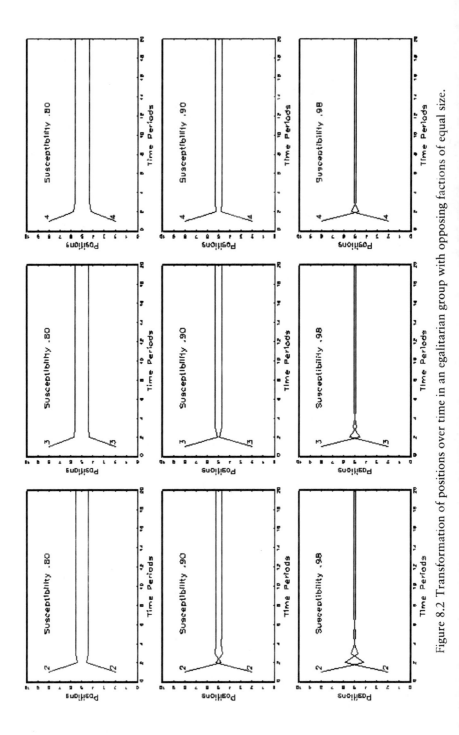

Figure 8.2 Transformation of positions over time in an egalitarian group with opposing factions of equal size.

groups of sizes 4, 6, and 8. The tendency of the group is to converge to the mean of the two initial positions. Indeed, in general, a homogeneous field of interpersonal influence (regardless of the number and sizes of the opposing factions) produces a convergence toward the mean of the initial attitudes (0.50), and this convergence is more or less pronounced depending on members' level of susceptibility to influence.

Social influence network theory suggests when effects of faction size would *not* be observed. Aggregation effects will be slight if the influence of a faction depends on the presence of particular highly influential persons in the faction. In the extreme case, all of the influence of the faction might be concentrated on one member. For example,

$$\mathbf{W} = \begin{bmatrix} w_{11} & w_{12} & 0 & 0 & w_{15} \\ w_{21} & w_{22} & 0 & 0 & w_{25} \\ 0 & 0 & 0 & 0 & 1 \\ 0 & 0 & 0 & 0 & 1 \\ 0 & 0 & 0 & 0 & 1 \end{bmatrix} \quad \mathbf{y}^{(1)} = \begin{bmatrix} \dot{y}^{(1)} \\ \dot{y}^{(1)} \\ \ddot{y}^{(1)} \\ \ddot{y}^{(1)} \\ \ddot{y}^{(1)} \end{bmatrix}$$

involves a situation in which all of the influence of the faction associated with the position $\ddot{y}^{(1)}$ is based on the interpersonal influence of person 5. Persons with a high degree of perceived authority, expertise, or charisma should increase the total influence of nearly any position that they happen to advocate, within reasonable limits, regardless of the number of persons who initially share their attitude or who initially disagree with them. Although most members of a faction may be without influence, the position that they hold may be highly influential, based on the influence of one or two persons who hold the same position that they do. Hence, an array of superficially confusing and contradictory findings on the effects of faction size may be produced if the influence network of the group is not taken into account.

8.1.2 Social Impact Theory

Social impact theory (Latané 1981) suggests that the influence of a source (whether it is a majority or minority faction) depends on the strength, immediacy, and number of the faction's members. Strength is a function of the power bases (status or resources) of the source. Immediacy is defined as the physical (geographical) proximity of the source to the target. In terms of these constructs, Latané's theory suggests that a simple formulation underlies both majority and minority effects.

> The impact experienced by [the] individual should be a direct function of the strength, immediacy, and number of people in the

opposing group and an inverse function of the strength, immediacy, and number of people in his own group. (Latané and Wolf 1981: 447)

The strength of a faction may rest on various power bases, but the influence mechanism is the same when it is defined in terms of these constructs. We also take the position that a simple interpersonal influence mechanism underlies the relative influence of different factions of a group.

Social impact theory views factions as coherent sources and targets of interpersonal influence. It does not allow for individual differences in susceptibility, and it does not allow for individual differences in the relative impact of different members of a majority faction. We also depart from social impact theory on the question of whether the *number* of members in a faction has any general relevance in the influence process, once the strengths of the various individual sources of influence have been taken into account. The presence of a powerful individual in a faction will make that faction influential regardless of the number of weaker sources of influence who share the same attitude. Along the same lines, although we do not discount the importance of the geographical proximity of influence sources and targets, we take the theoretical position that such proximity is only one of a number of conditions that may affect persons' susceptibilities and interpersonal influences. In the interpersonal influence process described by our standard model, the effects of individual-level and group-level conditions are transmitted through their effects on A, W, and $y^{(1)}$. Finally, social impact theory treats the source and target factions as occupying two discrete geographical locations. A more general approach, which treats geographical proximity as one among many variables that may affect persons' susceptibilities and interpersonal influences, allows individual differences in the geographical proximities of persons.

8.1.3 Social Positions and Interpersonal Agreements

Our approach provides a theoretical perspective on the observed tendency for faction members to maintain their interpersonal agreement with those persons who share their initial positions on an issue. In triads, we have found that the members of a faction (who share the same initial position on an issue) are likely to maintain their agreement even as they shift their position (Chapter 7). We will show that the same empirical tendency holds for tetrads. The tendency for faction members to remain in agreement during the influence process is obviously enhanced when there are strongly felt pressures to reach consensus; but we also find that factions are unlikely to be broken when the group fails to reach consensus. In this section, we develop a theoretical perspective on the conditions under which faction members will shift attitudes without breaking their interpersonal agreement. The mathematical foundations of the conclusions to be presented in this section are laid out in Appendix D.

Interpersonal influences make the correspondence between initial positions on issues and equilibrium interpersonal agreements somewhat more complex than might be thought. With a network of interpersonal influences at work, persons may have their attitudes directly or indirectly influenced (via intermediaries) by persons who are located elsewhere in the social structure. Initial disagreements among persons may be either enhanced or reduced by the interpersonal influences of these other persons. Initial agreements may be broken if the persons who are in initial agreement are subject to different interpersonal influences. Hence, the settled attitudes of persons are a potentially complex product of the entire social structure of social positions and interpersonal influences.

In our theoretical approach, the systemic equilibrium *implications* of an influence network are manifested in the matrix of total interpersonal influences, V, that is generated by the network of interpersonal influences, AW, as members repetitively respond to changes of attitude among the persons who are influencing them. Thus far, we have defined a social position as a position on an issue. However, persons not only have positions on an issue, but also have positions in the influence network. These two types of social positions have distinct roles in the development of individual and collective outcomes. Our present analysis focuses on how these two types of social positions bear on interpersonal agreements.

Our approach is to begin with social process and deduce the relevant positional concepts and relationships that bear on the reduction of variation in persons' attitudes. This theoretical approach leads to conclusions about the structural prerequisites of maintaining an initial interpersonal agreement and the interaction of social positions in producing such continuity. From our analysis, it is clear that a shared initial position on an issue does not ensure interpersonal agreement across time, and that persons with proximate initial positions on an issue may differ substantially in their equilibrium positions. The influence network in which two persons are embedded can disrupt any correspondence of an initial and equilibrium agreement between persons.

However, there are special cases in which initial agreement will be maintained. Trivially, for instance, if there is an initial consensus in the group as a whole, then that consensus also is the equilibrium consensus of the group, and if two persons are in initial agreement and are not susceptible to interpersonal influence, then their initial agreement also will be maintained. Less trivially, we show that if persons are structurally equivalent in the influence network, then any initial agreement of these persons will be maintained during the process of attitude change (Appendix D). In short, when a shared initial position on an issue is joined with a shared structural position in the influence network, then this implies that the occupants of the position will be "fellow travelers" in the social influence process that transforms their attitudes: they must always occupy the same position on an issue at every time t during the influence process.

8.2 Two Special Cases

Here, we situate both the Asch and reverse-Asch experimental designs as special cases of the influence networks that may form in groups-with-factions. In the Asch design, the members of the majority faction are confederates of the experimenter with susceptibilities that are constrained to zero; in the reverse-Asch design, the members of the minority faction are confederates of the experimenter with zero susceptibilities. In both designs, the subjects with unconstrained susceptibilities may or may not be influenced by the confederates who hold a fixed position on an issue.

8.2.1 Minority of One versus Unanimous Majority

In this section we develop a formal perspective on Asch's experiments (1951; 1952; 1956). Asch examined the response of a naïve subject who was faced with a discrepant unanimous attitude of two or more others on an issue. The response involved a choice among alternative responses one of which is objectively correct and the others incorrect. Specifically, an image of a line is displayed and then each subject (both naïve and confederate) voices his or her opinion on the best match from a set of alternative images of lines. Confederates unanimously voice the same incorrect alterantive.

Asch found that choice errors are negligible when subjects have no information about the choices of other persons and substantial when subjects are confronted with a unanimous selection of an incorrect alternative by others. These experiments complement the emphasis of Sherif (1936) and Festinger (1954) on *ambiguous* issues for which there is no obvious correct position on an issue:

> The subject knows (1) that the issue is one of fact; (2) that a correct result is possible; (3) that only one result is correct; (4) that the others and he are oriented to and reporting about the same objectively given relations; (5) that the group is in unanimous opposition at certain points with him. (Asch 1952: 461)

The employment of an issue that has an obvious correct answer has two consequences. First, it ensures the occurrence of an initial disagreement between the naïve subject and the confederate majority, who are instructed to choose an incorrect alternative. The subject "faced, possibly for the first time in his life, a situation in which a group unanimously contradicted the evidence of his senses" (Asch 1951: 178). Second, in variations of the standard experimental design where one confederate is instructed to select the correct alternative, it can be assumed that the naïve subject is likely to perceive that confederate's choice as supportive of his or her own initial position. This assumption is important because in the experiment minority subjects' initial attitudes are not directly ascertained prior to their encounter with the majority's attitude. This assumption is supported by evidence from control subjects, who formed their attitudes without any information about other persons' attitudes, and for whom the proportion of errors (incorrect choices) was less than 1%; 95% of the control subjects made no errors at all.

Asch showed that "when there is a disagreement between a single person and a group concerning a simple and clear matter of fact," a substantial fraction of persons placed in such a situation will adopt the group's position even though it is incorrect and is one that these persons would not have chosen otherwise" (Asch 1956: 1). In the presence of a unanimous but incorrect majority attitude, the error rate of subjects increased dramatically relative to the error rate of control subjects: only 25% of the subjects made no errors.[1] Asch's postexperiment interviews with subjects revealed that, despite the obvious correct alternative, subjects' perceptual hold on reality (i.e., their inclination to advocate the correct alternative) diminishes in the presence of a fallacious social construction by the group.

This experiment and closely related variants of it (Crutchfield 1955; Deutsch and Gerard 1955) have been replicated numerous times since the 1950s in the United States and other countries (Allen 1965, 1975; Bond and Smith 1996; Cialdini and Trost 1998; Kent 1994; Levine and Russo 1987). Several conclusions appear secure. First, despite the obvious nature of the correct alternative, there is a substantial probability that the subject will select an incorrect alternative given the circumstances in which he or she is placed. Second, the probability that a person will select an incorrect alternative under these circumstances increases at a declining rate as the number of persons in the majority position increases, although there is conflicting evidence on the magnitude of the declining marginal

[1] In Asch's experiments, subjects were given a choice among several alternatives, and the subject's choice was counted as an *error* if the subject selected either the alternative advocated by the majority or one that was in the *direction* of the majority position (Asch 1956: 9). Assuming that the subject's initial position is the correct position on an issue, *any* deviation from that position was counted as an error regardless of whether the subject adopted the position advocated by the majority. From Asch's results it is clear that the probability of maintaining a maximal self-weight ($w_{ii} = 1$) is relatively low for a single person who confronts a unanimous majority opinion; however, the average value of this self-weight could be considerably greater than 0 (indicating less than complete conformity) for most of the subjects during the critical trials on which they committed errors, to the extent that they adopted positions that were in the direction of the majority position but not exactly the majority position.

effect. Asch found no marginal effect of factions with more than three members. Third, the probability of selecting an incorrect alternative is dramatically diminished, regardless of the size of the majority, if there is at least *one* other person who also voices disagreement with the majority's position on the issue.[2] The probability of selecting an incorrect alternative is reduced whether or not the attitude of the additional deviant is the same as the subject's; breaking the opposing consensus is the important factor, rather than support for an opposing position. Fourth, the probability of selecting an incorrect alternative is substantially reduced when minority subjects are permitted to privately record their selections. Hence, the most secure finding is that noteworthy marginal effects of faction size appear with majority factions in triads and tetrads when subjects are forced to publicly announce their positions.

Formal Perspective. We now analyze the Asch experimental design as a special case of social influence network theory. For convenience, let the naïve subject be $i = 1$ in a group of size n and let the correct alternative be c. Hence, the influence network of an Asch-type situation is

$$
\mathbf{W} = \begin{bmatrix} w_{11} & w_{12} & \cdots & w_{1n} \\ 0 & 1 & \cdots & 0 \\ \vdots & \vdots & \ddots & \vdots \\ 0 & 0 & \cdots & 1 \end{bmatrix}
$$

with susceptibilities $a_{ii} = 1 - w_{ii}$ constrained so that only one person, person 1 in this case, may be susceptible to influence.

For qualitative comparisons, the issue may be represented by a row stochastic matrix of subjective probabilities that each element of a set of m alternatives is correct,

$$
\mathbf{Y}^{(1)}_{n \times m} = \begin{bmatrix} \mathbf{y}^{(1)}_1 & \mathbf{y}^{(1)}_2 & \cdots & \mathbf{y}^{(1)}_m \end{bmatrix} = \begin{bmatrix} 0 & \cdots & 0 & 1 \\ 1 & 0 & \cdots & 0 \\ \vdots & \vdots & \ddots & \vdots \\ 1 & 0 & \cdots & 0 \end{bmatrix},
$$

where each row i of $\mathbf{Y}^{(1)}_{n \times m} = [y^{(1)}_{ik}]$ describes the attitude of a group member i. Thus, members 2 through n are in agreement in their choice of

---

[2] The importance of social support in undermining powerful pressures to behave in an "incorrect" manner has also been documented in the studies of Milgram (1974) on obedience to authority. These countervailing effects of social support do not appear to be based on any substantive or intellectual engagement with an issue, but merely on the observation by the focal subject that there is another person who holds a position that is the same as or similar to his or her own position. But it is unclear whether this finding also holds for issues on which there is no obviously correct response.

some alternative (e.g, alternative 1 above) that is not the correct alternative ($c = m$ above), and person 1 holds an initial attitude different from these other members (here assumed to be $c = m$) on issues where the correct alternative is obvious. For qualitative attitudes, the impact of the majority is manifested in the subject's equilibrium *profile* of subjective probabilities, i.e., $\left[y_{11}^{(\infty)} \; y_{12}^{(\infty)} \; \dots \; y_{1m}^{(\infty)} \right]$ for subject 1. These equilibrium attitudes are derived from the initial attitudes by our model:

$$\mathbf{Y}^{(t+1)} = \mathbf{AWY}^{(t)} + (\mathbf{I} - \mathbf{A})\,\mathbf{Y}^{(1)}.$$

From this, the scalar equation for subject 1 is

$$y_{1k}^{(t+1)} = a_{11} \sum_{j=1}^{n} w_{1j} y_{jk}^{(t)} + (1 - a_{11})\, y_{1k}^{(1)}$$

for $k = 1, \dots, m$. In the present circumstances, subject 1's equilibrium profile is strictly a function of his or her susceptibility,

$$y_{1k}^{(\infty)} = a_{11} \sum_{j=1}^{n} w_{1j} y_{jk}^{(\infty)} + (1 - a_{11})\, y_{1k}^{(1)}$$

$$= a_{11}(1 - a_{11})\, y_{1k}^{(\infty)} + a_{11} \sum_{j=2}^{n} w_{1j} y_{jk}^{(\infty)} + (1 - a_{11})\, y_{1k}^{(1)},$$

whence

$$y_{1k}^{(\infty)} = \frac{a_{11}}{1 - a_{11} + a_{11}^2} \sum_{j=2}^{n} w_{1j} y_{jk}^{(\infty)} + \frac{1 - a_{11}}{1 - a_{11} + a_{11}^2} y_{1k}^{(1)}$$

$$= \frac{a_{11}^2}{1 - a_{11} + a_{11}^2} y_{*k}^{(\infty)} + \frac{1 - a_{11}}{1 - a_{11} + a_{11}^2} y_{1k}^{(1)},$$

because $y_{*k}^{(\infty)} = y_{2k}^{(\infty)} = y_{3k}^{(\infty)} = \dots = y_{nk}^{(\infty)}$. The result of no susceptibility to the influence of the majority ($a_{11} = 0$) is no change of attitude with certainty, i.e.,

$$\left[y_{11}^{(\infty)} \; y_{12}^{(\infty)} \; \dots \; y_{1m}^{(\infty)} \right] = [0 \; \cdots \; 0 \quad 1],$$

and the result of maximum susceptibility ($a_{11} = 1$) is an adoption of the majority's attitude with certainty,

$$\left[y_{11}^{(\infty)} \; y_{12}^{(\infty)} \; \dots \; y_{1m}^{(\infty)} \right] = [1 \quad 0 \; \cdots \; 0].$$

Intermediate susceptibilities produce levels of uncertainty between these two extremes, e.g.,

$$\left[y_{11}^{(\infty)} \quad y_{12}^{(\infty)} \quad \cdots \quad y_{1m}^{(\infty)} \right] = \left[0.08 \quad 0 \cdots 0 \quad 0.92 \right] \quad \text{for } a_{11} = 0.25,$$

$$\left[y_{11}^{(\infty)} \quad y_{12}^{(\infty)} \quad \cdots \quad y_{1m}^{(\infty)} \right] = \left[0.33 \quad 0 \cdots 0 \quad 0.67 \right] \quad \text{for } a_{11} = 0.50,$$

and

$$\left[y_{11}^{(\infty)} \quad y_{12}^{(\infty)} \quad \cdots \quad y_{1m}^{(\infty)} \right] = \left[0.69 \quad 0 \cdots 0 \quad 0.31 \right] \quad \text{for } a_{11} = 0.75$$

The point of *maximum uncertainty*,

$$\left[y_{11}^{(\infty)} \quad y_{12}^{(\infty)} \quad \cdots \quad y_{1m}^{(\infty)} \right] = \left[0.50 \quad 0 \cdots 0 \ 0.50 \right],$$

occurs at $a_{11} \approx 0.618$. How subjects choose an alternative based on these subjective probabilities would be the result of a decision rule that is outside the scope of our standard model. The model predicts only the *attitude* that underlies such choices, although it can easily be extended to an account of choice behavior on the basis of a function that links attitude to choice (Chapter 3). For example, with a measure of a_{11}, a simple decision rule might be that the majority's position will be adopted when $a_{11} > 0.618$ and the minority's position will be maintained when $a_{11} < 0.618$.

   In some of Asch's experiments, three or more line lengths were displayed as options. These options have a natural *rank order* in terms of lengths and can be embedded into the positive real numbers. Therefore, the range of the group's initial choices is defined by the initial choice of the naïve subject (which is assumed to be the correct line length, c) and the line length advocated by the majority, m. Not all of the available options necessarily fall within this range. For example, consider the following two sets of options:

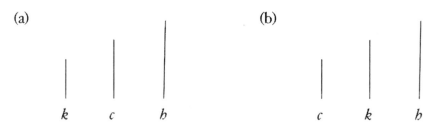

In situation (a) option k is outside the range defined by the initial attitudes c and h, and in situation (b) it is inside it. Options outside the range were never selected by subjects; however, incorrect final options within the range were sometimes selected that were not the majority's position. Asch found that for three alternative line lengths, in which the majority selected the line length most distant from the correct length, 81% of the naïve subjects' errors were choices of the majority's extreme position and 19% were choices of the available option between them. The tendency to select a moderate (compromise) position, rather than the extreme position of the majority, was increased when the subjects were allowed to record their choices privately.

We can now interpret c and h as numerical values in the positive real numbers, so that the attitude values of the group are given by the initial vector of these values

$$\mathbf{y}^{(1)} = \begin{bmatrix} c \\ h \\ \vdots \\ h \end{bmatrix}.$$

Such a vector would be directly applicable to experiments where persons were asked to publicly voice their judgments in terms of *numerical* values rather than categorical alternatives. This is the standard situation for our model

$$y_i^{(\infty)} = a_{ii} \sum_{j=1}^{n} w_{ij} y_j^{(\infty)} + (1 - a_{ii}) y_i^{(1)},$$

$i = 1, \ldots, n$, in which, for the unanimous majority,

$$y_j^{(\infty)} = y_j^{(1)} = h,$$

$j = 2, \ldots, n$, and for the minority of one, $i = 1$,

$$y_1^{(\infty)} = \left(\frac{a_{11}^2}{1 - a_{11} + a_{11}^2} \right) h + \left(\frac{1 - a_{11}}{1 - a_{11} + a_{11}^2} \right) c. \qquad (8.5)$$

Hence, the equilibrium attitude of the naïve subject is the weighted average of the initial attitudes of the subject and the majority. If $a_{11} = 1$, the naïve subject will adopt the fixed majority position and if $0 < a_{11} < 1$, he or she will move toward the majority position on the real number scale. The total influence of the majority position,

$$\left(\frac{a_{11}^2}{1 - a_{11} + a_{11}^2} \right),$$

is a function of the subject's susceptibility. As Figure 8.3 shows, the impact of the majority on the naïve subject is approximately a linear function

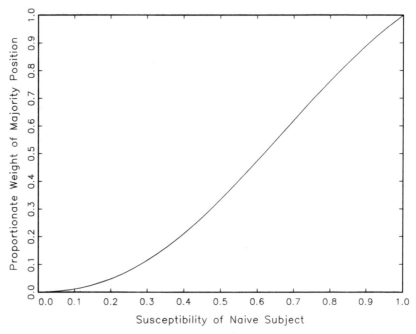

Figure 8.3 Proportionate weight of the majority position in the Asch influence system.

of the subject's susceptibility for most of the range of susceptibility, i.e., approximately $0.30 \leq a_{11} \leq 1$. When subjects' choices are constrained to two line lengths, they must choose either to adopt the majority position or not, but when subjects have an option or options that lie between these two initial positions, then they may move toward but not adopt the majority position.

Deriving Goldberg's Index of Proportional Conformity. Equation (8.5) allows for the case in which subjects move toward but do not completely comply with the majority faction's position. When persons reduce the differences of their positions on issues but do not entirely eliminate these differences, the concept of conformity needs to be relaxed to accommodate the spectrum of possible movements toward a position. Goldberg (1954) described such movements with an index of *proportional conformity* that is a measure of the *degree* of influence of a unanimous majority on a minority of one. His index is the absolute change in the minority position divided by the initial distance between the minority and majority positions. We now show that we can derive the index proposed by Goldberg (1954) from social influence network theory. Goldberg proposed the index *ad hoc*, without theoretical justification; our contribution is to provide a theoretical foundation for his index.

Consider

$$y_1^{(\infty)} = \sum_{j=2}^{n} v_{1j} y_j^{(1)}$$

with the additional stipulation of the existence of a consensus of initial attitudes among all persons other than person 1. If the *consensual attitude* of all persons $j \neq 1$ is κ, then

$$y_1^{(\infty)} = v_{11} y_1^{(1)} + \kappa \sum_{j=2}^{n} v_{1j} \tag{8.6}$$

and

$$\sum_{j=2}^{n} v_{1j} = 1 - v_{11} = \frac{y_1^{(\infty)} - y_1^{(1)}}{\kappa - y_1^{(1)}}. \tag{8.7}$$

The ratio described in (8.7) is Goldberg's index of proportional conformity. We see that this index describes the *aggregate* relative weight of the position held by others in determining the equilibrium position of person 1. The complement of this conformity index is simply v_{11}, that is, the weight person 1 places on his or her own position. This derivation does not assume that the unanimous majority position is fixed.

Under the conditions of Asch's experiments, the initial attitudes of the other group members are a fixed consensus, i.e., $a_{jj} = 1 - w_{jj} = 0$ and $y_j^{(1)} = \kappa$ for all $j \neq 1$. Person 1 cannot be influential, but may be influenced; hence, the only value of Goldberg's index that can be nonzero is the value of the index for person 1. Under the special condition of a fixed consensus, it also can be shown (Appendix E) that Goldberg's index of proportional conformity can be expressed in terms of person 1's susceptibility to interpersonal influence:

$$\sum_{j=2}^{n} v_{1j} = \frac{y_1^{(\infty)} - y_1^{(1)}}{\kappa - y_1^{(1)}} = \frac{a_{11}^2}{1 - a_{11} + a_{11}^2}. \tag{8.8}$$

It follows that

$$v_{11} = 1 - \frac{y_1^{(\infty)} - y_1^{(1)}}{\kappa - y_1^{(1)}} = \frac{1 - a_{11}}{1 - a_{11} + a_{11}^2} \tag{8.9}$$

and, from (8.5), that

$$y_1^{(\infty)} = \left(\frac{a_{11}^2}{1 - a_{11} + a_{11}^2} \right) m + \left(\frac{1 - a_{11}}{1 - a_{11} + a_{11}^2} \right) y_1^{(1)}$$

$$= \left(\sum_{j=2}^{n} v_{1j} \right) \kappa + (v_{11}) y_1^{(1)}. \tag{8.10}$$

The value of the index (8.8) will be 1 if person 1 adopts the consensual position κ of the other members, and it will be less than 1 depending on the extent of person 1's movement toward the fixed majority position. If he or she is not susceptible, then $a_{11} = 0$ and there is no change of attitude. If he or she is susceptible, then $0 < a_{11} \leq 1$ and some interpersonal influence is allocated to the consensual faction.

Although the consensual faction might be thought of as a coherent "collective other" that is allocated influence, from our perspective influence is always *interpersonal*. Membership in a majority or minority group may be conceptualized as a status characteristic of individuals that affects their susceptibilities and interpersonal influences. As such, it may add to or interact with other conditions, including other visible status characteristics (race, sex, age, etc.) of the minority and majority members. Our approach allows for the possibility that the members of the majority faction may have different interpersonal influences on person 1.

8.2.2 Reverse-Asch Design and Minority Influence

The generic social structure of a reverse-Asch situation is

$$\mathbf{W} = \begin{bmatrix} 1 & 0 & \cdots & 0 \\ w_{21} & w_{22} & \cdots & w_{2n} \\ \vdots & \vdots & \ddots & \vdots \\ w_{n1} & w_{n2} & \cdots & w_{nn} \end{bmatrix}$$

and either a row-stochastic matrix of initial subjective probabilities for m alternatives,

$$\mathbf{Y}_{n \times m}^{(1)} = \begin{bmatrix} 1 & 0 & \cdots & 0 \\ 0 & \cdots & 0 & 1 \\ \vdots & \vdots & \vdots & \vdots \\ 0 & \cdots & 0 & 1 \end{bmatrix},$$

or a vector of initial positions on an issue,

$$\mathbf{y}^{(1)} = \begin{bmatrix} h \\ c \\ \vdots \\ c \end{bmatrix}.$$

As in the Asch experiments, the issue may have an *obvious* correct response c, so that the initial attitudes among the naïve subjects are likely to be identical and correct; in contrast to this agreement, person 1 (the confederate) advocates an incorrect alternative h. Unlike an Asch-type experiment, where the consensual majority are confederates of the experimenter, who instructs them not to alter their initial positions, in the reverse-Asch situation, the deviate is the confederate, whose position is fixed, and the members of the consensual majority are the naïve subjects.

Asch (1952: 479–81) examined two special cases of this situation. First, in the case of a naïve majority of 15 members vs. an incorrect confederate minority of one, Asch found that the single deviate had no effect on the attitudes of the majority. In contrast to the tensions experienced by the naïve subject who was confronted with a unanimous incorrect majority, the naïve faction experienced no such problems:

> At the outset they greeted the estimates of the dissenter with incredulity. On the later trials there were smiles and impromptu comments. As the experiment progressed, contagious, and in some instances uncontrolled, laughter swept the group. (Asch 1952: 479)

Second, in the case of a naïve faction of 11 persons vs. a confederate faction of 9 persons, the members of the naïve faction were not influenced by the opposing position of the confederate faction.

> The naïve subgroup maintained confidence in their responses, and the main problem was why the others disagreed. The tenor of the reactions to the opposition was now quite different. The note of ridicule and derision, which previously was quite insistent, now occurred only rarely. The bulk of the comments were attempts to explain the cleavage in terms of relatively objective factors such as optical ability and misunderstanding of the instructions. The reactions of the naïve group changed from outright repudiation to a more respectful attitude as the ranks of the opposition increased. (Asch 1952: 480)

Moscovici's (1976, 1985) subsequent work on the reverse-Asch situation has stimulated a large number of studies (Cialdini and Trost 1998; Dreu and Vries 2001; Levine 1989; Levine and Moreland 1998; Levine and Russo 1987; Maass and Clark 1984; Maass, West, and Cialdini 1987; Martin and Hewstone 2001; Moscovici 1980, 1985; Moscovici, Mucchi-Faina, and Maass 1994; Wood, Lundgren, Ouellette, Busceme, and Blackstone 1994). These experiments support Asch's finding that the members of a majority position are unlikely to adopt the position of a minority; but unlike Asch's finding of no change of attitude, it is clear (as in our findings on triads, Chapter 7) that a minority may produce some change in majority members' initial position.

The literature on minority effects has become concentrated on questions related to (a) the basis of the effects of majority and minority influence, (b) the conditions under which minority influence might become more probable, and (c) the occurrence of hidden, delayed, or indirect changes of attitude among the majority of members. This body of work is controversial and unsettled (Baron, Kerr, and Miller 1992; Cramer 1975; Doms 1984; Doms and Avermaet 1980; Kelvin 1979; Latané and Wolf 1981; Levine 1989; Mackie 1987; Martin 1998; Martin and Hewstone 2001; Nemeth 1975; Sorrentino, King, and Leo 1980; Wood et al. 1994). Moscovici has argued that the main basis of majority influence is compliance (change of publicly displayed attitude without any change of the privately held attitude on an issue) and that the main basis of minority influence is conversion (change of privately held attitudes), and he has argued that conversion is a more enduring change than compliance. The argument rests on the following assumption: since the credibility of a minority is not based on numerical superiority, it is more likely to be based on argumentation and persuasion. However, minorities may coerce an accommodation to their positions when consensus is required or strongly desired and they may hold group consensus hostage to their special interests and intransigence. It may be overly generous to refer to such coercion as "behavioral consistency" as is often done in the literature on minority influence. Furthermore, a majority's influence may be based on sound arguments or broadly shared interests; indeed, majorities may form on particular positions because of the merits of those positions relative to alternatives (although this was not the case in the Asch experiments).

8.3 Findings on Naturally Occurring Factions

Our experiments provided some naturally occurring instances of factions. Denoting the initial and equilibrium attitudes of a faction's members by the subvectors $\mathbf{y}^{(1,f)}$ and $\mathbf{y}^{(\infty,f)}$, respectively, three types of factions may be discriminated: fixed, shifted, and broken. In fixed factions $\mathbf{y}^{(1,f)} = \mathbf{y}^{(\infty,f)}$; in shifted factions $\mathbf{y}^{(1,f)} \neq \mathbf{y}^{(\infty,f)}$ and the faction members have moved to a new shared position; in broken factions $\mathbf{y}^{(1,f)} \neq \mathbf{y}^{(\infty,f)}$ and the faction members are in disagreement at equilibrium.

Table 8.1 *Fixed, shifted, and broken initial factions in dyads, triads, and tetrads*

	Faction at equilibrium			
Faction size	Fixed	Shifted	Broken	Totals
Dyads				
2	5	3	0	8
Triads				
2	15	9	3	27
3	2	0	0	2
Tetrads				
2	32	63	4	99[a]
3	3	3	0	6
4	0	0	0	0
TOTALS	57	78	7	142

[a] These 99 tetrads do not include the factions of four tetrads that were split into two factions.

Table 8.1 reports the behavior of the factions that appeared in our dyads, triads, and tetrads. There are two especially noteworthy features of these data. First, the incidence of broken factions is low. Second, the incidence of shifted factions is substantial. Faction members tend to remain in agreement, but it cannot be assumed that their initial positions remain fixed.

We have previously analyzed triads with a majority and a minority of one. We noted that in only 2 of the 27 instances of a majority faction was a consensus formed on the initial position of the minority member. The tetrads provided only 6 cases of a naturally occurring majority: 2 resulted in a consensus on the position of the minority of one; 3 resulted in a consensus on the position of the majority; and 1 resulted in a consensus on a compromise position. However, the tetrads provided 107 naturally occurring two-person factions, 8 of which occurred in four groups that were split into two factions. We set these four tetrads aside and concentrate the analysis on the remaining 99 tetrads, each with one two-person faction and two disagreeing members. These cases provide an opportunity to analyze the effects of modal positions that are not majority positions. Table 8.2 describes the group outcomes of these 99 tetrads.

Given a *modal* position (that is not a majority) in a tetrad, consensus was reached in 87 (87.9%) of the groups, and in 74 of these 87 cases the consensus was *not* on an initial position of one of the minority members. However, the consensus that was produced under these circumstances involved a shift of the modal faction's initial position in 61 cases, which suggests that minority members frequently influence the members of modal factions. Minorities infrequently divide a modal faction; this

Table 8.2 *Group outcomes of tetrads with naturally occurring two-person factions*

	Attitude of faction members						
	Fixed position[a]		Shifted position		Broken position		Totals
Equilibrium pattern of attitudes	*N*	%	*N*	%	*N*	%	*N*
Consensus on boundary initial position	10	31.2	4[a]	6.3	—	—	14
Consensus on internal initial position	16	50.0	11[b]	17.5	—	—	27
Consensus on new internal position	0	0	46[c]	73.0	—	—	46
Disagreement in range of initial positions	6	18.8	2	3.2	4	100.0	12
TOTALS	32	100.0	63	100.0	4	100.0	99

[a]In 3 of these cases, the faction occupied an initial position between the two other members; hence, the group settled on a minority member's initial position in these 3 cases.

[b]In none of these cases did the faction occupy an initial position between the two other members; hence, the group settled on a minority member's initial position in all 11 of these cases.

[c]In 15 of these 46 cases, the faction occupied an initial position between the two other members.

—Logically impossible cases.

occurred in only four cases. Hence, it is clear that in tetrads, a faction consisting of two persons *cannot* be assumed to reliably anchor the faction on its initial position, but it *can* be assumed to reliably anchor the maintenance of a state of agreement.

8.4 Concluding Remarks

We propose, as others have, that a single influence process underlies majority and minority influence (Doms 1984; Latané and Wolf 1981; Tanford and Penrod 1984; Wolf 1987). The assertion of a single process does not imply that there is a single *basis* of influence. Indeed, there are usually multiple and various bases for the interpersonal influences that are shaping group members' attitudes; this is evident in Asch's (1951, 1952, 1956) analysis of the bases of conformity that were revealed in the postexperiment interviews with his subjects, in French and Raven's (1959) typology of power bases, and in other such typologies.

The theoretical contribution of social influence network theory is to elucidate the process by which attitudes are changed and consensus is produced, or not, in a group regardless of the bases on which group members' interpersonal influences rest. Findings indicating that particular bases predominate in certain circumstances, or that particular behavioral styles or persuasion tactics foster interpersonal influence under certain circumstances, are interesting and important, but they are of limited theoretical value to an understanding of how groups reach consensus. The assertion of a single process is an assertion that interpersonal influences operate through a small set of key theoretical constructs that are combined in one social process function. Our candidate for such a mechanism is the iterated weighted averaging of influential positions which unfolds within an influence network.

In this chapter, we have developed an influence network perspective on the faction-size effects that have been emphasized in the literature stemming from the Asch experiments. There is little doubt that there are effects on a substantial fraction of subjects' susceptibilities when they are confronted with the circumstances of the Asch experiments: some subjects questioned their own expertise, others could not tolerate the punishing tensions of disagreement, and still others sought reward and approval through agreement, or accepted the authority of the majority (Asch 1952). However, the influence of faction size is tenuous and its effects diminish radically if there are multiple dissenting attitudes. Moreover, our evidence indicates that factions do not operate to *fix* the attitudes of the occupants of a position. Given the likely presence of multiple sources of disagreement with any given position in a group, and the presence of bases of influence that foster inequalities of interpersonal influence, we think it is doubtful that faction size *per se* has a ubiquitous effect on persons' susceptibilities or interpersonal influences.

Our theoretical emphasis on the aggregation of a faction's interpersonal influences is built directly on the logic of our model. In essence, it is an approach that relaxes the viewpoint on a faction as a coherent social unit. The members of a faction share an identical position on an issue. But apart from that identity, they may differ in their susceptibilities to interpersonal influence, they may be influenced differently by persons within and outside the faction, and other group members (who are not members of the faction) may be influenced differently by particular members of the faction. An aggregation approach is sufficiently flexible to deal with such potential heterogeneity. This approach allows the analysis of factions in the influence process and, by directly addressing the interpersonal influences of individuals, presents a more nuanced theoretical treatment of factions than we find in the literature on majority and minority effects. The approach is not incompatible with an assertion of other effects of the faction structure of a group, including the relative size of a particular faction, on group decisions. With respect to the influence process that may modify group members' positions on an issue, such effects may occur when the visible faction structure of a group affects the influence network of the group, e.g., when membership in a large faction has a main effect in lowering susceptibilities, or when membership in a small faction has a main effect in elevating susceptibilities. Our theoretical analysis is restricted to the *implications* of the influence networks that are formed in groups with factions.

This chapter advances our general unification agenda by detailing how two prominent experimental designs in social psychology – dealing with majority and minority influences – may be situated as special cases of social influence network theory. We have shown how the two experimental designs may be formalized in terms of imposed constraints on the social structure of a group that includes not only its initial faction structure but also its influence network. We believe that this is a useful formal perspective on these designs. It emphasizes that they are special cases, amenable to experimental study, in a larger domain of social structures, defined by $\mathbf{A}$, $\mathbf{W}$, and $\mathbf{y}^{(1)}$, some which might also be examined in experimental settings and others which might be examined in field settings. It is difficult to see how such unification might be advanced without the construct of an influence *network* and a formalization of the influence process that unfolds in such networks.

9

Choice Shift and Group Polarization

In this chapter, we bring social influence network theory to bear on the explanation of choice shift and group polarization in small groups. A *choice shift* occurs when, after a group's interaction on an issue, the mean attitude of group members differs from the members' mean initial attitude. *Group polarization* occurs when the choice shift is in the same direction as the inclination of the mean initial attitude: for example, if on some issue the initial attitude of the average member is positive (negative), then the subsequent attitude of the average member after group discussion will be more positive (negative). An explanation of choice shift is fundamental because it would also explain group polarization. Group polarization always involves a choice shift, but a choice shift can occur that does not entail group polarization (e.g., a choice shift that is in the direction opposite to the initial inclination of the group). Research on choice shifts and group polarization originated with Stoner's (1961) finding on choice dilemmas (issues in which a level of acceptable risk on a course of action is being debated) in which he reported that the decisions of groups involved higher levels of risk-taking than the decisions of individuals. This finding, known as the "risky shift," stimulated a large number of studies:

> Rarely in the history of social psychology has a single study stim-
> ulated as much research as the master's thesis by Stoner (1961)
> which reported the discovery of "the risky shift." Its conclusion
> that groups are riskier than individuals was widely interpreted as
> being contrary to the findings of previous research on the effects
> of groups on individuals. It challenged conventional wisdom, and
> it appeared to have implications for those responsible for making
> important decisions involving risk. (Cartwright 1971: 361)

Although the idea that group discussion reliably produces greater acceptance of risk was discredited, the more general phenomenon of choice

211

shift (including group polarization) continued to motivate research (Cartwright 1971; 1973; Clark 1971; Dion, Baron, and Miller 1970; Hogg, Turner, and Davidson 1990; Isenberg 1986; Kaplan and Miller 1983; Lamm and Myers 1978; McGarty et al. 1992; Myers and Lamm 1976; Pruitt 1971; Turner, Wetherell, and Hogg 1989; Vinokur 1971).

Research on choice shift has developed as a *counterpoint* to classical perspectives on social influence that have emphasized mechanisms of accommodation and conformity. It is not clear why some researchers in the choice shift tradition believe that classical perspectives on social influence predict convergence to the mean initial position on an issue (e.g., McGarty et al. 1992: 2; Turner 1991: 50), but it is clear that these researchers view choice shifts as the product of a distinctive social process that requires the development of new theory. We believe that this viewpoint on choice shifts is incorrect and that both the convergence of attitudes on the mean initial attitude of a group and choice shifts (including group polarization) are special cases of a general process of interpersonal influence that may unfold in different influence networks.

The literature on choice shift has treated group discussion as a main effect on attitudes. None of the various theories that have competed to explain choice shifts has entertained the simple idea that choice shifts are generated by heterogeneous interpersonal influences and susceptibilities to such influences among the members of a group. We demonstrate that choice shifts and group polarization are readily explained by the group's influence network and the interpersonal influence process that unfolds in it, i.e., the process that is specified by our standard model. Near the beginning of our research on this model (Friedkin and Johnsen 1990), we included a group polarization parameter that operated to shift all group members' positions up or down the attitude scale. We dropped that parameter as we became convinced that there was no need for it.

Below, we demonstrate that our standard model is formally consistent with choice shifts. We then review the main theories on choice shifts that have been proposed. Finally, we present our empirical findings on choice shifts and group polarization, which have led us to the theoretical assertion of a single process underlying these phenomena.

9.1 Formal Analysis

We develop an account of choice shifts that was suggested by Cartwright (1971) in his analysis of the "risky shift" literature. Cartwright pressed for an analysis of the interpersonal influences that produce a choice shift. He suggested that a choice shift could be produced by the process of interpersonal accommodation itself (i.e., that no new process or separate group effect produces these shifts), and he pointed to the formal theory of social power developed by French (1956) and Harary (1959) as a possible starting point for such an explanation.[1] The models proposed by French and Harary are special cases of our model, as we showed in Chapter 2. We revisit Cartwright's (1971) arguments with our network theory of social influence.

In terms of social influence network theory, choice shifts (including group polarization) are produced by individual differences in susceptibilities and inequalities of interpersonal influence. Conditions (E) exogenous to our model may produce a choice shift as a consequence of their effects on group members' initial attitudes, susceptibilities to influence, and interpersonal influences:

$$\mathbf{y}^{(t+1)} = \mathbf{A}\mathbf{W}\mathbf{y}^{(t)} + (\mathbf{I} - \mathbf{A})\,\mathbf{y}^{(1)} \tag{9.1}$$

$$\underset{\mathrm{E_W}}{\uparrow} \qquad \underset{\mathrm{E_A}\ \mathrm{E_Y}}{\uparrow\ \uparrow}$$

As (9.1) suggests, any condition that affects $\mathbf{AW}$ may produce a choice shift. Heterogeneous individual susceptibilities and interpersonal influences may result in no choice shift, but the more likely outcome of such heterogeneity is a choice shift in which the mean equilibrium attitude of a group differs from the mean initial attitude. Choice shifts may be *ubiquitous* because individual differences in susceptibilities and inequalities of interpersonal influence in groups are ubiquitous.

The following example illustrates how our theory bears on choice shifts. The initial attitudes of the group members are

$$\mathbf{y}^{(1)} = \begin{bmatrix} 1{,}000 \\ 500 \\ 1{,}000 \\ 1{,}000 \end{bmatrix}$$

and the mean of these initial attitudes is $\bar{y}^{(1)} = 875$. The influence network of the group is

$$\mathbf{W} = \begin{bmatrix} 0 & 0.780 & 0.110 & 0.110 \\ 0 & 1 & 0 & 0 \\ 0.140 & 0.530 & 0 & 0.330 \\ 0 & 0.500 & 0.500 & 0 \end{bmatrix},$$

and describes the distribution of interpersonal influences. From the above $\mathbf{W}$, the susceptibilities of the group's members are $a_{22} = 0$ and $a_{11} = a_{33} =$

---

[1] Our analysis also builds on Kaplan and Miller's (1983) suggestion that a weighted averaging mechanism of information integration (Anderson 1981; Anderson and Graesser 1976) elucidates choice shift and group polarization; an iterated weighted averaging of influential attitudes is the engine that drives our network theory of social influence.

$a_{44} = 1$. The matrix of total influences that results from the influence process is

$$
\mathbf{V} = \begin{bmatrix} 0 & 1 & 0 & 0 \\ 0 & 1 & 0 & 0 \\ 0 & 1 & 0 & 0 \\ 0 & 1 & 0 & 0 \end{bmatrix}
$$

and the equilibrium attitudes of the group's members are

$$
\mathbf{y}^{(\infty)} = \mathbf{V}\mathbf{y}^{(1)} = \begin{bmatrix} 500 \\ 500 \\ 500 \\ 500 \end{bmatrix}.
$$

The mean of the final attitudes is $\bar{y}^{(\infty)} = 500$, and the choice shift $\left(\bar{y}^{(\infty)} - \bar{y}^{(1)} = -375\right)$ is substantial.

Choice shifts are a function of inequalities of interpersonal influence. Since

$$
y_i^{(\infty)} = \sum_{j=1}^{n} v_{ij} y_j^{(1)}, \quad 1 \le i \le n,
$$

it follows that

$$
\bar{y}_{\bullet}^{(\infty)} = \sum_{j=1}^{n} \bar{v}_{\bullet j} y_j^{(1)},
$$

where $\bar{v}_{\bullet j}$ is the average value of the entries in column j of $\mathbf{V}$ and $\sum_{j=1}^{n} \bar{v}_{\bullet j} = 1$. If the total influences of the group's members are heterogeneous, then a choice shift may occur.

Heterogeneity may be produced by *constraints* on the pattern of interpersonal influences. For example, consider a homogeneous group in which each person i is directly influenced by some number of persons $n_i < n$ and each of the interpersonal influences $w_{ij} > 0$ is $w_{ij} = \alpha/n_i$ and where $a_{ii} = \alpha$ for all i; that is, the influence network may be incomplete but otherwise homogeneous with respect to the relative influences on each person and the susceptibilities of each person. For instance, in a group with four members, if $\alpha = 1 - w_{ii} = 0.8$ for all i and

$$
\mathbf{W} = \begin{bmatrix} 0.2 & 0 & 0 & 0.8 \\ 0 & 0.2 & 0.4 & 0.4 \\ 0 & 0.8 & 0.2 & 0 \\ 0.4 & 0 & 0.4 & 0.2 \end{bmatrix} \quad \mathbf{y}^{(1)} = \begin{bmatrix} 108 \\ 6 \\ -97 \\ 28 \end{bmatrix},
$$

the equilibrium attitudes are

$$\mathbf{y}^{(\infty)} = \begin{bmatrix} 32.1 \\ -5.9 \\ -27.6 \\ 8.4 \end{bmatrix}$$

and the means of the initial and equilibrium attitudes (11.25 and 1.75, respectively) indicate a choice shift. Thus, a single influence process may be consistent with equilibrium attitudes that are either in agreement or disagreement, with mean final and mean initial attitudes that may be the same or different, and with a convergence of attitudes on a particular attitudinal position within the range of initial attitudes, including the mean initial attitude of the group and the initial attitude of a particular person.

9.2 Theories of Choice Shifts

Four main approaches have competed as explanations of choice shifts – *persuasive arguments theory*, *social comparison theory*, *self-categorization theory*, and *social decision scheme theory*. We describe each of these approaches and discuss its relationship (and possible theoretical integration) with social influence network theory. We begin with a formal definition of the choice shift phenomena that these theories are seeking to explain.

9.2.1 Types of Choice Shift

Group outcomes appear in a variety of forms in the distribution of group members' attitudes. Attitudes may settle on the mean of group members' initial attitudes. They may settle on a compromise attitude that differs from the mean of initial attitudes. They may settle on an initial attitude of a group member that differs from the mean of initial attitudes. They may settle on altered attitudes that do not form a consensus. All of these outcomes are common (Chapter 4). The literature on choice shifts defines group outcomes in terms of the *relative* positions of the mean initial and mean equilibrium attitudes of group members. If $\bar{y}^{(\infty)} = \bar{y}^{(1)}$ in a group, then there is no choice shift; otherwise, the choice shift is either a polarization (positive or negative), antipolarization (positive or negative), or nonpolarization (positive or negative).[2] The type of shift depends on

---

[2] Within the two categories of antipolarization (positive and negative), there are interesting special cases that seem to differ qualitatively as a function of the magnitude of the shift. The shift may or may not move through the neutral value of the scale and, in the latter case, it may or may not move to a value that is more distant from the neutral value than the mean initial attitude.

the position of the mean initial attitude relative to a neutral attitude θ and the mean equilibrium attitude in a group:

a. Positive Polarization $\quad \left\{ \bar{y}^{(1)} > \theta, \ \bar{y}^{(\infty)} > \bar{y}^{(1)} \right\}$

b. Negative Polarization $\quad \left\{ \bar{y}^{(1)} < \theta, \ \bar{y}^{(\infty)} < \bar{y}^{(1)} \right\}$

c. Positive Antipolarization $\quad \left\{ \bar{y}^{(1)} < \theta, \ \bar{y}^{(\infty)} > \bar{y}^{(1)} \right\}$

d. Negative Antipolarization $\quad \left\{ \bar{y}^{(1)} > \theta, \ \bar{y}^{(\infty)} < \bar{y}^{(1)} \right\}$

e. Positive Nonpolarization $\quad \left\{ \bar{y}^{(1)} = \theta, \ \bar{y}^{(\infty)} > \bar{y}^{(1)} \right\}$

f. Negative Nonpolarization $\quad \left\{ \bar{y}^{(1)} = \theta, \ \bar{y}^{(\infty)} < \bar{y}^{(1)} \right\}$

g. No Polarization $\quad \left\{ \bar{y}^{(\infty)} = \bar{y}^{(1)} \right\}.$

Given θ, we can describe the distribution of group outcomes on an issue across these possible types of choice shift. However, if there is no neutral point or one cannot be ascertained, then the concept of group polarization no longer applies. Instead, we may categorize choice shifts either as involving an increasing (escalating) or decreasing (deescalating) change in the mean attitude of group members:

a. Positive Escalation $\quad \left\{ \bar{y}^{(\infty)} > \bar{y}^{(1)} \right\}$

b. Negative Escalation $\quad \left\{ \bar{y}^{(\infty)} < \bar{y}^{(1)} \right\}$

c. No Escalation $\quad \left\{ \bar{y}^{(\infty)} = \bar{y}^{(1)} \right\},$

or, even more simply, as a difference between the mean initial and equilibrium attitudes of a group:

a. Choice Shift $\quad \left\{ \bar{y}^{(\infty)} \neq \bar{y}^{(1)} \right\}$

b. No Choice Shift $\quad \left\{ \bar{y}^{(\infty)} = \bar{y}^{(1)} \right\}.$

Various methods for detecting choice shift and group polarization on choice dilemma issues have been employed. These different methods in part reflect the changing focus of research questions that have motivated work on choice shifts. Are groups' decisions more risky than individuals' decisions? To address this question, studies have compared the mean of N individuals' initial attitudes with the mean of K groups' decisions (the unanimous or average attitude of a group after discussion) composed of the same N individuals. Does group discussion make individuals' decisions more risky? To address this question, studies have compared the mean of N individuals' initial attitudes with the mean of the same N individuals' attitudes after discussion of the issue. Does group discussion produce group polarization? To address this question, studies have compared the central tendencies of the distributions of group-level mean attitudes before and after discussion.

In contrast to the detection of a simple escalation or deescalation of attitudes, the detection of group polarization requires special methods.

The detection of group polarization must take into account the conditional (if–then) nature of the phenomenon: *if* there is an initial mean inclination of the group, *then* under the condition of group discussion the mean attitude of the group will become more extreme in the direction of the initial inclination. It follows that for a set of groups that are dealing with the *same* issue, some groups may shift toward greater caution and others toward great risk, depending on the location of each group's mean initial attitude on an issue. If *issues* vary in their likelihood of risky or cautious group polarization, then this can only be because the initial mean attitude of a group is likely to be either risky or cautious. The detection of group polarization is arguably more compelling if it occurs on the *same* issue for groups that differ in the direction of the initial inclination of their members' attitudes; otherwise, for the same issue, the phenomenon is indistinguishable from a simple escalation or deescalation of attitudes that occurs in the absence of a neutral point. Less arguably, group polarization is a group-level phenomenon, but with a few exceptions (e.g., Fraser, Gouge, and Billig 1971; Friedkin 1999), the assessment of group polarization has not been conducted at the group level.

In addition to a group-level analysis of group polarization, the detection of this phenomenon also necessarily involves a neutral value upon which the assertion rests that there is an initial *inclination* of the group. On attitude scales that include both positive and negative values, there is a natural neutral point (zero). On issues concerned with the assessment of risk, the neutral value might be 0.50 on a scale of subjective probability of risk. Note that there is a close formal correspondence between a probability scale, an odds scale, and an attitudinal scale, in which the neutral values are 0.50, 1, and 0 respectively. The odds of an event is $P/(1 - P)$, where P is the probability of the event, and if $P = (1 + e^{-Z})^{-1}$, where Z is any real number, then $Z = 0$ corresponds to $P = 0.50$, a large positive Z corresponds to $P \approx 1$, and a large negative Z corresponds to $P \approx 0$. If Z is an attitude, then P is the attitude displayed in the form of a subjective probability. However, although we can move in a consistent fashion between scales of attitudes, odds, and subjective probabilities, the literature on group polarization is not clear on the theoretical properties of the neutral value that defines a group's initial inclination. Is it 0.50 on a scale of subjective probabilities, or is it a range of values near 0.50? Might it be any value (e.g., the mean attitude of the population of persons from which the group members are drawn) or any range of values (e.g., 0.55–0.65) on a scale? Or might it be any value or range of values on the basis of which a tendency for group polarization is *revealed* in a particular sample? If the theoretical properties of the neutral threshold are uncertain, one must wonder whether the methodological ambiguities involved in the claim that group polarization has been observed are so great as to make any such assertion problematical.

9.2.2 Persuasive Arguments Theory

Persuasive arguments theory (Burnstein 1982; Burnstein and Vinokur 1973, 1977; Vinokur and Burnstein 1978) explains group polarization on the basis of the *content* of the arguments that arise during a discussion. The hypothesis is that there is a pool of arguments that could be applied to any issue and that discussants draw those arguments from the pool that support their initial attitudes. If the distribution of initial attitudes is biased in a particular direction, then the sample of arguments expressed will reflect this bias and affect the direction of a choice shift:

> When the preponderance of arguments in the pool favors a particular alternative, the average prior attitude reflects the direction and magnitude of this preponderance. Further thought or discussion leads to polarization toward the alternative that initially elicits more and/or better arguments. (Burnstein and Vinokur 1977: 316)

> The extent of this effect will depend on whether the argument samples initially generated by the members overlap or exhaust the larger pool. Polarization will approach a maximum when members begin to reconsider the issue and there still remain many arguments that have not yet come to mind, and/or they discuss the issues with each other and the arguments that have come to mind are only partially shared. (Vinokur and Burnstein 1978: 873)

Hence, group discussion serves to provide more complete information about the relative merits of alternative positions and, if the pool of position arguments upon which group members are drawing tends to favor a more extreme than the mean of initial positions, then some polarization is likely to occur.

This hypothesis has been refined in various ways (Lamm and Myers 1978), but the key idea is that choice shift and group polarization depend on the actual or implicit *arguments* for positions that result from group discussions or a rethinking of the issue. This theory does not address the structure of interpersonal interactions and the responses of group members to these arguments (who is being influenced by whom, and who is saying what to whom). Instead, it emphasizes the effect of the *set* of arguments that emerge on an issue on the initial attitudes of group members. The proponents of this approach emphasize that the *visibility* of group members' attitudes is not a sufficient condition for a choice shift and that information about the relative merits of different attitudes (usually conveyed through interpersonal communication) is necessary. In this respect, persuasive arguments theory sharply contrasts with the other three major theories (reviewed below) in which the *visibility* of the initial distribution of attitudes is a sufficient condition for choice shift and group polarization.

We believe that persuasive arguments can be conceptualized as a pattern of interpersonal influences. Knowing who is persuading whom should improve an account of the attitude changes that are taking place in a group. However, the idea that interpersonal influence is necessarily based on persuasive arguments is too limiting. An attitude must be both visible and salient in order to be influential, and persuasive arguments are only one of many possible bases of salience. For example, a person's attitude may be influential without accompanying argument, if that person has power bases (French and Raven 1959) or status characteristics (Berger et al. 1974; Blascovich, Ginsburg, and Veach 1975) that make the person's displayed attitude salient.

9.2.3 Social Comparison Theory

This theory hypothesizes that persons initially espouse attitudes that are less extreme than their true attitudes (i.e., a more attractive extreme position) because of a fear of being labeled deviant, and when group discussion reveals that others espouse similar but more extreme attitudes they shift their position toward their true values and may even leapfrog over the more extreme positions of others (Baron and Roper 1976; Baron et al. 1996; Brown 1965; Goethals and Zanna 1979; Sanders and Baron 1977):

> This realization either "releases" the moderate members from their fear of appearing extreme, or motivates moderate members to "compete" with the extreme members to see who can come closest to espousing the most admired position. In either case, the moderates are motivated to adopt more extreme positions, while there is no corresponding pressure on extreme members to moderate their opinions (although, of course, simple conformity pressure may lead to some small amount of moderation by extreme members). The net result is an overall polarization of opinions, that is, a choice shift. (Sanders and Baron 1977: 304)

Group discussion, by disclosing group members' attitudes, erodes moderate positions and reinforces the attractiveness of adopting extreme positions.

The postulated mechanism assumes that the extreme positions on one part of the attitude scale are more highly valued than the other moderate or opposing positions. The relative salience of these positions is determined by the broader culture of the group members that invests positions with positive, negative, or neutral attractiveness. Hence, the mechanism does not appear to require persuasive arguments, because it is based on the *visibility* of positions that have different culturally determined relative values. But persuasive arguments could be involved if cultural values were explicitly invoked in an argument, and an interpersonal influence network might arise based on the visibility (mere awareness) of the distribution of attitudes in a group when different initial positions have unequal salience for group members.

9.2.4 Self-Categorization Theory

Self-categorization theory explains group polarization on the basis of the persons' conformity to an extreme norm or prototypical position of the group (Abrams, Wetherell, Cochrane, and Hogg 1990; Hogg et al. 1990; Mackie 1986; McGarty et al. 1992; Turner 1985; Turner et al. 1989; Turner and Oakes 1989; Wetherell 1987). We have described this perspective in previous chapters. For our readers' convenience, we repeat the statement of the approach as it bears on group polarization:

> The basic argument of [self-categorization] theory relevant to polarization is that people are conforming to a shared in-group norm, but that the norm is not the pre-test average but rather the position most *prototypical* of the group. The prototypicality of in-group members is defined by means of the *meta-contrast principle*...: the less a person differs from in-group members and the more he or she differs from out-group members, the more representative is he or she of the in-group. Thus the prototype is the position which best defines what the group has in common *in contrast to other relevant out-groups*.... The most consensual, normative position is understood both as a defining categorical property of the group prior to interaction and as the position on which members converge through social interaction. Both convergence on the mean and polarization are explained as the result of members' moving towards the consensual position of their group. (McGarty et al. 1992: 3)

The out-group positions that enter into the definition of the prototypical in-group position are all the discrete positions that are not endorsed by any group member. Hence, self-categorization theory permits the prototypical or normative attitude to be any position in the range of group members' initial attitudes (e.g., a prototypical position could be the group's mean initial attitude or it could be one of the group's most extreme attitudes depending on the out-group frame of reference).[3] It

---

[3] Self-categorization theory does not appear to allow a process by which group members converge to a compromise position that is not one of the initial positions of the group members.

appears that the self-categorization mechanism requires only the *visibility* of group members' initial positions on an issue for the recognition of an attractive normative position, to which group members then gravitate. Proponents of self-categorization theory argue that group members modify their attitudes to reduce the discrepancy between their initial positions and an implicit group norm: they identify with the norm and find members' attitudes more or less persuasive depending on the extent to which a particular attitude embodies the norm. Thus, Turner et al. (1987: 154) state, "the informational value of a response or its 'persuasiveness' is *exactly equivalent* to the degree that it is perceived to be exemplary of some in-group norm or consensus." Mackie and Cooper (1984: 577) predict that "attitudes will extremitize in the direction of conveyed information only when the information is attributed to the subject's own group."

If a powerful normative position on an issue exists prior to group discussion, then it should be reflected in the group's *initial* distribution of attitudes. For example, generally accepted norms should produce consensus or near consensus in the distribution of a group's initial attitudes; if an initial consensus is present, then social influence network theory predicts that there will be no choice shift. If there is not a preexisting norm, and instead a group norm is established *immediately* by the display of initial attitudes, then our hypothesis is that the influence of such a norm is manifested in and mediated by the susceptibilities and interpersonal influences among group members. The influence network of a group may be affected by in-group out-group identifications or by the distances between members' initial positions and the prototypical position. When the sources of information are persons, who are either in the same or a different group relative to a focal person, the effect of group-membership categorizations will be on the differentiation of the relative weights of the interpersonal influences. Social categorization theorists argue that interpersonal influence is restricted to in-group members. We believe that this is not the case; indeed, reference group theory is based on the opposite premise (Merton 1968).

9.2.5 Social Decision Schemes

Social decision scheme theory postulates that group decisions can be understood in terms of the initial distribution of attitudes and a decision scheme, or decision rule, that members use to obtain a decision (Davis 1973; Kerr 1981; Stasser, Kerr, and Davis 1980, 1989). Given a demand for a group decision, disagreement triggers the employment of a particular decision rule: majority rule, the arithmetic mean of initial attitudes, the median of initial attitudes, the most extreme initial position, and so on (Laughlin 1980; Laughlin and Earley 1982; Zuber, Crott, and

Joachim 1992). Different rules may be involved depending on the initial distribution of attitudes in a group and the issue that is being considered. Choice shifts arise when decision-making rules produce a group decision that differs from the mean initial attitude of group members; the direction and magnitude of a choice shift is the byproduct of the decision rule.

Social decision scheme theory is not concerned with the information value or normative attraction of particular positions, except insofar as the number of persons who hold particular positions determines their salience. Although individual differences in interpersonal influence are acknowledged by social decision scheme theorists, they are not included in the formal theory:

> Clearly, in most groups there are some members who are more persuasive, knowledgeable, intimidating, indomitable, or able than others; in fact, some of the SDS [social decision scheme] research ... has empirically made this point. SDS and STS [social transition scheme] models can be modified to incorporate individual differences, but this involves considerable complexity. (Kerr 1992: 70)

In contrast, social influence network theory is based on individuals' distributions of accorded influence. From this individualistic start point, one can derive the main outcome of social decision scheme theory – the relative contribution of particular initial positions on an issue to a group decision. If a consensus is formed in a group and V has the form

$$\begin{bmatrix} v_{11} & v_{22} & \cdots & v_{nn} \\ v_{11} & v_{22} & \cdots & v_{nn} \\ \vdots & \vdots & \ddots & \vdots \\ v_{11} & v_{22} & \cdots & v_{nn} \end{bmatrix},$$

then each person's initial attitude makes a particular (uniform) relative contribution to the emergent consensus. As detailed in our analysis of factions (Chapter 8), the total effect of each alternative initial position can be aggregated (i.e., the total effects of the persons who hold a particular position can be summed) to obtain the relative weights of the various issue positions in determining the group outcome. If persons 1, 3, and 5 held the same initial attitude on an issue, then the total weight of that issue position in determining the group consensus would be $v_{11} + v_{33} + v_{55}$, for instance. The derivation of these weights shows that this approach achieves the same end as social decision scheme theory while taking into account *individual differences* in interpersonal influence. We also have previously demonstrated that there is some combination of individual susceptibilities and interpersonal influences consistent with most of the observed equilibrium attitudes of group members (Chapter 4). This demonstration has an important logical implication for social decision scheme theory: if one or more decision rules can be employed to account for most group decisions, then these decision rules might be replaced with a single underlying process that is played out in groups with different social structures. For instance, instead of understanding a group decision as a product of a decision scheme, it may be viewed as consequence of an influence process that unfolds in the group's influence network. In Chapter 10, on group decision-making, we directly demonstrate that the different schemes required to account for different group outcomes are consistent with a single influence process that unfolds in different influence networks. This re-conceptualization of social decision scheme theory does not encompass the *social choice* problem in which all group members' initial attitudes are fixed; in such cases, decision rules (e.g., voting procedures) may carry forward the process of convergence to a common collective outcome that was not attained by means of interpersonal influences.

9.3 Findings

In this section, we present our empirical findings on choice shifts and group polarization. Our experiments on dyads, triads, and tetrads involve a design that has frequently been employed in studies of choice shifts: persons' initial independent responses to an issue are recorded, interpersonal communication on the issue is opened, and persons' final attitudes on the issue are recorded. Three of the discussion issues in the experiments (i.e., the Sports, School, and Surgery issues) involve choice dilemmas that have been used by other investigators and for which there has been evidence of risky or cautious choice shifts. Although choice shifts are ubiquitous in these data, we find no compelling evidence for group polarization as a distinct fundamental process that systematically or powerfully biases the outcomes of issue resolution discussions. With respect to choice shifts, we show that the magnitude and direction of the shift is predicted by our standard model.

9.3.1 Group Polarization

We employed two methods for detecting group polarization. One method is based on defining the neutral point *a priori*, for instance, $\theta = 0.50$ on a subjective probability scale. The other is based on obtaining a fitted value for θ in an effort to reveal any tendency toward group polarization that may or may not be present in a sample of groups.

Table 9.1 *Distribution of groups across the typology of group polarization outcomes*

	Total trials	Polarization (a)	Antipolarization (b)	(c)	Condition for polarization is not satisfied (d)	(e)	No polarization (f)	(g)	Binomial test
Tetrads									
Sports	50	6	16	9	12	2	1	4	0.720
School	50	6	20	12	9	0	0	3	0.444
Surgery	50	25	2	2	18	0	1	2	0.284
Triads									
Sports	32	5	10	1	11	0	2	3	0.572
School	32	11	6	2	9	1	0	3	0.360
Surgery	32	14	0	4	9	0	0	5	0.811
Dyads									
School	52	9	7	7	15	2	0	12	0.997
Surgery	50	17	1	4	21	0	0	7	0.984

Note: For the binomial test: the sample size N is the number of trials in which the condition for group polarization is satisfied ($N = a + b + c + d + g$), the number of successes x is the number of trials in which group polarization is observed ($x = a + b$), and the baseline expected proportion of successes is 0.50.

   (a) Positive Polarization $\{\bar{y}^{(1)} > \theta, \bar{y}^{(\infty)} > \bar{y}^{(1)}\}$
   (b) Negative Polarization $\{\bar{y}^{(1)} < \theta, \bar{y}^{(\infty)} < \bar{y}^{(1)}\}$
   (c) Positive Anti-Polarization $\{\bar{y}^{(1)} < \theta, \bar{y}^{(\infty)} > \bar{y}^{(1)}\}$
   (d) Negative Anti-Polarization $\{\bar{y}^{(1)} > \theta, \bar{y}^{(\infty)} < \bar{y}^{(1)}\}$
   (e) Positive Non-Polarization $\{\bar{y}^{(1)} = \theta, \bar{y}^{(\infty)} > \bar{y}^{(1)}\}$
   (f) Negative Non-Polarization $\{\bar{y}^{(1)} = \theta, \bar{y}^{(\infty)} < \bar{y}^{(1)}\}$
   (g) No Polarization $\{\bar{y}^{(\infty)} = \bar{y}^{(1)}\}$

A Priori Neutral Value $\theta = 0.50$. On each of the choice dilemma issues – Sports, School, and Surgery – the neutral position is defined as the subjective probability $\theta = 0.50$. Hence, the occurrence of group polarization is defined in terms of the positions of the means of the group member's initial and final attitudes relative to this neutral position: If $\{\bar{y}^{(1)} > 0.50$ and $\bar{y}^{(\infty)} > \bar{y}^{(1)}\}$ or $\{\bar{y}^{(1)} < 0.50$ and $\bar{y}^{(\infty)} < \bar{y}^{(1)}\}$, then group polarization has occurred. If $\{\bar{y}^{(1)} < 0.50$ and $\bar{y}^{(\infty)} \geq \bar{y}^{(1)}\}$ or $\{\bar{y}^{(1)} > 0.50$ and $\bar{y}^{(\infty)} \leq \bar{y}^{(1)}\}$, then group polarization has *not* occurred. If $\bar{y}^{(1)} = 0.50$, then the condition for group polarization is not satisfied.

In the findings reported in Table 9.1, the condition for group polarization, i.e., $\bar{y}^{(1)} \neq 0.50$, is satisfied in most of the issue resolution trials, indicating that most groups have some initial inclination in one direction or another. Table 9.1 reports the distribution of group polarization outcomes. The binomial test is the probability of the observed number of group polarizations (or more) for a 0.50 probability of polarization. The test, for each issue and group size, indicates that the number of observed polarizations is within the domain of chance expectation. In general, the results do *not* support the idea that group polarization is a social process

Table 9.2 *95% confidence limits for the regression coefficients in the model* $\bar{y}^{(\infty)} = b_0 + b_1 \bar{y}^{(1)} + e$

	b_0	b_1	R^2	N
Tetrads				
Sports	−16.71, 6.33	0.78, 1.24	0.624	50
School	−15.30, 16.56	0.63, 1.30	0.417	50
Surgery	−10.86, 15.12	0.79, 1.17	0.697	50
Triads				
Surgery	3.03, 29.05	0.63, 0.99	0.743	32
Sports	−29.65, −0.11	0.91, 1.45	0.727	32
School	−22.88, 0.35	0.99, 1.40	0.828	32
Dyads				
School	3.28, 31.83	0.58, 0.98	0.646	36
Surgery	−13.63, 18.58	0.69, 1.25	0.586	36

that reliably operates, at the group level, to reinforce the initial inclination of group's members on issues that involve an assessment of risk.

Fitted Neutral Value. Is there a systematic departure from a baseline convergence-to-the-mean model ($\bar{y}_k^{(\infty)} = \bar{y}_k^{(1)}$) that is consistent with a group polarization process? Table 9.2 reports the results of a linear regression–modeling approach to address this question. This approach does not require an *a priori* definition of a neutral point. The neutral point, if it exists, is determined empirically, and group polarization detected, by regressing the group's mean final attitude on the group's mean initial attitude,

$$\bar{y}_k^{(\infty)} = \beta_0 + \beta_1 \bar{y}_k^{(1)} + e,$$

where $k = 1, 2, \ldots, K$ are the K groups that have dealt with a particular issue. If there is no choice shift, then the estimated regression coefficients should be $\beta_0 = 0$ and $\beta_1 = 1$; i.e., the expected value of the mean equilibrium attitude should be the mean initial attitude of the group. If there is a tendency to group polarization, then the estimated regression coefficient should be $\beta_1 > 1$; i.e., the estimated regression line should intersect the no–choice shift baseline at some point such that (a) above the point of intersection the expected value of a group's mean equilibrium attitude is greater than the group's mean initial attitude and (b) below the point of intersection the expected value of a group's mean equilibrium attitude is less than the group's mean initial attitude. As the confidence intervals for the estimated coefficient for β_1 show, none of the estimates correspond to the group polarization hypothesis.

Our findings conflict with those of Fraser et al. (1971: 20), who found that most choice shifts involved a group polarization rather than an antipolarization of the group-level mean attitudes. However, their finding was based on the pooled outcomes of groups dealing with different issues, and they did not demonstrate that, within each issue, a risky or cautious polarization occurred as a function of the particular inclination of a group's initial attitude on the issue. We should not accept the idea that there is a general tendency for group polarization to occur in discussion groups, unless it can be demonstrated in a group-level analysis that the direction of a group's choice shift is predicted by the inclination of a group's mean initial attitude, and that this prediction is supported to some extent for each issue. Currently, there is no compelling support for such an idea.

9.3.2 Escalation

Nor is there support for a systematic *escalation* or *deescalation* of issue positions. Most groups exhibited a choice shift, and such a shift must involve either a positive or a negative escalation of attitudes. Positive escalation occurs when $\bar{y}_k^{(\infty)} > \bar{y}_k^{(1)}$, negative escalation occurs when $\bar{y}_k^{(\infty)} < \bar{y}_k^{(1)}$, and no escalation occurs when $\bar{y}_k^{(\infty)} = \bar{y}_k^{(1)}$. On these risky-shift issues, positive escalation indicates a shift toward greater risk, and negative escalation a shift toward greater caution. Table 9.3 is constructed from the data reported in Table 9.1 and describes the frequency with which positive, negative, or no escalation occurred. The binomial test assesses whether the greater frequency of escalation in a particular direction relative to the mean of initial attitudes (toward greater or less risk) could have occurred by chance under the baseline assumption that they are equally likely outcomes. The assessment is restricted to groups in which there was an observed choice shift. The findings are mixed and indicate that, given a choice shift, there may or may not be a tendency to escalation (toward greater risk) or deescalation (toward greater caution) on a particular issue. There is no evidence to suggest a tendency toward greater risk or caution on the School issue; on the Surgery issue, a significant tendency toward greater risk appears only among the dyads; and on the Sports issue, a significant tendency toward greater risk appears only among the triads. The only general observation that might be made is that choice shifts, in some direction, are highly likely across all these issues among the tetrads, triads, and dyads

If the hypotheses of general tendencies toward group polarization and escalation (or deescalation) are dismissed, we are left only with an account of the *choice shifts* that have occurred among the groups, that is, an account of the changes in the distribution of attitudes within groups. The research question has now changed. The focus is now on choice shifts and the magnitude and direction of these shifts. As defined

Table 9.3 *Escalation and deescalation of issue positions*

	Total trials	Positive escalation (a)	Negative escalation (b)	No escalation (c)	Binomial test
Tetrads					
Sports	50	17	29*	4	0.052
School	50	18	29*	3	0.072
Surgery	50	27*	21	2	0.235
Triads					
Sports	32	6	23*	3	0.001
School	32	14	15*	3	0.500
Surgery	32	18*	9	5	0.061
Dyads					
School	52	18	22*	12	0.318
Surgery	50	11	22*	7	0.040

Note: For the binomial test: the sample size N is the number of trials in which escalation occurred ($N = a + b$), the number of successes x is the number of trials in which either positive or negative escalation occurred (whichever was more frequent ($x = *$), and the baseline expected proportion of successes is 0.50:

(a) Positive Escalation $\{\bar{y}^{(\infty)} > \bar{y}^{(1)}\}$
(b) Negative Escalation $\{\bar{y}^{(\infty)} < \bar{y}^{(1)}\}$
(c) No Escalation $\{\bar{y}^{(\infty)} = \bar{y}^{(1)}\}$

by the literature on choice shifts, these are group-level phenomena, and we analyze them as such.

9.3.3 Choice Shifts

Previously (Chapter 4, Table 4.4) we regressed groups' observed mean equilibrium attitudes on their predicted mean equilibrium attitudes from social influence network theory, controlling for their group's mean initial attitudes:

$$\bar{y}_k^{(\infty)} = \beta_0 + \beta_1 \hat{\bar{y}}_k^{(\infty)} + \beta_2 \bar{y}_k^{(1)} + e_k,$$ (9.2)

where $k = 1, 2, \ldots, K$ are the K groups that have considered a particular issue. Those results indicated that our network model predicts the direction and magnitude of group members' average distance from the mean of their initial attitudes on an issue. Table 9.4 regresses a direct measure of the observed choice shift in a group, $\bar{y}_k^{(\infty)} - \bar{y}_k^{(1)}$, on the choice shift that is predicted by the network model, $\hat{\bar{y}}_k^{(\infty)} - \bar{y}_k^{(1)}$:

$$\left(\bar{y}_k^{(\infty)} - \bar{y}_k^{(1)}\right) = \beta_0 + \beta_1 \left(\hat{\bar{y}}_k^{(\infty)} - \bar{y}_k^{(1)}\right) + e_k.$$ (9.3)

Table 9.4 *Group-level analysis of choice shifts* $(\bar{y}^{(\infty)} - \bar{y}^{(1)}) = \beta_0 + \beta_1(\hat{\bar{y}}^{(\infty)} - \bar{y}^{(1)}) + e$ *(OLS standard errors in parentheses)*

	β_0	β_1	R	N
Dyads surgery issue	1.040	0.671***	0.511	52
	(0.935)	(0.093)		
Dyads school issue	0.505	0.910***	0.543	52
	(1.253)	(0.118)		
Triads surgery issue	1.526	0.497***	0.403	32
	(1.101)	(0.110)		
Triads school issue	−0.330	0.857***	0.873	32
	(0.625)	(0.060)		
Triads sports issue	−1.369	0.940***	0.738	32
	(1.146)	(0.102)		
Tetrads surgery issue	−0.020	0.872***	0.494	50
	(0.798)	(0.127)		
Tetrads school issue	−0.229	1.069***	0.494	50
	(1.296)	(0.156)		
Tetrads sports issue	−1.064	1.032***	0.654	50
	(0.978)	(0.108)		
Tetrads asbestos issue	−0.079	0.899***	0.776	50
	(0.150)	(0.072)		
Tetrads disaster issue	−0.147	0.763***	0.287	50
	(0.117)	(0.175)		

Notes: ***$p < 0.001$; **$p < 0.01$; *$p < 0.05$; †$p < 0.10$.

Again, the results indicate that the network model is predicting the direction and magnitude of the observed choice shifts on each issue. Table 9.4 includes the two monetary issues for completeness and, for these two issues, the network model also predicts the direction and magnitude of the observed choice shifts.

9.3.4 Choice Shift in the Distribution of Individuals' Attitudes

We now compare the mean of N individuals' initial attitudes with the mean of the same N individuals' attitudes after discussion on an issue. Our subjects formed initial positions on an issue prior to group discussion: the numbers of subjects are $N = 104$, $N = 96$, and $N = 250$, respectively, for the dyads, triads, and tetrads. In Table 9.5, we assess whether the means of these subjects' observed end-of-trial attitudes significantly differ from the means of their initial attitudes. A significant difference indicates that the group discussion caused a shift in the central tendency of the individual-level distribution of attitudes on an issue – toward either greater risk or caution on Sports, School, and Surgery issues, or more generous or conservative monetary awards on the Asbestos and

Table 9.5 *Individual-level analysis of choice shifts*

(a) Individuals' final minus initial attitudes on issues

	Mean final-initial	Std. dev. final-initial	N	t
Asbestos	0.532	4.112	200	1.830[†]
Disaster	−0.303	1.819	200	−2.356*
Sports				
Triads	−5.417	19.691	96	−2.695**
Tetrads	−4.600	21.527	200	−3.022**
School				
Dyads	−0.865	19.700	104	−0.448
Triads	−0.625	19.005	96	−0.322
Tetrads	−1.025	21.468	200	−0.675
Surgery				
Dyads	1.231	16.237	104	0.773
Triads	2.490	16.962	96	1.438
Tetrads	0.950	18.193	200	0.738

(b) Correlations of individuals' initial attitudes with their self-weights and influences

	w_{ii}	$\sum_{j \neq i}^{n} w_{ji}$	v_{ii}	$\sum_{j \neq i}^{n} v_{ji}$
Asbestos	0.111	0.271***	0.159*	0.217**
Disaster	−0.044	−0.157*	−0.132[†]	−0.142*
Sports				
Triads	−0.179[†]	−0.199[†]	−0.273**	−0.226*
Tetrads	−0.101	−0.257***	−0.195**	−0.214**
School				
Dyads	−0.053	−0.016	−0.127	−0.082
Triads	−0.047	0.042	−0.042	0.000
Tetrads	0.026	−0.032	0.000	−0.075
Surgery				
Dyads	0.004	0.015	0.023	0.018
Triads	0.201*	0.004	0.178[†]	0.070
Tetrads	0.095	−0.048	0.089	0.055

Notes: ***$p < 0.001$; **$p < 0.01$; *$p < 0.05$; [†]$p < 0.10$.

Disaster issues. A significant shift toward greater risk occurred on the Sports issue in the triads and tetrads that considered this issue. No significant shift occurred on the School and Surgery issues in the dyads, triads, and tetrads that considered these issues. A significant shift toward greater generosity occurred on the Asbestos and toward greater conservatism on the Disaster issue in the tetrads that considered these two issues.

From our network theory, we expect that when a significant shift occurs, it is based on an association of individuals' initial positions on an issue with their net (total) interpersonal influence in the group discussion of the issue. Hence, on the Sports issues, where a shift toward greater risk occurred, we expect *negative* associations of individuals' initial positions $y_i^{(1)}$ with $\sum_{j \neq i}^{n} v_{ji}$, for $i = 1, 2, \ldots, N$. On the Asbestos issue, where a shift toward more generous monetary awards occurred, we expect *positive* associations of $y_i^{(1)}$ with $\sum_{j \neq i}^{n} v_{ji}$. On the Disaster issue, where a shift toward less generous monetary awards occurred, we expect *negative* associations of $y_i^{(1)}$ with $\sum_{j \neq i}^{n} v_{ji}$. Since these total influences are measures of the net implications of the influence process that occurred in each group, we expect that they, rather than the individuals' direct influences, reflect the emergent inequalities of the group process. The findings in Table 9.5 support these expectations and suggest that choice shifts, when they occur, are based on inequalities in the net influences of group members that are linked with the degree of extremeness of their initial positions on an issue.

9.4 Concluding Remarks

Social influence network theory contributes to the integration of the persuasive arguments, social comparison, self-categorization, and social decision scheme approaches to the extent that the effects of an argument, social comparison, prototypical position, or decision scheme can be represented directly as interpersonal influences in **AW** or as mediated by such influences. There are a host of different conditions that may produce a choice shift or group polarization. However, a coherent theoretical perspective is possible if all these conditions are conceptualized as antecedent conditions of one or more of the three constructs of social influence network theory – persons' initial attitudes, susceptibilities, and interpersonal influences.

Our evidence suggests that choice shifts are a ubiquitous product of interpersonal interactions on issues, but that group polarization (the tendency for such shifts to enhance the group's initial position) is neither a ubiquitous nor reliable product of group discussion per se. A choice shift can be viewed as a byproduct of the group's influence structure and as an outcome of the same type of process that sometimes produces convergence on the mean of the group's initial attitudes. Note that choice shifts do not deal with the phenomenon of consensus production or more generally with the reduction of the differences of attitudes among group members. The analysis of choice shift is only concerned with locations of the means of the distributions of initial and equilibrium attitudes. However, the process that may be producing a consensus is the *same* process that is determining the mean equilibrium attitude of a group's members as well as the location of this equilibrium mean relative to the mean of the group's initial attitudes.

Cartwright's (1971) analysis of the "risky shift" literature suggested that risky shifts were not reliable and that the work on risky shifts should be rethought. He argued that the relevant research question was not why group discussion produces riskier decisions, but rather why group discussion produces choice shifts. Although the field has moved to a broader conceptualization in which choice shifts are now the focus of study, our investigation suggests that choice shifts should be viewed as an aggregate manifestation of an interpersonal influence process, and that the focus should not be on the choice shift itself (which derives from the influence process) but on the attitude changes that occur for each individual in the group. From this perspective, the crucial ingredients are the network of interpersonal influence and the process by which these interpersonal influences modify persons' attitudes. Choice shifts are the byproducts (the aggregate-level consequences) of these individual attitude changes.

The theoretical importance of the choice-shift group-polarization phenomenon is that it appears to suggest that there is an *additional* important main effect of group discussion on attitude change that causes attitudes to shift or extremitize. This argument initially led us to include a special "group polarization" parameter in our model (Friedkin and Johnsen 1990). We dropped this parameter when we became convinced that there is no group polarization process that exerts a separate main effect on persons' attitudes (Friedkin 1999). We believe that a choice shift is the product of a group's social structure in which certain members have more influence than others during the attitude change process. Thus, the present perspective on choice shifts and group polarization reasserts an older theoretical tradition in social psychology in which the *structure* of a group's influence network is viewed as an important construct in the study of group dynamics.

A model of the social influence process must allow for inequalities of interpersonal influence, for situations in which there is not an initial consensus, for situations in which no person's attitude is fixed, and for situations in which the influence process does not necessarily produce a consensus. Group polarization is not a ubiquitous phenomenon because it depends on the group's structure of interpersonal influence. Choice shifts are a ubiquitous phenomenon because influence networks often involve inequalities of interpersonal influence, which in turn usually imply such shifts. Conditions that affect group members' susceptibilities to interpersonal influence (group cohesion, attitude strength) and conditions that affect the relative influence of the members of a group (members' power bases and status characteristics) may affect the direction and magnitude of a choice shift. Hence, social influence network theory provides a framework that is in line with classical studies of influence and conformity, for assessing hypotheses concerned with the origins of choice shift and group polarization.

Although we are skeptical of the idea that group polarization results from a fundamental process that is not captured by the iterated weighted averaging mechanism of social influence network theory, instances of group polarization do occur. Indeed, we have shown that group polarization (in the form of a simple escalation or deescalation of initial attitudes on an issue) does occur on some issues. Our theoretical perspective is consistent with the hypothesis that, under specified conditions, group polarization (including "risky shifts") is an *expected* outcome of group discussion. The key condition, we think, is an association of the extremeness of persons' initial positions and self-weights and interpersonal influences on others. However, note that any such prediction springs from a general framework in which group polarization is merely one of a number of special cases of group outcomes that might be observed in natural settings and reliably produced under suitable experimental conditions.

Part III

Linkages with Other Formal Models

10

Models of Group Decision-Making

A group decision occurs when group members select or settle upon one option from a set of alternatives and collectively consider that option to be the choice of the group (Brandstatter, Davis, and Stocker-Kreichgauer 1982; Castellan 1993; Levine and Moreland 1990, 1998; Moscovici and Doise 1994; Witte and Davis 1996). Social influence network theory has an important bearing on how groups make decisions, because it presents an account of how interpersonal influences produce the agreements that are the foundation of many group decisions. In this chapter, we describe how our theory is related to several lines of formal work on group decision-making in which a decision scheme or normative procedure is invoked to reach a group decision.

We concentrate our analysis on social decision scheme theory, arguably the most prominent approach among psychologists to group decisions, and this theory's application to jury outcomes. The extant literature on social decision scheme theory indicates that groups behave as if different decision schemes are invoked to reach a collective decision, depending on the type of issue that is being dealt with. We show that a social influence network perspective provides a unifying formal framework. A single social process suffices to account for these issue-contingent results.

We then consider the relationship of social influence network theory and several formal normative models of group decision-making. Interestingly, DeGroot's (1974) model, which is closely related to French's (1956) formal theory of social power, was proposed as a *device* that might be employed by a group for settling their disputes and reaching collective decisions. Similarly, Lehrer and Wagner's (1981) model of *rational consensus* is strikingly close to the formalization of group decision-making via a mechanism of iterated weighted averaging.

Secondarily, we also develop structural perspectives on (a) the group-think phenomenon (Janis 1982), in which pressures to reach consensus inhibit the thorough appraisal of options, and (b) ecological control

235

(Cartwright and Zander 1968; Whitmeyer 2000), in which group decisions are controlled through appointments of members to decision-making groups and the formal positions within such groups. Although groupthink is not a formalized approach to the study of social groups, we show that the conditions of groupthink and the implications of these conditions may be conceptualized and addressed within the formal framework of social influence network theory. Similarly, ecological control via appointment power may also be conceptualized and addressed in terms of the effects of control activities on the initial positions and influence networks of groups.

10.1 Social Decision Scheme Theory

Social decision scheme theory is the most prominent model in psychology of how groups make decisions (Davis 1973; Kerr 1981; Laughlin 1980; Stasser et al. 1989; Zuber et al. 1992). It postulates that group decisions can be explained by the initial distribution of attitudes and a decision scheme, or rule, that is explicitly or tacitly employed by the group's members to obtain a group decision from this initial distribution. The theory deals with group members' selections among qualitatively distinct options, such as the guilty vs. not guilty positions of jury members. We previously described Davis's (1996) related approach to quantitative attitudes as part of our assessment of social comparison theory (Chapter 7), and we found that it did not perform better than the baseline prediction of group decisions provided by the *mean* of group members' initial positions. As part of our analysis of choice shifts (Chapter 9), we noted that social decision scheme theory predicts choice shifts in *quantitative* attitudes as a byproduct of particular decision schemes involved in the production of group decisions. Now we focus on the central thrust of social decision scheme theory, an analysis of group decisions that involve a choice among a set of *qualitative* alternatives.

In its application to qualitative attitudes, social decision scheme theory is implemented in three steps. First, the *possible* distributions of initial attitudes (choices) in the group are listed. Second, depending on the decision scheme, collective outcomes of the scheme for the group are determined for each distribution of initial attitudes. Third, a probability is assigned to each of the possible initial distributions to obtain an expected value (expected relative frequency) for each group outcome.

Table 10.1 describes the application of the theory to a six-member jury, for which there are seven alternative initial distributions of Guilty (G) and Not Guilty (NG) votes, each with a collective outcome based on the rule that an initial 2/3 majority will prevail and that a jury in which there is no such initial majority will be Hung (H). The probabilities, $\pi' = \begin{bmatrix} \pi_1 & \pi_2 & \dots & \pi_7 \end{bmatrix}$, are obtained either directly from empirical data on

Table 10.1 *Social decision scheme theory*

Initial distribution			Outcomes (D)		
G	NG	π	G	NG	H
6	0	π_1	1.0	0.0	0.0
5	1	π_2	1.0	0.0	0.0
4	2	π_3	1.0	0.0	0.0
3	3	π_4	0.0	0.0	1.0
2	4	π_5	0.0	1.0	0.0
1	5	π_5	0.0	1.0	0.0
0	6	π_7	0.0	1.0	0.0
		$\pi'D$	0.024	0.875	0.101

Note: $\pi'D = [0.024 \quad 0.875 \quad 0.101]$, where

$\pi_1 = P(6,0) = 0.00011338$
$\pi_2 = P(5,1) = 0.00241190$
$\pi_3 = P(4,2) = 0.02137820$
$\pi_4 = P(3,3) = 0.10106059$
$\pi_5 = P(2,4) = 0.26872931$
$\pi_6 = P(1,5) = 0.38110702$
$\pi_7 = P(0,6) = 0.22519960.$

the observed relative frequency of each initial distribution in a sample of juries, or indirectly from data on the relative frequency of predeliberation positions in a sample of jury members. The latter approach requires data on the relative frequencies of G and NG initial positions ($\bar{p}_G$, $\bar{p}_{NG}$), from which the probability of each initial jury faction structure is determined by the multinomial function under the assumption of independence,

$$P(n_G, n_{NG}) = \frac{n!}{(n_G)!\,(n_{NG})!} (\bar{p}_G)^{x_G} (\bar{p}_{NG})^{x_{NG}}, \qquad (10.1)$$

where $n_G + n_{NG} = n$ and $\bar{p}_G + \bar{p}_{NG} = 1$. Based on the values $\bar{p}_G = 0.22$ and $\bar{p}_{NG} = 0.78$ observed among predeliberation individual jurors (Davis 1982: 49), the probability of each of the initial distributions derived from (10.1) is as shown in Table 10.1. Thus, $\pi'D = [0.024\ 0.875\ 0.101]$ gives the predicted probabilities of Guilty, Not Guilty, and Hung jury outcomes, respectively.[1]

Davis reports that "From amongst the predictions generated by various social decision scheme models suitable to juries (15 more or less plausible schemes were entertained) only one (2/3 majority, otherwise hung) closely predicted the outcome distributions of both six- and 12-person juries" (1982: 49). Note that social decision scheme theory provides a macro-level summary of the net consequences of whatever social process is occurring within a group. The theory does not describe the decision-making process, unless a jury actually counts the initial votes of

[1] The high predicted probability of NG verdicts appears extraordinary, with its implication that weak cases for conviction, whether mock or real, are being prosecuted.

its members and *immediately* applies a decision rule. If decision schemes described the social process by which juries reach collective decisions, then there would be no need for jury deliberation; but juries do deliberate, and their members' initial positions on a case may be modified as a result of such deliberation.

In contrast, social influence network theory is concerned with the *process* of interpersonal influence, and it explicitly incorporates individual differences of susceptibility and inequalities of interpersonal influence into the process of attitude change.[2] In the standard model of social influence network theory, the influence network, which describes these susceptibilities and influences, is not linked to the distribution of initial attitudes, although it may be. We will show that such a linkage is unnecessary to account for the power of large jury factions. An important question for us is whether our theory describes an influence process that, when applied to a large number of juries, results in a *distribution* of jury outcomes that is consistent with the observed distribution of jury outcomes. In principle, our theory goes well beyond this macro-account: it should be able to account not only for the distribution of jury outcomes, but also for the outcomes of specific juries and the individual positions of their members when they are Hung.

In addition, given Davis's (1982) observation that decision rules appear to vary across tasks (issues), another important question for us is whether a *single* influence process suffices to explain such variation:

> Overall, it is difficult to escape the impression that social decision schemes do depend to a considerable extent upon the task confronting the group. To what extent a social decision scheme is a picture of a social norm that is engaged by the task and context and to what extent the social decision scheme is an emergent consequence of other conditions in the group situation is not yet clear. (Davis 1982: 53–54)

From our perspective, if there are different group outcomes for different *types* of issues (e.g., differences in the distributions of G, NG, and H juries for different types of criminal cases), then it must be so because of differences in the typical initial positions of group members and the influence network, **W**, that occur in groups dealing with those issues.

Davis argues that the crucial dimension on which tasks vary is the level of uncertainty of group members concerning the correctness of their initial positions. For high-uncertainty tasks, his evidence suggests that an

---

[2] Social decision scheme theorists acknowledge that "in most groups there are some members who are more persuasive, knowledgeable, intimidating, indomitable, or able than others" (Kerr 1992). However, they also acknowledge that the theory does not easily accommodate such individual differences in interpersonal influence.

"equal-probability" decision rule is most accurate, where each faction's position (i.e., an initial position that is held by one or more members) is as likely to be the group's choice as any other faction's position. Under this rule, when two or more factions are present in a group, the relative sizes of factions have no effect on the probabilities of the possible group outcomes. For low-uncertainty tasks, Davis' evidence suggests that a "majority, otherwise proportionality" decision rule is most accurate. Under this rule, if there is no majority, then alternative positions are weighted according to the relative sizes of the factions that advocate them. For juries, which may deal with low- or high-uncertainty cases, Davis concludes, as we have seen, that a "2/3 majority, otherwise hung" rule provides the best overall fit. For social issues, which also may vary in their levels of uncertainty, Davis concludes that a "majority, otherwise averaging" rule is most accurate, but he notes that a "median" rule is also accurate. Under the former rule, if there is no majority faction, the mean of the group members' initial positions is the predicted group consensus; under the latter rule, the median of the group member's initial positions is the predicted outcome for the group. We believe that a theoretical integration of these findings may be possible, and offer preliminary findings that suggest the feasibility of a more integrative approach.

10.2 A Model for Qualitative Jury Outcomes

In this section, we focus on the influence process in juries and consider the consequences of variation among cases in their levels of uncertainty. We posit that uncertainty alters the expected structure of a group's influence network and, in turn, produces different distributions of group outcomes. We will show that under simple assumptions, the distribution of jury outcomes is altered in ways that conform to different decision schemes. *The illustrations and findings to be presented suggest the possibility of a general correspondence between our network theory of interpersonal influence and social decision scheme theory. Our analysis suggests that any decision scheme that is a macro-level description of observed group outcomes may be accounted for by a suitable micro-level interpersonal influence process.* Below we describe a set of ancillary assumptions that link our standard model to the special case of juries concerned with decisions on the guilt or innocence of defendants.

10.2.1 Influence Network Formalization

For the application of our standard model to juries, we assume that each juror *i* forms a predeliberation attitude about the merits of the prosecutor's case that is transformed, in the mind of the juror, into an initial position $y_i^{(1)}$ on the subjective probability of innocence and, in turn, into an individual decision (vote) in favor of guilt or innocence $\ddot{y}_i^{(1)} \in \{G, NG\}$. We also assume that *various* influence networks may be formed within juries, and that in a population of juries, the influence networks that get formed may be regarded as *random* structures, which are independent of the initial positions of the juries. This independence assumption is easily relaxed, and we entertain one plausible possibility in which jurors' susceptibilities are inversely associated with their degrees of initial certainty in either the guilt or innocence of the defendant. Moreover, given data on the influence networks that are formed in particular (e.g., mock) juries, the assumption of random structures can be discarded.

We assume that jurors' initial attitudes are a random draw from a transformed standard normal distribution $N(\beta_0, \beta_1)$ given by

$$\tilde{z}_i = \beta_0 + \beta_1 z_i \tag{10.2}$$

for all $1 \leq i \leq n$, where each z_i is a randomly selected z-score from the standard normal distribution $N(0, 1)$, β_0 is a bias parameter on the scale of real numbers, and $\beta_1 > 0$ is a variance multiplier. An expectation of positive or negative bias may occur when the cases made by the prosecution and defense are of unequal strength, or when the population from which the juries are formed is biased. An expectation of high or low variance among jurors' predeliberation attitudes arises when the cases made by the prosecution and defense are of unequal strength, or when the population from which the juries are formed is heterogeneous. Note that the mean and variance of the predeliberation attitudes may vary from jury to jury because they are sampled from an $N(\beta_0, \beta_1)$ population. Again, given data on the predeliberation attitudes of jurors in particular cases, this statistical approach to jurors' initial positions can be discarded.

We take positive attitudes as favoring innocence (NG), negative attitudes as favoring Guilty (G), and zero as indicating a neutral attitude. These initial attitudes are transformed into individual initial positions on the subjective probability of innocence (NG) scale,

$$y_i^{(1)} = \frac{1}{1 + \exp(-\tilde{z}_i)}, \tag{10.3}$$

for all $1 \leq i \leq n$, so that $0 < y_i^{(1)} < 1$ for all i. Hence, the more positive the attitude, the higher the subjective probability of NG in the mind of a juror; and the more negative the attitude, the lower the subjective probability of NG in the mind of a juror. The neutral (maximum uncertainty) attitude corresponds to a subjective probability of 0.50. On this basis we define the *personal uncertainty* of juror i as

$$pu_i = 1 - 2 \left| y_i^{(1)} - 0.50 \right|. \tag{10.4}$$

For criminal cases, we assume that a "burden of proof" or "beyond reasonable doubt" threshold $0 < \lambda < 1$ underlies a juror's decision to favor a guilty verdict, and we set that threshold at 0.40.[3] Accordingly, a juror will favor a guilty verdict only if his or her subjective probability of innocence is weak (i.e., $y_i^{(1)} < 0.40$). The consequences of different thresholds (and individual differences in threshold) could be analyzed, although we do not do so in the present analysis.

We construct a jury's influence network by drawing a sample of n^2 values from the uniform distribution over the range $[0, 1]$ and normalizing these values (dividing each value by its row sum) to obtain a row-stochastic matrix of relative influences, $\mathbf{W}$. The diagonal matrix of jurors' susceptibilities $\mathbf{A}$ is based on the main diagonal entries of $\mathbf{W}$, i.e., $a_{ii} = 1 - w_{ii}$ for all i. We also construct a *constrained* random influence network,

$$\mathbf{W} = \mathbf{AC} + \mathbf{I} - \mathbf{A}, \tag{10.5}$$

in which a juror i's susceptibility a_{ii} increases with his or her level of initial personal uncertainty, $a_{ii} = 1 - w_{ii} = pu_i$, and $\mathbf{C}$ is a matrix of normalized uniform random values with zeros on the main diagonal. Both the unconstrained and constrained $\mathbf{W}$ are random networks, the only difference between them being whether or not individuals' susceptibilities are governed by their personal uncertainties pu_i.

For this analysis, equilibrium subjective probabilities of innocence (NG) were derived from our standard model, $\hat{\mathbf{y}} = \mathbf{V}\mathbf{y}^{(1)}$, and transformed, according to the "burden of proof" threshold, into individual juror votes in favor of guilt or innocence. Group-level decisions are based on *unanimity*. Hence, if all the jurors' votes are for acquittal, the jury outcome is NG; if all the jurors' votes are for conviction, the jury outcome is G; and otherwise the jury is H. This model produces a jury outcome for *one* jury. Monte Carlo estimates of the *expected* proportion of NG, G, and H juries were based on 1,000 trials of the model for *different* bias values $-1 \leq \beta_0 \leq 1$ (this range could be relaxed) and a fixed variance multiplier β_1, which in most of the examples presented below we set to $\beta_1 = 0.5$.

10.2.2 Random Influence Networks

Figure 10.1 shows that, for juries of size 6, social influence network theory can generate predictions that are close to the expected proportions,

---

[3] This value is employed for didactic purposes to show that our model can produce the outcomes described by Davis (1982). The "burden of proof" levels for the average mock vs. real juror may differ significantly. If the "burden of proof" is considerably more stringent than 0.40 for real juries, then it would be reasonable to assume that prosecutors would only on average put forward very strong cases for conviction, i.e., $\beta_0 \ll 0$.

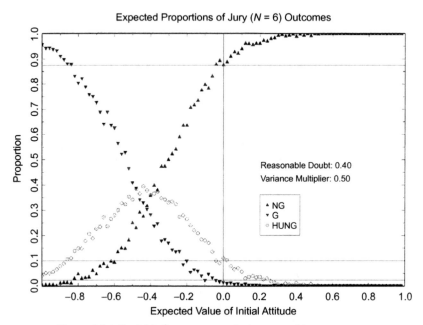

Figure 10.1 Social influence network theory and jury outcomes.

$\pi'D = [\,0.024\ 0.875\ 0.101\,]$, of social decision theory for Guilty, Not Guilty, and Hung jury outcomes (Table 10.1). Assuming that the expected value of jurors' initial attitudes is unbiased, the horizontal lines (running from the values 0.024, 0.875, 0.101) intersect the vertical *neutral* line for unbiased juries at locations that closely correspond to the predictions of social influence network theory for the expected proportions of Guilty, Not Guilty, and Hung jury outcomes (0.016, 0.881, and 0.104, respectively).

The important implication of this result is that the predictions of social decision scheme theory for jury outcomes may be derived from a model of the micro-process of interpersonal influence that occurs in juries. Recall that we assume a unanimity basis at equilibrium for a jury's decision, whereas social decision scheme theory derives its prediction based on a "2/3 majority, otherwise hung" rule. Our specification of the micro-process that underlies jury outcomes produces the outcome that a "2/3 majority, otherwise hung" rule would produce if it were immediately implemented by a jury. But how a jury proceeds from an initial 2/3 majority to a final decision is not specified by social decision scheme theory; the process is a black box. Our approach specifies the interpersonal influence process that takes jury members from their initial positions to their unanimous G or NG decision or their H irresolution. The final

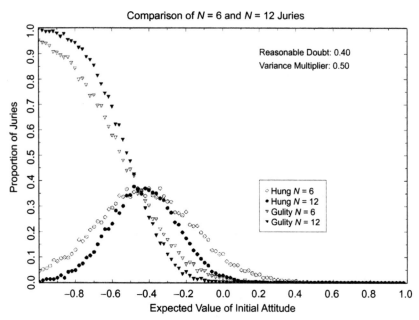

Figure 10.2 Effects of jury size.

disposition of the jury (G, NG, H) depends on the legally more realistic final status of unanimity-else-hung.

Juries should be *biased* in their initial attitudes if prosecutors tend to bring only especially strong cases for conviction to trial by jury. Hence, the evidence having been heard, the expected predeliberation bias of juries should be negative. Our model points to the existence of a point of maximum inefficiency, where the proportion of hung juries is at its maximum and the proportions of G and NG verdicts are equal. Figure 10.2 shows that this point of maximum inefficiency does not appear to be importantly affected by jury size (6 vs. 12). Within the region of negative bias, to the right and left of the point of maximum inefficiency, the proportion of hung juries is smaller for juries of size 12 than for juries of size 6. To the left of the point of maximum inefficiency, the proportion of guilty verdicts is higher for juries of size 12 than for juries of size 6; to the right of this point, the proportion of guilty verdicts is lower for juries of size 12 than for juries of size 6. In other words, stronger cases for conviction diminish the proportion of hung juries and increase the proportion of guilty verdicts; weaker cases increase the proportion of hung juries to a maximum, after which the proportion of hung juries declines while the proportion of nonguilty verdicts increases. This pattern is slightly more pronounced for juries of size 12 than for juries of size 6.

10.2.3 Task Uncertainty

The value of the decision threshold, which determines an individual juror's vote, may vary across individual jurors. For the results presented above, we set the threshold to a constant value of 0.40. The value of this threshold has an important bearing on the individual juror's *task uncertainty*, i.e., the uncertainty regarding the juror's *decision* to vote G or NG, defined as

$$tu_i = 1 - \left| y_i^{(1)} - \lambda \right|, \quad 0 \le y_i^{(1)} \le 1. \tag{10.6}$$

Depending on the threshold value $0 < \lambda < 1$, a juror with high personal uncertainty pu_i may or may not have high task uncertainty tu_i. For $\lambda = 0.40$, a juror i with the highest personal uncertainty, i.e., at $y_i^{(1)} = 0.50$, will vote NG with reduced task uncertainty. Thresholds lower than 0.40 will make casting a NG vote even easier for a juror. Clearly, if the threshold is such that almost *any* doubt in the mind of the juror requires a NG vote (say, based on a threshold of 0.05), then task uncertainty is dramatically reduced for a juror with $y_i^{(1)} = 0.50$.

The value of the bias parameter β_0 also has a closely related bearing on task uncertainty. This parameter determines the central tendency of jurors' initial attitudes in the population from which the jury is drawn; these attitudes are on the $\tilde{z}$ scale given by (10.2). The corresponding bias value on the scale of subjective probabilities β_0' is

$$\beta_0' = (1 + \exp(-\beta_0))^{-1}. \tag{10.7}$$

Since β_0 locates the mode of the $N(\beta_0, \beta_1)$ distribution of initial attitudes $\tilde{z}_i$, β_0' locates the mode of the distribution of the transformed attitudes $y_i^{(1)}$. When β_0' is sufficiently distant from the threshold λ, the task uncertainty of the modal juror will be low. For example, when the prosecutors of a local court system only bring very strong cases for conviction before juries, so that the bias value β_0' falls well below the "burden of proof" threshold, then it is more likely that the modal juror will begin his or her deliberation task with reduced uncertainty; obviously, a low level of task uncertainty for the modal juror is hard to achieve in such a court system when the threshold is very low. Hence, there may be a prosecutorial incentive to maximize jurors' threshold values, by various means, within the limits of accepted professional standards.

As Figure 10.3 shows, for the highest-uncertainty cases ($pu_i = tu_i = 1$) among unbiased juries ($\beta_0 = 0$) with a "burden of proof" threshold $\lambda = 0.50$, the expected proportions of G, NG, and H juries are approximately equal, with H juries being slightly more probable than both G and NG verdicts. Hence, any initial position (held by one or more members) is as likely to be the jury's decision choice as any other initial position (held

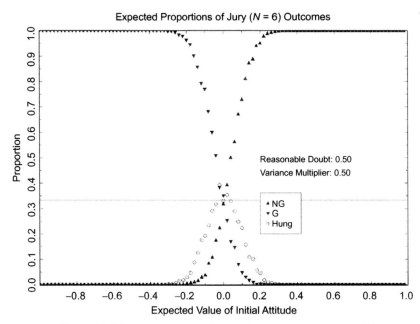

Figure 10.3 Jury outcomes under maximum uncertainty conditions.

by one or more members). Consistent with Davis's findings on uncertain tasks, an equal-probability decision rule is the most accurate macro-level summary of the resulting distribution. Davis has argued that *different* decision rules are involved for tasks that vary in their uncertainty. As our results suggest, different distributions of group outcomes may be produced by a single micro-process of interpersonal influence that unfolds under different conditions.

10.2.4 Variance Multiplier

Figure 10.4 indicates the effects of the variance multiplier that determines the expected value of the variance of jury members' initial attitudes. For juries with homogeneous initial attitudes, the proportions of G, NG, and H juries reach their ceilings (1) and floors (0) within a narrow range of bias values. Hence, *small* changes in the relative strength of the cases for acquittal and conviction may lead to very different expected distributions of jury outcomes; furthermore, homogeneous juries are more likely to acquit in the range of negative bias than are heterogeneous juries. For heterogeneous juries, the proportions of G, NG, and H juries reach their ceilings and floors over a broader range of expected bias. Large changes of bias are required to produce a substantial change in the expected distributions of jury outcomes.

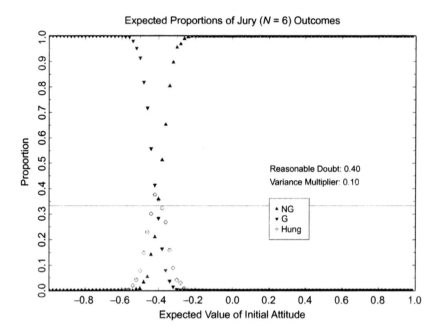

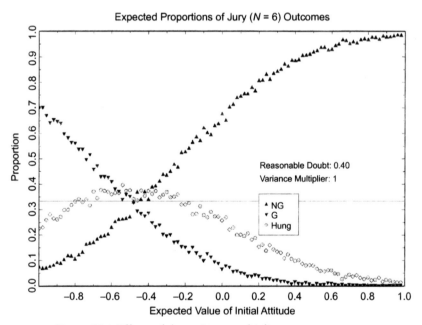

Figure 10.4 Effects of the variance multiplier.

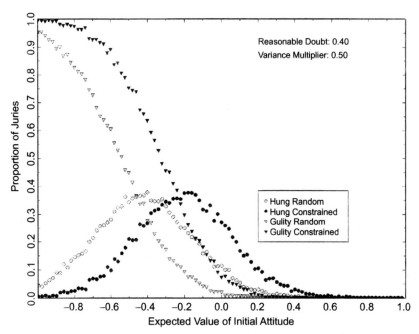

Figure 10.5 Random and constrained influence networks in $N = 6$ juries.

10.2.5 Constrained Influence Networks

Figure 10.5 shows the result of *constraining* the influence network of juries, so that jurors' susceptibilities to influence decline as their subjective certainties of guilt or innocence increase. A comparison of Figure 10.5 with Figure 10.1 shows that, for unbiased juries, the effect of the constraint is to increase the proportions of G verdicts and H juries and, thus, to lessen the proportion of NG verdicts. The constraint shifts the point of maximum inefficiency (equiprobable outcomes) to the right, so that for constrained networks weaker cases for conviction achieve the same likelihood of conviction (G) as for random networks, ceteris paribus. These results arise because, for negatively biased juries, the presence of a confident attitude favoring guilt, in one or more of the jurors, is more resistant to change in these constrained influence networks than in the entirely random networks. Confident attitudes favoring innocence also are more resistant to change, and also may contribute to the occurrence of H juries; however, a low decision threshold (e.g., 0.40) for adopting a NG position drives the expected proportion of NG verdicts toward 1 among juries with a weak positive bias, so that the effect of jurors who confidently advocate a NG verdict is to dampen the proportion of G verdicts among such positively biased juries.

Table 10.2 *Findings on jury factions*

Initial factions		Zeisel and Diamond			Kerr and MacCoun		
G	NG	G	NG	H	G	NG	H
6	0	1.00	0.00	0.00	1.00	0.00	0.00
5	1	0.95	0.02	0.01	0.81	0.00	0.19
4	2	0.83	0.13	0.04	0.31	0.26	0.42
3	3	0.42	0.46	0.12	0.11	0.46	0.43
2	4	0.12	0.85	0.03	0.00	0.84	0.16
1	5	0.02	0.97	0.01	0.00	0.89	0.11
0	6	0.00	1.00	0.00	0.00	1.00	0.00

Thus, entertaining a plausible *systematic* constraint on jury members' influence networks modifies the expectations of verdicts of guilty and not guilty and of hung juries. It should not be difficult to accept the hypothesis that the *idiosyncratic* influence networks that get formed in juries (and that are affected by the individual characteristics of jurors) also can have a potentially dramatic effect on jury outcomes. Although the voir dire phase of a trial provides an opportunity for inducing or mitigating bias, and affecting the influence network of a potential jury, and although prosecutors may be inclined to bring only strong cases for conviction to jury trial, jury outcomes are likely to depend heavily on the particular influence network that gets formed during the deliberation phase of a trial.

10.2.6 Factions in Juries

Based on its specification of the jury influence process, our approach allows an analysis of the expected outcomes of the *different* initial distributions of the G and NG factions in a jury. Table 10.2 shows the findings of Zeisel and Diamond (1978) for real juries and Kerr and MacCoun (1985) for mock juries. The findings of Kerr and MacCoun allow an assessment of the effects of factions under a *common* set of trial conditions. The findings of Zeisel and Diamond are difficult to interpret because they were compiled from trials that may have varied substantially in the conditions that affect the expected bias and variance of jurors predeliberation attitudes. The occurrence of particular faction structures is likely to be associated with the particular conditions under which trials occur. For example, the 3–3 faction structure is more likely to occur in close cases (i.e., zero-bias cases) and the negatively skewed faction structures (e.g., 4–2) are more likely to occur in cases where the prosecution has a strong case (i.e., negative-bias cases). Thus, it is unclear whether the Zeisel and Diamond findings are indicating the effects of different faction structures, the effects of the relative strengths of a case for conviction and acquittal, or both.

Our findings on the expected outcomes of different faction structures apply to a population of trials conducted under a specific set of conditions: a standard "burden of proof," and an expected bias (and variance) in jurors' predeliberation attitudes. The findings of Kerr and MacCoun (1985), therefore, are more relevant than those of Zeisel and Diamond (1978) and other similar findings, with respect to analysis of the effects of faction structures.

In social decision scheme theory, the group outcome is deterministic for a given set of initial factions (Table 10.1). In social influence network theory, the group outcome is deterministic only when both the group members' initial attitudes and their influence network have been specified, because the influence network mediates the effects of an initial distribution of attitudes on jury outcomes. Thus, unless the influence network is entirely determined by the distribution of initial attitudes (which we do not think is so), identical initial faction structures may have various outcomes. For a sample of juries, which may vary in their members' initial subjective probabilities of the defendant's innocence, but which have an *identical initial* (G, NG) faction structure, social influence network theory predicts the expected distribution of jury outcomes, which can then be compared to the observed proportions of G, NG, and H juries for each faction structure. Again, our assumption will be that the influence networks of juries are random structures.

To obtain a Monte Carlo estimate of the expected distribution of jury outcomes (conditional on a particular initial faction structure), we proceed exactly as outlined in the introduction to this section. However, we now also obtain the faction structure (G, NG) of the initial attitudes of a jury and partition the jury group outcomes by their initial faction structure. For this analysis of conditional expectations, the number of Monte Carlo trials is increased to provide a sufficient basis for estimating the expected values of low-probability faction structures; in juries with six members, for instance, the (6, 0) faction structure rarely occurs under a 0.40 "burden of proof" threshold.

Table 10.3 shows our findings for juries with six members (for which there are seven faction structures, as shown in Table 10.1) under the conditions of a 0.40 "burden of proof" threshold, zero bias, and a variance multiplier of 0.50. Recall that the unconditional Monte Carlo estimates of the expected proportions of G, NG, and Hung juries are 0.016, 0.881, and 0.104, respectively, under these conditions. Even with 20,000 Monte Carlo trials, we obtained an insufficient number of (6, 0) and (0, 6) faction structures upon which to base an estimate; however, we know from our theory that an initial consensus is maintained, so that the prediction in this case must be a G or NG jury outcome, respectively. Our predictions

Table 10.3 *Observed and expected faction-structure effects: Kerr and MacCoun's (1985) observed frequencies and social influence network theory's expected frequencies (in parentheses)*

G	NG	G	NG	H	Total
6	0	16	0	0	16
		(16)	(0)	(0)	
5	1	26	0	6	32
		(21.44)	(1.92)	(8.64)	
4	2	12	10	16	38
		(9.12)	(10.64)	(18.24)	
3	3	3	13	12	28
		(1.96)	(15.96)	(10.08)	
2	4	0	21	4	25
		(0.25)	(20.50)	(4.25)	
1	5	0	17	2	19
		(0.00)	(18.05)	(0.95)	
0	6	0	3	0	3
		(0.00)	(3.00)	(0.00)	

Note: Social influence network theory's expected proportions are

		G	NG	H
6	0	1.00	0.00	0.00
5	1	0.67	0.06	0.27
4	2	0.24	0.28	0.48
3	3	0.07	0.57	0.36
2	4	0.01	0.82	0.17
1	5	0.00	0.95	0.05
0	6	0.00	1.00	0.00

are shown in parentheses under the Kerr and MacCoun (1985) estimates. Kerr and MaCoun's observed relative frequencies appear close to our expected frequencies; unfortunately, a formal test of goodness of fit is precluded by the numerous low expected frequencies.

10.2.7 Summary

Our standard model presents a formalization of the interpersonal influence process that underlies jury deliberations and that results in different distributions of jury outcomes depending on the conditions under which the process unfolds. The constructs of our standard model – jury members' initial attitudes, susceptibilities, and interpersonal influences – mediate the effects of other variables on jury outcomes; these other variables include idiosyncratic (jury-specific) conditions and broader (jurisdictional) conditions under which juries are formed and cases argued in court. Jury outcomes may vary substantially across jurisdictions (state vs.

federal courts), locale (e.g., California vs. New York), case type (civil vs. criminal), and ambiguity (the relative strengths of cases for conviction and acquittal). Any theory of the expected distribution of jury outcomes must be general enough to accommodate these and other conditions, ideally in terms of a small set of formal parameters. Our approach to criminal cases employs three parameters: a "burden of proof" threshold, a bias parameter, and a variance parameter. Our analysis of juries suggests that the different macro-level descriptions of jury (and other group) outcomes of social decision scheme theory can be theoretically integrated on the basis of a micro-process of interpersonal influence that unfolds under different conditions. Given suitable data on specific criminal mock juries (e.g., analogous to our data for tetrads' discussions of the civil case described by the Disaster issue), our approach also could be employed to produce jury-level outcome predictions.

10.3 Normative Models of Group Decisions

We have noted that social decision schemes may be viewed as normative models of group decision-making to the extent that group members actually apply a decision rule in reconciling their members' initial positions on an issue. For example, "majority rule" is such a normative scheme when a group explicitly employs it (as a formal procedure) to achieve a collective decision based on a balloting of members' positions on an issue. The scope of normative models of group decision-making is large and, in this section, we informally address several lines of work related to such models.

10.3.1 DeGroot's Social Device for Consensus

In this section, we describe DeGroot's (1974) normative model, which he proposed as a *device* that might be employed by a group for settling their disputes and reaching collective decisions:

> Consider a group of k individuals who must act together as a team or committee, and suppose that each of these k individuals can specify his own subjective probability distribution for the unknown value of some parameter θ. In this article we shall present a model which describes how the group might reach a consensus and form a common subjective probability distribution for θ simply by revealing their individual distributions to each other and pooling their opinions. (p. 118)

DeGroot noted that a process of iterated weighted averaging, $y^{(t+1)} = Wy^{(t)}$, may result in consensus (depending on the structure of the weight matrix $\mathbf{W}$) and that the consensus is $\mathbf{y}^{(\infty)} = \mathbf{W}^{\infty}\mathbf{y}^{(1)}$.[4] DeGroot posits that $\mathbf{W}$ should be issue-specific (depending only on the relative perceived expertise of the group members) and constructed *a priori* (before group members have announced their positions on the issue):

> The weights should be chosen by individual i, before he is informed of the distributions of the other members of the group, on the basis of the relative importance that he assigns to the opinions of the various members of the group, including himself. For example, if individual i feels that individual j is a leading expert with regard to predicting the value of the parameter θ, then individual i will choose a large value for j. Alternatively, individual i may wish to assign a large weight to his own distribution and small total weight to the distributions of the others. (p. 119)

DeGroot's device is a *normative* model of consensus formation in an idealized sense. As Lehrer and Wagner (1981) have emphasized, this model is proposed for use by groups because it is viewed as a fair and rational method for collective decision-making. DeGroot noted that the mechanism of iterated weighted averaging provides a possible formalization of the Delphi method for reconciling differences of opinion and reaching agreements among a panel of experts (Dalkey 1972). Typically, the Delphi method involves a display of the distribution of initial attitudes (or the central tendency of that distribution) without any identification of which expert holds which attitude, followed by the development of revised attitudes and a second display of the distribution, and so on, until a collective consensual decision may be apparent to all involved.

10.3.2 Social Influence Network Theory as a Normative Model

The viewpoint of DeGroot (1974) and Lehrer and Wagner (1981) suggests that our standard model also might be employed as a *social device* for achieving a settled set of positions on an issue. This would be accomplished by computing $\mathbf{y}^{(\infty)} = \mathbf{V}\mathbf{y}^{(1)}$ based on a normative $\mathbf{W}$ with $a_{ii} = 1 - w_{ii}$ for all i. If a particular $\mathbf{W}$ were accepted by all group members and were consistent with the production of consensus, then such a group might short-circuit the influence process (and associated discussion) and simply employ the analytically derived $\mathbf{V}$ as a *decision scheme* to arrive at a group decision on all issues for which $\mathbf{W}$ is viewed as

---

[4] In applications of our standard model, we assume that $\mathbf{A} = \mathbf{I} - \text{diag}(\mathbf{W})$, which implies that $\text{diag}(\mathbf{W}) = 0$ when $\mathbf{A} = \mathbf{I}$. DeGroot's model assumes that $\mathbf{A} = \mathbf{I}$ and allows $0 \leq \text{diag}(\mathbf{W})$.

applicable. It is difficult to imagine a real group, with members who value discussion, doing that.

Nevertheless, an expert system, such as proposed by DeGroot (1974), could be implemented in situations where "time is of the essence" and quick decisions must be made. If the optimal influence network for an effective group decision could be prespecified for different classes of issues and circumstances under which these issues arise, based on past real or simulated experiences, then this social device would immediately transform members initial attitudes on an issue into a group decision without any deliberation. This procedure could only be justified if there were a strong relationship between the decisions reached by such a device and the outcomes of actual or preferred group deliberations.

The distinction between an idealized (normative) and actual (descriptive) W becomes blurred when the interpersonal influences and self-weights in the influence network of a group are based on group members' roles and expectations. Consider, for example, a deference hierarchy where there is a central source of influence (a leader or a dominant subgroup) with a single fixed initial position and where all subordinates defer completely to their immediate superiors. In a group with such a deference hierarchy, the outcome of an issue is a forgone conclusion and the collective decisions of the group might easily come to be viewed by all group members as the legitimate and sole responsibility of the central source of influence. In general, when groups allocate decision-making responsibilities on certain issues to particular individuals or subgroups, the underlying assumption (expectation) of the group members may be that the decisions of the responsible parties will be commensurate with the consensus that the full group would attain were it to engage the issue via a process of discussion and interpersonal influence. Hence, the social organization of decision-making in a group might be viewed as a legitimated social device that "short-circuits" the process of interpersonal influence on certain issues. The interpersonal foundations of the social organization of decision-making in a group become manifest when decision-makers, who have the formal authority to make decisions, secure a consensus via an interpersonal influence process prior to making their decisions.

10.3.3 *Social Choice*

Voting mechanisms allow group-level decisions in the absence of consensus. If consensus is produced, then any social choice mechanism is moot or pro forma. If consensus is not produced, then the legitimacy of the choice mechanism that is employed to produce a group decision becomes critical. At the foundations of the legitimacy of social choice mechanisms are formal procedural agreements and informal shared understandings. But how were these agreements and understandings first established, and how is their legitimacy maintained? It seems likely that these underlying agreements were established and are maintained on the basis of interpersonal influences that affect group members' attitudes about the circumstances of the group, its leadership, and their collective interests and concerns. In short, the employment of a formal decision rule to obtain a group decision is based on prior agreement that such a rule is legitimate and suitable under the circumstances in which the rule is applied. Social choice mechanisms do not reduce the importance of interpersonal influences; they fundamentally depend on such influences and on their capacity to form and maintain interpersonal agreements.

10.3.4 Groupthink

Janis's (1982) theory of groupthink is a controversial normative model of the conditions under which *flawed* group decisions are likely (Aldag and Fuller 1993; Kameda and Sugimori 1993; Mullen, Anthony, Salas, and Driskell 1994; Tetlock, Peterson, McGuire, Chang, and Feld 1992). Groupthink describes a situation in which pressures to reach consensus in a group inhibit a thorough consideration of options. Michener and Wasserman (1995: 338) state that "Groupthink is a form of premature consensus seeking. It produces an incorrect assessment of the options, which often leads to ill-considered decisions that eventuate in significant failure." Janis's case studies suggest that groupthink is fostered by (a) homogeneous initial positions on an issue, (b) highly directive leadership, and (c) a high level of group cohesion. However, the same conditions of groupthink that have been cited as encouraging flawed decisions (attitudinal homogeneity, strong leadership, and high cohesion) also are characteristic features of effective and efficient organizations, e.g., military units in field operations. An equal number of case studies also might be marshaled to support the argument that groups fail when their members are in substantial disagreement, their leaders are weak, and group cohesion is lacking. We briefly address each of the main conditions of groupthink from the perspective of social influence network theory.

Homogenous Initial Positions. Janis argues that groupthink is fostered by homogenous initial attitudes on issues. In terms of our theory, the effect of homogeneous initial positions is clear. Any consensus reached by a group must lie within the range of the initial positions of the group members. If the initial range of positions is narrow, then the consensus will fall somewhere in that range. For issues involving qualitative options, our conjecture is that no new options will be created by the influence process, unless the size or composition of the group is changed to include new members with other initial positions on an issue. Brainstorming (Osborn 1957; Sutton and Hargadon 1996) places the burden of generating new options on the members of a group. But our theory suggests that any option without an advocate will not be considered or generated by group members. Groups may consider a number of qualitative options greater than *n* if some members' distributions of subjective probabilities (indicating their relative confidence in different qualitative options) includes *multiple* options.

For example, if each group member views two options as having some merit, then in a group of size three as many as six options may be involved in the group's deliberation, e.g.,

$$\mathbf{Y}^{(1)} = \begin{bmatrix} 0.25 & 0 & 0.75 & 0 & 0 & 0 \\ 0 & 0.20 & 0 & 0.80 & 0 & 0 \\ 0 & 0 & 0 & 0 & 0.40 & 0.60 \end{bmatrix},$$

and, depending on the influence network, all of these options will be considered. Suppose the influence network of the group is

$$\mathbf{W} = \begin{bmatrix} 0 & 0.7 & 0.3 \\ 0.5 & 0 & 0.5 \\ 0.4 & 0.6 & 0 \end{bmatrix}$$

with $a_{ii} = 1 - w_{ii}$. This influence system will produce the following matrix of total influences:

$$\mathbf{V} = \begin{bmatrix} 0.314 & 0.395 & 0.291 \\ 0.314 & 0.395 & 0.291 \\ 0.314 & 0.395 & 0.291 \end{bmatrix},$$

and an equilibrium consensus on the following distribution of subjective probabilities:

$$\begin{bmatrix} 0.078 & 0.079 & 0.235 & 0.316 & 0.117 & 0.175 \end{bmatrix},$$

in which option 4 is slightly favored. Note that in this system, no one option emerges as the *confident* choice of the group. Hence, the range of options considered by a group may be enlarged if each group member is asked to present multiple options. While the efficiency of the deliberation process may decline, the quality of the collective decision may increase.

Directive Leadership. Janis suggests that groupthink is fostered by a directive leadership style. In terms of our theory, leadership is based on inequalities of interpersonal influence. Such inequalities may produce a matrix of total interpersonal influences in which consensus is reached on one option with high confidence. Consensual confidence in a single option can emerge under a variety of alternative influence networks, including a network in which group members concentrate their interpersonal influences on a single member. For example, in the extreme case where the influences in **W** are concentrated on one person, a group will *immediately* adopt the initial position (e.g., the subjective probability distribution or relative allocation preferences) of that person as the group's consensus:

$$\mathbf{W} = \begin{bmatrix} 1 & 0 & 0 \\ 1 & 0 & 0 \\ 1 & 0 & 0 \end{bmatrix}$$

with $a_{ii} = 1 - w_{ii}$. Such efficiency dampens deliberation, but does not necessarily result in the confident choice of a *single option*. If the influential member's initial position is not concentrated on any one option, then the group's consensus will mirror the uncertainty of the influential member. If group members seek to reach consensus on a single *confidently held* option, they may tend to allocate more influence to persons who strongly advocate one option; in doing so, they accept the confidence of that person in that option as their own.

If a diverse group of heavily self-weighted persons is assembled to deal with an issue, then the efficiency of the deliberation process will be low and the result is not likely to be a confident consensus on one option. But the quality of the collective decision may be higher in such a group than in a group without strong dissent. Inefficiency is undesirable when it entails enervating or destructive social conflict on an issue, or when quick decisions must be made. However, efficient influence networks are not necessarily desirable when they dampen discussion. A slower, more inefficient, social influence process may be desirable in allowing group members to fully *articulate* the bases of their initial positions on an issue, including the assumptions and beliefs upon which persons have arrived at, and advocate, their positions.

Group Cohesion. Janis suggests that the likelihood of groupthink increases with the cohesion of a group. Cohesion is a multifaceted condition that may affect the influence system of a group in different ways. In terms of our theory, cohesion may affect group outcomes by affecting either group members' initial positions on an issue, their network of interpersonal influences, or their susceptibilities to influence. If cohesion is achieved on the basis of members' homogeneity of initial positions on issues (i.e., if members are selected or self-selected because of their like-mindedness), then a limited range of options will be considered by a group. If cohesion fosters egalitarian influences, when inequalities of influence based on members' expertise ought to be decisive, then cohesion will dampen the group's ability to alter its influence network, depending on the specific issues on which members have different levels of expertise. Similarly, if the effect of cohesion is to support a single deference hierarchy regardless of the specific issues confronted by the group, then cohesion will dampen the group's capacity to modify the influence network of the group in ways that optimally weight members' expertise. If cohesion has the effect of increasing members' susceptibilities to interpersonal influence, then group members with high susceptibilities may quickly abandon their initial positions (without articulation of the bases of their position) in favor of the positions advocated by other persons and gravitate toward the positions of members who, for whatever reasons, are both intransigent and influential. In short, if cohesion (or the desire for it) fosters a homogeneous group membership and an efficient influence network, and if the group's social structure (its membership composition and influence network) is stable across issue domains, then, as Janis suggests, a *structural* basis exists for low quality decisions. The ironic conclusion is that important decisions should not be made by cohesive groups. Some U.S. presidents (Lincoln and FDR) intuitively reached the same conclusion.

10.3.5 Appointment Power

In many organizations, decisions are made by groups that are formally constituted to deal with a specific issue or class of issues. The extent to which the composition of such groups is shaped by normative, idealized models of group-membership composition will vary from case to case. Whitmeyer (2000) has defined *appointment power* as the ability to realize one's interests by appointing persons with similar attitudes to a decision-making group and (if interpersonal influence within the group is affected by members' structural positions) by assigning members of the group to particular positions. For Cartwright and Zander(1968), such appointment power is a special case of *ecological power* in which conditions exogenous to the group determine group outcomes. For Simon (1945), such appointment power is a component of the managerial administration of formal organizations, in which the conditions under which decisions are made in the different subgroups of a formal organization are structured by managers who may not directly participate in the decision-making processes of these subgroups. Clearly, control over the composition of decision-making groups may be based on a variety of considerations, including more or less widely accepted norms about who ought to be included in the group's deliberation of an issue. Some level of control and coordination of the decision-making process is a necessary feature of an effective and efficient formal organization. However, judgments of considerable complexity are involved in exercising power over the composition of decision-making groups, in part because of the various dimensions (technical, political, economic) that may be involved in group members' choice of particular options.

10.4 Concluding Remarks

In this chapter, we have shown that social influence network theory provides a process-oriented approach to an account of group decision-making, which is able to account for and integrate some of the results of social decision scheme theory. In doing so, we have shown how social influence network theory may be applied to juries. More generally, we have shown how a sociological approach in which influence networks are emphasized can contribute to an understanding of a line of social psychological work on group decision-making – social decision scheme theory – in which an attention to influence networks has been largely missing. We also have pointed to work on normative models of group decision-making that is closely related to our theory; however, lest there be some confusion, we again emphasize that our main interest in the mechanism of iterated weighted averaging is based on the possibility that it actually describes not what group members might do or ought to do, but approximately what they actually do to reach consensus.

Any attempt to link the social structure of a group with the quality of its decision is a troublesome enterprise, but we believe that there may be a reliable connection based on efficiency. A rapid reduction of the variance of initial positions may inhibit group members' opportunities to fully articulate the bases of initial attitudes on an issue, and such articulation is likely to bear on the quality of the group decision. It is not known whether such articulation serves to modify the influence network of the group, so that the group becomes focused more on the merits of the arguments of members than on their relative preexisting standing in the influence structure of the group. The discovery of reliable effects of groups' influence networks and initial positions on the quality of the groups' decisions would be very useful.

11

Expectation States and Affect Control Theory

In this chapter, we will describe a model in which $\mathbf{Y}^{(t)}$ affects $\mathbf{W}^{(t)}$ at each time $t = 1, 2, \ldots$. The $\mathbf{Y}^{(t)}$ that is involved in this model is an $n \times n$ matrix of group members' attitudes toward each other and themselves. Their $\mathbf{Y}^{(t)}$ attitudes determine $\mathbf{W}^{(t)}$ along with its coupled $\mathbf{A}^{(t)}$; and because these attitudes are subject to interpersonal influence, $\mathbf{W}^{(t)}$, together with its coupled $\mathbf{A}^{(t)}$, generates a $\mathbf{Y}^{(t+1)}$ matrix of attitudes, and so on. From this process, an equilibrium matrix of attitudes, susceptibilities, and interpersonal influences may be produced in the group. The equilibrium $\mathbf{W}^{(\infty)}$ and $\mathbf{A}^{(\infty)}$ that may emerge from this process constitute a stable influence network for the group, conditioned on the matrix of initial interpersonal attitudes $\mathbf{Y}^{(1)}$. Here, $\mathbf{Y}^{(1)}$, in the form of a matrix of interpersonal attitudes, appears as the core construct in determining a group's influence network. The explanation of the origins of stable influence networks in groups has been a longstanding sociological issue, and this model contributes to the theoretical integration of two lines of inquiry related to it – expectation states theory and affect control theory.

Recently, there have been efforts to develop linkages between some of the major lines of work in sociological social psychology – affect control theory, expectation states theory, and social identity theory. Ridgeway and Smith-Lovin (1994) have described possible linkages between affect control theory and expectation states theory. Kalkhoff and Barnum (2000) have described possible linkages between social identity theory and expectation states theory. These and other efforts (Deaux and Daniela 2003; Skvoretz and Fararo 1996) indicate points of intersection based on shared theoretical constructs and shed an integrative light on the domain of social psychology by linking different theoretical structures. Such efforts advance knowledge and understanding by developing links between extant theories, in contrast to advances that are predicated on competition through elimination or subsumption of theories.[1]

Our efforts are exactly in this vein of establishing productive linkages between theories. In this chapter, we link social influence network theory with affect control theory and expectation states theory. Social influence network theory and affect control theory intersect on *sentiments*, which in affect control theory are attitudes toward particular persons measured by semantic differential scales of evaluation, potency, and activity. Social influence network theory and expectation states theory intersect on *performance expectations*, which in expectation states theory are latent attitudes that affect interpersonal influence in task-oriented groups. As attitudes, both interpersonal sentiments and expectations are subject to interpersonal influence, and a network of endogenous interpersonal influences that affects them may be formed. However, neither affect control theory nor expectation states theory grapples directly with the implications of the presence of such networks. We currently do not have a good theoretical understanding of how the fundamental sentiments associated with persons' social identities or the performance expectations associated with persons' status positions are modified by the displayed attitudes of other group members, or how interpersonal influences in a group may generate equilibrium sentiments and expectations that are quite different from (and possibly more consensual than) their initial array of sentiments and expectations.

Social influence network theory does not add anything further to the accounts of affect control theory and expectation states theory when the *initial* attitudes of group members are consensual, i.e., when they view the same object in the same way. In affect control theory and expectation states theory, this is the typical situation analyzed. When there is an initial consensus, interpersonal influences are moot and the equilibrium attitude of each group member is the initial consensus. However, matters become more complex and interesting when the attitudes of group members toward the same objects are heterogeneous and there is a network of interpersonal influence that connects the members of the group. A contribution of social influence network theory is to show how an influence network may operate to modify attitudes toward other group members and how a more consensual set of interpersonal attitudes can emerge from a sequence of interpersonal influences. As a prelude to our analysis,

---

[1]   Joining theories sometimes requires raising the level of abstraction of their constructs so that a commonality and intersection can be established; it seems reasonable to believe that the less abstraction is required, the more concrete and useful the linkage will be for those engaged in the empirical research program of each theoretical structure. When abstraction is required, the "stress" produced by the juxtaposition of the theoretical structures can be productive in stimulating the growth and revision of the structures so that they dovetail more seamlessly.

we briefly sketch the main features of affect control theory and expectation states theory, and we develop some of the possible links between these theories and social influence network theory. Our main analytical emphasis will be on the linkage between affect control theory and social influence network theory. We will demonstrate how these theories, once joined, may bear on the account of the core constructs of expectation states theory (the performance expectations that are associated with persons' status positions and the influence networks in groups) and how an influence network may emerge from the process of attitude change about group members' interpersonal sentiments. We also will show how the standard prediction equation for persons' performance expectations in expectation states theory can be employed to predict influence networks in our social influence network–theory framework and how a relaxation of the assumption of consensual performance expectations is easily accommodated by our framework.

11.1 Three Theories

11.1.1 Affect Control Theory

Affect control theory deals with mechanisms and associated behaviors and emotions that underlie the formation, maintenance, and transformation of persons' definitions of situations in the particular social settings in which they are interacting (Heise 2002; Smith-Lovin and Heise 1988). Affect control theory posits that social situations entail a constellation of sentiments toward various objects, including the social setting (classroom, home, workplace), the social identities of the persons who are located in the setting (doctor, nurse, husband, child), the behaviors of the persons in the setting, and other salient characteristics of the persons (mood, gender, status) and their behaviors. Hence, for n persons with k-dimensional sentiments toward q objects, the social situation would be defined in terms of an $n \times q \times k$ matrix of scores that are indicative of persons' attitudes toward the q objects. Prior to any interaction among the persons involved in a social situation, a set of *fundamental* sentiments are triggered by persons' identification or recognition of the objects in the situation. Affect control theory assumes that these fundamental sentiments are *normative* in the sense that the same matrix of sentiments occurs for different persons in the same situation. This homogeneity is assumed to be based on a cultural consensus in the population from which the persons involved in the situation are drawn. Affect-control investigators have obtained empirical estimates from surveys of the fundamental sentiments for a large number of objects, so that in applications of the theory a matrix of fundamental sentiments can be obtained *a priori* for an immense number of theoretically possible social situations.

Affect control theory posits that each person in a social situation will have a normative *expectation* about the likelihood of various events that might occur in that setting, based on the fundamental sentiments that are entailed in the initial definition of the situation.[2] The events that occur in a social setting do not necessarily conform to these expectations, for a variety of reasons. Affect control theory posits that any such *deflection* (deviation) of actual events from expectation is *transitory* and that these deflections are diminished by homeostatic control or balancing mechanisms (involving actions or redefinitions) that bring experienced sentiments into closer conformity or fit with expected fundamental sentiments. Although perfect conformity with expectations may not be feasible, it is the movement toward greater conformity that is the fundamental social mechanism with which affect control theory is concerned. Events trigger felt and displayed emotions that signal the degree of deflection of events from expectations.

Persons may reduce deflections by altering their behavior (eventually bringing their behavior into closer accord with normative expectations) or by *redefining* the elements of the definition of the situation. If the social identities, setting, and other salient conditions of the situation are *fixed*, then a deflection can only be mitigated by new behaviors in subsequent events that bring the sentiments for these subsequent events closer to the fundamental sentiments for these fixed conditions. However, affect control theory also allows "reidentifications" that involve a relabeling of the setting or the identities and characteristics of persons and other objects. In effect, a "reidentification" may reduce deflection by changing fundamental sentiments, so that now the experienced events in a setting are more consistent with normative expectation and do not produce as much stress.

The balancing mechanisms of affect control theory are grounded on consensual understandings in the culture or subculture of a population that a particular set of fundamental sentiments are appropriate or correct for the situation. Without discounting this explanation, we point out that when there is a lack of initial consensus on what is appropriate or correct, interpersonal influences in a group may produce the shared meanings and the strong normative foundations that underlie the equilibrating behaviors postulated by affect control theory. That is, in a group of persons who find themselves interacting in a situation, a consensual understanding about what is expected and correct may be *constructed* by them on

---

[2] Behaviors of the person or the object (another person) conform more or less closely to the normative expectations associated with the particular social identities and other features of the setting and persons. For instance, persons would expect their friends to behave in particular ways toward them as a function of the setting, mood, and other attributes involved in the interaction. Thus, certain events (i.e., the nexus of a person–behavior–object) are expected and other events are not.

the basis of a network of interpersonal influences that is being formed in the group.

11.1.2 Introducing Influence Networks into Affect Control Theory

Social influence network theory and affect control theory intersect on the fundamental sentiments that deal with persons' attitudes toward objects in a social situation. In affect control theory, a semantic differential scale is employed to describe persons' sentiments toward the objects that define a situation and the events that take place in it. Semantic differential scales are among the most widely employed attitudinal scales in social psychology (Osgood, May, and Miron 1975; Osgood, Suci, and Tannenbaum 1957). Such scales are constructed from pairs of antonyms (good or bad, wise or foolish, and so forth) that might describe an object. For each pair of antonyms, a scale consisting of five, seven, or nine possible positions or locations indicates the attitude of a person toward the object; for example, a scale with nine positions would be coded $-4, -3, -2, -1, 0, 1, 2, 3, 4$, and the middle position would indicate that one adjective is not a better description than the other, or that both adjectives are irrelevant.

Semantic differential scales of attitudes are widely employed, in part, because they allow a standard or uniform set of antonym pairs to be applied to a large domain of different objects. The frequent and successful employment of this scaling approach to attitudes has suggested, in turn, that persons may be responding to a wide variety of different objects in terms of a common metric. From factor-analytic studies of semantic differential antonyms, it appears that the many possible word-items (pairs of antonyms) that have been employed in the construction of semantic differential scales are indicators of three underlying dimensions – *evaluation* (e.g., good vs. bad), *potency* (e.g., strong vs. weak), and *activity* (e.g., lively vs. quiet). A person's mean scores on the dimensions of evaluation, potency, and activity are referred to as the EPA profile for the target object from the point of view of the source person, who is the holder of the attitude. If the EPA profile is treated as a set of coordinates in 3-dimensional space, then a spatial model of the distribution of persons' attitudes toward a common target-object is produced.

Social influence network theory is introduced into affect control theory by allowing persons' fundamental sentiments to be affected by other persons' fundamental sentiments (cf. Robinson 1996). Heterogeneous fundamental sentiments toward the same object may arise in various ways: different subcultures (e.g., male vs. female subcultures) may have different sentiments toward the same object, persons with similar identities (e.g., female identity) from different cultures may have different sentiments toward the same object (e.g., male objects), or persons with similar identities may identify the same object differently. Thus, endogenous interpersonal influences – sentiments affecting sentiments – may modify persons' viewpoints about the objects in their social environments. An influence network is the *structure* in which such endogenous interpersonal responses occur.

Although affect control theory emphasizes that definitions of the situation are constructed on the basis of widely shared orientations toward identities and expected behaviors, the theory allows for within-group processes that modify the identities that persons attribute to themselves and others in a particular setting. We have previously noted that affect control theorists argue that such "reidentifications" redefine the situation so that there is a closer correspondence between the situated identities and their behaviors. We believe that there may also be some "reidentification" based on endogenous interpersonal influence, that is, as a direct response to the displayed sentiments of significant others toward the objects that define a situation.[3] Therefore, we introduce a process of endogenous interpersonal influence into the construction of a definition of a situation, based on the assumption that persons may take into account (to varying degrees) the fundamental sentiments of their significant others in refining their own fundamental sentiments about the salient objects involved in a social situation. Social influence network theory is nuanced in that it allows for individual differences in susceptibilities to interpersonal influence; hence, we do not stipulate that persons necessarily modify their sentiments through a process of interpersonal influence or that all persons involved in a situation will do so to the same extent.

Thus, our contribution to affect control theory is the idea that the fundamental sentiments upon which deflections are based are not always strictly based on the specification of the dyadic situation consisting of the identities of two persons, their modifying characteristics, and their setting. We are proposing that the normative foundations of the fundamental sentiments are not entirely specified by the fixed contextual conditions of the situation, but may to some extent be shaped by the interpersonal influences in the situation. Hence, the basis of deflections may not be the discrepancy between the *initial* fundamental sentiments and the transitory impressions that are associated with a particular behavior, but instead may involve a set of *influenced* fundamental sentiments that have been shaped by the interpersonal influences of significant others. When multiple persons are involved in a situation who are simultaneously forming sentiments about the salient objects in the setting, and when at least some of these persons are susceptible to interpersonal influence, then the normative sentiments (and expected behaviors) for the

---

[3] The sentiments may be communicated through behaviors, emotional expressions, gestures, or words.

situation may be "negotiated" within the group to some extent. Interpersonal influence among persons with heterogeneous identities may produce sentiments that are very different from the initial fundamental sentiments that are broadly associated with the identities in the population-level culture. Indeed, once endogenous interpersonal influences are introduced, it becomes at least a theoretical possibility that a person may come to hold sentiments that are radically different from his or her initial fundamental sentiments toward some object. Whether such persons experience stress as a consequence of such a structural deflection from their initial sentiments is an open question.

11.1.3 Expectation States Theory

Expectation states theory is a family of models concerned with the formation of inequalities of individual behavior and interpersonal interaction in task-oriented groups (Balkwell 1991; Berger et al. 1974; Berger, Fisek, Norman, and Zelditch 1977; Berger et al. 1985; Fisek, Berger, and Norman 1991; Fisek, Norman, and Nelson-Kilger 1992; Ridgeway 2001; Skvoretz et al.1999; Wagner and Berger 1993). Following Bales (1950), the initial emphasis of the theory was on an account of how inequalities of interpersonal influence emerged in status *homogenous* groups, where there were no differences among group members on certain sociodemographic characteristics; however, the theory was quickly extended to include an account of how the emergent inequalities of interpersonal influence in *heterogeneous* groups are shaped by members' sociodemographic characteristics.

In expectation states theory, the key construct in the explanation of influence inequalities is a latent attitude – a performance expectation – that a person forms about each group member, including him- or herself, concerning the value of a person's task-relevant opinions and actions. In status-*homogeneous* groups, expectation states theory posits that the main antecedents of a performance expectation are initial manifest differences in behavior (e.g., persons' self-assertion or quiescence).[4] In status-*heterogeneous* groups, the main antecedents of a performance expectation include general sociodemographic characteristics of the group's members (e.g., the members' age, sex, skin color, height, weight, attractiveness, and social class) and more specific task-related characteristics that suggest some relevant expertise. A major accomplishment of expectation states

---

[4] We are not convinced that status differentiation on some dimensions is ever entirely absent in human encounters, because physical differences always provide a basis (however misguided) for attributions and imputations about the character and intelligence of others; hence, task-relevant meaning will be generated on whatever differentiating features are apparent to the persons involved in the interaction. Pure homogeneity may be a theoretical, but not a realistic, possibility in human groups.

theory is the development of a "graph-analytic" model that predicts persons' performance expectations based on sociodemographic characteristics. Expectation states theory posits that group members compare each other in terms of their expected levels of task-related performance and that these comparisons govern their behavior toward one another, including their resistance to or acceptance of interpersonal influence from particular persons in the group. The empirical focus in expectation states research has been on the dyad, where influence outcomes have been measured as the proportion of disagreements resolved in favor of one member of the dyad or the other. Because expectation states theory assumes that the effects of status characteristics on performance expectations and interpersonal influence are based on population-level consensual understandings about the meaning and relevance of particular status characteristics, the predicted pattern of interpersonal influence that emerges in these dyads should tend to reflect the broader cultural consensus concerning the value of these different status characteristics in the population.

Whitmeyer (2002) has demonstrated that the graph-analytic models of expectation states theory, which have been employed to predict performance expectations, may be represented more parsimoniously by algebraic equations of the following form:

$$\Phi = \exp\left[-a \sum_r n_r g(r)\right] - \exp\left[-a \sum_r p_r g(r)\right], \qquad (11.1)$$

where Φ is the predicted performance expectation for a person with a given array of status characteristics, $r = \{1, 2, 3\}$ is the relevance level of a status condition, p_r is the number of status conditions of relevance r on which a person's status value is high (positive), n_r is the number of status conditions of relevance r on which a person's status value is low (negative), $a > 0$ is a constant, $g(r) > 0$ is one of the functions

$$g(r) = \begin{cases} c^{3-r} + c^{2-r} & \text{Berger et al. (1977)} \\ c^{6-r} + c^{5-r} & \text{Balkwell (1991)} \\ c^{1-r} + c^{-r} & \text{Fisek et al. (1992),} \end{cases}$$

and c is an estimated constant ($c \approx 3$). In turn, the performance expectations of group members $\{\Phi_1, \Phi_2, \ldots, \Phi_n\}$ are linearly transformed into a measure (B) of influence behavior; for instance, $B_{12} = \beta_0 + \beta_1 (\Phi_1 - \Phi_2)$ in the case of a dyad.

We note that an alternative expression for (11.1) is

$$\Phi = \exp\left[-\beta_0 \sum_r \beta_r n_r\right] - \exp\left[-\beta_0 \sum_r \beta_r p_r\right], \qquad (11.2)$$

where the β coefficients are estimatable constants.[5] This reformulation suggests that even simpler expressions may suffice. For example, if we take the two leading terms in the infinite series expansion of the exponential function $e^{-x} = 1 - \frac{x}{1!} + \frac{x^2}{2!} - \frac{x^3}{3!} + \cdots$, that is, $1 - x$, performance expectations might be adequately predicted by a simple linear combination of status variables, i.e.,

$$\Phi = \sum_k \beta_k X_k$$

$$= \beta_0 \sum_{r=1}^{3} \beta_r p_r - \beta_0 \sum_{r=1}^{3} \beta_r n_r = \beta_0 \sum_{r=1}^{3} \beta_r (p_r - n_r), \qquad (11.3)$$

where each status variable X_k involves a dichotomous coding (-1 for negative status, $+1$ for positive status) and there are only *three* homogeneous classes of these variables with three corresponding distinct effects ($\beta_1, \beta_2, \beta_3$). These, in turn, can be transformed into interpersonal influences according to a function that we shall specify. Whether such a reformulation captures all of the effects of the standard expectation states formulation is an open question that we believe is worth pursuing.[6]

11.1.4 Introducing Influence Networks into Expectation States Theory

We have mentioned that most of the empirical work in the expectation states tradition has concentrated on an analysis of dyads, and this focus is for us a major limitation of the tradition; see the work on larger discussion groups (e.g., Robinson and Balkwell 1995; Smith-Lovin, Skvoretz, and Hawkins 1986). We are interested in the analysis of systems of interpersonal influence of arbitrary size; moreover, we suspect that dyadic systems have certain atypical properties and that it may be misleading to concentrate analysis on them.[7] In the expectation states research

[5] Expectation states theorists argue that performance expectations are not observable. The estimation of these coefficients occurs in a reduced-form equation (predicting influence behavior as a function of status variables) in which performance expectations do not appear.

[6] Although attenuation effects (i.e., diminishing marginal effects of additional status characteristics) on influence outcomes have been noted in various studies, there is no direct evidence that there are attenuation effects on performance expectations. It is important to recognize that performance expectations have not been subject to direct measurement in the expectation states research tradition. Additionally, direct indicators of performance expectations would allow an assessment of the degree to which group members actually do *agree* in their expectations at the start of the group interaction. If such consensus actually exists in a group – and we doubt that it does in most groups – then endogenous interpersonal influences may not have any effect in modifying these expectations. It is when such consensus is *absent* that social influence network theory becomes interesting theoretically for an expectation-states theorist.

[7] See Friedkin and Johnsen (1999) and Chapter 6 of this book.

tradition, there has been some work on the effects of persons' performance expectations on other persons' performance expectations; it is assumed that the influential expectations are *fixed* conditions that are affecting the performance expectations of some focal person (Fisek, Berger, and Norman 1995; Troyer and Younts 1997; Webster and Sobieszek 1974; Webster and Whitmeyer 1999, 2002). However, unlike persons' status characteristics, influential performance expectations may not be fixed conditions. In a group, performance expectations of its members may change because of the various interpersonal influences present in the group, especially when there is substantial initial *disagreement* on appropriate expectations. In its account of the emergence of stable influence structures in newly formed task-oriented groups, we believe that expectation states theory has somewhat overstated the general extent of *initial consensus* on performance expectations. The theory assumes consensus as an initial condition, and it has not adequately detailed the *mechanism* by which interpersonal agreements on performance expectations are produced. We propose that such agreements arise through the interactions of the group members. Thus, when there is a consensus on performance expectations in a group, we believe that it often has been produced *within the group*, through a process of endogenous interpersonal influence among its members. When an observed consensus is not based on the simple importation of a population-level agreement, the intragroup process that has produced the consensus should be formally incorporated into expectation states theory.

Previous work on the effect of interpersonal influences on performance expectations has not described a mechanism by which the expectations of the sources of influence are also being influenced and has not shown how, in concrete mathematical terms and under what conditions, a consensus will arise as a result of a sequence of interpersonal influences among group members. The work that has been conducted on the diffusion of shared understandings of the performance value of different status characteristics has been motivated by the assumption (central to expectation states theory, but one that we question) that persons *enter into* groups with a substantial degree of consensus about the relevance and performance value of various status characteristics to task-oriented activities (Ridgeway 1991; Ridgeway & Balkwell 1997). For us, what is most fundamental about expectation states theory is *not* the assertion of an initial consensus of status beliefs. What is fundamental is (a) an assertion that status characteristics affect persons' attitudes about each other, e.g., their performance expectations, and (b) an assertion that, regardless of the degree of initial consensus of these attitudes, social processes operate within groups to generate such consensus and, in turn, a stable network of interpersonal influence. Our theoretical focus is on the social process within a group that generates such consensus and stable patterns of influence, where they do not exist *a priori*.

11.1.5 Social Influence Network Theory

During the past two decades, there has been a dramatic increase of work on how social networks form and change (Arrow 1997; Carley 1990, 1991; Doreian and Stokman 1997; Lazer 2001; Stokman and Berveling 1998). Our focus is on the *influence* networks in groups that shape group members' attitudes. We now develop a model of the evolution of such influence networks in which the set of attitudes that group members have about themselves (i.e., their sentiments) affect the network of interpersonal influences among them. In this model, the influence network in turn modifies persons' sentiments, and so on, until an equilibrium is reached. Thus, our theoretical orientation to network dynamics is distinctly social psychological, and our present effort is to link these dynamics to theoretical constructs that are the cornerstones of affect control theory (sentiments and identities) and expectation states theory (performance expectations and status characteristics).

In much of our previous work and in the present book, we have assumed that an influence network is a stable social context in which the process of attitude change unfolds:

$$\mathbf{y}^{(t+1)} = \mathbf{A}\mathbf{W}\mathbf{y}^{(t)} + (\mathbf{I} - \mathbf{A})\,\mathbf{y}^{(1)}, \tag{11.4}$$

where $\mathbf{y}^{(t)}$ is an $n \times 1$ vector of persons' attitudes on an issue at time t, $\mathbf{W} = \left[w_{ij}\right]$ is an $n \times n$ matrix of interpersonal influences, and $\mathbf{A} = \mathrm{diag}\,(a_{11}, a_{22}, \ldots, a_{nn})$ is an $n \times n$ diagonal matrix of the persons' susceptibilities to interpersonal influence on the issue. We have always viewed (11.4) as a special case of a more general model in which persons' susceptibilities and interpersonal influences might change over time (Friedkin and Johnsen 1990),

$$\mathbf{Y}^{(t+1)} = \mathbf{A}^{(t)}\mathbf{W}^{(t)}\mathbf{Y}^{(t)} + \left(\mathbf{I} - \mathbf{A}^{(t)}\right)\mathbf{Y}^{(1)}, \tag{11.5}$$

but did not until recently (Friedkin and Johnsen 2003) attempt to specify functions that govern the changes in the influence network.

The linkage between our theory and affect control theory is an $n \times n \times 3$ matrix of sentiments, $\mathbf{Y}^{(t)} = \left[y_{ijk}^{(t)}\right]$, where $\left(y_{ij1}^{(t)}, y_{ij2}^{(t)}, y_{ij3}^{(t)}\right)$ is the EPA profile of person j from the viewpoint of person i at time t. For $t = 1$, $\mathbf{Y}^{(1)} = \left[y_{ijk}^{(1)}\right]$ describes the *fundamental sentiments* of the group members toward themselves and each other. For $t > 1$, $\mathbf{Y}^{(t)} = \left[y_{ijk}^{(t)}\right]$ describes the revised sentiments of the group members at time t that may have been influenced by other members' sentiments. In our model of the evolution of the influence network that is detailed below, we assume that sentiments affect interpersonal influence via a latent construct – the *salience* of self and others – that is at the foundation of interpersonal influence.

Interpersonal influence depends on interpersonal visibility and salience. Person j's attitudes cannot directly influence person i's attitudes unless they are visible and salient for person i. Let $\mathbf{G}^{(t)} = \left[g_{ij}^{(t)} \right]$ be the *visibility* matrix for the group at time t,

$$
\mathbf{G}^{(t)} = \begin{bmatrix} 1 & g_{12}^{(t)} & \cdots & g_{1n}^{(t)} \\ g_{21}^{(t)} & 1 & \cdots & g_{2n}^{(t)} \\ \vdots & \vdots & \ddots & \vdots \\ g_{n1}^{(t)} & g_{n2}^{(t)} & \cdots & 1 \end{bmatrix},
\tag{11.6}
$$

where $g_{ij}^{(t)} = 1$ if person i is acquainted with person j and $g_{ij}^{(t)} = 0$ otherwise. We restrict our analysis to those groups in which every person is acquainted with at least one other person in the group; hence, we stipulate that $\sum_{k \neq i}^{n} g_{ik}^{(t)} > 0$ for all i. Let $\mathbf{S}^{(t)} = \left[s_{ij}^{(t)} \right]$ be the *salience* matrix for the group at time t,

$$
\mathbf{S}^{(t)} = \begin{bmatrix} s_{11}^{(t)} & s_{12}^{(t)} & \cdots & s_{1n}^{(t)} \\ s_{21}^{(t)} & s_{22}^{(t)} & \cdots & s_{2n}^{(t)} \\ \vdots & \vdots & \ddots & \vdots \\ s_{n1}^{(t)} & s_{n2}^{(t)} & \cdots & s_{nn}^{(t)} \end{bmatrix},
\tag{11.7}
$$

where $0 \leq s_{ij}^{(t)} \leq 1$ indicates the potential salience of person j's attitudes for person i. In terms of these constructs, the matrix of interpersonal influence, $\mathbf{W}^{(t)} = \left[w_{ij}^{(t)} \right]$ at time t,

$$
\mathbf{W}^{(t)} = \begin{bmatrix} w_{11}^{(t)} & w_{12}^{(t)} & \cdots & w_{1n}^{(t)} \\ w_{21}^{(t)} & w_{22}^{(t)} & \cdots & w_{2n}^{(t)} \\ \vdots & \vdots & \ddots & \vdots \\ w_{n1}^{(t)} & w_{n2}^{(t)} & \cdots & w_{nn}^{(t)} \end{bmatrix},
\tag{11.8}
$$

is specified as one in which the weight accorded to one's self *is* the perceived salience of one's self,

$$
w_{ii}^{(t)} = 1 - a_{ii}^{(t)} = s_{ii}^{(t)},
\tag{11.9}
$$

and the weight accorded to an acquaintance is a function of the *relative* salience of that acquaintance, $\mathbf{C}^{(t)} = \left[c_{ij}^{(t)} \right]$, where

$$
c_{ij}^{(t)} = \frac{g_{ij}^{(t)} s_{ij}^{(t)}}{\sum_{k \neq i}^{n} g_{ik}^{(t)} s_{ik}^{(t)}}.
\tag{11.10}
$$

for $\sum_{k \neq i}^{n} g_{ik}^{(t)} s_{ik}^{(t)} \neq 0$. For $\sum_{k \neq i}^{n} g_{ik}^{(t)} s_{ik}^{(t)} = 0$, we set $c_{ij}^{(t)} = 0$ ($j = 1, n$) and $a_{ii}^{(t)} = 1 - w_{ii}^{(t)} = 0$. Hence, $\mathbf{W}^{(t)} = \mathbf{A}^{(t)} \mathbf{C}^{(t)} + \mathbf{I} - \mathbf{A}^{(t)}$, consistent with the approach described in Chapter 3.[8]

We continue this formulation with a linkage of salience to constructs that are exogenous to the model. We employ the following functions with the understanding that their specific mathematical form is an open empirical issue. Here, we posit that salience is a monotonically nondecreasing function of a linear combination of conditions

$$s_{ij}^{(t)} = \begin{cases} \dfrac{\exp\left\{\lambda z_{ij}^{(t)}\right\} - 1}{\exp\left\{\lambda z_{ij}^{(t)}\right\} + 1} & \text{for} \quad z_{ij}^{(t)} \geq 0 \\[2mm] 0 & \text{for} \quad z_{ij}^{(t)} < 0, \end{cases} \tag{11.11}$$

where

$$z_{ij}^{(t)} = \beta_0 + \beta_1 x_{ij1}^{(t)} + \beta_2 x_{ij2}^{(t)} + \cdots, \tag{11.12}$$

$\lambda > 0$ is a constant, and $-\infty < z_{ij}^{(t)} < \infty$. The function (11.11) serves to map $-\infty < z_{ij}^{(t)} < \infty$ onto $0 \leq s_{ij}^{(t)} < 1$. Note that the function maps $z_{ij}^{(t)} = 0$ onto $s_{ij}^{(t)} = 0$ and all $z_{ij}^{(t)} < 0$ onto $s_{ij}^{(t)} = 0$ and is monotonically increasing for all $0 \leq z_{ij}^{(t)} < \infty$.

11.2 Formal Linkages and Illustrations

11.2.1 Linking to Affect Control Theory

In line with affect control theory, we posit per (11.12) that interpersonal sentiments toward one's self and particular others, on the dimensions of evaluation, potency, and activity, are among the immediate (direct) determinants of salience:

$$z_{ij}^{(t)} = \beta_0 + \beta_1 y_{ij1}^{(t)} + \beta_2 y_{ij2}^{(t)} + \beta_3 y_{ij3}^{(t)}.$$
$$\qquad\qquad\quad \uparrow \qquad\quad \uparrow \qquad\quad \uparrow$$
$$\text{Evaluation} \quad \text{Potency} \quad \text{Activity} \tag{11.13}$$

This equation may easily be elaborated to include other determinants of salience; for instance, bases of social power (French and Raven 1959), status characteristics, and other conditions directly affecting persons' salience. As we have illustrated in Figure 11.1, we believe that many of these conditions are *antecedents* of the sentiments that are at the core

---

[8] That is, as an extension of the formalization presented in Chapter 3, where $\mathbf{B} = [b_{ij}]$ is the basis of $\mathbf{W}$, here we have $b_{ij}^{(t)} = g_{ij}^{(t)} s_{ij}^{(t)}$ for all i and j.

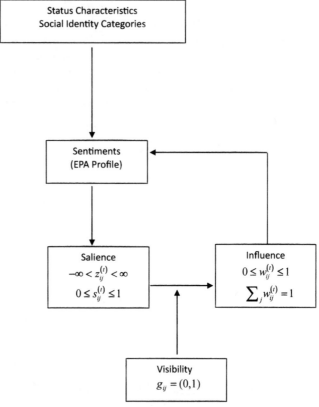

Figure 11.1 A model of the evolution of influence networks. The extent of the mediating role of sentiments is an open empirical issue.

of affect control theory (evaluation, potency, activity) and that these sentiments, in turn, affect salience. After controlling for persons' sentiments, there may or may not be any noteworthy *direct* effects of status characteristics and identity categories on salience. Our theoretical position (discussed later) is that persons' displayed sentiments toward themselves and others in a group have a major role in the determination of interpersonal influence networks, and that the effects of status characteristics and identity categories on salience are entirely mediated by persons' sentiments.

Hence, in this social influence process, the sentiments of group members towards themselves and others shape the group members' interpersonal influences, which, in turn, shape the sentiments of group members, and so on. The displayed attitudes of influential others toward person i describe a viewpoint on person i's identity that may change i's self-orientation depending on i's susceptibility to interpersonal influence. Person i's attitude toward self may be a reflected appraisal of the attitudes of others, but this interpersonal determination of i's self-orientation is governed by his or her susceptibility to influence. Interpersonal influences on i may either maintain, lower, or raise person i's self-orientation, depending on whose attitudes are influential. In this process, person i is a potential *recipient* of influence. However, person i is also is a potential *source* of influence. Hence, person i is simultaneously a recipient and an agent of influence and these "roles" are determined, respectively, by i's susceptibility to influence and by the amount of influence that is being accorded to i by others. Because person i may directly or indirectly influence those persons who are having some influence on him or her, person i may shape the social environment in which he or she is situated so that the definition of the situation as construed by *others* more closely corresponds to person i's own *initial* definition. Hence, the agents of influence are in competition with each other, whether or not they recognize it, in the determination of the definition of the situation for each person. This competition is especially clear when a *consensual* definition of the situation emerges from the process, because in that case each person's *initial* position (his or her initial fundamental sentiments) is a proportionate contribution to the content of the consensual understanding of the group as a whole.

If this process, (11.5), attains an equilibrium, then

$$\mathbf{Y}^{(\infty)} = \mathbf{A}^{(\infty)}\mathbf{W}^{(\infty)}\mathbf{Y}^{(\infty)} + \left(\mathbf{I} - \mathbf{A}^{(\infty)}\right)\mathbf{Y}^{(1)}$$
$$= \mathbf{V}^{(\infty)}\mathbf{Y}^{(1)}, \tag{11.14}$$

where $\mathbf{V}^{(\infty)} = \left[v_{ij}^{(\infty)}\right]$ is the matrix of total influences, $0 \leq v_{ij}^{(\infty)} \leq 1$ and $\sum_{j=1}^{n} v_{ij}^{(\infty)} = 1$, which transforms the initial fundamental sentiments of the group members into their equilibrium sentiments, $\mathbf{Y}^{(\infty)}$. These equilibrium sentiments are the more or less *influenced* fundamental sentiments of the n group members about each other on each of the three dimensions of evaluation, potency, and activity. Group members' sentiments and the pattern of interpersonal visibility determine persons' susceptibilities, $\mathbf{A}^{(\infty)}$, and influences, $\mathbf{W}^{(\infty)}$, so that the equilibrium influence structure of the group also is completely determined by the initial fundamental sentiments among the group members about one another and themselves, $\mathbf{Y}^{(1)}$, and by the fixed pattern of interpersonal visibility in the group, $\mathbf{G}$. The direct or total influences, $\mathbf{W}^{(\infty)}$ or $\mathbf{V}^{(\infty)}$ respectively, may involve either a consensual stratification of interpersonal influences or a more complex pattern of heterogeneous influences.

If a group's equilibrium sentiments and influences are formed during the discussion of a particular substantive issue, then the development of persons' positions on the substantive issue may evolve in parallel with the process that is forming the interpersonal sentiments and influences in the group. Such may be the case when a group of strangers assemble to discuss an issue. Once a stable influence network is formed, it may provide a fixed social context for a domain of subsequent issues that arise in the group,

$$\mathbf{Y}^{(t+1)} = \mathbf{A}^{(\infty)}\mathbf{W}^{(\infty)}\mathbf{Y}^{(t)} + \left(\mathbf{I} - \mathbf{A}^{(\infty)}\right)\mathbf{Y}^{(1)}, \tag{11.15}$$

where now $\mathbf{Y}^{(t)}$ represents any one of a number of issues that may arise in the group.

To illustrate the application of this approach, consider the following matrix of sentiments for a husband and wife:

Sentiments held by:		Sentiments about:					
		Male			Female		
Male		Husband			Wife		
		E	P	A	E	P	A
	$t = 1$	1.18	1.59	0.62	2.31	1.17	1.06
	$t = \infty$	1.39	1.57	0.75	2.19	1.14	1.02
Female		Husband			Wife		
		E	P	A	E	P	A
	$t = 1$	2.27	1.36	0.93	1.67	0.88	0.97
	$t = \infty$	2.17	1.44	0.86	1.73	0.98	0.99

Each set of three numbers contains the evaluation, potency, and activity sentiments of the row person for the column person. The $t = 1$ sentiments were obtained from David Heise's INTERACT data set. The $t = \infty$ sentiments are the equilibrium sentiments of the husband and wife that are predicted from the social influence network theory that we have described. For each dimension (E, P, A), we have based the salience of person j for person i on corresponding dimension of the EPA profile: setting $\lambda = 1$ in (11.11) for simplicity, and setting $z_{ij}^{(t)} = y_{ij1}^{(t)}$ for E, $z_{ij}^{(t)} = y_{ij2}^{(t)}$ for P, and $z_{ij}^{(t)} = y_{ij3}^{(t)}$ for A in (11.13). The predicted equilibrium networks of direct effects is

$$\mathbf{W}_E^{(\infty)} = \begin{bmatrix} 0.600 & 0.400 \\ 0.301 & 0.699 \end{bmatrix}, \quad \mathbf{W}_P^{(\infty)} = \begin{bmatrix} 0.655 & 0.345 \\ 0.545 & 0.455 \end{bmatrix},$$

$$\mathbf{W}_A^{(\infty)} = \begin{bmatrix} 0.358 & 0.642 \\ 0.542 & 0.458 \end{bmatrix}$$

and the corresponding networks of total effects are

$$\mathbf{V}_E^{(\infty)} = \begin{bmatrix} 0.810 & 0.190 \\ 0.093 & 0.907 \end{bmatrix}, \quad \mathbf{V}_P^{(\infty)} = \begin{bmatrix} 0.901 & 0.099 \\ 0.355 & 0.645 \end{bmatrix},$$

$$\mathbf{V}_A^{(\infty)} = \begin{bmatrix} 0.587 & 0.413 \\ 0.229 & 0.771 \end{bmatrix}.$$

The equilibrium networks $\mathbf{W}^{(\infty)}$, the total influence networks $\mathbf{V}^{(\infty)}$, and the equilibrium sentiments $\mathbf{Y}^{(\infty)}$ depend on the particular basis of the influence network, i.e., either E, P, or A. In this situation, regardless of the basis, interpersonal influences do not dramatically modify the fundamental sentiments of the husband and wife about themselves and each other. Below, we examine situations in which substantial modifications do arise.

11.2.2 Linking to Expectation States Theory

It is possible to link social influence network theory with expectation states theory directly. Let $z_{ij}^{(t)} = y_{ij}^{(t)}$, where $y_{ij}^{(t)}$ is person i's *performance expectation* for person j. An important special case of this occurs when all group members have a consensual initial performance expectation for every member of the group. In this special case, if the initial set of performance expectations are determined by (11.1), then the *initial* performance expectations are the predictions of the expectation states model, i.e., $y_j^{(1)} = \Phi_j$. Given an initial consensus of expectations, the predicted equilibrium performance expectations are simply the initial performance expectations of the group, and the equilibrium influence structure of the group is determined by these initial expectations. Thus, the constraints involved in this special case, i.e., consensual initial performance expectations, provide a straightforward dovetailing of expectation states theory and social influence network theory. From our perspective, it would be more interesting theoretically if *individual differences* were allowed and predicted in persons' performance expectations, that is, if (11.1) were modified so that different members of a group might have different performance expectations for the same target persons. But whether or not individual differences in performance expectations are allowed, if endogenous interpersonal influences are viewed as operating *directly* on persons' performance expectations, then an expectation states theorist may employ our approach to grapple with a larger domain of influence structures without incorporating into his or her theoretical account the *sentiments* that are the key constructs of affect control theory.

However, as Figure 11.1 suggests, we believe that a more interesting line of theoretical development would be to link expectation states theory and social influence network theory *through* the sentiments that are the focal constructs in affect control theory. In affect control theory, persons' fundamental sentiments are based on certain individual variables (identities and traits) and contextual conditions (situation, culture). These identities and traits include the specific and diffuse status characteristics considered by expectation states theory as being determinants of persons' *performance expectations* for themselves and others in a particular task domain. There is no theoretical limitation in affect control theory that would prohibit the inclusion of any specific or diffuse status characteristic. Moreover, a substantive application of affect control theory to *task-oriented* groups does not present any serious theoretical problems, because affect control theory is in principle applicable to such situations. Ridgeway and Smith-Lovin (1994: 225) suggest that task-specific status is "less easily handled by affect control theory," but this is not to say that fundamental sentiments that are the resultants of an interaction between status and task cannot be formed.

A key question is whether the performance expectations that are at the heart of expectation states theory have a theoretical status that is *independent* of the fundamental sentiments that are at the heart of affect control theory. Ridgeway and Smith-Lovin (1994: 225) state, "There is no simple translation between performance expectations and fundamental sentiments...." However, we believe that there may be a close relationship between these constructs (Driskell and Webster 1997; Fisek and Berger 1998; Lovaglia 1997; Shelly 1993). Performance expectations may involve evaluation (e.g., a perception of expertise) , potency (e.g., a perception of capacity to achieve a result), and activity (e.g., a perception of committed engagement) with respect to a task. In terms of Figure 11.1, we are suggesting that performance expectations are realizations of EPA sentiments. If this is so, then the effects of status characteristics on performance expectations are *mediated* by persons' fundamental sentiments. Performance expectations may be high because of a positive *evaluation* of a person's competence, or because of the perceived *forcefulness* or capability of a person to achieve or foster group tasks, or because of the perceived *activity* or participation of the person with the task, or because of a combination of these dimensions (Kemper and Collins 1990; Robinson 1996; Skvoretz and Fararo 1996).[9] If this general theoretical position has some merit, then it will establish a linkage between the three theories, and we think that this possibility is worthy of intensive investigation. It is premature in our view to dismiss the possibility of the existence of translation functions between persons' fundamental sentiments and performance expectations.

The following illustration shows how affect control theory incorporates status characteristics into its account of the definition of situations and how social influence network theory extends affect control theory to include an account of the emergence of an influence network. In this illustration, we again deal with a dyadic interaction between a husband and wife, but in this case the husband is educated and the wife is uneducated:

---

[9] We recognize that the simple linear combination described in (11–13) may not be sufficiently refined; for instance, a high level of activity may not substitute for low levels of evaluation or potency. This may or may not be the case for the status characteristics that affect performance expectations.

Sentiments held by:		Educated-Male			Uneducated-Female		
		Sentiments about:					
Educated-male		Husband			Wife		
		E	P	A	E	P	A
	$t = 1$	1.46	1.61	0.45	0.02	−0.73	0.51
	$t = \infty$	1.46	1.61	0.57	0.02	−0.73	0.39
Uneducated-female		Husband			Wife		
		E	P	A	E	P	A
	$t = 1$	1.88	1.77	0.93	−0.28	−0.94	0.04
	$t = \infty$	1.46	1.61	0.64	0.02	−0.73	0.32

We employ the same procedure here as in the previous example. The predicted equilibrium network of direct effects is

$$\mathbf{W}_E^{(\infty)} = \begin{bmatrix} 0.623 & 0.377 \\ 0.992 & 0.008 \end{bmatrix}, \quad \mathbf{W}_P^{(\infty)} = \begin{bmatrix} 0.667 & 0.333 \\ 1 & 0 \end{bmatrix},$$

$$\mathbf{W}_A^{(\infty)} = \begin{bmatrix} 0.279 & 0.721 \\ 0.839 & 0.161 \end{bmatrix}$$

and the corresponding networks of total effects are

$$\mathbf{V}_E^{(\infty)} = \begin{bmatrix} 0.998 & 0.002 \\ 0.990 & 0.010 \end{bmatrix}, \quad \mathbf{V}_P^{(\infty)} = \begin{bmatrix} 1 & 0 \\ 1 & 0 \end{bmatrix},$$

$$\mathbf{V}_A^{(\infty)} = \begin{bmatrix} 0.743 & 0.257 \\ 0.605 & 0.395 \end{bmatrix}.$$

The emergent influence networks for the evaluation and potency dimensions, $\mathbf{W}_E^{(\infty)}$ and $\mathbf{W}_P^{(\infty)}$, indicate that the husband accords little weight to the wife, whereas the wife accords substantial weight to the husband. The total influence networks for the evaluation and potency dimensions, $\mathbf{V}_E^{(\infty)}$ and $\mathbf{V}_P^{(\infty)}$, are highly stratified, with the total influence of the educated husband dominating the total influence of the uneducated wife. Note that although the fundamental sentiments of the husband have hardly changed, the wife's sentiments about her husband have come to more closely reflect his *own* initial sentiments about himself, and the wife's sentiments about *herself* have come to more closely reflect the husband's initial sentiments about her. Her susceptibility to influence is high and his is not. Thus, issue outcomes should substantially reflect the initial preferences of the husband. Finally, the activity dimension reflects these tendencies to a much lesser extent.

Expectation states theory also has been concerned with an account of the emergence of stratified influences in status *homogeneous* groups. The basic argument is that even when a group is homogeneous on various sociodemographic characteristics, there are individual differences that will generate unequal influence. Clearly, such an argument can be framed in terms of a translation of fundamental sentiments into salience. We believe that in most situations there will be some, more or less marked, degree of initial heterogeneity of sentiments (even among status peers). Hence, even in status homogeneous groups, variation among persons on the EPA sentiment dimensions may produce inequalities of interpersonal salience and influence.

To illustrate how individual differences among peers may generate a stable influence network consider the matrix of fundamental sentiments for four male engineers with different personality traits. Again, these sentiments are obtained from David Heise's INTERACT program:

	1	2	3	4
1	Confident (1.11,1.50,0.81)	Agreeable (1.19,0.18,0.36)	Indifferent (−0.12,−0.03,−0.18)	Stubborn (−0.61,1.06,0.44)
2	Intelligent (1.13,1.28,0.34)	Confused (−0.39,−0.32,0.68)	Thoughtful (1.51,0.74,0)	Experienced (0.97,1.01,−0.10)
3	Bossy (−1.12,1.37,0.64)	Stupid (−0.94,−0.44,0.51)	Bored (−0.70,−0.30,−0.50)	Insecure (−0.61,−0.68,0.32)
4	Reckless (−0.96,0.72,1.72)	Annoying (−1.10,0.32,1.21)	Apathetic (−0.57,−0.55,−0.25)	Cautious (0.82,0.32,−0.36)

Engineer 1 is confident, engineer 2 is confused, engineer 3 is bored, and engineer 4 is cautious. Their sentiments are heterogeneous. For instance, the confident engineer views his confused peer as agreeable, his bored peer as indifferent, and his cautious peer as stubborn; the cautious engineer views his confident peer as reckless, his confused peer as annoying, and his bored peer as apathetic; and so on.

We employ the same procedure as in the previous examples. Here, for convenience, we report only the emergent $W^{(\infty)}$ and equilibrium $V^{(\infty)}$, and we suppress the report of the equilibrium sentiments. If salience is determined by magnified raw scores of the corresponding dimensions of these fundamental sentiments, i.e., $\lambda = 5$ in (11.11), then the emergent influence networks are

$$
W_E^{(\infty)} = \begin{bmatrix} 0.992 & 0.008 & 0 & 0 \\ 0 & 0 & 0 & 1 \\ 0 & 0 & 0 & 1 \\ 0.011 & 0.011 & 0.011 & 0.967 \end{bmatrix} \quad W_P^{(\infty)} = \begin{bmatrix} 0.999 & 0 & 0 & 0.001 \\ 0.235 & 0.542 & 0 & 0.224 \\ 0.420 & 0.175 & 0 & 0.404 \\ 0.158 & 0.104 & 0 & 0.738 \end{bmatrix}
$$

$$
W_A^{(\infty)} = \begin{bmatrix} 0.966 & 0.016 & 0 & 0.018 \\ 0.065 & 0.935 & 0 & 0 \\ 0.413 & 0.396 & 0 & 0.191 \\ 0.506 & 0.494 & 0 & 0 \end{bmatrix}
$$

and the corresponding network of total influences is

$$
\mathbf{V}_E^{(\infty)} = \begin{bmatrix} 1 & 0 & 0 & 0 \\ 0 & 0 & 0 & 1 \\ 0 & 0 & 0 & 1 \\ 0 & 0 & 0 & 1 \end{bmatrix} \quad
\mathbf{V}_P^{(\infty)} = \begin{bmatrix} 1 & 0 & 0 & 0 \\ 0.151 & 0.724 & 0 & 0.125 \\ 0.470 & 0.137 & 0 & 0.394 \\ 0.056 & 0.025 & 0 & 0.919 \end{bmatrix}
$$

$$
\mathbf{V}_A^{(\infty)} = \begin{bmatrix} 0.999 & 0.001 & 0 & 0 \\ 0.005 & 0.995 & 0 & 0 \\ 0.551 & 0.489 & 0 & 0 \\ 0.508 & 0.492 & 0 & 0 \end{bmatrix}.
$$

Here the total interpersonal influences of the engineers substantially depend on the particular sentiment dimension that is the basis of the emergent network. With the evaluation basis, the cautious engineer emerges as the dominant person of the group. Although the confident engineer is heavily self-weighted and is not susceptible to the influence of the cautious engineer, the two other engineers are influenced exclusively by the cautious engineer. Consensus is not reached. If the final collective decisions, after discussion, are made by majority rule, then the decisions of this group will reflect the initial preferences of the cautious engineer. The social process that has produced this stratified influence network also has produced a modified set of equilibrium sentiments for engineers 2 and 3; their equilibrium sentiments are virtually identical to the *initial* fundamental sentiments of the cautious engineer. Hence, engineers 2 and 3 have *adopted* the viewpoint of the cautious engineer about the other group members. Note that a dramatically different set of outcomes emerge if the basis of the influence network is the activity dimension. This illustration shows that the social process that we have described easily generalizes to an account of influence networks in groups larger than a dyad and that it is consistent with the emergence of complex forms of stratification in which not all members "agree" on the relative influence of each member.

In the three examples that we have presented, we note that the results may be sensitive to the parameterization of the function (11.11). In the case of the dyads, we have set $\lambda = 1$ in order to apply a simple transformation of sentiments to salience; in the case of the engineers, we have set λ to the high value of 5 in order to operationalize a contextual condition of strong pressures toward consensus. In some situations, methodological and substantive criteria may be brought to bear *a priori* to constrain the values of λ. For example, if we require that an increase in the latent attitude ($z_{ij}^{(t)}$) should not result in an increase of the salience ($s_{ij}^{(t)}$) exceeding that of the latent attitude, then the value of λ is constrained to $0 < \lambda \leq 2$, and if we adopt the maximum sentiment value of $+4.3$ (given by affect control theory) as the value at which salience should be virtually 1, then the value of λ is further constrained to $\lambda \geq 1.77$; hence, we obtain the overall constraint $1.77 \leq \lambda \leq 2$.

11.3 Concluding Remarks

We believe that three formal theories in sociological social psychology – social influence network theory, affect control theory, and expectation states theory – can be formally linked and that these linkages enhance the power and scope of each theory. Each of these theories represents an attempt to grapple with concrete social processes and structures in groups. Our focus has been on the discovery of fundamental and parsimonious mechanisms and on the formal integration of theory. As part of our effort to link these three theories, we have extended social influence network theory so that the influence network is not only affecting, but also being affected by, the positions of group members on an issue – their sentiments about themselves and other group members. We have focused on persons' sentiments about themselves and others because of the importance of this construct in affect control theory and its close bearing (in our view) on the performance expectations that, in expectation states theory, underlie the formation of influence networks in task-oriented groups. More generally, as we suggested in Chapter 3, we believe that attitudes involving *persons-as-objects*, i.e., persons' attitudes about others and themselves as objects, are the proximate conditions of their susceptibilities to interpersonal influence and the interpersonal influences of particular persons upon them. If attitudes are being formed about persons during the course of interactions on other issues (or if such person-as-object attitudes *are* the issue), then an equilibrium influence network may be formed that reflects the outcomes of the interpersonal influences that have shaped group members' attitudes about each other. This basic idea has a domain of application that is larger than the linkage to affect-control and expectation-states models.

Two features of our operationalization warrant emphasis. First, we currently do not know how the three dimensions of sentiment (evaluation, potency, and activity) may combine to determine the salience of self and particular others. Thus, in our illustrations of the theory, we have employed the individual dimensions of sentiment separately as bases of salience. Substantively, this corresponds to analyses of groups that have distinctive dominant dimensions as the bases of their influence networks. Second, in the present operationalization, we have assumed that the pattern of interpersonal visibility is complete and stable during the process in which the equilibrium influence network of the group is being formed; i.e., $\mathbf{G}^{(1)} = \mathbf{G}^{(2)} = \cdots = \mathbf{G}^{(\infty)} = \mathbf{J}$, the matrix of all 1's. In small groups, group members are often acquainted with each other, so that $\mathbf{G}^{(t)} = \mathbf{J}$

for all t is plausible. In large groups, visibility may be patterned and the pattern may be changing; for instance, if $G^{(t)}$ and $S^{(t)}$ become linked because persons are establishing ties with persons who are salient to them (Stokman and Berveling 1998), then some function would have to be specified that describes this linkage over time, in order to understand the evolution of the influence network $W^{(t)}$.

In conclusion, the cornerstone of our effort has been the analysis of sentiments that, in affect control theory, are the elementary foundations of persons' definition of a situation. Our theory introduces an influence network into affect control theory by allowing these fundamental sentiments to be modified by the sentiments of others. Thus, persons take into account not only the "macro-structural" normative information that is evoked by a given situation, but also the "micro-structural" individual differences of sentiment that are displayed by the persons who are involved in a particular situation. As a result of persons' interactions in a particular situation, endogenous interpersonal influences on sentiments can operate to form a set of within-group normative expectations that are conditional upon the particular social structure of a group and its setting.

12

Individuals in Groups

In this chapter, we examine the implications of interpersonal influences for issues that occur in small groups that are (a) homophilous with respect to a particular sociodemographic characteristic, (b) assembled in a large-scale population, and (c) disjoint in their memberships. These groups are "small" ($n = 2, 3, 4, \ldots, 12, \ldots 20, \ldots 100, \ldots, 1,000, \ldots$) relative to the size of the population in which they are assembled. We treat these groups as disjoint influence systems with respect to a particular issue (Section 1.3.3), which need not involve direct interpersonal influences or contacts between all pairs of members.[1] The empirical analysis that we present in this chapter addresses the implications of interpersonal influences within small same-sex (i.e., gender-homophilous) groups of dyads, triads, and tetrads for the distribution of issue positions in the *population* of individuals in which these small groups are embedded.

We focus on a circumstance in which individuals of the same sex randomly assemble into disjoint groups (i.e., groups with no overlapping memberships), enter into their groups with independently formed positions on an issue, proceed to discuss the issue with other members of their groups, and terminate their discussion of an issue after some period of time with either a modified or unmodified position on the issue. Such a set of circumstances describes a common experimental design for the study of small group social processes. These designs have typically been employed to investigate hypotheses concerned with within-group phenomena and, thus far, we have concentrated on such phenomena. In this final chapter, our focus shifts to the macro-level individual distribution of issue positions in the population in which small groups are formed. Although different in its theoretical emphasis, our analysis of the

---

[1] For example, geographically separated overlapping subsets of individuals, with direct or indirect interpersonal influences between all pairs of members, fall under our definition of an influence system that is a group.

282

macro-level distributions of issue positions is intimately coupled to the internal dynamics that unfold within groups. Here our theoretical interest focuses on the macro-level integration of populations governed by the principle of homophily and, specifically, on the contributions of gender homophily and small group dynamics to such integration.

Blau's (1977) macro-level analysis of social heterogeneity describes a population as distributed in sociodemographic space and develops the implications of a generalized form of homophily in which the probability of interpersonal contact declines with the distance between persons in this space. His analysis has been employed to buttress the hypothesis that the direct effects of sociodemographic positions on attitudes and interpersonal ties often suffice to account for interpersonal agreements between persons who are in contact (McPherson et al. 2001). However, Blau's analysis points to the opposite conclusion – that homophily on one sociodemographic dimension (gender, race, religion, age, etc.) often involves contact between persons who differ on other sociodemographic dimensions and who have different positions on issues. McPherson et al. acknowledge the challenging aspects of Blau's analysis, and they point to those aspects as an arena of future work on homophily. Here, we enter into that arena.

Blau's analysis of structural heterogeneity entertained both *consolidated* social structures, in which persons find themselves in interaction only with other persons who have the same profile of sociodemographic characteristics, and *unconsolidated* social structures, in which persons find themselves in interaction with persons in the same social position on one or more dimensions and different social positions on other dimensions. He took the latter – multiform heterogeneity – as the basis of social integration:

> Actual social structures are characterized by multiform heterogeneity...Multiple nominal parameters that intersect increase heterogeneity exponentially, and thereby reduce the size of perfectly homogeneous subgroups to the vanishing point....Multiform heterogeneity compels people to have associates outside their own group, because it implies that ingroup relations are simultaneously intergroup relations in terms of different parameters. We cannot help engaging in social intercourse with outsiders, because our ingroup associates in one dimension are, in several others, members of groups other than our own.
>
> (Blau 1977: 83–4)

In unconsolidated social structures, individuals cannot escape heterogeneity in their social associations. Blau emphasizes the structural dualities involved in interpersonal contacts; i.e., status-homogeneous encounters are typically also status-heterogeneous encounters. If contact occurs between two persons with a shared status on one social dimension and different statuses on another dimension, and if these statuses are inconsistent with respect to their characteristic attitudes on an issue, then the interaction between the two persons cannot be automatically treated as a vehicle of reinforcement of the characteristic attitudinal position associated with the shared status condition.

McPherson et al. suggest that once we have taken into account the tendency for contact to occur among persons with a shared status on a sociodemographic dimension (i.e., homophily), the theoretical importance of interpersonal influences on persons' attitudes is dramatically reduced. Their viewpoint implicitly assumes a generalized form of homophily in which shared status on one sociodemographic dimension implies shared statuses on other salient sociodemographic dimensions, i.e., a consolidated social structure. Their viewpoint also assumes that the sociodemographic positions of individuals heavily constrain persons' selection of interpersonal contacts and persons' attitudes. Under these assumptions, persons are likely to encounter and interact with others who are in substantial agreement on issues. Below we outline an alternative viewpoint consistent with the circumstances of unconsolidated social structures.

Blau (1977) carefully contrasts consolidated and unconsolidated social structures. In a consolidated social structure, social dimensions are highly intercorrelated; hence, in such structures, status on one dimension is informative of a person's status on other dimensions and status occupants' positions and interpersonal agreements on issues. In a consolidated structure, if sociodemographic variables strongly constrain individuals' issue positions and interpersonal contacts, then interpersonal contacts and agreements will be concentrated within generalized social positions that correspond to specific subpopulations with differentiated characteristic positions on issues. In unconsolidated social structures, the associations among sociodemographic variables are weaker and the effects of these variables do not combine to produce differentiated subpopulations with small variances of position on issues within each subpopulation. In such a circumstance, when a contact is made with a geographically proximate other, the other may differ dramatically in his or her sociodemographic characteristics. If a homophilous contact is made with a high-income similar other, the two may differ in their race, religion, and education. Gender homophily does not imply that two females in contact will be homogeneous in race, income, and education; same-sex contacts may link persons with different profiles of characteristics. Thus, two females in contact may also be two females who, via their contact, are structurally integrating a population whose members differ in income, education, race, and religion. This is the thrust of Blau's argument. Blau also suggests, along the lines of Simmel (1950), that sociodemographic effects on individuals' behaviors and attitudes weaken as the consolidation of a social structure diminishes, but this tendency is not essential to his argument. The empirical relevance of Blau's analysis is that the assumption of an unconsolidated social structure, for a large-scale population, provides a more accurate description of many large-scale communities than does the assumption of a consolidated social structure.

Blau's theory is structural in that he does not delve into what occurs in interpersonal contacts. The contact may be weak or strong. It may involve discussions about important matters or not. The contact may involve an initial agreement or disagreement. For Blau, contact presents integrative opportunities. Under the assumption that some noteworthy proportion of these contacts reduce interpersonal disagreements, the population's aggregate mass of cross-cutting contacts contributes to social integration. Nowhere does he take the position that such contacts are likely to involve persons who agree *a priori* on issues. Such *a priori* agreement is unlikely in an unconsolidated social structure. Persons who are involved in homophilous contacts are likely to differ on a number of sociodemographic dimensions that will generate a difference of positions on issues. In addition, it is likely that persons will differ in their initial viewpoints on issues based on their idiosyncratic life experiences and inclinations.

The most powerful constraint on contact is geographic location, e.g., placement of individuals in a region, a city, a neighborhood, or a workplace, or in the departments and hallways of the buildings where they live or work. In an unconsolidated social structure, these social foci (Feld 1981) bring people into contact who may differ in a variety of ways. Hence, based on the logic of multiform heterogeneity, the structural integration that occurs via contacts tends to be both geographically localized and idiosyncratically patterned within these geographic foci.

Here, we emphasize that homophily includes not only isolated dyadic encounters but also small groups of persons who are homogeneous on one or more dimensions and heterogeneous on others. Different initial viewpoints on issues are to be expected in such small groups. Whether they are task-oriented or informal, small groups are settings in which interpersonal differences may be influenced and negotiated. Small groups are sites of intense symbolic interaction, where positions on issues are altered, and interpersonal agreements are formed. In these respects, they are rightly taken as primary groups for the individuals who are involved in them (Blumer 1969; Cooley 1962). In addition, depending on the manner in which such small groups are assembled, they may have larger macro-level implications. The mass of local accommodations that arise within such small groups, and the enduring and transitory agreements that are formed in them, generate movements of individuals' positions on issues – changes of attitude about various objects in the social environments of these persons. These movements may reduce the variance of the large-scale population's distribution of issue positions. Although such attitude changes do not alter individuals' sociodemographic profiles, they may reduce the distance between their viewpoints on issues and disrupt the correspondence between sociodemographic and cognitive positions on issues.

The mass of small groups in a large-scale population thus contributes to a haphazard social integration that stitches together the larger-scale social structure of differentiated sociodemographic positions. Homophilous small groups contribute to social integration in a manner that is akin to formal meetings of disputants who assemble to resolve their differences. Based on homophily, we have a mass of informal groups that are being assembled in a population at any given time. The shifts of attitudes and the formation of interpersonal agreements that occur in these informal groups are no less constitutive of the social integration of the larger population than are formal meetings aimed at settling intergroup conflicts. We advance the hypothesis that the attitude changes and agreements generated by the mass of assembled small groups in a population are a key informal foundation of the social integration of differentiated social structures. We view this argument as a straightforward extension and deepening of the theoretical perspective outlined by Blau (1977) and as an effort to dovetail Blau's macro-level structural analysis with the meso-level of subgroups and with the micro-level interactionist tradition in social psychology that attends to small group dynamics.

12.1 Analytical Framework

In this analysis, we set aside the two monetary issues in our data and concentrate on the three choice dilemma issues – Sports, School, and Surgery issues – on which we find a consistent gender effect. We develop a group dynamics perspective on attitude changes in gender-homogeneous small groups that have assembled to consider these issues of appropriate risk on two alternative courses of action. One course of action entails higher risk of failure and greater rewards from success than the other course of action, which entails lower risk of failure and lesser rewards from success. As we have previously noted, a large literature has developed on such issues. The literature has been concerned with the effects of small group discussion on individual and group-level positions on such issues. Not surprisingly, group discussion frequently generates individual attitude changes of position and differences between a small group's mean initial (prediscussion) position and the group's mean final (postdiscussion) position on such issues. With interpersonal influences that generate attitude changes in a group, average postdiscussion positions on an issue are sometimes more risky and sometimes less risky than the average prediscussion positions on the issue. Such average differences between pre- and postdiscussion positions are referred to as choice shifts, and a number of alternative hypotheses have been investigated that might explain them. Most of the hypothesized mechanisms reflect the cognitive theoretical interests of the psychologists who have developed them. In Chapter 9, we advanced a sociological perspective on choice shifts that attends to the influence network structures formed within groups. We draw on social influence network theory for the development and support of the thesis of the present chapter.

The starting point of this empirical analysis is a finding that, on each of the three choice dilemma issues, the average female (in the sample of all females from all groups) adopts a more conservative postdiscussion position than does the average male (in the sample of all males from all groups). We probe the foundations and implications of the observed postdiscussion distributions on these issues and, via a set of additional findings, develop a theoretical perspective on these distributions that attends to the small group dynamics that were involved in them. The macro-level implications of these postdiscussion distributions reside in the extent and nature of the attitude changes of the individuals who compose these distributions. The extent to which same-sex peer groups contribute to the cognitive integration of the population from which these individuals were drawn depends on whether the observed postdiscussion distributions of positions masks movements of individual positions on the issue that (a) reshuffle individuals' relative positions in the population's distribution of positions on an issue and (b) reduce the variance of the macro-level issue distributions. We will demonstrate that the observed gender differentiation on risk aversion/acceptance is, from a sociological perspective, the least interesting aspect of these data.

Homophily in unconsolidated social structures operates to assemble same-sex contact groups with members who hold different positions on issues, and these small groups may generate attitude changes that reduce the variance of issue positions in the population from which these small groups are assembled. We further show that the attitude changes generated by these small groups may or may not reinforce a differentiation of characteristic norms for the male and female subpopulations; instead, we show that small groups operate under their own local constraints and emergent social constructions. The local constraints and constructions include the range of the group members' initial positions on an issue and the influence network that is formed in the group. These two conditions vary across groups and generate large and small movements of issue positions in a variety of different directions. The idiosyncratic array of initial positions taken by members of these small groups, in combination with the construction of the influence networks within them, operate to reshuffle individuals into cognitive positions on an issue that they would not otherwise have held. Hence, the postdiscussion distributions are often less a manifestation of characteristic differences between males and females and more a manifestation of the accommodative sociality described by Mead (1934) occurring in the unconsolidated social structures described by Blau (1977).

12.2 Findings

We begin with cross-sectional observations that are the basis of most sociological field studies – the positions of individuals on issues that may or may not have been affected by prior interpersonal influences and the statuses of these individuals on a sociodemographic dimension. Then we bring into the analysis the available data on the initial positions of the individuals on the issues and the group dynamics that have affected them. We structure the analysis in this fashion in order to emphasize the shift in theoretical perspective on macro-level distributions of issue positions that occurs when the small group dynamics that have affected these distributions are taken into account.

12.2.1 Gender Differentiation of Postdiscussion Positions

Table 12.1 presents the gender effects on individuals' postdiscussion positions for the three choice dilemma issues. On each issue, females on average adopt a more conservative (less risky) position than do males on average. Although this finding suggests a characteristic difference between the average male and female in their levels of risk aversion/acceptance, it is also the case that gender accounts for modest proportions of the variance in individuals' positions on these issues, with R^2 of 0.171, 0.022, and 0.010 on the Sports, School, and Surgery issues, respectively.

12.2.2 Individuals Nested in Small Groups

The analysis of Table 12.1 ignores the obvious fact and implications of the nesting of males and females in these small groups, where their positions on the issues may have been affected by the localized endogenous interpersonal influences. Here, the *intraclass correlation coefficient* provides a measure of the extent to which the variation of postdiscussion positions is attributable to group membership. The intraclass correlations on each issue are substantial: 0.940, 0.840, and 0.563 on the Sports, School, and Surgery issues, respectively. There are two immediate and important implications of these substantial correlations. One is methodological and the other is theoretical.

For investigators who are attentive to the literature on multilevel modeling, these substantial intraclass correlations seriously invalidate the standard approaches of statistical analysis that assume individuals'

Table 12.1 *Gender effects on postdiscussion positions for three choice dilemmas (two-sample* t *test with equal variances)*

		Mean	Std. Dev.	N
Sports issue				
	Females	53.007	18.806	148
	Males	37.230	16.049	148
	TOTAL	45.118	19.158	296

Mean(Females) − Mean(Males) = 15.777
($t = 7.763$; $df = 294$; $p = 0.000$)

School issue				
	Females	52.500	18.597	212
	Males	46.622	21.141	188
	TOTAL	49.738	20.025	400

Mean(Females) − Mean(Males) = 5.878
($t = 2.958$; $df = 398$; $p = 0.003$)

Surgery issue				
	Females	72.453	17.716	212
	Males	68.963	16.364	188
	TOTAL	70.813	17.161	400

Mean(Females) − Mean(Males) = 3.490
($t = 2.038$; $df = 398$; $p = 0.042$)

independent responses (Hox 2002). Here the responses of individuals are interdependent not only because individuals have been assembled in small groups with members who share the same gender status, but also because (as we have shown) endogenous interpersonal influences within these groups often substantially reduce the variance of individuals' positions within each group on each issue. The methodological implication is a dramatic inflation of false findings of statistical significance; i.e., in the present case, the observed differences between males and females (Table 12.1) do not provide compelling evidence of gender differentiation in the population from which the individuals were drawn. This problem is reduced, but not necessarily eliminated, by an analysis of individuals' prediscussion positions on the issues. These initial positions were formed prior to the interpersonal influences that occurred within the groups; hence, the intraclass correlations on prediscussion positions strictly reflect interdependencies based on the assembly of individuals into gender-homophilous groups. On the prediscussion positions, the intraclass correlations are 0.118, 0.075, and 0.045 on the Sport, School, and Surgery issues, respectively. Unfortunately, even these seemingly modest correlations may have marked effects in biasing statistical tests (Kreft and De Leeuw 1998: 9–10).

Here, unlike the typical field setting situation, it is *known* that individuals were randomly selected into small groups based on a single sociodemographic dimension – gender. Moreover, here, unlike the typical field setting situation, measures of individuals' prediscussion positions are available. In field settings, investigators typically do not possess data that locate individuals in small groups with known memberships and characteristics, including their initial positions on issues. Where the foundations of group formations are unclear and data are lacking on group members' positions on issues prior to group discussion, the methodological challenges of obtaining trustworthy findings are daunting.

The theoretical implication of a strong intraclass correlation is that the small group becomes the primary unit of analysis. This must be so whenever the interpersonal interactions in small groups have substantially reduced within-group variances. A multilevel modeling approach is justified by strong intraclass correlation coefficients, which indicate that a disproportionate amount of the variance in individual postdiscussion positions on these issues is *between* groups. The standard application of multilevel modeling pursues an account of the between-group variance based on group-level characteristics, e.g., the mean initial positions of the groups and other group-level characteristics. *However, multilevel models specify the interdependency among group members without a theory that attends to the small group dynamics that have contributed to the interdependency.* Instead, multilevel models base such explanations on contextual group-level characteristics. Here, one such variable is simply whether a group is a male or female peer group. Another such variable is the within-group mean prediscussion position of the group's members on an issue. When endogenous interpersonal influence is the major process that generates interdependent responses, such group-level contextual variables are theoretically weak substitutes for an analysis that directly attends to the small group dynamics that generated a reduction of within-group variance. The shared positions that emerge from these dynamics cannot be adequately understood in terms of group members' responses to shared contextual conditions. Instead, they are responses that are formed via a system of endogenous interpersonal influences in which group members' positions are affected by other group members' positions on an issue. The males and females have entered into their small groups and confront group members who express different positions on the issue. The interpersonal influence process operates to modify these initial positions and reduce these initial differences.

With respect to the between-group variation that is arguably the most important feature of the postdiscussion distributions of positions on the issues, we take a different theoretical approach than is afforded by standard forms of contextual analysis. The gender distinction between the small groups provides a modest purchase on the variation of the group-level means. These group-level means are governed by the array of initial positions adopted by group members, the influence network that occurs within each group, and the influence process that unfolds in these networks. Our analysis is motivated and constrained by our theoretical specification of the interpersonal process that occurs within our groups. Below we will show that the means and variances of the postdiscussion distributions of issue positions for males and females may be derived from (explained by) the within-group influence process. Moreover, we show that the interpersonal influence process has the important theoretical implication of reshuffling the positions of individuals in the distribution of positions and reducing the variance of the macro-level distribution of issue positions.

12.2.3 Contributions of Small Group Dynamics

When issue positions are subject to interpersonal influences within disjoint small groups, the macro-level distribution of postdiscussion positions depends entirely on the initial positions expressed by each group's members, the influence networks that are formed in these groups, and the influence processes that unfolds in these networks and that transform initial prediscussion positions into postdiscussion positions. This perspective allows for persons within small groups who have no susceptibility to interpersonal influence (i.e., persons who have not been influenced by other members of their group and whose postdiscussion positions are their prediscussion positions). It also allows for within-group dynamics that substantially move persons into positions distant from their initial positions, which may alter (a) the distribution of their subpopulation's (here, male and female) positions on the issue and (b) the associations of sociodemographic dimensions with issue positions. Given powerful within-group interpersonal influences on many group members, postdiscussion positions are largely derivative of these influences rather than of the postdiscussion effects of sociodemographic variables on these positions.

Our standard model of the influence process generates individual-level predictions of persons' postdiscussion positions:

$$\hat{y}_{ig}^{(\infty)} = \sum_{j=1}^{n_g} v_{ijg} y_{jg}^{(1)}, \qquad (12.1)$$

where $\hat{y}_{ig}^{(\infty)}$ is the predicted postdiscussion position of member i of group g, with n_g members ($j = 1, 2, \ldots, n_g$), $y_{jg}^{(1)}$ is the initial prediscussion position of group g member j on the issue, and v_{ijg} is the total (direct and indirect) interpersonal influence of j on i in the determination of i's postdiscussion position in group g. These total influences are such that $0 \leq v_{ijg} \leq 1$ for all $i, j,$ and g and $\sum_{j=1}^{n_g} v_{ijg} = 1$ for all i and g. Hence, for a

Table 12.2 *Regressing observed postdiscussion positions on predicted positions, with the predictions derived from the within-group interpersonal influence systems of the small groups*

| | Regression coefficients (standard errors in parentheses) | | | |
	Constant	Predicted position	R^2	N
Sports issue	−0.097	0.977***	0.851	296
	(1.183)	(0.024)		
Females	0.728	0.976***	0.851	148
	(1.910)	(0.034)		
Males	0.946	0.931***	0.787	148
	(1.679)	(0.040)		
School issue	1.263	0.974***	0.791	400
	(1.329)	(0.025)		
Females	1.276	0.982***	0.783	212
	(1.954)	(0.036)		
Males	1.399	0.960***	0.792	188
	(1.842)	(0.036)		
Surgery issue	10.307***	0.858***	0.738	400
	(1.858)	(0.026)		
Females	11.749***	0.846***	0.761	212
	(2.428)	(0.033)		
Males	8.898***	0.869***	0.707	188
	(2.909)	(0.041)		

particular group member i, if $v_{iig} = 1$, then $\hat{y}_{ig}^{(\infty)} = y_{ig}^{(1)}$ and the prediction is that i's position does not change; and if $v_{ikg} = 1$, then $\hat{y}_{ig}^{(\infty)} = y_{kg}^{(1)}$ and the prediction is that i adopts k's position. In general, $\hat{y}_{ig}^{(\infty)}$ is a weighted average of the initial positions of the members of group g. As detailed in Chapter 2, the total interpersonal influences of a group's members $\mathbf{V}_g$ may be derived from the influence network of the group $\mathbf{W}_g$ (and $\mathbf{A}_g$) that describes the direct interpersonal influences among all members of the group. Social influence network theory is based on a social process that specifies how persons combine the direct influences on them to form a revised position on an issue, and from this theory the total interpersonal influence of each group member j on each member i (for all i and j) may be derived. The prediction of individuals' postdiscussion positions, as given by (12.1), is deduced directly from the theory based on empirical measures of group members' direct influences and initial positions. There is no optimization of fit involved in these predictions.

Table 12.2 shows that the predicted postdiscussion positions, based on our model of endogenous interpersonal influences, explain 70.7–85.1% of the variance of postdiscussion positions for both males and females on the three issues. Table 12.3 shows that pooling all males and females,

Table 12.3 *Predicting postdiscussion means and variances*

(a) Predicting the means of the postdiscussion distributions (standard errors in parentheses)

	Observed mean	Predicted mean	Difference	Paired t–test
Sports issue	45.118 (1.114)	46.272 (1.051)	−1.154	$t = -2.684$ ($df = 295; p = 0.008$)
Females	53.007 (1.546)	53.564 (1.461)	−0.558	$t = -0.932$ ($df = 147, p = 0.353$)
Males	37.230 (1.319)	38.979 (1.257)	−1.750	$t = -2.843$ ($df = 147, p = 0.005$)
School issue	49.738 (1.001)	49.779 (0.915)	−0.041	$t = -0.090$ ($df = 399; p = 0.928$)
Females	52.500 (1.277)	52.137 (1.150)	0.363	$t = 0.610$ ($df = 211, p = 0.543$)
Males	46.622 (1.542)	47.119 (1.429)	−0.497	$t = -0.704$ ($df = 187, p = 0.482$)
Surgery issue	70.813 (0.858)	70.516 (0.859)	0.297	$t = 0.651$ ($df = 399; p = 0.515$)
Females	72.453 (1.217)	71.729 (1.253)	0.724	$t = 1.156$ ($df = 211, p = 0.249$)
Males	68.963 (1.193)	69.148 (1.155)	−0.185	$t = -0.279$ ($df = 187, p = 0.781$)

(b) Predicting the variances of the postdiscussion distributions

	Observed std. dev.	Predicted std. dev.	Variance ratio test
Sports issue	19.158	18.090	$f = 1.122$ ($df = 295, 295; p = 0.325$)
Females	18.806	17.771	$f = 1.120$ ($df = 147, 147; p = 0.493$)
Males	16.049	15.293	$f = 1.101$ ($df = 147, 147; p = 0.559$)
School issue	20.025	18.294	$f = 1.198$ ($df = 399, 399; p = 0.071$)
Females	18.597	16.749	$f = 1.233$ ($df = 211, 211; p = 0.129$)
Males	21.141	19.599	$f = 1.164$ ($df = 187, 187; p = 0.301$)
Surgery issue	17.161	17.187	$f = 0.997$ ($df = 399, 399; p = 0.976$)
Females	17.716	18.251	$f = 0.942$ ($df = 211, 211; p = 0.666$)
Males	16.364	15.839	$f = 1.067$ ($df = 187, 187; p = 0.656$)

Table 12.4 *Regressing observed postdiscussion group-level means on predicted group-level means, with the predictions based on our standard model*

	Regression coefficients (standard errors in parentheses)		
	Sports issue	School issue	Surgery issue
Predicted position	1.008***	0.980***	0.817***
	(0.043)	(0.040)	(0.033)
Sex composition	−0.972	−0.910	−1.948[†]
(F = 0, M = 1)	(1.505)	(1.407)	(1.075)
Constant	−1.077	1.516	14.281***
	(2.498)	(2.284)	(2.478)
Groups (N)	82	134	134
R^2	0.897	0.827	0.824

[†] $p < 0.10$. *$p < 0.05$. **$p < 0.01$. ***$p < 0.001$.

to obtain a predicted macro-level distribution, generates *predicted* means and variances for each issue that do not significantly differ from the *observed* postdiscussion means and variances. The exception is a significant difference between the predicted and observed means on the Sports issue. Table 12.3 also shows that pooling the predictions for both males and females *within each subpopulation,* to obtain predicted male and female postdiscussion distributions, generates predicted means and variances for each subpopulation on each issue that do not significantly differ from the observed postdiscussion means and variances. The exception is a significant difference between the predicted and observed means for males on the Sports issue.

We have seen that most of the variance of individuals' postdiscussion positions occurs between the small groups. In the multilevel modeling framework, strong intraclass correlations direct attention to explanations of the variation of the groups' means in terms of group-level contextual variables. Our approach to such explanation is based on the *internal dynamics* of the groups, that is, the endogenous system of interpersonal influences that transforms group members' initial positions into their postdiscussion positions. Table 12.4 presents a group-level analysis in which the units of analysis are the small groups, the dependent variable is the observed mean postdiscussion position of a group, and the explanatory variable is the predicted mean postdiscussion position of the group members based on social influence network theory. Note that the explanation of the group means is grounded on individual-level predictions that result from taking into account the *influence system* of each small group. On each issue, the predicted mean outcome of the influence process significantly contributes to the explanation of the observed mean. The sex composition of the group does not contribute to such explanation,

Table 12.5 *The association of individuals' pre- and postdiscussion positions depends on individuals' susceptibilities to interpersonal influence*

	Regression coefficients (standard errors in parentheses)		
	Sports issue	School issue	Surgery issue
Prediscussion position	0.678*** (0.059)	0.632*** (0.047)	0.537*** (0.032)
Susceptibility × prediscussion position	−0.323*** (0.060)	−0.232*** (0.050)	−0.081** (0.081)
Constant	22.297*** (2.093)	25.272*** (1.945)	36.873*** (2.040)
Groups (N)	296	400	400
R^2	0.358	0.351	0.447

† $p < 0.10$. *$p < 0.05$. **$p < 0.01$. ***$p < 0.001$.

except marginally on the Surgery issue. Over 80% of the variance of the group-level means is accounted for on each of the issues.

The interpersonal influence process that occurs within a group may substantially alter individuals' initial (prediscussion) positions on an issue. Individuals' postdiscussion positions depend on who they accord influence to within the group, and these interpersonal influences are potentially heterogeneous within groups. Persons vary in both the extent to which they are influenced, and by whom. On this point, Table 12.5 returns to the *individual-level analysis* and shows that the contribution of individuals' initial positions to their postdiscussion positions *interacts* with the individuals' susceptibilities to interpersonal influence as follows:

$$\hat{y}_i^{(\infty)} = \beta_0 + \beta_1 y_i^{(1)} + \beta_2 a_{ii} y_i^{(1)},$$

where the effect of $y_i^{(1)}$ is $\beta_1 + \beta_2 a_{ii}$ with $\beta_1 > 0$ and $\beta_2 < 0$. Thus, the greater an individual's susceptibility, the less informative is the individual's initial position about the individual's postdiscussion position.[2]

For individuals who have been influenced by others, an important macro-level implication of these small influence systems is that they shuffle the relative positions of individuals in the distributions of positions taken on an issue. Group discussion shifts individual positions in various directions and by different amounts; hence, the collection of these individual movements within all the independent groups may not be accurately portrayed in terms of a coherent additive (or subtractive) main effect on the movement of individuals' positions. Consider individuals'

[2] Here, it makes no theoretical sense to include a direct effect of susceptibility on individuals' postdiscussion positions, because susceptibility only permits interpersonal influence to a certain degree.

relative postdiscussion positions (i.e., positions that have been standard-ized with respect to the mean and standard deviation of the grand distri-bution of postdiscussion positions) and their relative prediscussion posi-tions (i.e., positions that have been standardized with respect to the mean and standard deviation of the grand distribution of prediscussion posi-tions). Regressing the former on the latter, the standardized regression coefficients (i.e., correlations) are 0.544, 0.562, and 0.660 for the Sports, School, and Surgery issues, respectively, with R^2 of 0.296, 0.317, and 0.436, respectively.

There are two important implications of the above findings. First, it is plain from the correlations that there is a moderate level of consistency between the relative positions of individuals in their pre- and postdiscus-sion distributions of positions on an issue; an individual who is above (below) the mean in the prediscussion distribution is, on average, also above (below) the mean in the postdiscussion distribution. This consis-tency occurs in the context of a regression toward the mean. In this regression toward the mean, it is not only the case that extreme ini-tial positions have been moderated, on average, but also more generally the case that all initial positions also have been moderated, on average. Second, it is plain from the R^2 values that there is a substantial level of unexplained individual-level variability. The moderate R^2 values indicate that there is substantial variability in the relative postdiscussion positions of persons with the same initial positions; i.e., the small group dynam-ics within homophilous groups has induced substantial "mobility" of positions in the macro-level distribution of positions on an issue.

Small group dynamics has shuffled individuals' issue positions. The shuffling of issue positions is a consequence of the interpersonal contacts that were realized by assembling homophilous small groups. Such would be Blau's (1977) *structural* perspective on what has occurred. However, such a structural viewpoint is enriched when we directly attend to what these homophilous contacts entail, i.e., to the influence systems that were constructed within the settings of these contacts and that operated to modify individuals' initial positions.

12.3 Law of Total Variance

The generality of the above theoretical perspective and findings may be assessed on the basis of the law of total variance. The law of total vari-ance, with respect to a variable y, states that if a set with N members is partitioned into K subsets according to a discrete variable x, then the vari-ance of the set on y is equal to the weighted mean of the variances of the subsets plus the variance of the K weighted means, where the variances of the subsets are weighted proportionally to their size. In the present application, for each issue, we have two subpopulations (females and males), each of which is partitioned into small gender-homophilous small groups of dyads, triads, and tetrads. The total variance of positions on a particular issue is a weighted average of the within-group variances of the female and male small groups, plus a weighted average of the variances of the female and male small-group means, plus the variance of the male and female subpopulation means. See Appendix F, where we derive the following decomposition:

$$
\begin{aligned}
\text{var}(y) = {} & w_1[w_{11}\text{var}(y_{11}) + w_{12}\text{var}(y_{12}) + \cdots + w_{1F}\text{var}(y_{1F})] \\
& + w_2[w_{21}\text{var}(y_{21}) + w_{22}\text{var}(y_{22}) + \cdots + w_{2M}\text{var}(y_{2M})] \\
& + w_1\text{var}(\bar{y}_{11}, \bar{y}_{12}, \ldots, \bar{y}_{1F}) \\
& + w_2\text{var}(\bar{y}_{21}, \bar{y}_{22}, \ldots, \bar{y}_{2M}) \\
& + \text{var}(\bar{y}_1, \bar{y}_2),
\end{aligned}
$$

in which

(a) $w_1 = n_1/N$ and $w_2 = n_2/N$ are the proportions of females and males, respectively, in the population,

(b) $\bar{y}_1$ and $\bar{y}_2$ are the means of the female and male subpopulations, respectively,

(c) $\text{var}(\bar{y}_1, \bar{y}_2) = w_1(\bar{y}_1 - \bar{y})^2 + w_2(\bar{y}_2 - \bar{y})^2$,

(d) $f = 1, 2, \ldots, F$ are the indices for the female small groups, and $m = 1, 2, \ldots, M$ are the indices for the male small groups,

(e) w_{1f} is the proportion of all females located in group f, $\text{var}(y_{1f})$ is the variance of issue positions among the females within group f, and $\bar{y}_{1f}$ is the mean of the issue positions within group f, and

(f) w_{2m} is the proportion of all males located in group m, $\text{var}(y_{2m})$ is the variance of issue positions among the males within group m, and $\bar{y}_{2m}$ is the mean of the issue positions within group m.

Note that the weights $w_1 + w_2 = 1$ and $\sum_{f=1}^{F} w_{1f} = \sum_{m=1}^{M} w_{2m} = 1$. Hence,

$$
w_1 \sum_{f=1}^{F} w_{1f} + w_2 \sum_{m=1}^{M} w_{2m} = 1.
$$

This decomposition shows that, *ceteris paribus*, holding all the means constant, reductions of the variances within gender-homophilous small groups must decrease the total variance $\text{var}(y)$ of the population and, hence, must increase the homogeneity of issue positions in the population. That is, when the endogenous interpersonal influences within small groups have not substantially altered the means,

$$
\begin{aligned}
\text{Pre-var}(\bar{y}_{11}, \bar{y}_{12}, \ldots, \bar{y}_{1J}) &\approx \text{Post-var}(\bar{y}_{11}, \bar{y}_{12}, \ldots, \bar{y}_{1J}) \\
\text{Pre-var}(\bar{y}_{21}, \bar{y}_{22}, \ldots, \bar{y}_{2K}) &\approx \text{Post-var}(\bar{y}_{21}, \bar{y}_{22}, \ldots, \bar{y}_{2K}) \\
\text{Pre-var}(\bar{y}_1, \bar{y}_2) &\approx \text{Post-var}(\bar{y}_1, \bar{y}_2),
\end{aligned}
$$

Table 12.6 *Variance decompositions of pre- and postdiscussion issue positions*

Variance components	Prediscussion	% total	Postdiscussion	% total
(a) Sports issue				
Within-group	361.486	64.1	15.977	4.4
Between-group	177.278	31.4	263.907	72.1
Between-subpopulation	25.509	4.5	85.896	23.5
TOTAL	564.273		365.780	
(b) School issue				
Within-group	330.484	61.7	42.969	10.7
Between-group	198.788	37.1	347.632	86.9
Between-subpopulation	6.462	1.2	9.393	2.3
TOTAL	535.734		399.994	
(c) Surgery issue				
Within-group	335.734	63.7	85.781	29.2
Between-group	188.616	35.8	203.023	69.1
Between-subpopulation	2.748	0.5	4.973	1.7
TOTAL	527.099		293.777	

Notes:

$$\text{Within-Groups: } w_1 \sum_{f=1}^{F} w_{1f}\, \text{var}(y_{if}) + w_2 \sum_{m=1}^{M} w_{2m}\, \text{var}(y_{2m}).$$

$$\text{Between-Groups: } w_1 \sum_{f=1}^{F} \text{var}(\bar{y}_{1f}) + w_2 \sum_{m=1}^{M} w_{2m}\, \text{var}(\bar{y}_{2m}).$$

Between Subpopulations: $\text{var}(\bar{y}_1 . \bar{y}_2)$.

then the reduction of the total variance, Pre-var(y) − Post-var(y), will depend mainly on the reductions of variance generated by the within-group endogenous influences that occur within *each* of the gender-homophilous small groups.

Table 12.6 compares the variance decompositions of the pre- and postdiscussion issue positions for the three issues. On the Sports issue, the total variance is reduced by 35.2%. Endogenous interpersonal influences have dramatically redistributed the total variance: the percentage of within-group variance has dropped from 64.1% to 4.4%, and the percentage of between-group variance has increased from 31.4% to 72.1%. On this Sports issue, there is also a noteworthy increase of the between-subpopulations (female and male) variance from 4.5% to 23.5%. On the School issue, the total variance is reduced by 25.3%. Again, endogenous interpersonal influences have dramatically redistributed the total variance to between-groups, but here without a noteworthy increase in the between-subpopulations variance. On the Surgery issue, the total variance is reduced by 44.3%. As with the School issue, endogenous interpersonal influences have dramatically redistributed the total variance to between-groups without a noteworthy increase in the between-sub-populations variance. Thus, the statistically significant effects of gender on subjects' postdiscussion positions are based on different implications of the influence process. On each issue, the detected effect is based on variances that have been dramatically affected by within-group social processes. On the Sports issue, these within-group influences also have served to further differentiate the female and male subpopulations. On the two other issues, within-group influences have modest effects on subpopulation differentiation. Hence, with the possible exception of the Sport issue, interpersonal influences within same-sex small groups have substantially reduced the population's diversity of issue positions, i.e., the total variance, without generating a substantial increase in the social differentiation of the female and male subpopulations.

12.4 Concluding Remarks

Blau (1977) contrasts consolidated social structures, in which there are strong associations among sociodemographic variables, with unconsolidated structures, in which these associations are weak. In an unconsolidated social structure, contacts with similar others on one social dimension typically involves contacts with persons who differ on other social dimensions. Blau refers to such contacts as instances of multiform heterogeneity, suggests that such heterogeneity is a typical characteristic of actual social structures, and takes such contacts as a basis of the structural integration of the social structure. But how, and in what ways, do contacts foster integration? We argue that contacts foster integration when they trigger interpersonal influences that reduce the total variance of issue positions in a population. Such reductions of the total variance of issue positions in a population may occur on the basis of small group dynamics. This integration may be an inelegant, even ramshackle, social construction based on cross-cutting local, often transitory and frequently modified, interpersonal agreements.

In this chapter, we deepen Blau's insight on the integrative implications of multiform heterogeneity. Contacts often arise in small group settings, and the contacts that occur in such settings often entail multiform heterogeneity. For instance, the females involved in gender-homophilous small groups may also be involved in religion-homophilous small groups of males and females. The interpersonal influence systems within small groups may not only substantially reduce the within-group variances of issue positions, but also reduce the total variance of issue positions in the population. In a population, small groups are being assembled on *various* social dimensions (sex, race, religion, age, etc.) and engaged in symbolic interactions, i.e., negotiations of interpersonal disagreements, the definition of common objectives, and the organization of coordinated activities. Hence, there is a massive collection of small groups that may be contributing to the reduction of the total variance of issue positions in the population. The reduction of total variance on issue positions that we have observed, in our constrained analytical setting, is a telltale sign of a more general effect of small group dynamics in unconsolidated social structures that can shuffle individuals into different positions on issues and reduce the population-level variance on issue positions.

The influence systems of small groups may substantially reduce within-group variances on issues. Under the experimental conditions of the present analysis, most of the small groups reached consensus: 76.8% of 82 groups, 67.9% of 134 groups, and 61.9% of 134 groups on the Sports, School, and Surgery issues, respectively. In the postdiscussion distributions, with modest contributions of the within-group variances to the total variance, the total variance on each issue mainly rests on the between-group and between-subpopulation (female and male) variances. From a circumstance in which the prediscussion total variance is mainly within-group variance, group dynamics has operated to modify the allocation of the total variance dramatically and to reduce the total variance significantly.

From a multilevel modeling perspective, our strong intraclass correlations at the group-level for the postdiscussion issue positions would trigger the pursuit of an explanation of the distribution of the groups' postdiscussion means. However, as we noted in the introduction to this chapter, multilevel models typically explain the variation among group means in terms of group-level variables. Our approach is different, although not entirely inconsistent with a multilevel modeling approach. From our perspective, explanations that rely on group-level variables (such as a group's size or density of contacts) must attend to how these group-level features translate into the group's influence network. The effects of group-level variables depend on the interpersonal influence process that unfolds within the network. The macro-level features of the distribution of post-discussion positions on issues (their means and variances) are derivatives of the within-group influence processes.

In the present analysis, we have placed emphasis on the reduction of variance within-groups via interpersonal influences. It is also the case that the influence networks of small groups may modify the means of the macro-level distributions of issue positions, i.e., the mean of the total population and the means of the separate female and male subpopulations. In our data, such an effect is most manifest on the Sport issue. Small group influence processes have two ubiquitous characteristics that pertain to the values of these postdiscussion means.

First, within-group influence processes do not, as rule, generate convergence to the mean of the group members' prediscussion positions. Choice shifts are common, i.e., a difference between the means of the within-group pre- and postdiscussion positions. The direction and magnitude of the choice shift within a group depend on the influence network. It may be the case, for example, that the holders of risky initial positions are less susceptible to interpersonal influence than the holders of cautious positions, and that group members tend to accord more influence to the holders of risky initial positions than to the holders of cautious positions. However, the influence network of a small group is affected by many other factors, including idiosyncratic individual differences in susceptibility and persuasiveness. The influence networks of small groups may collectively affect the total population mean of the postdiscussion distribution of positions, or these networks may increase or decrease the difference between the means of female and male distributions of postdiscussion positions. There is evidence in the present data that they may do so. Recall that these effects are aggregate derivatives of the small group influence processes.

Second, the range of within-group initial positions on an issue may vary dramatically from one small group to another. The outcomes of small group influence processes are strongly constrained to the ranges of initial positions within groups. This constraint is virtually never violated in groups with three or more members; in dyads, the constraint is less pronounced, with a low incidence of violations. Thus, the group members' initial positions on an issue are an important feature of the influence system. Individual outcomes are a weighted average of the members' prediscussion positions. Within this constraint, it is the network that determines individual outcomes. Thus, the means of small group postdiscussion positions may be affected by the initial arrays of positions. Constraints on the initial ranges place constraints on the final ranges and, in turn, on the feasible absolute difference in the means of the macro-level distributions of the females and males.

Although the theoretical perspective outlined in this chapter is broad, the data that we have marshaled to support it are narrow in scope. This is both a limitation and a strength of the present analysis. We have sought to advance our perspective on the contribution of small group dynamics to the macro-level integration of populations with an analysis of a simple situation. The elaboration and implications of our perspective are more fully realized when small groups of all sorts, involving different bases of homophily (sex, age, race, religion, etc.), are allowed to enter into the analysis. Individuals are involved in arrays and sequences of small groups with different compositions on the same and different issues. It is the disorderly mass of such small group formations that must be taken into account. Simmel concluded that the important effect of intersecting social circles is an increase of individualism and autonomy – freedom from the constraints of sociodemographic conditions. This conclusion is, of course, consistent with Blau's analysis of unconsolidated social structures. However, the implications of Simmel's conclusion depend on whether the individualism that is fostered by intersecting social circles implies a diminution of susceptibilities to interpersonal influence. Our viewpoint on this matter is that small groups retain their status as the primary sites of symbolic interaction, accommodation, and negotiation, regardless of any broad restructuring of the social organization of contacts in a population.

Epilogue

Small groups take many forms in natural settings and generally involve discussions of issues of interest to their members. In sociology, at least since Cooley's (1983 [originally published 1902]) observations on primary and secondary groups, various types of groups (families, gangs, communes, work-groups, etc.) have been investigated in field settings as possible sites of important symbolic interactions and the formation of interpersonal agreements. Interpersonal influence networks are implicated in all such groups and, therefore, the development of our understanding of the implications of such networks is a fundamental problem. When group size is scaled upward to the meso-level (e.g., organizations and communities) and to the macro-level (e.g., large populations), influence networks also are present for issues of general salience to the members of these larger collectivities. In such meso and macro collectivities, when interpersonal influences affect members' attitudes toward particular objects and, in turn, their object-related behaviors, influence networks are also fundamental to an understanding of collective action, social diffusion, and behavioral cascades.

Our work, in this volume, focuses on the basic mechanism by which an influence network becomes a meaningful construct, and through which we might analyze the implications of influence networks. We are not exclusively wedded to the experimental settings in which we have examined the implications of influence networks. It appears evident to us that the analysis of interpersonal influences within groups in field settings will be placed on firmer theoretical grounds when it can be demonstrated that particular approaches to the construct of an influence network provide accurate predictions of small group outcomes in experimental settings.

Under specialized conditions, and for issues that involve a collective choice of one position from a small number of mutually exclusive alternative positions, many investigations have demonstrated that such choices depend on the distribution of group members' initial positions on the issue and the conditions under which the members of the group are communicating about the issue. It also is clear that the transformation of group members' initial positions into their collective choice is amenable to formalization. Bibb Latané's social impact theory and James Davis's social decision scheme theory are prominent approaches to a formalized model of the group process that is involved in such transformations, but there are other applicable formalizations as well in the literatures of the social and physical sciences. The relative merits of these alternative approaches will eventually become a more settled matter than they are at present, as more empirical data are brought to bear on the extent to which particular models present accurate predictions in a large domain of applications that include both quantifiable and categorical positions on issues.

We believe that advancement toward a broadly applicable formalization will require the specification of the social process over time that is involved in the maintenance or modification of group members' issue positions. Ideally, we should be able to theoretically ground a static-equilibrium analysis of groups (i.e., an explanation of their final states when such states occur) on a dynamic analysis of the changes over time of individuals' issue positions. Our efforts in this book have been to describe, analyze, and evaluate a discrete-time ($t = 1, 2, \ldots$) interpersonal influence process that is *dynamic* in its formal foundations, *specific* in its attention to individual differences among group members, and *generally applicable* to both quantifiable and categorical issue positions.

We concentrate our analysis on the implications of influence networks for individuals' changes of position on issues. Our focus is on networks of endogenous interpersonal influences that involve the effects of issue positions, held by particular individuals at a given time, on the issue positions of other particular individuals. We place emphasis on the embodiment of *issue-positions* within the *individuals* who hold these positions; i.e., a particular person j expresses a held position on an issue that may influence another particular person i based on i's accord of influence to j. Such embodiment of issue positions has important implications for the bases of the interpersonal influences that are involved in the formation of a group's influence network – individuals are responding to other individuals as complex social agents under a particular set of contextual conditions. Hence, the influence network of a group is, we believe, more typically an idiosyncratic social construction of individuals than it is an *a priori* (received or imposed) social structure. Influence networks are conditional on a specific set of individuals, on the issue that concerns them, and on the circumstances in which the issue is being considered. Building on a line of formalization concerned with such influence networks (DeGroot 1974; French 1956; Harary 1959), we conceptualize the *realized* influence network of a group with n members as an $n \times n$ matrix of relative weights $\mathbf{W}$, in which $0 \leq w_{ij} \leq 1$ for all i and j and $\sum_{k=1}^{n} w_{ik} = 1$ for all i.

The individual differences that may appear in a comparison of the rows and columns of this matrix are consequential and, we believe, essential to an explanation of the issue-position changes that occur in groups.

In special cases, a group may begin the discussion of an issue with a fixed influence network. More generally, the influence network may be modified and become fixed during the discussion of an issue. In special cases, the influence network that is constructed during the discussion may be constrained by group members' initial positions on an issue and by their formal or informal status characteristics. More generally, such constraints are mediated by the attitudes of group members about themselves and others as *objects* during the discussion of an issue. Although, as sociologists, we have an interest in explaining the origins of influence networks, and have touched on these origins in this book, our primary analytical focus has been on the *implications* of a realized stable influence network (whatever the antecedent bases of this network might be) for the attitude changes that occur in a group on an issue.

Our *positive thesis* is that, when group members modify their positions on an issue, their final positions emerge from a process of endogenous interpersonal influence, involving a weighted averaging of members' positions, unfolding in an influence network. If this thesis is accepted, based on the evidence presented in this book, then the influence networks of groups, and the specification of the influence processes that unfold in these networks, become theoretically central in the explanation of individual and group outcomes. Our *negative thesis* is that group members' final destinations on an issue are often not determined by their initial positions on the issue. If this thesis is accepted, based on the evidence presented in this book, then we must delve more deeply into the "black box" of the group's social process for an explanation of individual and group outcomes on an issue.

In developing to the above theses, we have revisited work in the classical tradition of group dynamics in order to reshape theoretical perspectives on that work and to promote new advances. Initial issue positions, by themselves, do not appear to constrain group outcomes strongly, except in special cases. However, initial positions, in *combination* with the group's influence network, do predict group members' attitude changes on issues; specifically, $y^{(\infty)} = Vy^{(1)}$, where V is the emergent matrix of total (direct and indirect) influences that arises from a process of endogenous interpersonal influences unfolding in the group's influence network W. Although initial positions do not appear to strongly constrain W, they sometimes strongly constrain the outcomes of the influence process, regardless of W, when the initial range of group members' initial positions is sufficiently limited. However, by the same token, the initial positions of group members should *not* be expected to predict group outcomes given a sufficiently large range of initial positions on the issue.

As reviewers of the literature on small group dynamics have repeatedly pointed out, studies of small groups have appeared disconnected in the absence of a formal theory that establishes links between different lines of work. We have pursued a formal integration of the *cognitive* and *structural* emphases of current investigations on small groups in psychology and sociology, and we have done so with a formalization of an individual-level social cognition mechanism of attitude change:

$$y_i^{(t+1)} = a_{ii} \sum_{i=1}^{n} w_{ij} y_j^{(t)} + (1 - a_{ii}) y_i^{(1)} \qquad (a_{ii} = 1 - w_{ii}).$$

In a group with n members, this mechanism, unfolding over time $(t = 1, 2, \ldots)$, implies an endogenous *system* of interpersonal influences in which an influence *network* (i.e., the collection of w_{ij} for all i and j) is theoretically implicated in the attitude changes of group members. Thus, the influence network construct that we introduce is intrinsic to the postulated social cognition mechanism of attitude change when this mechanism is considered as part of a system of individual responses. The *group context* is likely to generate intersections of the subsets of group members who are directly influencing the positions of each group member. Such intersections allow flows of influence between persons in two overlapping subsets via intermediaries in the intersection of the subsets; this implication extends to chains of pairwise overlapping subsets of influentials. Interdependent responses arise from these intersections and from the influence process that unfolds, via these intersections, in the group.

We also have pursued an integration of two research programs in sociology – affect control theory and expectation states theory. For this integration, we *relax* the assumption of a fixed influence network, allowing interpersonal influences to vary over time. We draw on the three fundamental dimensions of interpersonal sentiment – evaluation, potency, and activity (Osgood, Suci, and Tannenbaum 1957) – as the initial bases of an influence network that, in turn, affects group members' interpersonal sentiments that, in turn, affect their influence network, and so on, over time. In a group that has reached equilibrium, there exists a stable matrix of interpersonal sentiments and a corresponding stable influence network. Such an equilibrium may or may not be reached rapidly and may or may not involve the generation of consensual sentiment and influence structures. We do not assume the prior existence of such consensual structures. When group members' initial sentiments are consensual, the process that we describe will maintain the consensus. When group members' initial sentiments disagree, the interpersonal influence process that is affecting their sentiments may generate the stable consensual social structure that has been assumed a priori by expectation states and affect control theorists. With this approach, we suggest that various bases of interpersonal influence (expertise, punishment, reward, authority, identification, information) are located in a coordinate space defined by evaluation, potency, and activity attitudinal dimensions. One or more of these bases, via interpersonal sentiments, enter into individuals' accord of weight to themselves and to particular others. Hence, the influence network of a group on an issue is an *attitudinal construct* that is an expression of the interpersonal sentiment structure of a group. The influence networks formed to deal with issues that arise in groups are highly idiosyncratic social constructs because of their foundation on the manifold conditions that affect interpersonal sentiments prior to and during the discussion of issues.

Numerous formalizations of interpersonal influence have been proposed in the literatures of the social sciences and, increasingly, in the literatures of the natural sciences. We have empirically assessed some of these formalizations and not attended to others. The work presented in this book is embedded in the social psychological literature, wherein we limit our analysis to an investigation of endogenous interpersonal influences on attitudes. Our colleagues in sociology will recognize that this work has not attended to important lines of formal theory in sociology, economics, and political science concerned with collective action, social diffusion, and behavioral cascades. In an early (much larger and entirely unwieldy) version of this book, we addressed these lines of inquiry (e.g., Gould 1993; Granovetter 1978; Kaufer and Carley, 1993; Laumann and Pappi 1976; Marsden 1981; Stokman, van Assen, Knoop, and Oosten 2000; Valente 1995; Watts and Dodds 2007) from the perspective of social influence network theory. Behavioral cascades may be linked to underlying attitudes and, when they are, endogenous interpersonal influences on attitudes may generate local and global behavioral cascades (social diffusion and collective action) in small- and large-scale groups. Our particular substantive focus here does not imply a lack of interest in these lines of work.

Here we only note that the prominent formalization of the attitude–behavior linkage proposed by Fishbein and Ajzen (Ajzen 1988; Fishbein and Ajzen 1975) has a close relationship to our formalization. Their line of work on the attitude–behavior linkage suggests that there are attitudinal antecedents to behavior and that this linkage is mediated by a *behavioral intention* to manifest a particular object-related behavior. In their model, the immediate antecedent of a suitably specific volitional behavior is a person's intention (I) to engage in the behavior and, in turn, the immediate antecedents of a behavioral intention are (a) a person's *favorable or unfavorable attitude* (A_B) toward the behavior and (b) a person's *subjective norm* (SN), that is, the person's perception of the extent to which significant others believe that the person should manifest the behavior. Each component (the person's attitude and subjective norm) has a relative weight in determining the person's behavioral intention:

$$B \leftarrow I = w_1 (SN) + w_2 (A_B) .$$

A person's subjective norm is determined by his or her perceptions of the attitudes of others, and by his or her motivation to comply with the attitudes of these referents, $SN = \sum_{j=1}^{n} b_j m_j$, where b_j is the perceived attitude of j toward the behavior, and m_j is i's motivation to comply with j's attitude. A person's evaluative attitude toward the behavior is determined by his or her beliefs that the behavior will lead to particular outcomes and by his or her evaluation of those outcomes, $A_B = w_2 \sum_{j=1}^{k} o_j e_j$, where o_j is the believed outcome j and e_j is the evaluation of that outcome. Combining these equations, we have

$$B \leftarrow I = w_1(SN) + w_2(A_B)$$

$$= w_1 \sum_{j=1}^{n} b_j m_j + w_2 \sum_{j=1}^{k} o_j e_j$$

for the behavioral intention that is taken as the immediate antecedent of the individual's behavior. If we interpret the above in terms of our constructs, then $w_1 = 1 - w_2 = a_{ii}$, $\sum_{j=1}^{k} o_j e_j = y_i^{(1)}$, and $\sum_{j=1}^{n} m_j b_j = \sum_{j=1}^{n} w_{ij} y_j^{(\infty)}$, so that

$$B \leftarrow I \leftarrow y_i^{(\infty)} = a_{ii} \sum_{j=1}^{n} w_{ij} y_j^{(\infty)} + (1 - a_{ii}) y_i^{(1)}.$$

This approach suggests that the person's equilibrium attitude $y_i^{(\infty)}$ toward the behavior is the immediate antecedent of a behavioral intention that, in turn, is a factor in whether or not the person adopts the behavior. The association of the antecedent attitude, $y_i^{(1)} = \sum_{j=1}^{k} o_j e_j$, with intention I and behavior B depends on a person's susceptibility to interpersonal influence.

We also have not developed the linkage of our standard model with the canonical mixed regressive–autoregressive model of endogenous interpersonal influence that is currently employed in field studies of such influences (Anselin 1988; Doreian 1981; Erbring and Young 1979; Marsden and Friedkin 1994; Ord 1975). This model is

$$y = \alpha Wy + X\beta + e,$$

where X is an $n \times k$ matrix with its first column consisting of ones, β is a $k \times 1$ vector of parameters, W is an $n \times n$ matrix of weights, α is a scalar parameter, and $e \sim N(0, \sigma^2 I)$. For endogenous interpersonal influences on attitudes, the closely related mixed regressive–autoregressive specification based on social influence network theory is

$$y = AWy + (I - A)(X\beta + e).$$

An implication of this model is that the contribution of fixed exogenous variables X to y depends on individual differences, i.e., on individuals' self-weights $w_{ii} = 1 - a_{ii}$ for each i. With $y^{(1)} = X\beta + e$, the empirical analysis presented in the *previous chapter* supports this specification.

Prior to our formal work and empirical investigations, the line of theory on social influence networks pursued by DeGroot (1974), French (1956), and Harary (1959) was undeveloped and untested. Our contribution to this theory is a program of investigation in which formal theory and empirical findings have been placed in an intimate relation. In closing, we highlight six instances of this fundamental relation and the role that is has played in our work.

First, our empirical evidence indicates that attitude changes are importantly constrained by the range of initial attitudes of a group's members. A breach of the range of group members' initial positions occurred in only 2 instances of the 346 issue trials in triads and tetrads. The constraint appears to be weaker for dyads, for reasons that have we have probed; we have achieved some tentative understanding of this phenomenon, but this understanding is not complete. The intensive analysis of dyadic influence systems presented in Chapter 6 reflects our empirical discovery that the influence systems of dyads are not only *different* from those of larger groups (à la Simmel 1950) but also surprisingly *complex* social systems in their own right.

Second, small group discussions sometimes result in a consensus on either an initial position or a compromise position, or in an unresolved disagreement. In our data, each of these outcomes occurs with a substantial frequency. This mundane observation has had an important role in the development of our theory. A credible formal theory of endogenous interpersonal influences on attitudes should be consistent with *all* of these outcomes. We have allowed for a continuing direct contribution of an individual's initial position on an issue to the individual's developing positions in order to enlarge the domain of influence networks to include those in which endogenous interpersonal influences will *not* result in consensus. Formally, this is not a trivial matter, as Abelson learned to his apparent consternation:

> Since universal ultimate agreement is an ubiquitous outcome of a very broad class of mathematical models, we are naturally led to inquire what on earth one must assume in order to generate the bimodal outcomes of community cleavage studies. (Abelson 1964: 153)

We must have a formal model that is consistent with unresolved disagreement and with the formation of consensus that is not restricted to a consensual choice of an *initial* position.

Third, in our original formalization (Friedkin and Johnsen 1990), we entertained a parameter for group polarization, which we subsequently have dropped, based on our empirical findings. We have concluded that the influence network construct suffices to account for this phenomenon of concern in the empirical literature on choice shifts and group polarization.

Fourth, we originally entertained a homogeneous susceptibility value (Friedkin and Johnsen 1990). We relaxed this homogeneity assumption because our empirical evidence suggested that the contribution of others' attitudes to an individual's attitude importantly depends on the individual's particular susceptibility to influence.

Fifth, we originally did not couple susceptibilities and self-weights. The coupling of these constructs ($w_{ii} = 1 - a_{ii}$) has been the subject of long hours of debate. We impose and work with the coupling assumption in part because it is an elegant simplifying assumption and in part because of its empirical usefulness; i.e., a single empirical measure suffices to operationalize the main diagonals of $\mathbf{W}$ and $\mathbf{A}$.

Sixth, our formalization postulates that susceptibility is a continuous dimension on which individuals vary. We have maintained this assumption throughout our analysis. However, interestingly, our empirical evidence suggests that susceptibilities may often be viewed as binary states. This is a fascinating possibility that emerged from our analysis of susceptibility values *derived* from measures of group members' initial positions $\mathbf{y}^{(1)}$, end-of-trial positions $\mathbf{y}^{(\infty)}$, and reported relative interpersonal influences $\mathbf{C}$. If susceptibility is a binary variable, then an individual's equilibrium attitude is either (a) strictly generated by the individual's adoption of the "normative" position of others $\sum_{j \neq i} w_{ij} y_j^{(t)}$ at each time t during the influence process or (b) a fixed initial position generated by the antecedent conditions that determined the individual's initial position.

We find it remarkable that the social cognition mechanism $y_i^{(t+1)} = a_{ii} \sum_{i=1}^{n} w_{ij} y_j^{(t)} + (1 - a_{ii}) y_i^{(1)}$, which was obtained by a generalization of the French, Harary, and DeGroot models, may also be obtained from "first principles" of information integration theory in cognitive science, which postulates that an individual's response is a *weighted average of units of information. The* derivation is presented in Chapter 2, Section 2.2.1. We are intrigued by the possibility that the cognitive algebra involved in the weighted averaging of information may have a neurological basis. The more general point that might be made here is that it is not unrealistic to suppose that a theory of social structure and social process grounded on cognitive science might be developed. The circumstances of individuals may vary within and between cultures and times. These different circumstances may affect the issues of concern, who persons interact with, and the weights accorded to others and to themselves. But the social cognition mechanism with which individuals integrate information may be invariant.

Appendix A

Fundamental Constructs and Equations

In this appendix, we present the fundamental constructs and equations upon which our work is based. In this presentation, we also embed a glossary of the terms that we employ to describe these constructs and equations.

A.1 Constructs and Their Relations

A.1.1 Social Group

A *social group* of size n is defined as a set of n individuals $\{1, 2, \ldots, n\}$ among whom an influence process is operating over time $(t = 1, 2, \ldots)$, such that the set includes *all* persons who directly or indirectly (i.e., via intermediaries) influence the attitude of others in the group on an issue.

A.1.2 Attitude Construct

The *attitude* construct is represented by the matrix

$$
\mathbf{Y}^{(t)} = \begin{bmatrix} y_{11}^{(t)} & y_{12}^{(t)} & \cdots & y_{1m}^{(t)} \\ y_{21}^{(t)} & y_{22}^{(t)} & \cdots & y_{2m}^{(t)} \\ \vdots & \vdots & \vdots & \vdots \\ y_{n1}^{(t)} & y_{n2}^{(t)} & \cdots & y_{nm}^{(t)} \end{bmatrix} \equiv \left[y_{ik}^{(t)} \right], \tag{A.1}
$$

where entry $y_{ik}^{(t)}$ quantitatively characterizes the position of individual i on dimension k of an issue at time t; $(i = 1, n; k = 1, m; t = 1, 2 \ldots)$. We refer to $y_{ik}^{(1)}$ as the *initial position* or initial attitude of i on dimension k of the issue. The matrix of initial positions may be reinitialized at some time t during the influence process on an issue, e.g., as a consequence of an exogenous shock on the influence process.

313

A.1.3 Influence Network Construct

The *direct* influence construct is represented by the matrix

$$\mathbf{W}^{(t)} = \begin{bmatrix} w_{11}^{(t)} & w_{12}^{(t)} & \cdots & w_{1n}^{(t)} \\ w_{12}^{(t)} & w_{22}^{(t)} & \cdots & w_{2n}^{(t)} \\ \vdots & \vdots & \ddots & \vdots \\ w_{n1}^{(t)} & w_{n2}^{(t)} & \cdots & w_{nn}^{(t)} \end{bmatrix} \equiv \left[w_{ij}^{(t)} \right], \qquad (A.2)$$

where each entry $w_{ij}^{(t)}$ satisfies $0 \leq w_{ij}^{(t)} \leq 1$ for all i and j, and $\sum_{j=1}^{n} w_{ij}^{(t)} = 1$ for all i, for each time $t = 1, 2, \ldots$. The set $\left\{ w_{ij}^{(t)} \mid j = 1, 2, \ldots, n \right\}$ are the *influence weights* that each individual i assigns to the members of the group at time t for all i. We refer to the weight $w_{ij}^{(t)}$ for $i \neq j$ as an *interpersonal weight* and to the weight $w_{ii}^{(t)}$ as a *self-weight*. We refer to $1 - w_{ii}^{(t)} = \sum_{j \neq i}^{n} w_{ij}^{(t)}$ as the *aggregate interpersonal weight* of the $n - 1$ other group members on i. In general, we refer to the weight $w_{ij}^{(t)}$ as the *relative unmediated influence* of j on i for $j = 1, 2, \ldots, n$.

A.1.4 Susceptibility Construct

The *susceptibility* construct is represented by the matrix $\mathbf{A}^{(t)} = \mathrm{diag}[a_{ii}^{(t)}]$,

$$\mathbf{A}^{(t)} = \begin{bmatrix} a_{11}^{(t)} & 0 & \cdots & 0 \\ 0 & a_{22}^{(t)} & \cdots & 0 \\ \vdots & \vdots & \ddots & \vdots \\ 0 & 0 & \cdots & a_{nn}^{(t)} \end{bmatrix} \equiv \mathrm{diag}\left[a_{11}^{(t)}, a_{22}^{(t)}, \ldots, a_{nn}^{(t)} \right], \quad (A.3)$$

where $0 \leq a_{ii}^{(t)} \leq 1$ for all i and t. We refer to $a_{ii}^{(t)}$ as i's time t *susceptibility* or *influenceability*.

A.1.5. General Form of the Model

We assume that each individual i in a group of n members maintains or modifies his or her position, on each dimension of an m-dimensional issue, as follows:

$$\text{member 1: } y_{1k}^{(t+1)} = a_{11}^{(t)} \sum_{j=1}^{n} w_{1j}^{(t)} y_{jk}^{(t)} + \left(1 - a_{11}^{(t)} \right) y_{1k}^{(1)} \qquad (A.4)$$

$$\text{member 2: } y_{2k}^{(t+1)} = a_{22}^{(t)} \sum_{j=1}^{n} w_{2j}^{(t)} y_{jk}^{(t)} + \left(1 - a_{22}^{(t)} \right) y_{2k}^{(1)}$$

$$\vdots$$

$$\text{member n: } y_{nk}^{(t+1)} = a_{nn}^{(t)} \sum_{j=1}^{n} w_{nj}^{(t)} y_{jk}^{(t)} + \left(1 - a_{nn}^{(t)} \right) y_{nk}^{(1)}$$

for $k = 1, 2, \ldots, m$ and $t = 1, 2, \ldots$. In matrix form, this system is described by the equation

$$\mathbf{Y}^{(t+1)} = \mathbf{A}^{(t)}\mathbf{W}^{(t)}\mathbf{Y}^{(t)} + \left(\mathbf{I} - \mathbf{A}^{(t)}\right)\mathbf{Y}^{(1)}, \tag{A.5}$$

where the construction of the equation has been defined above. Here, we do not index the susceptibilities and interpersonal weights according to the dimension k.

A.1.6 Coupling Constraint

The coupling constraint links individuals' self-weights and susceptibilities,

$$w_{ii}^{(t)} = 1 - a_{ii}^{(t)}, \tag{A.6}$$

for all $i = 1, n$. This constraint may or may not be invoked. When it is invoked, the *aggregate interpersonal weight* of the $n - 1$ other group members is equivalent to i's susceptibility,

$$a_{ii}^{(t)} = 1 - w_{ii}^{(t)} = \sum_{\substack{j \neq i}}^{n} w_{ij}^{(t)}, \tag{A.7}$$

for all i and t. Hence, under coupling, the specification of $\mathbf{W}^{(t)}$ determines $\mathbf{A}^{(t)}$.

A.1.7 Decomposition of the Influence Network Construct

When the coupling constraint is invoked, the influence network construct may be viewed as consisting of a susceptibility component $\mathbf{A}^{(t)}$ and an interpersonal influence component

$$\mathbf{C}^{(t)} = \begin{bmatrix} 0 & c_{12}^{(t)} & \cdots & c_{1n}^{(t)} \\ c_{21}^{(t)} & 0 & \cdots & c_{2n}^{(t)} \\ \vdots & \vdots & \ddots & \vdots \\ c_{n1}^{(t)} & c_{n2}^{(t)} & \cdots & 0 \end{bmatrix} \equiv \left[c_{ij}^{(t)} \right], \tag{A.8}$$

where $c_{ij}^{(t)}$, $0 \leq c_{ij}^{(t)} \leq 1$, describes the *relative direct strictly interpersonal influence* of j on i at time t, for all i and j, and, $c_{ii}^{(t)} = 0$, and $\sum_{k=1}^{n} c_{ik}^{(t)} = 1$ or 0 for all i. This construct may be viewed either as an additional fundamental construct or as a derivative of $\mathbf{W}^{(t)}$. Given $\mathbf{W}^{(t)}$,

$$c_{ij}^{(t)} = \frac{w_{ij}^{(t)}}{\sum_{k \neq i} w_{ik}^{(t)}} = \frac{w_{ij}^{(t)}}{1 - w_{ii}^{(t)}} \qquad j \neq i, \tag{A.9}$$

for $w_{ii}^{(t)} < 1$. For $w_{ii}^{(t)} = 1$, where $w_{ij}^{(t)} = 0$ for all $j \neq i$, we define $c_{ij}^{(t)} = 0$ for all $j \neq i$ and set $a_{ii}^{(t)} = 0$ so that $a_{ii}^{(t)} = 1 - w_{ii}^{(t)}$. Then, given $\mathbf{A}^{(t)}$, $\mathbf{C}^{(t)}$, and $a_{ii}^{(t)} = 1 - w_{ii}^{(t)}$ for all i, we can construct

$$\mathbf{W}^{(t)} = \mathbf{A}^{(t)}\mathbf{C}^{(t)} + \mathbf{I} - \mathbf{A}^{(t)}. \tag{A.10}$$

Thus, *without* a direct measure of $\mathbf{W}^{(t)}$, but *with* separate suitably scaled measures of $\mathbf{A}^{(t)}$ and $\mathbf{C}^{(t)}$, we can form $\mathbf{W}^{(t)}$ under the coupling assumption.

A.1.8 Equilibrium State of the System

In its general form, $\mathbf{A}^{(t)}$ and $\mathbf{W}^{(t)}$ may be modified at each time t. If $\lim_{t \to \infty} \mathbf{A}^{(t)} = \mathbf{A}^{(\infty)}$, $\lim_{t \to \infty} \mathbf{W}^{(t)} = \mathbf{W}^{(\infty)}$, and $\lim_{t \to \infty} \mathbf{Y}^{(t)} = \mathbf{Y}^{(\infty)}$ exist, then from (A.5) we have

$$\mathbf{Y}^{(\infty)} = \mathbf{A}^{(\infty)}\mathbf{W}^{(\infty)}\mathbf{Y}^{(\infty)} + \left(\mathbf{I} - \mathbf{A}^{(\infty)}\right)\mathbf{Y}^{(1)} \tag{A.11}$$

or

$$\left(\mathbf{I} - \mathbf{A}^{(\infty)}\mathbf{W}^{(\infty)}\right)\mathbf{Y}^{(\infty)} = \left(\mathbf{I} - \mathbf{A}^{(\infty)}\right)\mathbf{Y}^{(1)}, \tag{A.12}$$

and if $\mathbf{I} - \mathbf{A}^{(\infty)}\mathbf{W}^{(\infty)}$ is nonsingular, then

$$\mathbf{Y}^{(\infty)} = \mathbf{V}^{(\infty)}\mathbf{Y}^{(1)}, \tag{A.13}$$

where $\mathbf{V}^{(\infty)} = \left[\mathbf{I} - \mathbf{A}^{(\infty)}\mathbf{W}^{(\infty)}\right]^{-1}\left(\mathbf{I} - \mathbf{A}^{(\infty)}\right)$.

A.2 Standard Form

The standard form of the influence system assumes a fixed influence network $\mathbf{W}^{(t)} = \mathbf{W}$ for $t = 1, 2, \ldots$ and the coupling constraint $a_{ii}^{(t)} = 1 - w_{ii}^{(t)}$ for all i; hence, $\mathbf{A}^{(t)} = \mathbf{A}$ is also fixed. Thus,

$$y_{ik}^{(t+1)} = a_{ii} \sum_{j=1}^{n} w_{ij} y_{jk}^{(t)} + (1 - a_{ii}) y_{ik}^{(1)} \tag{A.14}$$

$$a_{ii} = 1 - w_{ii} = \sum_{j \neq i}^{n} w_{ij}$$

for all i, t, and k. In general, for this special case,

$$\mathbf{Y}^{(t+1)} = \mathbf{V}^{(t)}\mathbf{Y}^{(1)}, \tag{A.15}$$

where, for all t,

$$\mathbf{V}^{(t)} = \mathbf{AWV}^{(t-1)} + (\mathbf{I} - \mathbf{A})$$

$$= (\mathbf{AW})^t + \left[\sum_{k=0}^{t-1}(\mathbf{AW})^k\right](\mathbf{I} - \mathbf{A}), \tag{A.16}$$

$\mathbf{V}^{(0)} \equiv \mathbf{I}$, and $(\mathbf{AW})^0 = \mathbf{I}$; see Appendix B. The scalar equation for (A.15) is

$$y_{ik}^{(t+1)} = v_{i1}^{(t)}y_{1k}^{(1)} + v_{i2}^{(t)}y_{2k}^{(1)} + \cdots + v_{in}^{(t)}y_{nk}^{(1)} \tag{A.17}$$

for all i, t, and k. The coefficients in $\mathbf{V}^{(t)}$ are nonnegative $(0 \le v_{ij}^{(t)} \le 1)$ and each row of $\mathbf{V}^{(t)}$ sums to unity $(\sum_{k=1}^n v_{ik}^{(t)} = 1)$. Hence, at every point in time during the influence process, including $t = \infty$, persons' attitudes are weighted averages of the group members' initial attitudes.

Assuming that the process reaches *equilibrium*, which henceforth will mean that $\lim_{t\to\infty}\mathbf{V}^{(t)} = \mathbf{V}^{(\infty)} \equiv \mathbf{V}$ exists, then by (A.16)

$$\mathbf{V} = \lim_{t\to\infty}\left\{(\mathbf{AW})^t + \left[\sum_{k=0}^{t-1}(\mathbf{AW})^k\right](\mathbf{I} - \mathbf{A})\right\}, \tag{A.18}$$

or, when $\mathbf{I} - \mathbf{AW}$ is nonsingular,

$$\mathbf{V} = (\mathbf{I} - \mathbf{AW})^{-1}(\mathbf{I} - \mathbf{A}) \tag{A.19}$$

and by (A.15)

$$\mathbf{Y}^{(\infty)} = \mathbf{VY}^{(1)}. \tag{A.20}$$

Here, for $V = [v_{ij}]$, the scalar equation for (A.20) is

$$y_{ik}^{(\infty)} = v_{i1}y_{1k}^{(1)} + v_{i2}y_{2k}^{(1)} + \cdots + v_{in}y_{nk}^{(1)}. \tag{A.21}$$

Thus, $\mathbf{V}$ is a matrix of the *total interpersonal* influences (direct and indirect) that transform group members' initial attitudes into their final equilibrium attitudes.

Appendix B

Total Influnces and Equilibrium

In this appendix, we address two features of our model of the social influence process in a group:

$$\mathbf{y}^{(t+1)} = \mathbf{A}\mathbf{W}\mathbf{y}^{(t)} + (\mathbf{I} - \mathbf{A})\mathbf{y}^{(1)}, \quad t = 1, 2, \dots, \tag{B.1}$$

where $\sum_{k=1}^{n} w_{ik} = 1$ for all $i = 1, 2, \dots, n$, $0 \leq w_{ij} \leq 1$ for all i and j, $\mathbf{y}^{(t)}$ is the $n \times 1$ vector of attitudes at time $t = 1, 2, \dots$, and $\mathbf{A} = \mathrm{diag}(a_{11}, a_{22}, \dots, a_{nn})$ is a diagonal matrix in which a_{ii} is person i's susceptibility to interpersonal influence. Here we deal with the case of a fixed $\mathbf{A}$ and $\mathbf{W}$ that may or may not be coupled by $a_{ii} = 1 - w_{ii}$ for all i. First, we show that at each of the time points $t = 1, 2, \dots$ there exists a matrix $\mathbf{V}^{(t)} = [v_{ij}^{(t)}]$ that transforms the initial attitudes into the attitudes at time $t + 1$. Second, we describe the conditions under which the influence process of this model attains an equilibrium.

B.1 Total Influences

In this section, we run out the process given by (B.1) to obtain the attitudes that are formed at each point in time, and show that at each of these time points there exists a matrix $\mathbf{V}^{(t)} = [v_{ij}^{(t)}]$ that transforms the initial attitudes into the attitudes at time $t + 1$. Subtracting the two sides of (B.1) for t from the corresponding sides of this equation for $t + 1$ yields

$$\mathbf{y}^{(t+1)} - \mathbf{y}^{(t)} = \mathbf{A}\mathbf{W}(\mathbf{y}^{(t)} - \mathbf{y}^{(t-1)}), \quad t = 2, 3, \dots. \tag{B.2}$$

Repeatedly back-substituting the left side of (B.2) into its right side, for decreasing values of t, produces

$$\mathbf{y}^{(t+1)} - \mathbf{y}^{(t)} = (\mathbf{A}\mathbf{W})^{t-1}(\mathbf{y}^{(2)} - \mathbf{y}^{(1)}), \quad t = 1, 2, \dots, \tag{B.3}$$

318

where $(\mathbf{AW})^0 \equiv \mathbf{I}$. Since (B.1) with $t = 1$ yields

$$\mathbf{y}^{(2)} - \mathbf{y}^{(1)} = (\mathbf{AW} - \mathbf{A})\mathbf{y}^{(1)}, \tag{B.4}$$

(B.3) then becomes

$$\mathbf{y}^{(t+1)} - \mathbf{y}^{(t)} = (\mathbf{AW})^{t-1}(\mathbf{AW} - \mathbf{A})\mathbf{y}^{(1)}, \quad t = 1, 2, \ldots. \tag{B.5}$$

Summing the corresponding sides of (B.5) for the time index values $1, 2, \ldots, t$, we obtain

$$
\begin{aligned}
\mathbf{y}^{(t+1)} - \mathbf{y}^{(1)} &= \left\{ \sum_{k=0}^{t-1} (\mathbf{AW})^k \right\} (\mathbf{AW} - \mathbf{A})\mathbf{y}^{(1)} \\
&= \left\{ \sum_{k=1}^{t} (\mathbf{AW})^k - \sum_{k=0}^{t-1} (\mathbf{AW})^k \mathbf{A} \right\} \mathbf{y}^{(1)}, \quad t = 1, 2, \ldots, \tag{B.6}
\end{aligned}
$$

from which we obtain, since $\mathbf{y}^{(1)} = (\mathbf{AW})^0 \mathbf{y}^{(1)}$,

$$\mathbf{y}^{(t+1)} = \left[\sum_{k=0}^{t} (\mathbf{AW})^k - \left\{ \sum_{k=0}^{t-1} (\mathbf{AW})^k \right\} \mathbf{A} \right] \mathbf{y}^{(1)}, \quad t = 1, 2, \ldots. \tag{B.7}$$

Letting $\mathbf{V}^{(t)} = \sum_{k=0}^{t} (\mathbf{AW})^k - \{\sum_{k=0}^{t-1} (\mathbf{AW})^k\}\mathbf{A}$, we have

$$\mathbf{V}^{(t)} = (\mathbf{AW})^t + \sum_{k=0}^{t-1} (\mathbf{AW})^k (\mathbf{I} - \mathbf{A}), \quad t = 1, 2, \ldots, \tag{B.8}$$

where $\sum_{k=0}^{0} (\mathbf{AW})^k = (\mathbf{AW})^0 = \mathbf{I}$, so we have

$$\mathbf{y}^{(t+1)} = \mathbf{V}^{(t)}\mathbf{y}^{(1)}, \quad t = 1, 2, \ldots. \tag{B.9}$$

The matrix $\mathbf{V}^{(t)}$ captures the flows of interpersonal influence occurring in the group that have transformed $\mathbf{y}^{(1)}$ into $\mathbf{y}^{(t+1)}$. Thus, by (B.9) and (B.8), for $t = 1, 2, 3, \ldots$, we have

$$
\begin{aligned}
\mathbf{y}^{(2)} &= \mathbf{V}^{(1)}\mathbf{y}^{(1)} = [\mathbf{AW} + (\mathbf{I} - \mathbf{A})]\mathbf{y}^{(1)}, \\
\mathbf{y}^{(3)} &= \mathbf{V}^{(2)}\mathbf{y}^{(1)} = [(\mathbf{AW})^2 + (\mathbf{AW} + \mathbf{I})(\mathbf{I} - \mathbf{A})]\mathbf{y}^{(1)},
\end{aligned}
$$

and

$$\mathbf{y}^{(4)} = \mathbf{V}^{(3)}\mathbf{y}^{(1)} = [(\mathbf{AW})^3 + \{(\mathbf{AW})^2 + \mathbf{AW} + \mathbf{I}\}(\mathbf{I} - \mathbf{A})]\mathbf{y}^{(1)},$$

etc. The question now arises as to whether the influence process described by (B.1) attains an equilibrium.

B.2 Conditions of Equilibrium

If the influence process (B.1) reaches an equilibrium, i.e., the sequence $\{y^{(t)}; t = 1, 2, \ldots\}$ converges, then, from (B.9), it is given by the limit

$$y^{(\infty)} \equiv \lim_{t\to\infty} y^{(t+1)} = \lim_{t\to\infty} \left(V^{(t)} y^{(1)} \right). \tag{B.10}$$

If $V^{(\infty)} \equiv \lim_{t\to\infty} V^{(t)}$ exists then, since $y^{(1)}$ is constant, $\lim_{t\to\infty}(V^{(t)} y^{(1)}) = (\lim_{t\to\infty} V^{(t)}) y^{(1)}$, whence $y^{(\infty)}$ also exists and

$$y^{(\infty)} = V^{(\infty)} y^{(1)}. \tag{B.11}$$

However, by the following example, we can see that if $y^{(\infty)}$ exists it need not be true that $V^{(\infty)}$ exists.

Consider a group with $n = 4$, $A = \text{diag}(1, 1, 0.5, 0)$, $I - A = \text{diag}(0, 0, 0.5, 1)$,

$$W = \begin{bmatrix} 0 & 1 & 0 & 0 \\ 1 & 0 & 0 & 0 \\ 0.5 & 0 & 0 & 0.5 \\ 0 & 0.5 & 0 & 0.5 \end{bmatrix}, \quad AW = \begin{bmatrix} 0 & 1 & 0 & 0 \\ 1 & 0 & 0 & 0 \\ 0.25 & 0 & 0 & 0.25 \\ 0 & 0 & 0 & 0 \end{bmatrix},$$

$$\text{and} \quad y^{(1)} = \begin{bmatrix} 8 \\ 8 \\ 0 \\ 24 \end{bmatrix}.$$

In this group

$$y^{(2)} = y^{(3)} = \cdots = y^{(\infty)} = \begin{bmatrix} 8 \\ 8 \\ 8 \\ 24 \end{bmatrix},$$

but since

$$V^{(t)} = \begin{bmatrix} 0 & 1 & 0 & 0 \\ 1 & 0 & 0 & 0 \\ 0.25 & 0 & 0.5 & 0.25 \\ 0 & 0 & 0 & 1 \end{bmatrix}, \quad t \geq 1 \text{ odd,}$$

and

$$V^{(t)} = \begin{bmatrix} 1 & 0 & 0 & 0 \\ 0 & 1 & 0 & 0 \\ 0 & 0.25 & 0.5 & 0.25 \\ 0 & 0 & 0 & 1 \end{bmatrix}, \quad t \geq 2 \text{ even,}$$

$\{V^{(t)}; t = 1, 2, \ldots\}$ does not converge, so $V^{(\infty)}$ does not exist. We note that here the convergence of $\{y^{(t)}; t = 1, 2, \ldots\}$ depends on the fact that persons 1 and 2 have a common attitude in the initial attitude vector. If this were not so, this sequence would not converge. Thus, the convergence of the sequence here depends on the structure of $\mathbf{y}^{(1)}$. If we require that the sequence $\{\mathbf{y}^{(t)}; t = 1, 2, \ldots\}$ converge independent of $\mathbf{y}^{(1)}$, i.e., for every possible $\mathbf{y}^{(1)}$, then we can show that the sequence $\{\mathbf{V}^{(t)}; t = 1, 2, \ldots\}$ also converges. The converse was already shown above.

LEMMA B.1. *If the sequence* $\{\mathbf{y}^{(t)}; t = 1, 2, \ldots\}$ *for the influence process* (B.1) *converges for every possible initial attitude vector* $\mathbf{y}^{(1)}$, *then the sequence* $\{\mathbf{V}^{(t)}; t = 1, 2, \ldots\}$ *converges also.*

Proof. Assume $\lim_{t\to\infty} \mathbf{y}^{(t+1)} = \lim_{t\to\infty}(\mathbf{V}^{(t)}\mathbf{y}^{(1)})$ exists for every initial attitude vector $\mathbf{y}^{(1)}$. Then this limit exists for the particular choices $\mathbf{I}^{(1)} = [1 \ 0 \ 0 \ \cdots \ 0]^{\mathrm{T}}$, $\mathbf{I}^{(2)} = [0 \ 1 \ 0 \ \cdots \ 0]^{\mathrm{T}}, \ldots,$ $\mathbf{I}^{(n)} = [0 \ 0 \ 0 \ \cdots \ 1]^{\mathrm{T}}$. Here $\mathbf{V}^{(t)}\mathbf{I}^{(k)}$ is $\mathbf{V}_k^{(t)}$, the kth column of $\mathbf{V}^{(t)}$; hence, the sequence $\{\mathbf{V}_k^{(t)}; t = 1, 2, \ldots\}$ converges to a column vector $\mathbf{V}_k^{(\infty)} = \lim_{t\to\infty}(\mathbf{V}^{(t)}\mathbf{I}^{(k)})$ for every k, $1 \le k \le n$. Arranging these column vectors in order from left to right, we obtain that

$$\left[\mathbf{V}_1^{(\infty)}, \mathbf{V}_2^{(\infty)}, \ldots, \mathbf{V}_n^{(\infty)}\right] = \left[\lim_{t\to\infty}\mathbf{V}^{(t)}\mathbf{I}^{(1)}, \lim_{t\to\infty}\mathbf{V}^{(t)}\mathbf{I}^{(2)}, \ldots, \lim_{t\to\infty}\mathbf{V}^{(t)}\mathbf{I}^{(n)}\right]$$
$$= \lim_{t\to\infty}\left[\mathbf{V}^{(t)}\mathbf{I}^{(1)}, \mathbf{V}^{(t)}\mathbf{I}^{(2)}, \ldots, \mathbf{V}^{(t)}\mathbf{I}^{(n)}\right]$$
$$= \lim_{t\to\infty}\left[\mathbf{V}^{(t)}\mathbf{I}\right] = \lim_{t\to\infty}\mathbf{V}^{(t)}$$

exists. ∎

Now, in approaching the analysis of an influence process in a group, we generally do not have a priori knowledge of, nor control over, the initial attitudes of the group's members on a particular issue. In most cases, under such circumstances, we will not want the results of our analysis to depend on the accident of particular initial attitudes. Thus, henceforth, we shall assume that convergence of the process (B.1) means that convergence occurs for any initial attitude vector $\mathbf{y}^{(1)}$. This shifts the issue of the convergence of the sequence $\{\mathbf{y}^{(t)}; t = 1, 2, \ldots\}$ to that of the sequence $\{\mathbf{V}^{(t)}; t = 1, 2, \ldots\}$.

By (B.8), if both $\{(\mathbf{AW})^t; t = 1, 2, \ldots\}$ and $\sum_{k=0}^{t-1}(\mathbf{AW})^k(\mathbf{I} - \mathbf{A}); t = 1, 2, \ldots\}$ converge, then so does the sequence $\{\mathbf{V}^{(t)}; t = 1, 2, \ldots\}$. Now $\{\sum_{k=0}^{t-1}(\mathbf{AW})^k(\mathbf{I} - \mathbf{A}); t = 1, 2, \ldots\}$ is a sequence of sums of nonnegative matrices where, by equation (B.8), each matrix sum entry for index value t is bounded above by the corresponding matrix entry in the stochastic matrix $\mathbf{V}^{(t)}$ which, in turn, is bounded above by 1. Since each matrix entry sequence in $\{\sum_{k=0}^{t-1}(\mathbf{AW})^k(\mathbf{I} - \mathbf{A}); t = 1, 2, \ldots\}$ is nondecreasing and bounded above by 1, it converges; hence $\{\sum_{k=0}^{t-1}(\mathbf{AW})^k(\mathbf{I} - \mathbf{A}); t = 1, 2, \ldots\}$ converges. Thus, the convergence of $\{\mathbf{V}^{(t)}; t = 1, 2, \ldots\}$ depends completely on the convergence of $\{(\mathbf{AW})^t; t = 1, 2, \ldots\}$ and we now have

LEMMA B.2. *The sequence* $\{\mathbf{V}^{(t)}; t = 1, 2, \ldots\}$ *converges if and only if the sequence* $\{(\mathbf{AW})^t; t = 1, 2, \ldots\}$ *converges.*

We continue along this line, first for the very useful special case where $\{(\mathbf{AW})^t; t = 1, 2, \ldots\}$ converges to 0. Now $\mathbf{AW}$ is a nonnegative matrix with all its row sums less than or equal to 1. Because every nonnegative matrix of order n is the limit of some sequence of irreducible nonnegative matrices of order n, $\mathbf{AW}$ has a real nonnegative eigenvalue λ_M that has the maximum absolute value among all its eigenvalues and, since $\mathbf{AW}$ is substochastic, $\lambda_M \leq 1$ (Gantmacher, p. 68, *Note* before Subsection 2).

THEOREM B.3. *The following are equivalent conditions:*

(a) $\{(\mathbf{AW})^t; t = 1, 2, \ldots\}$ converges to 0,
(b) $\{\sum_{k=0}^{t-1} (\mathbf{AW})^k; t = 1, 2, \ldots\}$ converges,
(c) $\mathbf{I} - \mathbf{AW}$ is nonsingular,
(d) $\lambda_M < 1$.

Further, when any of these conditions hold we have $\sum_{k=0}^{\infty} (\mathbf{AW})^k = (\mathbf{I} - \mathbf{AW})^{-1}$, *whence* $\mathbf{V}^{(\infty)} = (\mathbf{I} - \mathbf{AW})^{-1}(\mathbf{I} - \mathbf{A})$.

Proof. Suppose we have (b). Since the sum in (b) must converge entry by entry in the resulting matrix, the term from $(\mathbf{AW})^t$ in each entry must converge to 0, which means that $\{(\mathbf{AW})^t; t = 1, 2, \ldots\}$ converges to 0, and we have (a). Now assume (a). Since λ_M^t is an eigenvalue of $(\mathbf{AW})^t$, this implies that $\{\lambda_M^t; t = 1, 2, \ldots\}$ converges to 0, which means that $\lambda_M < 1$, and we have (d). Now assume (d). Then $\mathbf{I} - \mathbf{AW} = 1 \cdot \mathbf{I} - \mathbf{AW}$ is nonsingular and we have (c). Finally, suppose we have (c). Since $\lambda_M \leq 1$ and $\lambda_M \neq 1$, we have $\lambda_M < 1$. Then $\{\lambda_M^t; t = 1, 2, \ldots\}$ converges to 0, whence $\{\lambda_k^t; t = 1, 2, \ldots\}$ converges to 0 for every eigenvalue λ_k of $\mathbf{AW}$. Now by the Hamilton–Cayley Theorem for a positive integer q, $(\mathbf{AW})^q$, of order n, satisfies its characteristic equation

$$0 = \det(\lambda \mathbf{I} - (\mathbf{AW})^q) = \prod_{k=1}^{n} (\lambda - \lambda_k^q), \tag{B.12}$$

which, in matrices, becomes

$$0 = \prod_{k=1}^{n} ((\mathbf{AW})^q - \lambda_k^q \mathbf{I}) \tag{B.13}$$

$$= (\mathbf{AW})^{qn} - \left(\sum_{i_1=1}^{n} \lambda_{i_1}^q\right)(\mathbf{AW})^{q(n-1)} + \left(\sum_{\forall i_1 < i_2} \lambda_{i_1}^q \lambda_{i_2}^q\right)(\mathbf{AW})^{q(n-2)} - \cdots$$

$$+ (-1)^k \left(\sum_{\forall i_1 < i_2 < \cdots < i_k} \lambda_{i_1}^q \lambda_{i_2}^q \cdots \lambda_{i_k}^q\right)(\mathbf{AW})^{q(n-k)} + \cdots + (-1)^n \left(\prod_{j=1}^{n} \lambda_j^q\right)\mathbf{I}.$$

Now, for any ε, $0 < \varepsilon < 1$, there exists an integer $s > 0$ such that for all $q > s$, $|\lambda_i^q| < \varepsilon \cdot 2^{-n}$, and for all i, $1 \leq i \leq n$, and for the $n \times n$ all-ones matrix $\mathbf{J}$, we have $(\mathbf{AW})^p \leq \mathbf{J}$ for all integers $p \geq 0$ (note that $(\mathbf{AW})^0 = \mathbf{I}$). Thus,

$$|(\mathbf{AW})^{nq} - \mathbf{0}| \leq \left| \sum_{i_1=1}^{n} \lambda_{i_1}^q \right| (\mathbf{AW})^{nq-q} + \left| \sum_{\forall i_1 < i_2} \lambda_{i_1}^q \lambda_{i_2}^q \right| (\mathbf{AW})^{nq-2q} + \cdots$$

$$+ \left| \sum_{\forall i_1 < i_2 \cdots < i_k} \lambda_{i_1}^q \lambda_{i_2}^q \cdots \lambda_{i_k}^q \right| (\mathbf{AW})^{nq-kq} + \cdots + \left| \prod_{j=1}^{n} \lambda_j^q \right| \mathbf{I} \qquad \text{(B.14)}$$

$$< \{ n(\varepsilon \cdot 2^{-n}) + \binom{n}{2} (\varepsilon \cdot 2^{-n})^2 + \cdots$$

$$+ \binom{n}{k} (\varepsilon \cdot 2^{-n})^k + \cdots + \binom{n}{n-1} (\varepsilon \cdot 2^{-n})^{n-1} + (\varepsilon \cdot 2^{-n})^n \} \mathbf{J}$$

$$< (\varepsilon \cdot 2^{-n}) \{ 1 + n + \binom{n}{2} + \cdots + \binom{n}{k} + \cdots + n + 1 \} \mathbf{J}$$

$$= (\varepsilon \cdot 2^{-n}) \cdot 2^n \mathbf{J} = \varepsilon \cdot \mathbf{J}.$$

Now, every integer $k \geq n$ can be expressed as $k = nq + r$, for integer r, $0 \leq r < n$. Since $(\mathbf{AW})^r \mathbf{J} \leq \mathbf{J}$ for all such values of r, (B.14) implies that

$$(\mathbf{AW})^{qn+r} = (\mathbf{AW})^r (\mathbf{AW})^{nq} \leq (\mathbf{AW})^r \cdot \varepsilon \mathbf{J} = \varepsilon (\mathbf{AW})^r \mathbf{J} \leq \varepsilon \mathbf{J}$$

for every $q > s$ and every integer r, $0 \leq r < n$. Thus $\{(\mathbf{AW})^k; k = 1, 2, \ldots\}$ converges to 0. Now

$$(\mathbf{I} - \mathbf{AW}) \left(\sum_{k=0}^{t-1} (\mathbf{AW})^k \right) = \mathbf{I} - (\mathbf{AW})^t, \qquad \text{(B.15)}$$

and, since $\mathbf{I} - \mathbf{AW}$ is nonsingular, by (B.15) we have

$$\sum_{k=0}^{t-1} (\mathbf{AW})^k = (\mathbf{I} - \mathbf{AW})^{-1} - (\mathbf{I} - \mathbf{AW})^{-1} (\mathbf{AW})^t. \qquad \text{(B.16)}$$

Thus $\{ \sum_{k=0}^{t-1} (\mathbf{AW})^k; t = 1, 2, \ldots \}$ converges to $(\mathbf{I} - \mathbf{AW})^{-1}$, and we have (b). Under any of the conditions (a), (b), (c), or (d), and taking the limit on both sides of (B.8) as $t \to \infty$, we have $\mathbf{V}^{(\infty)} = (\mathbf{I} - \mathbf{AW})^{-1}(\mathbf{I} - \mathbf{A})$, which completes the proof. ∎

We now turn to the more general case in which $\mathbf{V}^{(\infty)}$ exists under conditions that may or may not be covered by Theorem B.3. This general case depends on the convergence of the sequence $\{(\mathbf{AW})^t; t = 1, 2, \ldots\}$ to a matrix that may or may not be 0.

THEOREM B.4. *(Oldenburger 1940). The infinite power of a complex matrix* H *exists if and only if the eigenvalues of* H *corresponding to elementary divisors of degree greater than 1 (taken with respect to the complex field) are in absolute value less than 1 and the remaining eigenvalues (with elementary divisors of degree 1) are equal to 1 or in absolute value less than 1.*

Thus H^∞ exists if and only if the following all hold:

(i) no eigenvalue λ of H satisfies $|\lambda| > 1$,
(ii) no eigenvalue λ of H satisfies $|\lambda| = 1$ with $\lambda \neq 1$, and
(iii) no eigenvalue $\lambda = 1$ of H corresponds to an elementary divisor of degree > 1.

We note that no restriction is attached to any eigenvalue λ of H for which $|\lambda| < 1$.

If we apply these criteria to $H = AW$ we find that criteria (i) and (iii) are automatically satisfied, as follows. As an $n \times n$ complex matrix, $H = AW$ can be represented in its Jordan canonical form as $P^{-1}HP = \widehat{J}$, for some complex nonsingular $n \times n$ matrix P,

$$\widehat{J} = \begin{bmatrix} \widehat{J}_1 & 0 & \cdots & 0 \\ 0 & \widehat{J}_2 & \cdots & 0 \\ \vdots & \vdots & \ddots & \vdots \\ 0 & 0 & \cdots & \widehat{J}_m \end{bmatrix}, \tag{B.17}$$

where each square submatrix $\widehat{J}_k$ corresponds to an eigenvalue λ_k of H and is of the form

$$\widehat{J}_k = \begin{bmatrix} \lambda_k & 1 & 0 & \cdots & 0 \\ 0 & \lambda_k & 1 & \cdots & 0 \\ 0 & 0 & \lambda_k & \ddots & 0 \\ \vdots & \vdots & \vdots & \ddots & 1 \\ 0 & 0 & 0 & \cdots & \lambda_k \end{bmatrix} \tag{B.18}$$

of size $r_k \times r_k$, where $r_k \geq 1$, $1 \leq k \leq m$ (this is an alternative, but equivalent, block form to that in Oldenburger 1940). Now $\widehat{J}^t = (P^{-1}HP)^t = P^{-1}H^tP$, so that $\{H^t; t = 1, 2, \ldots\}$ converges if and only if $\{\widehat{J}^t; t = 1, 2, \ldots\}$

converges, if and only if $\{\widehat{\mathbf{J}}_k^t; t = 1, 2, \ldots\}$ converges for each k, $1 \leq k \leq m$. Now, we have $\widehat{\mathbf{J}}_k^t = [\lambda_k^t]$ for $r_k = 1$, and

$$
\widehat{\mathbf{J}}_k^t =
\begin{bmatrix}
\lambda_k^t & c_1\lambda_k^{t-1} & c_2\lambda_k^{t-2} & c_3\lambda_k^{t-3} & \cdots & c_{r_k-1}\lambda_k^{t-r_k+1} \\
0 & \lambda_k^t & c_1\lambda_k^{t-1} & c_2\lambda_k^{t-2} & \cdots & c_{r_k-2}\lambda_k^{t-r_k+2} \\
0 & 0 & \lambda_k^t & c_1\lambda_k^{t-1} & \ddots & \vdots \\
0 & 0 & 0 & \lambda_k^t & \ddots & c_2\lambda_k^{t-2} \\
\vdots & \vdots & \vdots & \vdots & \ddots & c_1\lambda_k^{t-1} \\
0 & 0 & 0 & 0 & \cdots & \lambda_k^t
\end{bmatrix}
\tag{B.19}
$$

for $r_k > 1$ and $t \geq r_k - 1$, where $c_i = C(t, i)$, the binomial coefficient, is positive.

Here, $\{\widehat{\mathbf{J}}_k^t; t = 1, 2, \ldots\}$ converges if and only if $\lim_{t\to\infty}\lambda_k^t$ exists and $\lim_{t\to\infty} c_i\lambda_k^{t-i}$ exists for all i, $1 \leq i \leq r_k - 1$. This requires that $|\lambda_k| \leq 1$ for each k, $1 \leq k \leq m$, which is satisfied for $\mathbf{H} = \mathbf{AW}$. Thus, criterion (i) is automatically satisfied here. Next, if $\lambda_k = 1$ and $r_k \geq 2$, then, for $1 \leq i \leq r_k - 1$, $\lim_{t\to\infty} c_i\lambda_k^{t-i} = \lim_{t\to\infty} \frac{t(t-1)\cdots(t-i+1)}{i!} = \infty$, so all entries above the main diagonal of $\widehat{\mathbf{J}}_k^t$ diverge to infinity. However, since $(\mathbf{AW})^t \leq \mathbf{J}$ for all $t = 1, 2, \ldots$, no entries in $(\mathbf{AW})^t$ diverge to infinity as $t \to \infty$, and since the entries in $\mathbf{P}$ and $\mathbf{P}^{-1}$ are fixed, no entries in any power t of a Jordan block of $\widehat{\mathbf{J}}$ can diverge to infinity as $t \to \infty$. Hence, in any $\mathbf{H} = \mathbf{AW}$ for our model, the elementary divisors corresponding to eigenvalue 1 must all have degree 1. Thus, for each $r_k \geq 2$, $\lambda_M = \lambda_k = 1$ is eliminated. Thus criterion (iii) is automatically satisfied for $\mathbf{H} = \mathbf{AW}$. Furthermore, all other eigenvalues λ corresponding to elementary divisors of degree 1 must satisfy $|\lambda| < 1$. For $|\lambda_k| < 1$ in (B.19), we see that $\lim_{t\to\infty}\lambda_k^t = 0$ and, applying a variant of L'Hôpital's Rule, we find that $\lim_{t\to\infty} c_i\lambda_k^{t-i} = 0$ for each i, $1 \leq i \leq r_k - 1$. Thus, if every eigenvalue λ_k of $\mathbf{H}$ satisfies $|\lambda_k| < 1$, then $\mathbf{H}^\infty = \mathbf{0}$, and conversely, which shows again the equivalence of (a) and (d) in Theorem B.3.

Since $\mathbf{H} = \mathbf{AW}$ is a real matrix, if $\lim_{t\to\infty} \mathbf{H}^t = \mathbf{H}^\infty$ exists, then $\mathbf{H}^\infty$ is real and, to within a permutation of the rows and corresponding permutation of the columns, the Jordan canonical form for $\mathbf{H}^\infty$ is

$$
\mathbf{P}^{-1}\mathbf{H}^\infty\mathbf{P} = \begin{bmatrix} \mathbf{I}_\mu & \mathbf{0} \\ \mathbf{0} & \mathbf{0} \end{bmatrix},
\tag{B.20}
$$

where $\mathbf{I}_\mu$ is the $\mu \times \mu$ identity matrix, and μ is the multiplicity of the eigenvalue 1 for $\mathbf{H}$. Thus, we have

COROLLARY B.5. $\{(\mathbf{AW})^t; t = 1, 2, \ldots\}$ *converges, and hence* $\{\mathbf{V}^{(t)}; t = 1, 2, \ldots\}$ *converges, if and only if the eigenvalues* λ *of* $\mathbf{AW}$ *for which* $|\lambda| = 1$ *are all* $\lambda = \lambda_M = 1$. *Here, if* μ *is the multiplicity of the eigenvalue*

1 for AW, then $\{(\mathbf{AW})^t; t = 1, 2, \ldots\}$ converges, to within a permutation of the rows and corresponding permutation of the columns of its Jordan canonical form, to

$$(\mathbf{AW})^{\infty} = \mathbf{P}\begin{bmatrix} \mathbf{I}_{\mu} & \mathbf{0} \\ \mathbf{0} & \mathbf{0} \end{bmatrix}\mathbf{P}^{-1},$$

where the first μ diagonal blocks of the form are 1×1 and equal to [1].

By Lemma B.2, Corollary B.5 provides an exact criterion for the existence of $\mathbf{V}^{(\infty)}$. To illustrate this, we continue the discussion of the example presented earlier in this section. Here, for

$$\mathbf{AW} = \begin{bmatrix} 0 & 1 & 0 & 0 \\ 1 & 0 & 0 & 0 \\ 0.25 & 0 & 0 & 0.25 \\ 0 & 0 & 0 & 0 \end{bmatrix}$$

we have $\det(\lambda\mathbf{I} - \mathbf{AW}) = \lambda^2(\lambda - 1)(\lambda + 1)$, so that the complete set of eigenvalues for $\mathbf{AW}$ is $\{0, 0, 1, -1\}$, which includes an eigenvalue λ for which $|\lambda| = 1$ but $\lambda = -1 \neq 1$. Here $\{(\mathbf{AW})^t; t = 1, 2, \ldots\}$ does not converge and thus $\mathbf{V}^{(\infty)} = \lim_{t\to\infty} \mathbf{V}^{(t)}$ does not exist.

Having determined, on the basis of Corollary B.5, that $\mathbf{V}^{(\infty)}$ exists, one is still faced with the potentially nontrivial problem of accurately obtaining $\mathbf{V}^{(\infty)}$ numerically, which is related to the value of $D = \det(\mathbf{I} - \mathbf{AW})$. When $D \neq 0$ and D is not close to 0, $\mathbf{I} - \mathbf{AW}$ is clearly nonsingular, and $\mathbf{V}^{(\infty)}$ can be accurately determined by $\mathbf{V}^{(\infty)} = (\mathbf{I} - \mathbf{AW})^{-1}(\mathbf{I} - \mathbf{A})$. If $D \neq 0$ but D is close to 0 ($\mathbf{I} - \mathbf{AW}$ is nearly singular), the determination of $\mathbf{V}^{(\infty)}$ by $\mathbf{V}^{(\infty)} = (\mathbf{I} - \mathbf{AW})^{-1}(\mathbf{I} - \mathbf{A})$ may be subject to unacceptable errors because the computed entry values in $(\mathbf{I} - \mathbf{AW})^{-1}$ are highly sensitive to very small changes in the entry values of $\mathbf{A}$ and $\mathbf{W}$, such as measurement and round-off errors; i.e., $\mathbf{I} - \mathbf{AW}$ is ill-conditioned. One rule of thumb here is that ill-conditioning should be suspected when any entries in the computed $(\mathbf{I} - \mathbf{AW})^{-1}$ are much larger than 1.0 (Maron 1982; 154). Another is that ill-conditioning may be present when the magnitude of $\det(\mathbf{I} - \mathbf{AW})$ is small compared to the magnitudes of the entries of $\mathbf{I} - \mathbf{AW}$ (Maron 1982; 155). Finally, when $D = 0$ we need to find an efficient computational algorithm that produces $\mathbf{V}^{(\infty)} = \mathbf{V}^{(t^*)}$ accurately for a sufficiently large value $t = t^*$. Approaching this directly, we see that we can compute the sequence $\mathbf{V}^{(1)}, \mathbf{V}^{(2)}, \mathbf{V}^{(3)}, \ldots$ by specifying the starting matrix

$$\mathbf{V}^{(1)} = \mathbf{AW} + (\mathbf{I} - \mathbf{A}) \tag{B.21a}$$

and then recursively applying the formula

$$\mathbf{V}^{(t+1)} = \mathbf{AW}\mathbf{V}^{(t)} + (\mathbf{I} - \mathbf{A}); \qquad t = 1, 2, \ldots \tag{B.21b}$$

until we reach a $V^{(t^*)}$ for which there is essentially no change in successive values of t, i.e., $V^{(t^*+1)} = V^{(t^*)}$, to within, say, $10^{-5} = 0.00001$ for each matrix entry.

When a numerical approach using equations (B.21a) and (B.21b) is the only option, it may present nontrivial concerns when applied to very large groups. For small-scale groups, $V^{(\infty)}$ is usually ascertained, as above, by assessing whether the values obtained from equations (B.21a) and (B.21b) settle down as t increases. For the $V^{(\infty)}$ matrices computed for this book, none of the difficulties discussed here were encountered.

Appendix C

Formal Analysis of Dyadic Influence Systems

For $n = 2$, the vector–matrix equation for our standard model of the social influence process in a group is

$$\mathbf{y}^{(t+1)} = \mathbf{A}\mathbf{W}\mathbf{y}^{(t)} + (\mathbf{I} - \mathbf{A})\mathbf{y}^{(1)} \tag{C.1}$$

or, assuming coupling $a_{ii} = 1 - w_{ii}$ for $i = 1, i = 2$,

$$
\begin{bmatrix} y_1^{(t+1)} \\ y_2^{(t+1)} \end{bmatrix} =
\begin{bmatrix} a_{11} & 0 \\ 0 & a_{22} \end{bmatrix}
\begin{bmatrix} w_{11} & 1 - w_{11} \\ 1 - w_{22} & w_{22} \end{bmatrix}
\begin{bmatrix} y_1^{(t)} \\ y_2^{(t)} \end{bmatrix}
$$
$$
+ \begin{bmatrix} 1 - a_{11} & 0 \\ 0 & 1 - a_{22} \end{bmatrix}
\begin{bmatrix} y_1^{(1)} \\ y_2^{(1)} \end{bmatrix}
$$
$$
= \begin{bmatrix} a_{11}(1 - a_{11}) & a_{11}^2 \\ a_{22}^2 & a_{22}(1 - a_{22}) \end{bmatrix}
\begin{bmatrix} y_1^{(t)} \\ y_2^{(t)} \end{bmatrix}
\tag{C.2}
$$
$$
+ \begin{bmatrix} 1 - a_{11} & 0 \\ 0 & 1 - a_{22} \end{bmatrix}
\begin{bmatrix} y_1^{(1)} \\ y_2^{(1)} \end{bmatrix},
$$

which is equivalent to the pair of scalar equations

$$
\begin{aligned}
y_1^{(t+1)} &= a_{11}(1 - a_{11})\, y_1^{(t)} + a_{11}^2 y_2^{(t)} + (1 - a_{11})\, y_1^{(1)} \\
y_2^{(t+1)} &= a_{22}(1 - a_{22})\, y_2^{(t)} + a_{22}^2 y_1^{(t)} + (1 - a_{22})\, y_2^{(1)}
\end{aligned}
\tag{C.3}
$$

for $t = 1, 2, 3, \ldots$.

For a dyad in which there is an initial disagreement ($y_1^{(1)} \neq y_2^{(1)}$), it can be shown that the influence process will reach an *equilibrium*

$$
\begin{aligned}
\mathbf{y}^{(\infty)} &= \mathbf{A}\mathbf{W}\mathbf{y}^{(\infty)} + (\mathbf{I} - \mathbf{A})\,\mathbf{y}^{(1)} \\
&= \mathbf{V}\mathbf{y}^{(1)}
\end{aligned}
\tag{C.4}
$$

328

if and only if $A \neq I$. For $A \neq I$, the equilibrium equations are

$$y_1^{(\infty)} = a_{11} (1 - a_{11}) y_1^{(\infty)} + a_{11}^2 y_2^{(\infty)} + (1 - a_{11}) y_1^{(1)} \qquad \text{(C.5)}$$

$$y_2^{(\infty)} = a_{22} (1 - a_{22}) y_2^{(\infty)} + a_{22}^2 y_1^{(\infty)} + (1 - a_{22}) y_2^{(1)}$$

or alternatively, in terms of V,

$$y_1^{(\infty)} = v_{11} y_1^{(1)} + (1 - v_{11}) y_2^{(1)} \qquad \text{(C.6)}$$

$$y_2^{(\infty)} = (1 - v_{22}) y_1^{(1)} + v_{22} y_2^{(1)}.$$

Eq. (C.6) describes the relative weight of the two persons' initial attitudes in determining the equilibrium attitude of each person i.

C.1 Total Influences

Group members' total interpersonal influences, v_{ij}, are a consequence of the flows of influence that are generated by the sequence of attitude changes that arise from the influence process. We have shown that these total interpersonal influences are a function of AW. In this section, we analyze the relationship between the interpersonal influences in V and AW. This relationship is simplified in the case of dyads, where $a_{ii} = w_{ij}$, i.e., where group members' susceptibilities and interpersonal influences are confounded. Assuming equilibrium, either $\{a_{ii} = 1$ and $a_{jj} < 1\}$ or $\{a_{ii} < 1$ and $a_{jj} < 1\}$, because $\{a_{ii} = 1$ and $a_{jj} = 1\}$ is inconsistent with equilibrium. In the former circumstance, one member (j) attaches some weight to his or her own initial attitude whereas the other member (i) adopts whatever attitude the other holds. In the latter circumstance, both members attach some weight to their own initial attitudes. We will consider each of these situations and derive measures of direct and total interpersonal effects.

C.1.2 Special Case $a_{ii} = 1$ and $a_{jj} < 1$

If person 1 is completely susceptible ($a_{11} = 1$) and person 2 is not ($a_{22} < 1$), then Eq. (C.5) simplifies to

$$y_1^{(\infty)} = y_2^{(\infty)} \qquad \text{(C.7)}$$

$$y_2^{(\infty)} = y_2^{(1)}$$

and the total influence matrix is

$$V = \begin{bmatrix} 0 & 1 \\ 0 & 1 \end{bmatrix}.$$

Hence, a consensus is formed that is the initial attitude of person 2 *regardless* of the weight $w_{21} = a_{22} < 1$ that person 2 accords to person 1! The closer a_{22} is to 1, the longer the process takes to reach equilibrium.

C.2.2 Special Case $a_{ii} < 1$ and $a_{jj} < 1$

In this case, the total influence v_{ij} of person j on person i may be larger or smaller than the net direct influence $a_{ii}w_{ij} = a_{ii}^2$ of person j on person i. This, perhaps, is counterintuitive. Several examples illustrate the rank-order possibilities. An instance where one member's net direct interpersonal influence is less than the member's corresponding total influence and the other member's net direct interpersonal influence is greater than the member's corresponding total influence $(a_{11}w_{12} < v_{12}$ and $a_{22}w_{21} > v_{21})$ is

$$AW = \begin{bmatrix} 0.86 & 0 \\ 0 & 0.09 \end{bmatrix} \begin{bmatrix} 0.14 & 0.86 \\ 0.09 & 0.91 \end{bmatrix} = \begin{bmatrix} 0.120 & 0.740 \\ 0.008 & 0.082 \end{bmatrix}$$

$$\Rightarrow V = \begin{bmatrix} 0.160 & 0.840 \\ 0.001 & 0.999 \end{bmatrix}$$

for person 1. An instance where *both* net direct interpersonal influences are greater than the corresponding total influences $(a_{11}w_{12} > v_{12}$ and $a_{22}w_{21} > v_{21})$ is

$$AW = \begin{bmatrix} 0.95 & 0 \\ 0 & 0.87 \end{bmatrix} \begin{bmatrix} 0.05 & 0.95 \\ 0.87 & 0.13 \end{bmatrix} = \begin{bmatrix} 0.0475 & 0.9025 \\ 0.7569 & 0.1131 \end{bmatrix}$$

$$\Rightarrow V = \begin{bmatrix} 0.2743 & 0.7257 \\ 0.2341 & 0.7659 \end{bmatrix}.$$

An instance where *both* net direct interpersonal influences are less than the corresponding total influences $(a_{11}w_{12} < v_{12}$ and $a_{22}w_{21} < v_{21})$ is

$$AW = \begin{bmatrix} 0.49 & 0 \\ 0 & 0.49 \end{bmatrix} \begin{bmatrix} 0.51 & 0.49 \\ 0.49 & 0.51 \end{bmatrix} = \begin{bmatrix} 0.250 & 0.240 \\ 0.240 & 0.250 \end{bmatrix}$$

$$\Rightarrow V = \begin{bmatrix} 0.758 & 0.242 \\ 0.242 & 0.758 \end{bmatrix}.$$

Hence, any rank-order combination of direct and total influences is possible. In the last case (where $v_{12} - a_{11}w_{12} > 0$ and $v_{21} - a_{22}w_{21} > 0$), numerical analysis indicates that the differences are generally modest.

If neither person is completely susceptible $\{a_{11} < 1$ and $a_{22} < 1\}$, then the equilibrium is a disagreement between the two persons, $y_1^{(\infty)} \neq y_2^{(\infty)}$, which may be substantial or negligible. In this circumstance, since $y_1^{(\infty)} \neq y_2^{(\infty)}$ and $0 \leq a_{ii} < 1$,

$$\frac{a_{ii}^2}{1 - a_{ii}} = \frac{y_i^{(\infty)} - y_i^{(1)}}{y_j^{(\infty)} - y_i^{(\infty)}}. \tag{C.8}$$

Here, since $a_{ii} = w_{ij}$, the influence network in the dyad may be derived strictly in terms of the two members' initial and equilibrium attitudes. A similar result is obtained for the total influence matrix. With respect to total influences,

$$v_{ij} = \frac{y_i^{(\infty)} - y_i^{(1)}}{y_j^{(1)} - y_i^{(1)}} \tag{C.9}$$

for $y_i^{(1)} \neq y_j^{(1)}$. Thus, the total influence of j on i is the *ratio* of the change in i's attitude over the initial distance separating the attitudes of the two persons:

$$V = \begin{bmatrix} 1 - \dfrac{y_1^{(\infty)} - y_1^{(1)}}{y_2^{(1)} - y_1^{(1)}} & \dfrac{y_1^{(\infty)} - y_1^{(1)}}{y_2^{(1)} - y_1^{(1)}} \\[3mm] \dfrac{y_2^{(\infty)} - y_2^{(1)}}{y_1^{(1)} - y_2^{(1)}} & 1 - \dfrac{y_2^{(\infty)} - y_2^{(1)}}{y_1^{(1)} - y_2^{(1)}} \end{bmatrix}. \tag{C.10}$$

Furthermore,

$$y_i^{(\infty)} - y_i^{(1)} = v_{ij} \left(y_j^{(1)} - y_i^{(1)} \right). \tag{C.11}$$

Hence, the *change* in person i's attitude is a proportion of the discrepancy between person i's and person j's initial attitudes, and this proportion is equal to the *total* influence of person j upon person i.

Alternatively, since $\mathbf{I} - \mathbf{AW}$ is nonsingular,

$$V = [\mathbf{I} - \mathbf{AW}]^{-1} (\mathbf{I} - \mathbf{A}), \tag{C.12}$$

where

$$[\mathbf{I} - \mathbf{AW}]^{-1} = \begin{bmatrix} \dfrac{1 - a_{22}w_{22}}{D} & \dfrac{a_{11}w_{12}}{D} \\[3mm] \dfrac{a_{22}w_{21}}{D} & \dfrac{1 - a_{11}w_{11}}{D} \end{bmatrix} \tag{C.13}$$

and $D = (1 - a_{11}w_{11})(1 - a_{22}w_{22}) - (a_{11}w_{12})(a_{22}w_{21})$ is the determinant of $\mathbf{I} - \mathbf{AW}$. Hence,

$$v_{ij} = \frac{a_{ii}w_{ij}\left(1 - a_{jj}\right)}{\left(1 - a_{ii}w_{ii}\right)\left(1 - a_{jj}w_{jj}\right) - \left(a_{ii}w_{ij}\right)\left(a_{jj}w_{ji}\right)} \tag{C.14}$$

$$= \frac{a_{ii}^2\left(1 - a_{jj}\right)}{\left(1 - a_{ii} + a_{ii}^2\right)\left(1 - a_{jj} + a_{jj}^2\right) - \left(a_{ii}^2\right)\left(a_{jj}^2\right)}$$

for $\{a_{ii}, a_{jj}\}$, in which at most one susceptibility is equal to 1. From (C.9) and (C.14), when $0 < a_{11} < 1$ and $0 < a_{22} < 1$, we can express the ratio of the total interpersonal influences in a dyad in terms of the ratio of direct influences and attitude changes:

$$0 < \frac{v_{ij}}{v_{ji}} = \frac{y_i^{(\infty)} - y_i^{(1)}}{y_j^{(1)} - y_j^{(\infty)}} = \frac{a_{ii}w_{ij}\left(1 - a_{jj}\right)}{a_{jj}w_{ji}\left(1 - a_{ii}\right)} = \frac{a_{ii}^2\left(1 - a_{jj}\right)}{a_{jj}^2\left(1 - a_{ii}\right)}. \tag{C.15}$$

Hence, in a dyad, although there is no constraint on the rank order of $a_{ii}w_{ij}$ and v_{ij}, it is always the case that, in terms of their attitude changes, the person whose attitude changes *less* has the greater total influence of the two. It also can be shown that the total interpersonal influences in the dyad are always less than the corresponding relative interpersonal influences ($v_{ij} < w_{ij}$ and $v_{ji} < w_{ji}$).

In addition, from (C.14), it follows that

$$\frac{v_{ij}}{w_{ij}} > \frac{v_{ji}}{w_{ji}} \Leftrightarrow a_{ii} > a_{jj} \tag{C.16}$$

for $0 < a_{11} < 1$ and $0 < a_{22} < 1$, which implies that if person j is less susceptible than person i, then person j's interpersonal influence is less attenuated than that of person i as the influence process proceeds to equilibrium. Furthermore, it follows that

$$\frac{v_{ji}}{v_{ij}} < \frac{w_{ji}}{w_{ij}} \Leftrightarrow \frac{v_{ij}}{v_{ji}} > \frac{w_{ij}}{w_{ji}} \Leftrightarrow a_{ii} > a_{jj}; \tag{C.17}$$

i.e., the relative total influence of j on i (compared to i on j) is greater than the corresponding relative direct influence of j on i (compared to i on j) if and only if j is less susceptible than i.

C.2 Conditions of Consensus Formation

In this section, we analyze the conditions of consensus formation in the dyad. If a consensus is formed, then the columns of $\mathbf{V}$ are homogeneous, because

$$v_{11} = \frac{y_1^{(\infty)} - y_2^{(1)}}{y_1^{(1)} - y_2^{(1)}} = \frac{y_2^{(\infty)} - y_2^{(1)}}{y_1^{(1)} - y_2^{(1)}} = v_{21} \tag{C.18}$$

$$v_{22} = \frac{y_2^{(\infty)} - y_1^{(1)}}{y_2^{(1)} - y_1^{(1)}} = \frac{y_1^{(\infty)} - y_1^{(1)}}{y_2^{(1)} - y_1^{(1)}} = v_{12}.$$

Two possible patterns of homogeneity are

$$\mathbf{W}_1 = \begin{bmatrix} 1 - a_{11} & a_{11} \\ 1 & 0 \end{bmatrix} \Rightarrow \mathbf{V}_1 = \begin{bmatrix} 1 & 0 \\ 1 & 0 \end{bmatrix} \Rightarrow \mathbf{y}^{(\infty)} \begin{bmatrix} y_1^{(1)} \\ y_1^{(1)} \end{bmatrix}$$

for $0 \le a_{11} < 1$ and

$$\mathbf{W}_2 = \begin{bmatrix} 0 & 1 \\ a_{22} & 1 - a_{22} \end{bmatrix} \Rightarrow \mathbf{V}_2 = \begin{bmatrix} 0 & 1 \\ 0 & 1 \end{bmatrix} \Rightarrow \mathbf{y}^{(\infty)} = \begin{bmatrix} y_2^{(1)} \\ y_2^{(1)} \end{bmatrix}$$

for $0 \le a_{22} < 1$. The third pattern emerges for $\mathbf{A}$ that is very close to $\mathbf{I}$. For a_{11} and a_{22} that are both close to 1, the coordinates (a_{11}, a_{22}) and $(1, 1)$ in the plane determine a line passing through $(1, 1)$ with some slope γ, $0 < \gamma < \infty$, given by the linear equation $a_{22} = \gamma a_{11} + (1 - \gamma)$. For such values $\{a_{11}, a_{22}\}$, the corresponding direct influence matrix is

$$\mathbf{W}_3 = \begin{bmatrix} 1 - a_{11} & a_{11} \\ 1 - \gamma (1 - a_{11}) & \gamma (1 - a_{11}) \end{bmatrix}.$$

For this $\mathbf{W}_3$, the resulting $\mathbf{V}_3$ is

$$\mathbf{V}_3 \approx \begin{bmatrix} \dfrac{1}{1+\gamma} & \dfrac{\gamma}{1+\gamma} \\ \dfrac{1}{1+\gamma} & \dfrac{\gamma}{1+\gamma} \end{bmatrix} \Rightarrow \mathbf{y}^{(\infty)} \approx \begin{bmatrix} \dfrac{\left(y_1^{(1)} + \gamma y_2^{(1)}\right)}{1+\gamma} \\ \dfrac{\left(y_1^{(1)} + \gamma y_2^{(1)}\right)}{1+\gamma} \end{bmatrix}.$$

In the special case where $a_{11} = a_{22}$ and $\gamma = 1$, we have

$$\mathbf{V}_3 \approx \begin{bmatrix} 0.5 & 0.5 \\ 0.5 & 0.5 \end{bmatrix} \Rightarrow \mathbf{y}^{(\infty)} \approx \begin{bmatrix} \dfrac{\left(y_1^{(1)} + y_2^{(1)}\right)}{2} \\ \dfrac{\left(y_1^{(1)} + y_2^{(1)}\right)}{2} \end{bmatrix}. \tag{C.19}$$

In the first two cases, a consensus is reached on the initial position of person 1 and of person 2, respectively. In the third case, the consensus can only be approached, and the approach is to a weighted mean of the members' initial attitudes, as $\mathbf{A} \to \mathbf{I}$. When both members have supersusceptibilities, V_3 is *highly sensitive* to small differences between the susceptibilities, and *any* approximate stratification of influence and corresponding approximate consensus values are possible. For $a_{11} = 0.95$ and $a_{22} = 0.90$ ($\gamma = 0.5$), the effect is stratification, in which the initial attitude of person 2 is weighted approximately twice that of person 1,

$$V_3 = \begin{bmatrix} 0.335 & 0.665 \\ 0.298 & 0.702 \end{bmatrix}$$

but if $a_{11} = a_{22} = 0.95$, then

$$V_3 = \begin{bmatrix} 0.513 & 0.487 \\ 0.487 & 0.513 \end{bmatrix},$$

and the effect is a near equality that produces an approximate consensus near the mean of the members' initial attitudes.

Thus, in W_1, W_2, and W_3, consensus requires that at least one member be maximally, or near-maximally, susceptible to interpersonal influence. In the case of W_1 and W_2, the susceptibility of the more influential member may be at any level, short of the susceptibility of the other member, for consensus to be attained. Substantial disagreement may occur when neither member is maximally, or near-maximally, susceptible to influence.

Appendix D

Social Positions in Influence Networks

Two persons i and j are defined as *structurally equivalent* in the influence network if $a_{ii} = a_{jj}$ and $w_{ik} = w_{jk}$ for all $k \neq i, j$. Such persons are structurally equivalent in that their susceptibilities are the same and that they are subject to an identical set of relative interpersonal influences from all other members of the group, excluding themselves. We let the common value of susceptibility be $a_{ii} = a_{jj} = \alpha$ for two persons, i and j. Below we show that if two persons are structurally equivalent in the influence network then the difference between the attitudes of the two persons at time $t + 1$ is

$$y_i^{(t+1)} - y_j^{(t+1)} = \left[(1 - \alpha) \left(1 + \alpha\gamma + \alpha^2\gamma^2 + \cdots + \alpha^{t-1}\gamma^{t-1} \right) \right.$$
$$\left. + \alpha^t\gamma^t \right] \left(y_i^{(1)} - y_j^{(1)} \right) \tag{D.1}$$

for $t = 1, 2, \ldots$, where $\gamma = w_{ii} - w_{ji} = w_{jj} - w_{ij}$. Here $-1 \leq \alpha\gamma < 1$, because α and γ cannot both be 1 under the assumption that $a_{kk} = 1 - w_{kk}$ for $k = i, j$. When $\alpha\gamma = -1$ (so that $\alpha = 1$ and $\gamma = -1$) and $y_i^{(1)} \neq y_j^{(1)}$, there is no equilibrium, because persons i and j continually interchange their initial attitudes $(\alpha = 1, w_{ij} = w_{ji} = 1)$. Hence, our interest is focused on the case $-1 < \alpha\gamma < 1$, for which we show that

$$y_i^{(t+1)} - y_j^{(t+1)} = \left[\left(\frac{1 - \alpha}{1 - \alpha\gamma} \right) + \left(1 - \frac{1 - \alpha}{1 - \alpha\gamma} \right) (\alpha\gamma)^t \right] \left(y_i^{(1)} - y_j^{(1)} \right) \tag{D.2}$$

for $t = 1, 2, \ldots$. and

$$y_i^{(\infty)} - y_j^{(\infty)} = \left(\frac{1 - \alpha}{1 - \alpha\gamma} \right) \left(y_i^{(1)} - y_j^{(1)} \right) \tag{D.3}$$

for $t \to \infty$. Clearly, for a structurally equivalent i and j, an initial agreement $y_i^{(1)} - y_j^{(1)} = 0$ implies their agreement at every stage of the process. We now establish (D.1).

335

LEMMA D.1. *If two persons i and j are structurally equivalent in an influence network* $(\mathbf{A}, \mathbf{W})$, *then*

$$y_i^{(t+1)} - y_j^{(t+1)} = \left[(1-\alpha)\left(1 + \alpha\gamma + \alpha^2\gamma^2 + \cdots + \alpha^{t-1}\gamma^{t-1}\right) \right. $$
$$\left. + \alpha^t\gamma^t\right]\left(y_i^{(1)} - y_j^{(1)}\right),$$

where $\gamma = w_{ii} - w_{ji} = w_{jj} - w_{ij}, t = 1, 2, \ldots$.

Proof. If persons i and j are structurally equivalent in the influence network, then $w_{ii} + w_{ij} = w_{ji} + w_{jj}$ and so

$$w_{ii} - w_{ji} = w_{jj} - w_{ij} \equiv \gamma, \tag{D.4}$$

where $|\gamma| \le 1$ because $\max|w_{ii} - w_{ji}| = \max|w_{jj} - w_{ij}| = 1$.

If the difference in the initial attitudes of the persons i and j is $y_i^{(1)} - y_j^{(1)}$, then in $\mathbf{y}^{(2)} = \mathbf{A}\mathbf{W}\mathbf{y}^{(1)} + (\mathbf{I} - \mathbf{A})\,\mathbf{y}^{(1)}$ we have

$$y_i^{(2)} = \alpha \sum_{k=1}^{n} w_{ik}y_k^{(1)} + (1-\alpha)y_i^{(1)}$$

$$y_j^{(2)} = \alpha \sum_{k=1}^{n} w_{jk}y_k^{(1)} + (1-\alpha)y_j^{(1)},$$

whence

$$y_i^{(2)} - y_j^{(2)} = [1 - \alpha + \alpha\gamma]\left(y_i^{(1)} - y_j^{(1)}\right). \tag{D.5}$$

In $\mathbf{y}^{(3)} = \mathbf{A}\mathbf{W}\mathbf{y}^{(2)} + (\mathbf{I} - \mathbf{A})\,\mathbf{y}^{(1)}$ we have

$$y_i^{(3)} = \alpha \sum_{k} w_{ik}y_k^{(2)} + (1-\alpha)y_i^{(1)}$$

$$y_j^{(3)} = \alpha \sum_{k} w_{jk}y_k^{(2)} + (1-\alpha)y_j^{(1)},$$

whence

$$y_i^{(3)} - y_j^{(3)} = \left[(1-\alpha)(1+\alpha\gamma) + \alpha^2\gamma^2\right]\left(y_i^{(1)} - y_j^{(1)}\right). \tag{D.6}$$

Thus, we have established (D.1) for $t = 1, 2$.

Inductively, assume that (D.1) holds for some value $t = r$. Then in $\mathbf{y}^{(r+2)} = \mathbf{A}\mathbf{W}\mathbf{y}^{(r+1)} + (\mathbf{I} - \mathbf{A})\,\mathbf{y}^{(1)}$ we have

$$y_i^{(r+2)} = \alpha \sum_{k} w_{ik}y_k^{(r+1)} + (1-\alpha)y_i^{(1)},$$

$$y_j^{(r+2)} = \alpha \sum_{k} w_{jk}y_k^{(r+1)} + (1-\alpha)y_j^{(1)},$$

whence

$$y_i^{(r+2)} - y_j^{(r+2)}$$

$$= \alpha \sum_k \left(w_{ik} - w_{jk}\right) y_k^{(r+1)} + (1 - \alpha)\left(y_i^{(1)} - y_j^{(1)}\right)$$

$$= \alpha \left[\left(w_{ii} - w_{ji}\right) y_i^{(r+1)} + \left(w_{ij} - w_{jj}\right) y_j^{(r+1)}\right] + (1 - \alpha)\left(y_i^{(1)} - y_j^{(1)}\right)$$

$$= \alpha\gamma \left[y_i^{(r+1)} - y_j^{(r+1)}\right] + (1 - \alpha)\left(y_i^{(1)} - y_j^{(1)}\right)$$

$$= \left[(1 - \alpha)(1 + \alpha\gamma + \alpha^2\gamma^2 + \cdots + \alpha^r\gamma^r) + \alpha^{r+1}\gamma^{r+1}\right]\left(y_i^{(1)} - y_j^{(1)}\right),$$

$$\text{(D.7)}$$

which establishes (D.1) for all $t = 1, 2, \ldots .$ ∎

Given (D.1), where $-1 < \alpha\gamma < 1$,

$$y_i^{(t+1)} - y_j^{(t+1)} = \frac{(1 - \alpha\gamma)}{(1 - \alpha\gamma)}\left[(1 - \alpha)\left(1 + \alpha\gamma + \alpha^2\gamma^2 + \cdots + \alpha^{t-1}\gamma^{t-1}\right)\right.$$

$$\left. + \alpha^t\gamma^t\right]\left(y_i^{(1)} - y_j^{(1)}\right)$$

$$= \left[\frac{(1 - \alpha)}{(1 - \alpha\gamma)}(1 - \alpha\gamma)\left(1 + \alpha\gamma + \alpha^2\gamma^2 + \cdots + \alpha^{t-1}\gamma^{t-1}\right)\right.$$

$$\left. + \frac{(1 - \alpha\gamma)}{(1 - \alpha\gamma)}\alpha^t\gamma^t\right]\left(y_i^{(1)} - y_j^{(1)}\right)$$

$$= \left[\frac{(1 - \alpha)}{(1 - \alpha\gamma)}\left(1 - \alpha^t\gamma^t\right) + \frac{(1 - \alpha\gamma)}{(1 - \alpha\gamma)}\alpha^t\gamma^t\right]\left(y_i^{(1)} - y_j^{(1)}\right)$$

or

$$y_i^{(t+1)} - y_j^{(t+1)} = \left[\left(\frac{1 - \alpha}{1 - \alpha\gamma}\right) + \left(1 - \frac{1 - \alpha}{1 - \alpha\gamma}\right)(\alpha\gamma)^t\right]\left(y_i^{(1)} - y_j^{(1)}\right)$$

for $t = 1, 2, \ldots$, which establishes (D.2).

Hence, for a structurally equivalent i and j, an initial agreement $y_i^{(1)} - y_j^{(1)} = 0$ implies their agreement at every stage of the process. Taking the limit $t \to \infty$, we obtain

$$y_i^{(\infty)} - y_j^{(\infty)} = \left(\frac{1 - \alpha}{1 - \alpha\gamma}\right)\left(y_i^{(1)} - y_j^{(1)}\right),$$

which establishes (D.3). Note that this proof applies not only to the case of our standard model, which assumes coupling (i.e., $a_{kk} = 1 - w_{kk}$ for all k), but also to the more general model, which does not assume such coupling.

Appendix E

Goldberg's Index of Proportional Conformity

Here we show that under the special condition of a fixed consensus Goldberg's (1954) index of proportional conformity can be expressed in terms of deviant person i's susceptibility to interpersonal influence:

$$\sum_{j \neq i}^{n} v_{ij} = \frac{y_i^{(\infty)} - y_i^{(1)}}{\kappa - y_i^{(1)}} = \frac{a_{ii}^2}{1 - a_{ii}(1 - a_{ii})}, \qquad (E.1)$$

where κ is the *consensual fixed attitude* of all persons $j \neq i$, which differs from i's initial position; i.e., $\kappa - y_i^{(1)} \neq 0$.

When all persons in a group other than person i have an identical and fixed initial opinion, i.e., $y_j^{(1)} = y_j^{(\infty)} = \kappa$ for all $j \neq i$, we can derive

$$\frac{y_i^{(\infty)} - y_i^{(1)}}{\kappa - y_i^{(1)}} = \frac{a_{ii}(1 - w_{ii})}{1 - a_{ii}w_{ii}}$$

as follows:

$$y_i^{(\infty)} = a_{ii} \sum_{j=1}^{n} w_{ij} y_j^{(\infty)} + (1 - a_{ii}) y_i^{(1)} \qquad (E.2)$$

$$= a_{ii} w_{ii} y_i^{(\infty)} + a_{ii}\kappa \sum_{j \neq i}^{n} w_{ij} + (1 - a_{ii}) y_i^{(1)}$$

$$= a_{ii} w_{ii} y_i^{(\infty)} + a_{ii}\kappa (1 - w_{ii}) + (1 - a_{ii}) y_i^{(1)}$$

and

$$y_i^{(\infty)} - y_i^{(1)} = a_{ii} w_{ii} y_i^{(\infty)} + a_{ii}(1 - w_{ii})\kappa - a_{ii} y_i^{(1)} \qquad (E.3)$$

$$= a_{ii} w_{ii} y_i^{(\infty)} + a_{ii}\kappa - a_{ii} w_{ii}\kappa - a_{ii} y_i^{(1)}.$$

Adding $a_{ii} w_{ii} y_i^{(1)}$ to both sides and rearranging terms,

$$y_i^{(\infty)} - y_i^{(1)} - a_{ii} w_{ii} y_i^{(\infty)} + a_{ii} w_{ii} y_i^{(1)} = -a_{ii} y_i^{(1)} + a_{ii} \kappa - a_{ii} w_{ii} \kappa + a_{ii} w_{ii} y_i^{(1)}$$

$$y_i^{(\infty)} - y_i^{(1)} - a_{ii} w_{ii} \left(y_i^{(\infty)} - y_i^{(1)} \right) = a_{ii} \kappa \left(1 - w_{ii} \right) - a_{ii} y_i^{(1)} \left(1 - w_{ii} \right)$$

$$\left(1 - a_{ii} w_{ii} \right) \left(y_i^{(\infty)} - y_i^{(1)} \right) = a_{ii} \left(1 - w_{ii} \right) \left(\kappa - y_i^{(1)} \right).$$

Hence,

$$\frac{y_i^{(\infty)} - y_i^{(1)}}{\kappa - y_i^{(1)}} = \frac{a_{ii} \left(1 - w_{ii} \right)}{1 - a_{ii} w_{ii}} = \frac{a_{ii}^2}{1 - a_{ii} \left(1 - a_{ii} \right)} \tag{E.4}$$

for $w_{ii} = 1 - a_{ii}$.

Appendix F

Gender-Homophilous Small Groups

The law of total variance, with respect to a variable y, states that if a set with N members is partitioned into K subsets according to a discrete variable x, then the variance of the set on y is equal to the weighted mean of the variances of the subsets plus the variance of the K weighted means, where the variances of the subsets are weighted in proportion to their size:

$$\frac{1}{N}\sum_k\sum_i (y_{ik} - \bar{y})^2 = \frac{1}{N}\sum_k\sum_i (y_{ik} - \bar{y}_k)^2 + \frac{1}{N}\sum_k n_k (\bar{y}_k - \bar{y})^2. \quad \text{(F.1)}$$

Here, gender partitions the population into two subsets ($K = 2$):

$$\frac{1}{N}\sum_{k=1}^{2}\sum_i (y_{ik} - \bar{y})^2 = \frac{n_1}{Nn_1}\sum_i (y_{i1} - \bar{y}_1)^2$$
$$+ \frac{n_2}{Nn_2}\sum_i (y_{i2} - \bar{y}_2)^2 + \frac{n_1}{N}(\bar{y}_1 - \bar{y})^2 + \frac{n_2}{N}(\bar{y}_2 - \bar{y})^2.$$

Hence

$$\text{var}(y) = w_1 \, \text{var}(y_1) + w_2 \, \text{var}(y_2) + \text{var}(\bar{y}_1, \bar{y}_2), \quad \text{(F.2)}$$

where $w_1 = n_1/N$ and $w_2 = n_2/N$ denote the proportions of females and males, respectively, in the population, $\bar{y}_1$ and $\text{var}(y_1)$ are the mean and variance of the female subpopulation, respectively, $\bar{y}_2$ and $\text{var}(y_2)$ are the mean and variance of the male subpopulation, respectively, and $\text{var}(\bar{y}_1, \bar{y}_2) = w_1(\bar{y}_1 - \bar{y})^2 + w_2(\bar{y}_2 - \bar{y})^2$.

The macro-level decomposition described by (F.2) reflects only the sociodemographic partitioning of the population and ignores the partitioning of the subpopulations into small groups. The variance of the

340

female subpopulation is decomposable as follows:

$$\text{var}(y_1) = w_{11}\,\text{var}(y_{11}) + w_{12}\,\text{var}(y_{12}) + \cdots \tag{F.3}$$
$$+ w_{1F}\,\text{var}(y_{1F}) + \text{var}(\bar{y}_{11}, \bar{y}_{12}, \ldots, \bar{y}_{1F}),$$

where $f = 1, 2, \ldots, F$ are the indices for the female small groups, w_{1f} is the proportion of the females located in group f, $\text{var}(y_{1f})$ is the variance of issue positions among the females within group f, and $\bar{y}_{1f}$ is the mean of the issues positions within group f. Similarly, the decomposition of the variance of the male subpopulation is

$$\text{var}(y_2) = w_{21}\,\text{var}(y_{21}) + w_{22}\,\text{var}(y_{22}) + \cdots \tag{F.4}$$
$$+ w_{2M}\,\text{var}(y_{2M}) + \text{var}(\bar{y}_{21}, \bar{y}_{22}, \ldots, \bar{y}_{2M}),$$

where $m = 1, 2, \ldots, M$ are the indices for the male small groups.

Elaborating (F.2) with these two equations, (F.3) and (F.4), we have

$$\text{var}(y) = w_1 \left[w_{11}\,\text{var}(y_{11}) + w_{12}\,\text{var}(y_{12}) + \cdots + w_{1F}\,\text{var}(y_{1F}) \right]$$
$$+ w_2 \left[w_{21}\,\text{var}(y_{21}) + w_{22}\,\text{var}(y_{22}) + \cdots + w_{2M}\,\text{var}(y_{2M}) \right]$$
$$+ w_1\,\text{var}(\bar{y}_{11}, \bar{y}_{12}, \ldots, \bar{y}_{1F}) \tag{F.5}$$
$$+ w_2\,\text{var}(\bar{y}_{21}, \bar{y}_{22}, \ldots, \bar{y}_{2M})$$
$$+ \text{var}(\bar{y}_1, \bar{y}_2).$$

Note that the weights $w_1 + w_2 = 1$ and $\sum_{f=1}^{F} w_{1f} = \sum_{m=1}^{M} w_{2m} = 1$. Hence, $w_1 \sum_{f=1}^{F} w_{1f} + w_2 \sum_{m=1}^{M} w_{2m} = 1$. This decomposition shows that, *ceteris paribus*, holding all the means constant, reductions of the variances within gender-homophilous small groups must decrease the total variance $\text{var}(y)$ of the population and, hence, must increase the homogeneity of issue positions in the population.

Consider $\text{Prevar}(y) - \text{Postvar}(y)$ for the *baseline case* in which endogenous interpersonal influences within the small groups produce a consensus on the *mean initial position within each group*. In this baseline case, the change of variance is

$$\text{Prevar}(y) - \text{Postvar}(y) \tag{F.6}$$
$$= w_1 \left[w_{11}\,\text{var}(y_{11}) + w_{12}\,\text{var}(y_{12}) + \cdots + w_{1F}\,\text{var}(y_{1F}) \right]$$
$$+ w_2 \left[w_{21}\,\text{var}(y_{21}) + w_{22}\,\text{var}(y_{22}) + \cdots + w_{2M}\,\text{var}(y_{2M}) \right];$$

i.e., the change is entirely determined by the initial within-group variances of issue positions. For this baseline case, in which there is no change in the pre- and postdiscussion means, (F.6) is the expected change of variance.

References

Abelson, R. P. and A. Levi. 1985. "Decision making and decision theory." Pp. 231–308 in *Handbook of Social Psychology*, vol. 1, edited by G. Lindzey and E. Aronson. New York: Random House.

Abelson, R. P. 1964. "Mathematical models of the distribution of attitudes under controversy." Pp. 142–60 in *Contributions to Mathematical Psychology*, edited by N. Frederiksen and H. Gulliksen. New York: Holt, Rinehart & Winston.

Abrams, D. and M. A. Hogg. 1990a. "Social identification, self-categorization and social influence." Pp. 195–228 in *European Review of Social Psychology*, vol. 1, edited by W. Stroebe and M. Hewstone. Chichester: Wiley.

————. 1990b. *Social Identity Theory: Constructive and Critical Advances.* Hemel Hempstead: Harvester Wheatsheaf.

Abrams, D., M. S. Wetherell, S. Cochrane, and M. A. Hogg. 1990. "Knowing what to think by knowing who you are: Self-categorization and the nature of norm formation, conformity and group polarization." *British Journal of Social Psychology* 29:97–119.

Ajzen, I. 1988. *Attitudes, Personality, and Behavior*. Chicago: Dorsey Press.

Aldag, R. J. and S. R. Fuller. 1993. "Beyond fiasco: A reappraisal of the group-think phenomenon and a new model of group decision processes." *Psychological Bulletin* 113:533–52.

Alexander, J. C., B. Giesen, R. Munch, and N. J. Smelser. 1987. *The Micro–Macro Link*. Berkeley: University of California Press.

Allen, V. L. 1965. "Situational factors in conformity." Pp. 133–75 in *Advances in Experimental Social Psychology*, vol. 2, edited by L. Berkowitz. New York: Academic Press.

————. 1975. "Social support for nonconformity." Pp. 2–43 in *Advances in Experimental Social Psychology*, vol. 8, edited by L. Berkowitz. New York: Academic Press.

Allison, S. T. and D. M. Messick. 1987. "From individual inputs to group outputs, and back again." Pp. 111–43 in *Group Processes*, edited by C. Hendrick. Newbury Park: Sage.

Allport, F. H. 1924. *Social Psychology*. New York: Houghton Mifflin.

———. 1962. "A structuronomic conception of behavior: Individual and collective." *Journal of Abnormal and Social Psychology* 64:3–30.

Allport, F. H. and D. A. Hartman. 1925. "The measurement and motivation of atypical opinion in a certain group." *American Political Science Review* 19:753–63.

Anderson, N. H. 1981. *Foundations of Information Integration Theory*. New York: Academic Press.

———. 1991a. *Contributions to Information Integration Theory, Vol. I: Cognition*. Hillsdale, NJ: Lawrence Erlbaum.

———. 1991b. *Contributions to Information Integration Theory, Vol. II: Social*. Hillsdale, NJ: Lawrence Erlbaum.

———. 1996. *A Functional Theory of Cognition*. Mahwah, NJ: Lawarence Erlbaum.

Anderson, N. H. and C. C. Graesser. 1976. "An information integration analysis of attitude change in group discussion." *Journal of Personality and Social Psychology* 34:210–22.

Anderson, N. H. and C. Hovland. 1957. "The representation of order effects in communication research." Pp. 158–69 in *The Order of Presentation in Persuasion*, edited by C. Hovland. New Haven: Yale University Press.

Anselin, L. 1988. *Spatial Econometrics: Methods and Models*. Dordrecht: Kluwer Academic.

Aronson, E., J. A. Turner, and J. M. Carlsmith. 1963. "Communicator credibility and communication discrepancy as determinants of opinion change." *Journal of Abnormal and Social Psychology* 67:31–6.

Arrow, H. 1997. "Stability, bistability, and instability in small group influence patterns." *Journal of Personality and Social Psychology* 72:75–85.

Asch, S. E. 1951. "Effects of group pressure upon the modification and distortion of judgment." Pp. 117–90 in *Groups, Leadership and Men*, edited by M. H. Guetzkow. Pittsburgh: Carnegie Press.

———. 1952. *Social Psychology*. Englewood Cliffs, NJ: Prentice-Hall.

———. 1956. "Studies of independence and conformity: A minority of one against a unanimous majority." *Psychological Monographs* 70:1–70.

Back, K. W. 1951. "Influence through social communication." *Journal of Abnormal and Social Psychology* 46:9–23.

Bales, R. F. 1950. *Interaction Process Analysis*. New York: Addison-Wesley.

Balkwell, J. W. 1991. "From expectations to behavior: An improved postulate for expectation states theory." *American Sociological Review* 56:355–69.

Bargh, J. A. and M. J. Ferguson. 2000. "Beyond behaviorism: On the automaticity of higher mental processes." *Psychological Bulletin* 126:925–45.

Barnlund, D. C. 1959. "A comparative study of individual, majority, and group judgment." *Journal of Abnormal Psychology* 58:55–60.

Baron, R. S. and G. Roper. 1976. "Reaffirmation of social comparison views of choice shifts: Averaging and extremity effects in an autokinetic situation." *Journal of Personality and Social Psychology* 33:521–30.

Baron, R. S., S. I. Hoppe, C. F. Kao, B. Brunsman, B. Linneweh, and D. Rogers. 1996. "Social corroboration and opinion extremity." *Journal of Experimental Social Psychology* 32:537–60.

Baron, R. S., N. L. Kerr, and N. Miller. 1992. *Group Process, Group Decision, Group Action*. Pacific Grove, CA: Brooks/Cole.

Berger, J., T. L. Conner, and M. H. Fisek. 1974. "Expectation states theory: A theoretical research program." Cambridge, MA: Winthrop.

Berger, J., M. H. Fisek, R. Z. Norman, and M. Zelditch Jr. 1977. *Status Characteristics and Social Interaction*. New York: Elsevier.

Berger, J., D. G. Wagner, and M. Zelditch Jr. 1985. " Expectation states theory: Review and assessment." Pp. 1–72 in *Status, Rewards and Influence*, edited by J. Berger and M. J. Zelditch. San Francisco: Jossey-Bass.

Berger, R. L. 1981. "A necessary and sufficient condition for reaching a consensus using DeGroot's method." *Journal of the American Statistical Association* 76:415–18.

Bergin, A. E. 1967. "The effect of dissonant persuasive communications upon changes in a self-referring attitude." *Journal of Personality* 30:423–38.

Berkowitz, L. 1989. "Frustration–aggression hypothesis: Examination and reformulation." *Psychological Bulletin* 106: 59–73.

Blascovich, J., G. P. Ginsburg, and T. L. Veach. 1975. "A pluralistic explanation of choice shifts on the risk dimension." *Journal of Personality and Social Psychology* 31:422–9.

Blau, P.M. 1977. *Inequality and Heterogeneity*. New York: The Free Press.

Blumer, H. 1969. *Symbolic Interactionism*. Englewood Cliffs, NJ: Prentice-Hall.

Bochner, S. and C. A. Insko. 1966. "Communicator discrepancy, source credibility, and opinion change." *Journal of Personality and Social Psychology* 4:614–21.

Bond, R. and P. B. Smith. 1996. "Culture and conformity: A meta-analysis of studies using Asch's (1952b, 1956) line judgment task." *Psychological Bulletin* 119:111–37.

Bonner, H. 1959. *Group Dynamics: Principles and Applications*. New York: Ronald Press.

Bourgeois, M. and N. E. Friedkin. 2001. "The distant core: Social solidarity, social distance and interpersonal ties in core–periphery structures." *Social Networks* 23:245–60.

Bovard, E. W. 1948. "Social norms and the individual." *Journal of Abnormal and Social Psychology* 43:62–9.

Brandstatter, H., J. H. Davis, and G. Stocker-Kreichgauer. 1982. *Group Decision Making*. London: Academic Press.

Brodbeck, M. 1956. "The role of small groups in mediating the effects of propaganda." *Journal of Abnormal and Social Psychology* 52:166–70.

Brown, R. 1965. *Social Psychology*. New York: Free Press.

Bryk, A. S. and S. W. Raudenbush. 1992. *Hierarchical Linear Models: Applications and Data Analysis Methods*. Newbury Park, CA: Sage.

Burnstein, E. 1982. "Persuasion as argument processing." Pp. 103–24 in *Contemporary Problems in Group Decision-Making*, edited by J. H. Davis and G. Stocker-Kreichgauer. New York: Academic Press.

Burnstein, E. and A. Vinokur. 1973. "Testing two classes of theories about group-induced shifts in individual choice." *Journal of Experimental Social Psychology* 9:123–37.

_____. 1977. "Persuasive argumentation and social comparison as determinants of attitude polarization." *Journal of Experimental Social Psychology* 13:315–32.

Burt, R. S. 1987. "Social contagion and innovation: Cohesion versus structural equivalence." *American Journal of Sociology* 92:1287–1335.

Cantril, H. 1946a. *Gauging Public Opinion.* Princeton, NJ: Princeton University Press.

_____. 1946b. "The intensity of an attitude." *Journal of Abnormal and Social Psychology* 41:129–35.

Carley, K. 1990. "Group stability: A socio-cognitive approach." *Advances in Group Processes* 7:1–44.

_____. 1991. "A theory of group stability." *American Sociological Review* 56:331–54.

Cartwright, D. 1958. "Some things learned: An evaluative history of the research center for group dynamics." *The Journal of Social Issues* 12:3–19.

_____. 1971. "Risk taking by individuals and groups: An assessment of research employing choice dilemmas." *Journal of Personality and Social Psychology* 20:361–78.

_____. 1973. "Determinants of scientific progress: The case of research on the risky shift." *American Psychologist* 28:222–31.

Cartwright, D. and F. Harary. 1956. "Structural balance: A generalization of Heider's theory." *Psychological Review* 63: 277–93.

Cartwright, D. and A. Zander. 1968. *Group Dynamics: Research and Theory.* New York: Harper & Row.

Castellan, N. J., Jr. 1993. *Individual and Group Decision Making: Current Issues.* Hillsdale, NJ: Erlbaum.

Chaiken, S., W. Wood, and A. H. Eagly. 1996. "Principles of persuasion." Pp. 702–42 in *Social Psychology: Handbook of Basic Principles*, edited by E. T. Higgins and A. W. Kruglanski. New York: Guilford.

Charon, J. M. 2001. *Symbolic Interactionism.* Upper Saddle River, NJ: Prentice-Hall.

Chatterjee, S. and E. Seneta. 1977. "Towards consensus: Some convergence theorems on repeated averaging." *Journal of Applied Probability* 14:89–97.

Cialdini, R. B. and M. R. Trost. 1998. "Social influence: Social norms, conformity, and compliance." Pp. 151–92 in *The Handbook of Social Psychology*, vol. 2, edited by D. T. Gilbert, S. T. Fiske, and G. Lindzey. Boston: McGraw-Hill.

Clark, R. D. 1971. "Group-induced shift toward risk." *Psychological Bulletin* 76:251–70.

Cohen, A. R. 1959. "Communication discrepancy and attitude change." *Journal of Personality* 27:386–96.

Coleman, J. S. 1990. *Foundations of Social Theory.* Cambridge, MA: Harvard University Press.

Coleman, J. S., E. Katz, and H. Menzel. 1966. *Medical Innovation: A Diffusion Study.* Indianapolis: Bobbs-Merrill.

Cooley, C. H. 1962. *Social Organization.* New York: Schocken.

_____. [1902] 1983. *Human Nature and the Social Order.* Piscataway, NJ: Transaction.

Coombs, C. H. 1964. *A Theory of Data.* New York: Wiley.

Cramer, D. 1975. "A critical note on two studies of minority influence." *European Journal of Social Influence* 5:257–60.

Crutchfield, R. S. 1955. "Conformity and character." *American Psychologist* 10:191–8.

Dalkey, N. C. 1972. *Studies in the Quality of Life.* Lexington, MA: Lexington Books.

David, B. and J. C. Turner. 1996. "Studies in self-categorization and minority conversion: Is being a member of the outgroup an advantage?" *British Journal of Social Psychology* 38:115–34.

Davis, J. A. 1970. "Clustering and hierarchy in interpersonal relations: Testing two graph theoretical models on 742 sociomatrices." *American Sociological Review* 35:843–52.

Davis, J. H. 1973. "Group decision and social interaction: A theory of social decision schemes." *Psychological Review* 80:97–125.

———. 1982. "Social interaction as a combinatorial process in group decision." Pp. 27–58 in *Group Decision Making*, edited by H. Brandstatter, J. H. Davis, and G. Stocker-Kreichgauer. London: Academic Press.

———. 1996. "Group decision making and quantitative judgments: A consensus model." Pp. 35–59 in *Understanding Group Behavior: Consensual Action by Small Groups*, edited by E. H. Witte and J. H. Davis. Mahwah, NJ: Lawrence Erlbaum.

Davis, J. H., P. R. Laughlin, and S. S. Komorita. 1976. "The social psychology of small groups: Cooperative and mixed-motive interaction." *Annual Review of Psychology* 27:501–41.

Deaux, K. and M. Daniela. 2003. "Interpersonal networks and social categories: Specifying levels of context in identity processes." *Social Psychology Quarterly* 66:101–17.

DeGroot, M. H. 1974. "Reaching a consensus." *Journal of the American Statistical Association* 69:118–21.

Deutsch, M. and H. B. Gerard. 1955. "A study of normative and informational social influences upon individual judgment." *Journal of Abnormal and Social Psychology* 51:629–36.

Dion, K. L., R. S. Baron, and N. Miller. 1970. "Why do groups make riskier decisions than individuals?" Pp. 305–77 in *Advances in Experimental Social Psychology*, edited by L. Berkowitz. San Diego: Academic Press.

Doms, M. 1984. "The minority influence effect: An alternative approach." Pp. 1–33 in *Current Issues in European Social Psychology*, vol. 1, edited by W. Doise and S. Moscovici. Cambridge: Cambridge University Press.

Doms, M. and E. V. Avermaet. 1980. "Majority influence, minority influence and conversion behavior: A replication." *Journal of Experimental Social Psychology* 16:283–92.

Doreian, P. 1981. "Estimating linear models with spatially distributed data." Pp. 359–88 in *Sociological Methodology*, edited by S. Leinhardt. San Fransico: Jossey-Bass.

Doreian, P. and F. N. Stokman. 1997. *Evolution of Social Networks.* Amsterdam: Gordon and Breach.

348   *References*

Dreu, C. K. W. D. and N. K. D. Vries. 2001. *Group Consensus and Minority Influence: Implications for Innovation.* Oxford: Blackwell.

Driskell, J. E. and M. Webster Jr. 1997. "Status and sentiment in task groups." Pp. 179–200 in *Status, Network, and Structure*, edited by J. Szmatka, J. Skvoretz, and J. Berger. Stanford, CA: Stanford University Press.

Duncan, B. and O. D. Duncan. 1978. "Interaction of spouses with respect to an unobserved attitude." Pp. 291–6 in *Sex Typing and Social Roles.* New York: Academic Press.

Duncan, O. D., A. O. Haller, and A. Portes. 1968. "Peer influences on aspirations: A reinterpretation." *American Journal of Sociology* 74:119–37.

Eagly, A. H. and S. Chaiken. 1993. *The Psychology of Attitudes.* Fort Worth, TX: Harcourt Brace & Company.

Erbring, L. and A. A. Young. 1979. "Individuals and social structure: Contextual effects as endogenous feedback." *Sociological Methods & Research* 7:396–430.

Feld, S. L. 1981. "The focused organization of social ties." *American Journal of Sociology* 86:1015–35.

Ferguson, D. A. and N. Vidmar 1971. "Effects of group discussion on estimates of culturally appropriate risk levels." *Journal of Personality and Social Psychology* 20: 436–45.

Festinger, Leon. 1950. "Informal social communication." *Psychological Review* 57:271–82.

_____. 1953. "An analysis of compliant behavior." Pp. 232–56 in *Group Relations at the Crossroads*, edited by M. Sherif and M. O. Wilson. New York: Harper.

_____. 1954. "A theory of social comparison processes." *Human Relations* 7:117–40.

_____. 1957. *A Theory of Cognitive Dissonance.* Evanston, IL: Row, Peterson.

_____. 1964. *Conflict, Decision, and Dissonance.* Stanford, CA: Stanford University Press.

Festinger, L. and E. Aronson. 1968. "Arousal and reduction of dissonance in social contexts." Pp. 125–36 in *Group Dynamics*, edited by D. Cartwright and A. Zander. New York: Harper & Row.

Festinger, L., H. B. Gerard, B. Hymovitch, H. H. Kelley, and B. Raven. 1952. "The influence process in the presence of extreme deviates." *Human Relations* 5:327–46.

Festinger, Leon, S. Schachter, and K. W. Back. 1950. *Social Pressures in Informal Groups: A Study of Human Factors in Housing.* New York: Harper.

Fink, E. L., S. A. Kaplowitz, and C. L. Bauer. 1983. "Positional discrepancy, psychological discrepancy, and attitude change: Experimental tests of some mathematical models." *Communication Monographs* 50:413–30.

Fisek, M. Hamit and Joseph Berger. 1998. "Sentiment and task performance expectations." Pp. 23–40 in *Advances in Group Processes*, edited by J. Skvoretz and J. Szmatka. Greenwich, CT: JAI Press.

Fisek, M. H., J. Berger, and R. Z. Norman. 1991. "Participation in heterogeneous and homogeneous groups: A theoretical integration." *American Journal of Sociology* 97:114–42.

_____. 1995. "Evaluations and the formation of expectations." *American Journal of Sociology* 101:721–46.

Fisek, M. H., R. Z. Norman, and M. Nelson-Kilger. 1992. "Status characteristics and expectation states theory: A priori model parameters and test." *Journal of Mathematical Sociology* 16:285–303.

Fisek, M. H. and R. Ofshe. 1970. "The process of status evolution." *Sociometry* 33:327–46.

Fishbein, M. and I. Ajzen. 1975. *Belief, Attitude, Intention, and Behavior: An Introduction to Theory and Research.* Reading, MA: Addison-Wesley.

Fisher, S. and A. Lubin. 1958. "Distance as a determinant of influence in a two-person serial interaction situation." *Journal of Abnormal and Social Psychology* 56:230–38.

Fraser, C., C. Gouge, and M. Billig. 1971. "Risky shifts, cautious shifts, and group polarization." *European Journal of Social Psychology* 1:7–30.

Freeman, L. C. 1992. "The sociological concept of 'group' : An empirical test of two models." *American Journal of Sociology* 98:152–66.

French, J. R. P. Jr. 1956. "A formal theory of social power." *The Psychological Review* 63:181–94.

French, J. R. P. Jr. and B. Raven. 1959. "The bases of social power." Pp. 150–67 in *Studies of Social Power*, edited by D. Cartwright. Ann Arbor, MI: Institute for Social Research.

Friedkin, Noah E. 1986. "A formal theory of social power." *Journal of Mathematical Sociology* 12:103–26.

———. 1990. "Social networks in structural equation models." *Social Psychology Quarterly* 53:316–28.

———. 1991. "Theoretical foundations for centrality measures." *American Journal of Sociology* 96:1478–1504.

———. 1998. *A Structural Theory of Social Influence.* Cambridge: Cambridge University Press.

———. 1999. "Choice shift and group polarization." *American Sociological Review* 64:856–75.

———. 2001. "Norm formation in social influence networks." *Social Networks* 23:167–89.

Friedkin, N. E. and K. S. Cook. 1990. "Peer group influence." *Sociological Methods & Research* 19:122–43.

Friedkin, N. E. and E. C. Johnsen. 1990. "Social influence and opinions." *Journal of Mathematical Sociology* 15:193–206.

———. 1997. "Social positions in influence networks." *Social Networks* 19:209–22.

———. 1999. "Social influence networks and opinion change." *Advances in Group Processes* 16:1–29.

———. 2002. "Control loss and Fayol's gangplanks." *Social Networks* 24:395–406.

———. 2003. "Attitude change, affect control, and expectation states in the formation of influence networks." *Advances in Group Processes* 20:1–29.

Galam, S. and S. Moscovici. 1991. "Towards a theory of collective phenomena: Consensus and attitude changes in groups." *Eurpean Journal of Social Psychology* 21:49–74.

Gantmacher, F. R. 1959. *The Theory of Matrices, Vol. Two.* New York: Chelsea.

Gerard, H. B. 1954. "The anchorage of opinions in face-to-face groups." *Human Relations* 7:313–25.

Gerard, H. B. and N. Miller. 1967. "Group dynamics." *Annual Review of Psychology* 18:287–332.

Goethals, G. R. 1972. "Consensus and modality in the attribution process: The role of similarity and information." *Journal of Personality and Social Psychology* 21:84–92.

Goethals, G. R. and J. M. Darley. 1977. "Social comparison theory: An attributional approach." Pp. 259–78 in *Social Comparison Processes: Theoretical and Empirical Perspectives*, edited by J. M. Suls and R. L. Miller. Washington, DC: Halsted-Wiley.

Goethals, G. R. and R. E. Nelson. 1973. "Similarity in the influence process: The belief–value distinction." *Journal of Personality and Social Psychology* 25:117–22.

Goethals, G. R. and M. P. Zanna. 1979. "The role of social comparison in choice shifts." *Journal of Personality and Social Psychology* 37:1469–76.

Goldberg, S. C. 1954. "Three situational determinants of conformity to social norms." *Journal of Abnormal and Social Psychology* 49:325–9.

Gordon, B. F. 1966. "Influence and social comparison as motives for affiliation." *Journal of Experimental Social Psychology, Supplement I*: 55–65.

Gould, R. V. 1993. "Collective action and network structure." *American Sociological Review* 58: 182–96.

Graesser, C. C. 1991. "A social averaging theorem for group decision making." Pp. 1–40 in *Contributions to Information Integration Theory*, vol. 2, edited by N. H. Anderson. Hillsdale, NJ: Lawrence Erlbaum.

Granovetter, M. S. 1973. "The strength of weak ties." *American Journal of Sociology* 78: 1360–80.

———. 1978. "Threshold models of collective behavior." *American Journal of Sociology* 83: 1420–43.

Greenwald, A. G. 1966. "Effects of prior commitment on behavior change after a persuasive communication." *Public Opinion Quarterly* 29:595–601.

Harary, F. 1959. "A criterion for unanimity in French's theory of social power." Pp. 168–82 in *Studies in Social Power*, edited by D. Cartwright. Ann Arbor, MI: Institute for Social Research.

Harary, F., R. Z. Norman, and D. Cartwright. 1965. *Structural Models: An Introduction to the Theory of Directed Graphs*. New York: Wiley.

Hastie, R., S. Penrod, and N. Pennington. 1983. *Inside the Jury*. Cambridge, MA: Harvard University Press.

Heider, F. 1946. "Attitudes and cognitive organization." *Journal of Psychology* 21:107–12.

Heise, D. R. 2002. "Understanding social interaction with affect control theory." Pp. 17–40 in *New Directions in Sociological Theory*, edited by J. Berger and M. Zelditch. Boulder, CO: Rowman and Littlefield.

Helmreich, R., R. Bakeman, and L. Scherwitz. 1973. "The study of small groups." *Annual Review of Psychology* 24:337–54.

Hewitt, J. P. 2000. *Self and Society*. Boston: Allyn and Bacon.

Himmelfarb, S. 1974. "Resistance to persuasion induced by information integration." Pp. 413–19 in *Readings in Attitude Change*, edited by S. Himmelfarb and A. H. Eagly. New York: Wiley.

Hogg, M. A. 1992. *The Social Psychology of Group Cohesiveness*. New York: New York University.

Hogg, M. A. and D. Abrams. 1988. *Social Identification: A Social Psychology of Intergroup Relations and Group Processes*. London/New York: Routledge.

Hogg, M. A. and R. S. Tindale. 2001. "Social categorization, depersonalization, and group behavior." Pp. 56–85 in *Blackwell Handbook of Social Psychology: Group Processes*, edited by M. A. Hogg and R. S. Tindale. Oxford: Blackwell.

Hogg, M. A., J. C. Turner, and B. Davidson. 1990. "Polarized norms and social frames of reference: A test of the self-categorization theory of group polarization." *Basic & Applied Social Psychology* 11:77–100.

Homans, G. C. 1950. *The Human Group*. New York: Harcourt, Brace & World.

————. 1961. *Social Behavior: Its Elementary Forms*. New York: Harcourt, Brace & World.

————. 1964. "Bringing men back in." *American Sociological Review* 29:809–18.

Horowitz, Irving L. 1962. "Consensus, conflict and cooperation: A sociological inventory." *Social Forces* 41:177–88.

Hovland, C. 1959. "Reconciling conflicting results derived from the experimental and survey studies of attitude change." *The American Psychologist* 46:92–100.

Hovland, C. I., O. J. Harvey, and M. Sherif. 1957. "Assimilation and contrast effects in reactions to communication and attitude change." *Journal of Abnormal and Social Psychology* 55:244–52.

Hovland, C. I., I. L. Janis, and H. H. Kelley. 1953. *Communication and Persuasion*. New Haven, CT: Yale University Press.

Hovland, C. and H. Pritzker. 1957. "Extent of opinion change as a function of amount of change advocated." *Journal of Abnormal and Social Psychology* 54:257–61.

Hox, J. 2002. *Multilevel Analysis*. Mahwah, NJ: Lawrence Erlbaum.

Hubbell, C. H. 1965. "An input–output approach to clique identification." *Sociometry* 28:377–99.

Hunter, F. 1953. *Community Power Structure*. Durham, NC: University of North Carolina.

Hunter, J. E., J. E. Danes, and S. H. Cohen. 1984. *Mathematical Models of Attitude Change*. Orlando, FL: Academic Press.

Hutchinson, B. 1949. "Some problems of measuring the intensiveness of opinion and attitude." *International Journal of Opinion and Attitude Research* 3:123–31.

Insko, C. A., F. Murashima, and M. Saiyadain. 1966. "Communicator discrepancy, stimulus ambiguity, and balance." *Journal of Personality and Social Psychology* 34:262–74.

Isenberg, D. J. 1986. "Group polarization: A critical review and meta-analysis." *Journal of Personality and Social Psychology* 50:1141–51.

Janis, I. L. 1982. *Groupthink: Psychological Studies of Policy Decisions and Fiascoes*. Boston: Houghton Mifflin.

Johnson, D. M. 1940. "Confidence and the expression of opinion." *Journal of Social Psychology* 12:213–20.

Jones, E. E. 1985. "Major developments in social psychology during the past five decades." Pp. 47–107 in *Handbook of Social Psychology*, vol. 1, edited by G. Lindzey and E. Aronson. New York: Random House.

Kalkhoff, W. and C. Barnum. 2000. "The effect of status-organizing and social identity processes on patterns of social influence." *Social Psychology Quarterly* 63:95–115.

Kameda, T. and S. Sugimori. 1993. "Psychological entrapment in group decision making: An assigned decision rule and a groupthink phenomenon." *Journal of Personality and Social Psychology* 65:282–92.

Kaplan, M. F. and C. E. Miller. 1983. "Group discussion and judgment." Pp. 65–94 in *Basic Group Processes*, edited by P. B. Paulus. New York: Springer-Verlag.

Kaplowitz, S. A. and E. L. Fink. 1991. "Disentangling the effects of discrepant and disconfirming information." *Social Psychology Quarterly* 54:191–207.

Katz, D. and R. L. Kahn. 1978. *The Social Psychology of Organizations*. New York: Wiley.

Kaufer, D. and K. Carley. 1993. *Communication at a Distance: The Effect of Print on Sociocultural Organization and Change*. Hillsdale, NJ: Erlbaum.

Kelley, H. H. 1955. "Salience of membership and resistance to change of group-anchored attitudes." *Human Relations* 8:275–89.

_____. 1967. "Attribution theory in social psychology." Pp. 410–14 in *Nebraska Symposium on Motivation*, edited by D. Levine. Lincoln: University of Nebraska.

Kelley, H. H. and T. W. Lamb. 1957. "Certainty of judgment and resistance to social influence." *Journal of Abnormal and Social Psychology* 55:137–9.

Kelley, H. H. and E. H. Volkart. 1952. "The resistance to change of group-anchored attitudes." *American Sociological Review* 17:453–65.

Kelly, F. P. 1981. "How a group reaches agreement: A stochastic model." *Mathematical Social Sciences* 2:1–8.

Kelvin, P. 1979. "Review of Moscovici (1976) 'Social Influence and Social Change.'" *European Journal of Social Psychology* 9:441–6.

Kemper, T. D. and R. Collins. 1990. "Dimensions of Microinteraction." *American Journal of Sociology* 96:32–68.

Kent, M. V. 1994. "Conformity." Pp. 107–37 in *Small Group Research: A Handbook*, edited by A. P. Hare and H. H. Blumberg. Norwood, NJ: Ablex.

Kerr, Norbert L. 1981. "Social transition schemes: Charting the group's road to agreement." *Journal of Personality and Social Psychology* 41:684–702.

_____. 1992. "Group decision making at a multialternative task: Extremity, interfaction distance, pluralities, and issue importance." *Organizational Behavior and Human Decision Processes* 52:64–95.

Kerr, N. L. and R. J. MacCoun. 1985. "The effects of jury size and polling method on the process and product of jury deliberation." *Journal of Personality and Social Psychology* 48: 349–63.

Kreft, I. and J. D. Leeuw. 1998. *Introducing Multilevel Modeling*. London: Sage.

Lamm, H. and D. G. Myers. 1978. "Group-induced polarization of attitudes and behavior." *Advances in Experimental Social Psychology* 11:145–95.

Latané, B. 1966. "Studies in social comparison: Introduction and overview." *Journal of Experimental Social Psychology Supplement* 1:1–5.

———. 1981. "The psychology of social impact." *American Psychologist* 36:343–56.

Latané, B. and S. Wolf. 1981. "The social impact of majorities and minorities." *Psychological Review* 88:438–53.

Laughlin, P. R. 1980. "Social combination processes of cooperative problem-solving groups on verbal intellective tasks." Pp. 127–55 in *Progress in Social Psychology*, edited by M. Fishbein. Hillsdale, NJ: Erlbaum.

Laughlin, P. R. and P. C. Earley. 1982. "Social combination models, persuasive arguments theory, social comparison theory, and choice shift." *Journal of Personality and Social Psychology* 42:273–80.

Laumann, E. O. and F. U. Pappi. 1976. *Networks of Collective Action: A Perspective on Community Influence Systems.* New York: Academic Press.

Lawler, E. J., C. Ridgeway, and B. Markovsky. 1993. "Structural social psychology and the micro–macro problem." *Sociological Theory* 11:268–90.

Lazer, D. 2001. "The co-evolution of individual and network." *Journal of Mathematical Sociology* 25:69–108.

Lee, M. T. and P. Ofshe. 1981. "The impact of behavioral style and status characteristics on social influence: A test of two competing theories." *Social Psychology Quarterly* 44:73–82.

Lehrer, K. and C. Wagner. 1981. *Rational Consensus in Science and Society.* Dordrecht: D. Reidel.

Levine, J. M. 1989. "Reaction to opinion deviance in small groups." Pp. 187–231 in *Psychology of Group Influence*, edited by P. B. Paulus. Hillsdale, NJ: Erlbaum.

Levine, J. M. and R. L. Moreland. 1990. "Progress in small group research." *Annual Review of Psychology* 41:585–634.

———. 1998. "Small groups." Pp. 415–69 in *The Handbook of Social Psychology*, vol. 2, edited by D. T. Gilbert, S. T. Fiske, and G. Lindzey. New York: McGraw-Hill.

Levine, J. M. and E. M. Russo. 1987. "Majority and minority influence." Pp. 13–54 in *Review of Personality and Social Psychology: Group Processes*, vol. 8, edited by C. Hendrick. Newbury Park, CA: Sage.

Levinger, G. and D. J. Schneider. 1969. "A test of the 'risk as a value' hypothesis." *Journal of Personality and Social Psychology* 11:165–9.

Lewin, K. 1951. *Field Theory in Social Science.* New York: Harper.

———. 1958. *Group Decision and Social Change.* New York: Holt, Rinehart and Winston.

Likert, R. 1967. *The Human Organization.* New York: McGraw-Hill.

Lovaglia, M. J. 1997. "Status, emotion, and structural power." Pp. 159–78 in *Status, Network, and Structure: Theory Development in Group Processes*, edited by J. Szmatka, J. Skvoretz, and J. Berger. Stanford, CA: Stanford University Press.

Lundberg, G. A. and M. Lawsing. 1937. "The sociography of some community relations." *American Sociological Review* 2:318–35.

Luus, E. C. and G. L. Wells. 1994. "The malleability of eyewitness confidence: Cowitness and perseverance effects." *Journal of Applied Psychology* 79:714–23.

Maass, A. and R. D. Clark III. 1984. "Hidden impact of minorities: Fifteen years of minority influence research." *Psychological Bulletin* 95:428–50.

Maass, A., S. G. West, and R. B. Cialdini. 1987. "Minority influence and conversion." Pp. 55–79 in *Review of Personality and Social Psychology*, vol. 8, edited by C. Hendrick. Newbury Park, CA: Sage.

Mackie, D. M. 1986. "Social identification effects in group polarization." *Journal of Personality and Social Psychology* 50:720–28.

———. 1987. "Systematic and nonsystematic processing of majority and minority persuasive communications." *Journal of Personality and Social Psychology* 53:41–52.

Mackie, D. M. and J. Cooper. 1984. "Attitude polarization: Effects of group membership." *Journal of Personality and Social Psychology* 46:575–85.

Mackie, D. M. and J. J. Skelly. 1994. "The social cognition analysis of social influence: Contributions to the understanding of persuasion and conformity." Pp. 259–89 in *Social Cognition: Impact on Social Psychology*, edited by P. G. Devine, D. L. Hamilton, and T. M. Ostrom. San Diego: Academic Press.

MacCoun, R. J. and N. L. Kerr. 1988. "Asymmetric influence in mock jury deliberations: Jurors' bias for leniency." *Journal of Personality and Social Psychology* 54: 21–33.

Maron, M.J. 1982. *Numerical Analysis: A Practical Approach*. New York: Macmillan.

Marquis, D. G. 1962. "Individual responsibility and group decisions involving risk." *Industrial Management Review* 3: 8–23.

Marsden, P. 1981. "Introducing influence processes into a system of collective decisions." *American Journal of Sociology* 86: 1203–35.

Marsden, P. V. and N. E. Friedkin. 1994. "Network studies of social influence." Pp. 3–25 in *Advances in Social Network Analysis*, edited by S. Wasserman and J. Galaskiewicz. Thousand Oaks, CA: Sage.

Martin, R. 1998. "Majority and minority influence using the afterimage paradigm: A series of attempted replications." *Journal of Experimental Social Psychology* 34:1–26.

Martin, R. and M. Hewstone. 2001. "Conformity and independence in groups: Majorities and minorities." Pp. 209–34 in *Blackstone Handbook of Social Psychology: Group Processes*, edited by M. A. Hogg and R. S. Tindale. Oxford: Blackwell.

McGarty, C., J. C. Turner, M. A. Hogg, B. David, and M. S. Wetherell. 1992. "Group polarization as conformity to the prototypical group member." *British Journal of Social Psychology* 31:1–20.

McGrath, J. E. and D. A. Kravitz. 1982. "Group research." *Annual Review of Psychology* 33:195–230.

McPherson, M., L. Smith-Lovin, and J. Cook. 2001. "Birds of a feather: Homophily in social networks." *Annual Review of Sociology* 27:415–44.

Mead, G. H. 1934. *Mind, Self, and Society.* Chicago: University of Chicago Press.

Merton, R. K. 1968. *Social Theory and Social Structure.* New York: The Free Press.

H. A. Michener and M. Wasserman 1995. "Group decision making." Pp. 335–61 in *Sociological Perspectives on Social Psychology*, edited by K. S. Cook, G. A. Fine, and J. S. House. Boston: Allyn and Bacon.

Milgram, S. 1974. *Obedience to Authority.* New York: Harper & Row.

Mills, T. M. 1958. "Some hypotheses on small groups from Simmel." *American Journal of Sociology* 63:642–50.

Moreland, R. L., M. A. Hogg, and S. C. Hains. 1994. "Back to the future: Social psychological research on groups." *Journal of Experimental Social Psychology* 30: 527–55.

Moscovici, S. 1976. *Social Influence and Social Change.* London: Academic Press.

———. 1980. "Toward a theory of conversion behavior." Pp. 209–39 in *Advances in Experimental Social Psychology*, vol. 13, edited by L. Berkowitz. New York: Academic Press.

———. 1985. "Social influence and conformity." Pp. 347–412 in *Handbook of Social Psychology*, vol. 2, edited by G. Lindzey and E. Aronson. New York: Random House.

Moscovici, S. and W. Doise. 1994. *Conflict and Consensus.* London: Sage.

Moscovici, S., A. Mucchi-Faina, and A. Maass. 1994. *Minority Influence.* Chicago: Nelson-Hall.

Moscovici, S. and G. Mugny. 1983. "Minority influence." Pp. 41–64 in *Basic Group Processes*, edited by P. B. Paulus. New York: Springer-Verlag.

Mugny, G. 1982. *The Power of Minorities.* London: Academic Press.

Mullen, B. 1983. "Operationalizing the effect of the group on the individual." *Journal of Experimental Social Psychology* 19:295–322.

Mullen, B., T. Anthony, E. Salas, and J. E. Driskell. 1994. "Group cohesiveness and quality of decision making: An integration of tests of the groupthink hypothesis." *Small Group Research* 25:189–204.

Myers, D. G. and H. Lamm. 1976. "The group polarization phenomenon." *Psychological Bulletin* 83:602–27.

Nagel, E. 1961. *The Structure of Science: Problems in the Logic of Scientific Explanation.* London: Routledge & Kegan Paul.

Nemeth, C. J. 1975. "Understanding minority influence: A reply and digression." *European Journal of Social Psychology* 5:265–7.

———. 1986. "Differential contributions of majority and minority influence." *Psychological Review* 93: 23–32.

Newcomb, T. M. 1951. "Social psychological theory: Integrating individual and social approaches." Pp. 31–49 in *Social Psychology at the Crossroads*, edited by J. H. Rohrer and M. Sherif. New York, Harper.

———. 1953. "An approach to the study of communicative acts." *Psychological Review* 60:393–402.

———. 1961. *The Acquaintance Process.* New York: Holt, Rinehart and Winston.

Nowak, A., J. Szamrej, and B. Latané. 1990. "From private attitude to public opinion: A dynamic theory of social impact." *Psychological Review* 97:362–76.

Oldenburger, R. 1940. "Infinite powers of matrices and characteristic roots." *Duke Mathematical Journal* 6: 357–61.

Ord, K. 1975. "Estimation methods for models of spatial interaction." *Journal of the American Statistical Association* 70:120–26.

Osborn, A. F. 1957. *Applied Imagination.* New York: Scribner.

Osgood, C. E., W. H. May, and M. S. Miron. 1975. *Cross-Cultural Universals of Affective Meaning.* Urbana, IL: University of Illinois Press.

Osgood, C. E., G. J. Suci, and P. H. Tannenbaum. 1957. *The Measurement of Meaning.* Urbana, IL: University of Illinois Press.

Pattee, H. H. 1973. *Hierarchy Theory: The Challenge of Complex Systems.* New York: George Braziller.

Penrod, S. and R. Hastie. 1980. "A computer model of jury decision making." *Psychological Review* 87:133–59.

Perloff, R. M. 1993. *The Dynamics of Persuasion.* Hillsdale, NJ: Erlbaum.

Petty, R. E. and J. T. Cacioppo. 1986a. *Communication and Persuasion.* New York: Springer-Verlag.

———. 1986b. "The elaboration likelihood model of persuasion." *Advances in Experimental Social Psychology* 19:123–205.

Petty, R. E. and D. T. Wegener. 1997. "Attitude change: Multiple roles for persuasion variables." Pp. 323–90 in *Handbook of Social Psychology,* edited by D. Gilbert, S. Fiske, and G. Lindzey. New York: McGraw-Hill.

Petty, R. E., D. T. Wegener, and L. R. Fabrigar. 1997. "Attitudes and attitude change." *Annual Review of Psychology* 48:609–47.

Pruitt, D. G. 1971. "Choice shifts in group discussion: An introductory review." *Journal of Personality and Social Psychology* 20:339–60.

Radloff, R. 1961. "Opinion evaluation and affiliation." *Journal of Abnormal and Social Psychology* 62:578–85.

Ridgeway, C. L. 1991. "The social construction of status-value: Gender and other nominal characteristics." *Social Forces* 70:367–86.

———. 2001. "Social status and group structure." Pp. 352–7 in *Blackwell Handbook of Social Psychology: Group Processes,* edited by M. A. Hoog and R. S. Tindale. Malden, MA: Blackwell.

Ridgeway, C. L. and J. W. Balkwell. 1997. "Group processes and the diffusion of status beliefs." *Social Psychology Quarterly* 60:14–31.

Ridgeway, C. and L. Smith-Lovin. 1994. "Structure, culture, and interaction: Comparing two generative theories." *Advances in Group Processes* 11:213–39.

Riland, L. H. 1959. "Relationship of Guttman components of attitude intensity and personal involvement." *Journal of Applied Psychology* 43:279–84.

Robinson, D. T. 1996. "Identity and friendship: Affective dynamics and network formation." *Advances in Group Processes* 13:91–111.

Robinson, D. T. and J. W. Balkwell. 1995. "Density, transitivity, and diffuse status in task-oriented groups." *Social Psychology Quarterly* 58:241–54.

Rohrer, J. H., S. H. Baron, E. L. Hoffman, and D. V. Swander. 1954. "The stability of autokinetic judgments." *Journal of Abnormal and Social Psychology* 49:595–7.

Rosenberg, M. 1969. *The Logic of Survey Analysis*. New York: Basic Books.

Saltiel, J. and J. Woelfel. 1975. "Inertia in cognitive processes: The role of accumulated information in attitude change." *Human Communication Research* 1:333–44.

Sanders, G. S. and R. S. Baron. 1977. "Is social comparison irrelevant for producing choice shifts?" *Journal of Experimental Social Psychology* 13:303–14.

Schachter, S. 1951. "Deviation, rejection and communication." *Journal of Abnormal and Social Psychology* 46:190–207.

Shavitt, S. and T. C. Brock. 1994. *Persuasion: Psychological Insights and Perspectives*. Needham Heights, MA: Allyn-Bacon.

Shaw, M. E. 1961. "Group dynamics." *Annual Review of Psychology* 12:129–56.

———. 1976. *Group Dynamics: The Psychology of Small Group Behavior*. New York: McGraw-Hill.

Shelly, R. K. 1993. "How sentiments organize interaction." Pp. 113–32 in *Advances in Group Processes*, vol. 10, edited by E. J. Lawler et al. Greenwich, CT: JAI Press.

Sherif, C. W., M. Sherif, and R. E. Nebergall. 1965. *Attitude and Attitude Change: The Social Judgment-Involvement Approach*. Philadelphia: W. B. Saunders.

Sherif, M. 1936. *The Psychology of Social Norms*. New York: Harper.

Sherif, M. and C. I. Hovland. 1961. *Social Judgement: Assimilation and Contrast Effects in Communication and Attitude Change*. New Haven, CT: Yale University Press.

Simmel, G. 1950. *The Sociology of Georg Simmel*, translated by K. H. Wolff. New York: The Free Press.

Simon, H. A. 1945. *Administrative Behavior*. New York: Free Press.

———. 1953. "Notes on the observation and measurement of political power." *Journal of Politics* 15:500–516.

Singer, J. E. 1966. "Social comparison: Progress and issues." *Journal of Experimental Social Psychology* Supplement 1:103–10.

Skvoretz, J. and T. J. Fararo. 1996. "Status and participation in task groups: A dynamic network model." *American Journal of Sociology* 101:1366–1414.

Skvoretz, J., M. Webster Jr., and J. Whitmeyer. 1999. "Status orders in task discussion groups." *Advances in Group Processes* 16:199–218.

Smith-Lovin, L. and D. R. Heise. 1988. *Analyzing Social Interaction: Advances in Affect Control Theory*. New York: Gordon and Breach.

Smith-Lovin, L., J. V. Skvoretz, and C. Hawkins. 1986. "Social status and participation in six-person groups: A test of Skvoretz's comparative status model." *Social Forces* 64:992–1005.

Sniezek, J. A. and R. A. Henry. 1989. "Accuarcy and confidence in group judgment." *Organizational Behavior and Human Decision Processes* 43: 1–28.

———. 1990. "Revision, weighting, and commitment in consensus group judgment." *Organizational Behavior and Human Decision Processes* 45: 66–84.

Sorrentino, R. M., G. King, and Gloria Leo. 1980. "The influence of the minority on perception: A note on a possible alternative explanation." *Journal of Experimental Social Psychology* 16:293–301.

Stasser, G., N. L. Kerr and R. M. Bray 1982. "The social psychology of jury deliberation: Structure, process, and product." Pp. 221–256 in *The Psychology of the Count-room*, edited by N. L. Kerr and R. M. Bray, New York: Academic Press.

Stasser, G., N. L. Kerr, and J. H. Davis. 1980. "Influence processes in decision-making groups: A modeling appraoch." Pp. 431–77 in *Psychology of Group Influence*, edited by P. B. Paulus. Hillsdale, NJ: Lawrence Erlbaum.

———. 1989. "Influence processes and consensus models in decision-making groups." Pp. 279–326 in *Psychology of Group Influence*, edited by P. B. Paulus. Hillsdale, NJ: Lawrence Erlbaum.

Steiner, I. D. 1964. "Group dynamics." *Annual Review of Psychology* 15:421–46.

———. 1974. "Whatever happened to the group in social psychology?" *Journal of Experimental Social Psychology* 10:94–108.

———. 1986. "Paradigms and groups." *Journal of Experimental Social Psychology* 19:251–89.

Stogdill, R. M. 1959. *Individual Behavior and Group Achievement: A Theory, the Experimental Evidence*. New York: Oxford University Press.

Stokman, F. N. and J. Berveling. 1998. "Dynamic modeling of policy networks in Amsterdam." *Journal of Theoretical Politics* 10:577–601.

Stokman, F. N., M. A. L. M. van Assen, J. V. D. Knoop, and R. C. H. V. Oosten. 2000. "Strategic decision making." *Advances in Group Processes* 17:131–53.

Stoner, J. A. 1961. *A Comparison of Individual and Group Decisions Involving Risk*. M. A. Thesis, Sloan School of Management, Massachusetts Institute of Technology, Cambridge, MA.

Stryker, S. 1981. "Symbolic interactionism: Themes and variations." Pp. 3–29 in *Social Psychology*, edited by M. Rosenberg and R. H. Turner. New York: Basic Books.

Stryker, S. and A. Statham. 1985. "Symbolic interaction and role theory." Pp. 311–78 in *Handbook of Social Psychology*, vol. 1, edited by G. Lindzey and E. Aronson. New York: Random House.

Suchman, E. A. 1950. "The intensity component in attitude and opinion research." Pp. 213–76 in *Measurement and Prediction* (vol. 4 of *The American Soldier*), edited by S. A. Stouffer, L. Guttman, E. A. Suchman, P. F. Lazarfeld, S. A. Star, and J. A. Clausen. New York: Wiley.

Suls, J. and R. L. Miller. 1977. *Social Comparison Processes: Theoretical and Empirical Perspectives*. Washington, DC: Hemisphere.

Suls, J. and T. A. Wills. 1991. *Social Comparison: Contemporary Theory and Research*. Hillsdale, NJ: Lawrence Erlbaum.

Suls, J., R. Martin, and L. Wheeler. 2000. "Three kinds of opinion comparison: The triad model." *Personality and Social Psychology Review* 4:219–37.

Sutton, R. I. and A. Hargadon. 1996. "Brainstorming groups in context: Effectiveness in a product design firm." *Administrative Science Quarterly* 41: 685–718.

Tanford, S. and S. Penrod. 1984. "Social influence model: A formal integration of research on majority and minority influence processes." *Psychological Bulletin* 95: 189–225.

Tannenbaum, P. H. 1956. "Initial attitude toward source and concept as factors in attitude change through communication." *Public Opinion Quarterly* 20: 413–25.

Taylor, M. 1968. "Towards a mathematical theory of influence and attitude change." *Human Relations* 21:121–39.

Tetlock, P. E., R. S. Peterson, C. McGuire, S. Chang, and P. Feld. 1992. "Assessing political group dynamics: A test of the groupthink model." *Journal of Personality and Social Psychology* 63:403–25.

Thorndike, R. L. 1938. "The effect of discussion upon the correctness of decisions, when the factor of majority influence is allowed for." *Journal of Social Psychology* 9:343–63.

Tindale, R. S. and J. H. Davis. 1983. "Group decision making and jury verdicts." Pp. 9–38 in *Small Groups and Social Interaction*, edited by H. H. Blumberg, A. P. Hare, V. Kent, and M. F. Davies. Chichester: Wiley.

——. 1985. "Individual and group reward allocation decisions in two situational contexts: The effects of relative need and performance." *Journal of Personality and Social Psychology* 48: 1148–61.

Tindale, R. S., J. H. Davis, D. A. Vollrath, D. H. Nagao, and V. B. Hinsz. 1990. "Asymmetrical social influence in freely interacting groups: A test of three models." *Journal of Personality and Social Psychology* 58:438–49.

Tindale, R. S., C. M. Smith, L. S. Thomas, J. Filkins, and S. Sheffey. 1996. "Shared representations and asymmetric social influence processes in small groups." Pp. 81–103 in *Understanding Group Behavior: Consensual Action by Small Groups*, edited by E. H. Witte and J. H. Davis. Mahwah, NJ: Lawrence Erlbaum.

Troyer, L. and C. W. Younts. 1997. "Whose expectations matter? The relative power of first- and second-order expectations in determining social influence." *American Journal of Sociology* 103:692–732.

Turner, John C. 1985. "Social categorization and the self-concept: A social cognitive theory of group behavior." Pp. 77–122 in *Advances in Group Processes*, vol. 2, edited by E. J. Lawler. Greenwich, CT: JAI Press.

——. 1991. *Social Influence*. Pacific Grove, CA: Brooks/Cole.

Turner, J. C., M. A. Hogg, P. J. Oakes, S. D. Reicher, and M. S. Wetherell. 1987. *Rediscovering the Social Group: A Self-Categorization Theory*. Oxford: Basil Blackwell.

Turner, J. C. and P. J. Oakes. 1989. "Self-categorization theory and social influence." Pp. 233–275 in *Psychology of Group Influence*, edited by P. B. Paulus. Hillsdale, NJ: Lawrence Erlbaum.

Turner, J. C., M. S. Wetherell, and M. A. Hogg. 1989. "Referent informational influence and group polarization." *British Journal of Social Psychology* 28:135–47.

Valente, T. W. 1995. *Network Models of the Diffusion of Innovations*. Cresskill, NJ: Hampton Press.

Vinokur, A. 1971. "Review and theoretical analysis of the effects of group processes upon individual and group decisions involving risk." *Psychological Bulletin* 76:231–50.

Vinokur, A. and E. Burnstein. 1978. "Depolarization of attitudes in groups." *Journal of Personality and Social Psychology* 36:872–85.

Wagner, Carl. 1978. "Consensus through respect: A model of rational group decision-making." *Philosophical Studies* 34:335–49.

———. 1982. "Allocation, Lehrer models, and the consensus of probabilities." *Theory and Decision* 14:207–20.

Wagner, D. G. and J. Berger. 1993. "Status characteristics theory: Growth of a research program." Pp. 23–63 in *Theoretical Research Programs: Studies in the Growth of Theory*, edited by J. Berger and M. J. Zelditch. Stanford, CA: Stanford University Press.

Wasserman, S. and K. Faust. 1994. *Social Network Analysis: Methods and Applications*. New York: Cambridge University Press.

Watts, D. J. and P. S. Dodds. 2007. "Influentials, networks, and public opinion formation." *Journal of Consumer Research* 34: 441–58.

Weber, M. 1947. *The Theory of Social and Economic Organization*. Translated by A. M. Henderson and T. Parsons. New York: The Free Press.

Webster, M. and B. I. Sobieszek. 1974. *Sources of Self-Evaluation*. New York: Wiley.

Webster, M. and J. M. Whitmeyer. 1999. "A theory of second-order expectations and behavior." *Social Psychology Quarterly* 62:17–31.

———. 2002. "Modeling second-order expectations." *Sociological Theory* 20:306–27.

Weksel, W. and J. D. Hennes. 1965. "Attitude intensity and the semantic differential." *Journal of Personality and Social Psychology* 2:91–4.

Wetherell, M. S. 1987. "Social identity and group polarization." Pp. 142–70 in *Rediscovering the Social Group*, edited by J. C. Turner, M. A. Hogg, P. J. Oakes, S. D. Reicher, and M. S. Wetherell. Oxford: Blackwell.

Whitmeyer, J. M. 2000. "Power through Appointment." *Social Science Research* 29:535–55.

———. 2002. "The mathematics of expectation states theory." *Social Psychology Quarterly* 66: 238–53.

Witte, E. H. and J. H. Davis. 1996. *Understanding Group Behavior: Consensual Action by Small Groups*. Mahwah: Lawrence Erlbaum.

Wolf, S. 1987. "Majority and minority influence: A social impact analysis." Pp. 207–35 in *Social Influences: The Ontario Symposium*, vol. 5, edited by M. P. Zanna, J. M. Olson, and C. P. Herman. Hillsdale, NJ: Erlbaum.

Wood, J. 1989. "Theory and research concerning social comparisons of personal attributes." *Psychological Bulletin* 106:231–71.

Wood, W., S. Lundgren, J.A. Ouellette, S. Busceme, and T. Blackstone. 1994. "Minority influence: A meta-analytic review of social influence processes." *Psychological Bulletin* 115:323–45.

Yeung, K.-T. and J. L. Martin. 2003. "The looking glass self: An empirical elaboration." *Social Forces* 81: 843–79.

Zajonc, R. B. 1980. "Feeling and thinking: Preferences need no inferences." *American Psychologist* 35: 151–75.

Zander, A. F. 1979. "The psychology of group processes." *Annual Review of Psychology* 30:417–51.

Zeisel, H. and S. S. Diamond. 1974. "Convincing empirical evidence on the six-member jury." *University of Chicago Law Review* 41: 281–95.

Zimbardo, P. G. 1960. "Involvement and communication discrepancy as determinants of opinion conformity." *Journal of Abnormal and Social Psychology* 60:86–94.

Zuber, J., H. Crott, and W. Joachim. 1992. "Choice shift and group polarization: An analysis of the status of arguments and social decision schemes." *Journal of Personality and Social Psychology* 62:50–61.

Index

CPSIA information can be obtained at www.ICGtesting.com
Printed in the USA
LVOW12s0742270614

392011LV00005B/13/P